THE PROBLEM OF
LIFE & DESTINY

THE PROBLEM OF
LIFE &
DESTINY

© Copyright 2018 by the United States Spiritist Council

Scripture quotations are from the ESV Bible (The Holy Bible, English Standard Version), copyright © 2001 by Crossway Bibles, a publishing ministry of Good News Publishers. Used by permission. All rights reserved.

ISBN 978-1948109109
LCCN 2018957947
Proofreading: Jussara Korngold
Book design: Helton Mattar Monteiro
Cover design: Mauro de Souza Rodrigues

International data for cataloging in publication (CIP)

D395p Denis, Léon, 1846-1927
The problem of life and destiny: experimental studies / Léon Denis. Translator: Helton Mattar Monteiro. – New York: United States Spiritist Council, 2018.
480 pp.; 21.59 cm.

Original title: Le problème de l'être e de la destinée (new rev., augm. ed., 1922).

ISBN: 978-1948109109

1. Mediumship. 2. Spiritism. 3. New Spiritualism. I. Title. II. Title.

LCCN: 2018957947   DDC 133.93   UDC 133.7

1st edition, 1st print – October 2018

All rights reserved to
United States Spiritist Council
http://www.spiritist.us – info@spiritist.us

Manufactured in the United States of America

No part of this book may be reproduced or transmitted in any form or by any means, electronic or mechanical, including photocopying, recording, or by any information storage and retrieval system, without the prior permission in writing from the copyright holder.

The name "United States Spiritist Federation" is a trade mark registered of the United States Spiritist Council.

Léon Denis

THE PROBLEM OF
LIFE &
DESTINY

Experimental Studies

Translated by H. M. Monteiro

UNITED STATES
SPIRITIST FEDERATION
New York
2018

CONTENTS

INTRODUCTION 1

PART ONE
THE PROBLEM OF LIFE

I. EVOLUTION OF THOUGHT 17
II. THE CRITERION OF SPIRITISM 29
III. THE NATURE OF BEING 57
IV. THE INTEGRAL PERSONALITY 67
V. THE SOUL AND THE DIFFERENT STATES OF SLEEP 81
VI. OUT-OF-BODY EXPERIENCES, EXTERIORIZATIONS, AND TELEPATHIC PROJECTIONS 99
VII. MANIFESTATIONS AFTER DEATH 109
VIII. VIBRATIONAL STATES OF THE SOUL, ONE'S MEMORY ... 123
IX. EVOLUTION AND THE ULTIMATE OBJECTIVE OF THE SOUL ... 131
X. ON DEATH 145
XI. LIFE IN THE HEREAFTER 167
XII. MISSIONS AND A HIGHER LIFE 181

PART TWO
THE PROBLEM OF DESTINY

XIII. SUCCESSIVE LIVES, REINCARNATION LAWS 189
XIV. SUCCESSIVE LIVES, SCIENTIFIC EXPERIMENTS, REGRESSION OF MEMORY 211
XV. SUCCESSIVE LIVES, CHILD PRODIGIES AND HEREDITY ... 271
XVI. SUCCESSIVE LIVES, OBJECTIONS AND CRITICISMS 289
XVII. SUCCESSIVE LIVES, HISTORICAL EVIDENCE 305
XVIII. JUSTICE AND ACCOUNTABILITY, THE PROBLEM OF EVIL ... 327
XIX. THE LAW OF DESTINY 343

PART THREE
THE POWERS OF THE SOUL

XX. WILLPOWER 359
XXI. CONSCIENCE AND INNER AWARENESS 371
XXII. FREE WILL 395
XXIII. THOUGHT 403
XXIV. DISCIPLINE OF THOUGHT AND INNER TRANSFORMATION .. 411
XXV. LOVE 421
XXVI. PAIN 431
XXVII. REVELATION THROUGH PAIN 451

PROFESSION OF FAITH OF THE 20TH CENTURY 467
TESTIMONIES OF SCIENTISTS AND EXPERTS 471

INTRODUCTION

A PAINFUL REALIZATION strikes today's thinkers in the evening of life. It becomes even more poignant with the impressions they get after returning to the spiritual plane. It is then that they realize that the education provided by human institutions in general, that is, religions, schools and universities, while teaching many superfluous things, teach almost nothing of the things one most needs to know in order to conduct oneself, to direct one's earthly life, and to be prepared for the Hereafter.

Those with the high mission of enlightening and guiding the human soul seem to ignore its nature and its actual destinies.

In academic circles, a complete uncertainty still reigns over the solution of the most important problem humans have ever encountered during their time on Earth. This uncertainty is reflected particularly in teaching. Most professors and teachers systematically separate from their lessons all that concerns life problems, objective questions of goal and purpose.

We find the same impotence in the religious priest. By their affirmations devoid of evidence, they are hardly able to communicate to the souls in their charge a belief that no longer meets the standards of sound criticism or the demands of reason.

In reality, in the University as in the Church, the modern soul encounters only obscurity and contradiction in all that touches on the problem of its nature and future. It is to this state of affairs that most of the ills of our time should be ascribed: the incoherence of ideas, the disorder of consciences, the moral and social anarchy.

The education that is dispensed to the new generations is complicated; but it does not enlighten the way of life for them; it does not give them the mettle to the struggle of their lifetimes. Classical education can teach how to cultivate, to adorn one's intellect; but you never learn how to take action, how to love or to devote yourself. You learn even less to form a conception of destiny that may develop the deep energies of the self and direct your driving forces, your efforts toward a lofty goal. Yet this conception is indispensable to every being, to every society, for it is the support, the supreme consolation in hard times, the source of virile virtues and high inspirations.

Carl du Prel reports the following fact:[1]

"A friend of mine, a university professor, suffered the pain of losing his daughter, which revived in him the problem of immortality. He consulted his colleagues, professors of philosophy, hoping to find some consolation in their answers. What a bitter disappointment: he had asked for bread, he was offered a stone instead; he was looking for a certainty, all they gave him was a 'maybe'!"

Francisque Sarcey, this model of an accomplished university professor, once wrote:[2]

"So I am on this Earth. I do not really know how I wound up here and why I was thrown in this place. I have no idea either of how I will leave it or what will happen to me when I am gone."

It could not be put more frankly: the philosophy taught at school, after so many centuries of study and toil, is still a doctrine without light, without heat, without

---

[1] C. DU PREL (born Karl Ludwig August Friedrich Maximilian Alfred, Baron von Prel), *La Mort, l'Au-delà, la Vie dans l'Au-delà* (Trans. A. Hœmmerlé, Paris: Chacornac, 1905), p. 7.

[2] *Le Petit Journal*, column, Paris, March 7, 1894.

life.³ Our children's souls are tossed between different and contradictory systems: Auguste Comte's positivism, Hegel's naturalism, Stuart Mill's materialism, Cousin's eclecticism, etc., an uncertain fleet without an ideal or a precise aim.

Hence the early discouragement and enervating pessimism, both maladies of decadent societies and dreadful threats to the future, to which is added the bitter and mocking skepticism of so many young men who believe in nothing but fortune, and court only material success.

The eminent professor Raoul Pictet points out this state of mind in the introduction of his latest work on the physical sciences.⁴ He speaks of the disastrous effect produced by materialist theories on the frame of mind of his students, and concludes thus:

"These poor young people believe that all that is happening in the world is the necessary and fatal effect of primary conditions, where their will does not intervene; they consider that their own existence is inevitably the plaything of inevitable fatality, to which they are attached, bound hand and foot."

"These young people stop fighting when the first adversities are encountered. They do not believe in themselves anymore. They become living tombs, where they huddle together their hopes, their efforts, their wishes; a common grave of all that made their hearts beat until the day they were poisoned."

---

³ On the subject of university examinations, M. Ducros, dean of the Faculty of Aix, wrote the following in the *Journal des Débats*, May 3, 1912: "It seems that there is like a screen between the pupil and things; I do not know exactly what cloud of learned words, of scattered and opaque facts. It is especially in philosophy that one feels this painful impression."

⁴ R. PICTET, *Étude Critique du Matérialisme et du Spiritualisme, par la Physique Expérimentale* (Paris: Félix Alcan, 1896).

All this is not only applicable to part of our youth, but also to many adults of our time and our generation, in whom we can detect a certain moral lassitude and subsidence.

F. W. H. Myers[5] acknowledges in turn that there is a worry, a discontent, a lack of confidence in the true value of life; and that pessimism is the moral malady of our time.

From Germany, the philosophical theories of Nietzsche, Schopenhauer, Haeckel, and others, have also contributed to the development of this state of affairs. Their influence has been felt everywhere. To a large extent this deed must be ascribed to them, an obscure work of skepticism and discouragement, which continues to impact the contemporary soul.

It is time to react vigorously against these disastrous doctrines and to seek, outside the official rut and old established beliefs, new methods of teaching which can meet the pressing needs of the present age. It is necessary to prepare our souls for the necessities, the struggles of our current life and subsequent lives; above all, it is necessary to teach humans to know themselves, to develop, for their ends, the latent forces that lie asleep in them.

So far, thought has been confined to narrow circles: religions, schools or systems that exclude and fight each other. Hence this deep division of minds, these violent and contrary currents which disturb and upset the social environment.

Let us learn how to get out of these rigid circles and give free rein to our thoughts. Each system contains part of the truth; none contains the whole reality. The universe and life have too many facets, too numerous for any system of thought to encompass them all. From these disparate conceptions, it is necessary to separate the

---

[5] *Cf.* F. W. H. MYERS, *Human Personality* (London: Longmans, 1903).

INTRODUCTION

fragments of truth which they contain, and to bring them together and into agreement with one another. Then, by uniting them to the various new aspects of truth that we discover every day, eventually move toward a majestic unity and harmony of thought.

Much of the moral crisis and decadence of our times comes largely from the fact that the human mind has been immobilized for too long. It must be snatched from inertia, from age-old routines, and carried to high altitudes, without losing sight of the solid foundations that a growing and renewed science has to offer. This science of tomorrow, we are working to build it. It will provide us with indispensable criteria, the means of verification and control, without which the thought, left to itself, will always risk going astray.

The confusion and uncertainty that we see in teaching is reflected and found, as I said, in the entire social order.

Everywhere, inside and out, there is a worrying state of crisis. Beneath the brilliant surface of a refined civilization lies a deep uneasiness. Anger and frustration increase in the social classes. The conflict of interests, the struggle for life become more and more bitter every day. The feeling of duty has diminished in the popular consciousness, to the point that many individuals do not even know where duty lies. The law of numbers, that is to say, blind force, dominates more than ever. Perfidious demagogues try to unleash the passions, the bad instincts of the crowd, spreading unhealthy, sometimes criminal theories. Then, when the tide rises and the wind blows in a storm, they shirk or evade all responsibility.

Where is the explanation for this enigma, for this striking contradiction between the generous aspirations of our time and the brutal reality of the facts? Why a regime that has raised so many hopes threatens to lead to anarchy, a breakdown of all social equilibrium?

An inexorable logic is going to answer us: radical or socialist democracy, both in its deep masses and their directing spirit, also inspired by negative doctrines, could only yield a negative outcome to the happiness and elevation of humanity. An ideal is just as good as the people behind it; a nation is as good as its citizens!

Negative doctrines, with their extreme consequences, inevitably lead to anarchy, that is, social nothingness, and the void. Human history has already gone through this painful experience several times.

As long as it entailed the destruction of the remains of the past, of giving the last blow to the class privileges left standing, democracy has cleverly used its means of action. But today, it is important to build the city of tomorrow, the future city, the vast building that should house the thinking of generations. And in view of this task, the negative doctrines show their insufficiency and reveal their frailty; we see our best workers struggling in a sort of material and moral impotence.

No human work can be great and lasting unless it is inspired, in theory and practice, in its principles and applications, by the eternal laws of the universe. All that is conceived and built outside the higher laws is built on sand and will inevitably collapse.

Now, the doctrines of present-day socialism have a capital flaw. They want to impose a rule in contradiction with the nature of the true law of humanity: egalitarian leveling.

Individual and progressive evolution is the fundamental law of nature and life. This is the reason of being for humans, the norm of the universe. To rebel against it, substituting its true finality, would be as insane as wishing to stop the movement of the Earth or the ebb and flow of the oceans.

The weakest part of the socialist doctrine is the absolute ignorance of humans, of their essential principle, of the laws which preside over their destinies. And when one does not know the individual human being, how can one govern the social being?

The source of all our troubles lies in our lack of knowledge and our moral inferiority. Every society will remain weak and divided as long as distrust, doubt, selfishness, envy, and hatred dominate it. We do not transform a society with laws. Laws and institutions are nothing without morals, without elevated beliefs. Whatever may be the form of government and the legislation of a human population, if it possesses good morals and firm convictions, it will always be happier and mightier than another, morally inferior population.

Since a society is the result of individual forces, whether good or bad, we must first act upon the intelligence and the conscience of its individuals, if we want to improve the structure of a given society.

But, for socialist democracy, the inner being, the human of individual consciousness does not exist; the community absorbs it entirely. The principles it adopts are no more than a negation of all high philosophy and all higher causes. One thinks only of conquering rights. And yet the enjoyment of such rights cannot go without the practice of duties. A law without duty, which would limit and correct it, will only cause new tears and sorrows.

This is why the formidable thrust of socialism only displaces appetites, lusts, causes of discomfort, and substitutes the oppressions of the past with a still more intolerable, new form of despotism. We see this happening for example in Russia.

Already we can measure the extent of the disasters caused by negative doctrines. Determinism and materialism, by denying human freedom and responsibility, undermine the very foundations of universal ethics. The moral world is no more than an annex of physiology, that is to say, the reign, the manifestation of a blind and irresponsible force. Elite's minds profess metaphysical nihilism, and the human mass, the populace, without beliefs, without fixed principles, is delivered into the hands of individuals who exploit its passions and speculate on its cupidity.

Positivism, albeit less absolute, is no less fatal in its consequences. With its theory of the unknowable, it suppresses notions of purpose and broad evolution. It sees humans into the current phase of their lives, a mere fragment of their destiny, and prevents them from seeing before and after it; a sterile and dangerous method, made, it seems, for the blind of mind, and which has been falsely proclaimed as the most beautiful conquest of the modern mind.

This is the current state of society. The danger is enormous, and if some great spiritualistic and scientific breakthrough does not occur soon, the world will sink into incoherence and confusion.

Our government authority are already feeling the effects of living in a society where the essential bases of morals are shaken, where sanctions are fake or impotent, where everything is confused, even the elementary notion of good and evil.

It is true that religions, in spite of their worn out forms and retrograde spirit, are still able to group around them many sensible souls; but they have become incapable of warding off the danger, because of their avowed inability of accurately defining human destiny and the Hereafter, the latter supported by evidence.

Humanity, tired of dogmas and speculation without proof, has either plunged into materialism or fallen into indifference. There is no salvation for thought outside a philosophical doctrine based on experience and the testimony of facts.

Where will this philosophical doctrine come from? From the abyss into which we are slipping, what power will it draw? What new ideal will come to give humans confidence in the future and an ardent wish for good? At the tragic moments of history, when everything seemed hopeless, help never faltered. The human soul cannot become bogged down completely and perish. The moment the beliefs of the past are dimmed and veiled, a new conception of life and destiny, based on the science of facts, reappears. The great tradition lives again in enlarged forms, fresher and more beautiful. It shows everyone a future full of hope and promise. Let us salute the new reign of the Ideal, victorious over matter, and work together to prepare its paths!

The task at hand is huge, human education will have to be redone completely. Such an education, as we have seen, neither the University nor the Church can provide, since they no longer possess the necessary syntheses to enlighten the progress of new generations. Only one body of thought can offer this synthesis, that of scientific spiritualism. It is already rising on the horizon of the intellectual world and will seemingly illuminate the future.

To this philosophy, to this science, free, independent, and freed from all official pressure, from all political compromise, contemporary discoveries bring new and valuable contributions every day. The phenomena of magnetism, radioactivity, and telepathy are all applications of the same principle, that is, manifestations of the same law which governs living beings, all things, and the whole universe.

A few more years of patient labor, conscientious experimentation, and persevering research will lead this new education to encounter its scientific formula, its essential basis. This event will be the greatest occurrence in history since the appearance of Christianity.

Education, as we know, is the mightiest factor of progress; it contains in germ the entire future. But to be complete, it must be inspired by the study of life in its two alternating forms, the visible and the invisible: life in its fullness, in its ascending evolution to the summits of Nature and thought.

Therefore, the preceptors of humanity have an immediate duty to fulfill. It is to put Spiritualism at the base of education, to work in order to remake the inner human being and moral health. It is necessary to awaken the human soul, asleep by fatal rhetoric; to show it its hidden powers, to force it to become aware of itself and accomplish its glorious destinies.

Modern science has analyzed the external world; its advances in the objective universe are deep: they will be its honor and glory. However, she knows nothing yet about the unseen universe and the inner world. This is a boundless empire that remains to be conquered. To know by what links humans are attached to the whole, to descend into the mysterious recesses of being, where shadow and light mingle as in Plato's cave; to go through the labyrinths, the secret nooks, to examine both the normal self and the deep self, the consciousness and the subconsciousness – no study is more necessary. As long as the Schools and Colleges do not introduce it in their curricula, they will have done nothing for a definitive education of humanity.

Yet already we see the emergence and creation of a wholly wonderful and unexpected psychology, from which will emerge a new conception of being and the notion of a superior law that embraces and resolves all the problems related to evolution and the coming times.

An era is coming to an end; new times are ahead. We are going through a period of crisis and labor pains. The exhausted forms of the past will fade and collapse to make room for new ones, at first vague and confusing, but which are gradually becoming more precise. In them, the expanding thought of humanity is being sketched out.

The human spirit is at work: everywhere, under an apparent decomposition of ideas and principles; everywhere, in science, in art, in philosophy and even within religions; the attentive observer can detect the occurrence of a slow and painful gestation. Science, above all, has been planting richly promising seeds. The century that now begins will be one of powerful outbreaks.[6]

Forms and conceptions of the past, as said above, are no longer enough. As respectable as this legacy appears, and in spite of the pious feeling inspired by the teachings bequeathed by our ancestors, one generally feels and understands that this teaching was not enough to dispel the distressing mystery of the reason for life.

However, we want to live and act, in our time, with more intensity than ever; but can one fully live and act without being conscious of the goal to be attained? The state of the contemporary soul calls for a science, an art, and a religion of light and freedom that come to liberate it from its doubts, to free it from the old servitudes and miseries of thought, to guide it towards radiant horizons where she it carried away by its very nature, and by the impetus of irresistible forces.

---

[6] [Trans. note] Léon Denis was referring to the 20th century.

We often talk about progress; but what does progress mean? Is it an empty but sonorous word in the mouths of the majority of materialistic speakers, or does it have a definite meaning? Twenty civilizations have passed on the Earth, illuminating the march of humanity with their glow. Their great buildings shone in the darkness of ages, and then died out. Yet humans still cannot discern behind the limited horizons of their thought the limitless beyond where lies the door to their destinies. Powerless to dispel the mystery that surround them, humans concentrate their strength in the works of the Earth while evading the splendors of their spiritual tasks, which would make their true greatness.

Faith in progress cannot not dispense with faith in the future, in the coming times of each and everyone. Humans progress and advance only if they believe in this future and if they march with confidence and assurance of the ideal they have glimpsed.

Progress is not to be found only in material works, in the creation of powerful machines and all industrial tools; nor does it consist in finding new methods of art, literature, or forms of eloquence. Its highest objective should be to seize, to reach the master idea, the mother idea that will fecundate all human life, the high and pure source from which all truths, principles and feelings will flow at the same time, and which will inspire powerful works and noble actions.

It is time to spell it out: no civilization can grow, no society can ascend without an ever higher thought, an ever brighter light inspiring and enlightening the souls, and touching the hearts while renovating them. The idea alone, the thought, is the mother of action. The will to realize the fullness of being, always better, always greater, can only lead us to these distant summits where science, art, in one word, the whole human work, will find its flourishing, its regeneration.

Everything tells us that the universe is governed by the law of evolution; this is what I mean by the word progress. And we, ourselves, in the principle of our life, in our soul and our conscience, are forever subject to this law. Nowadays we cannot ignore this sovereign force which carries the soul and its works through the infinite time and space, toward an ever higher goal. But such a law can only be fulfilled through our own efforts.

To perform some useful work, to cooperate with the general evolution, and to reap all the fruits thus produced, it is necessary above all to learn how to discern, to grasp the reason, the cause and the purpose of this evolution, to know where it leads, so as to participate in the fullness of the forces and faculties that lie dormant in us, in this magnificent ascension.

Our duty is to trace our way for future humanity, of which we will still be an integral part, as we learn from the communion of souls, the revelations made by our great invisible Instructors, and also with Nature, which also teaches us through its thousands of voices, through the perpetual renewal of all things for those who know how to study and understand it.

Let us move, then, toward the future, to the life that is always reborn, on the immense path opened to us by a regenerated Spiritualism!

May the faith in the past, in the sciences, philosophies, religions, enlighten you with a new flame; shake your old shrouds and the ashes that cover them. Listen to the revealing voices from the grave; they bring us a renewal of thought with the secrets of the Hereafter, that humans need to know so as to live better, act better and die better!

PART ONE

THE PROBLEM OF LIFE

I
EVOLUTION OF THOUGHT

A SINGLE LAW, as I have said, governs the evolution of thought as well as the physical evolution of beings and worlds; our understanding of the universe develops with the progress of the human mind.

This general conception of the universe and of life as a whole has been expressed in a thousand manners, and under a thousand different guises in the past. Today it is described in broader terms, and it will always be increasingly wide-ranging, as humanity goes up the steps of its ascension.

Science is constantly expanding its field of inquiry. Everyday, using its powerful instruments of observation and analysis, it discovers new aspects of matter, force, and life. But what these instruments see, the spirit had long since discerned, for the growth of thought always overtakes and exceeds the means of action of positive science. Furthermore, such instruments would be nothing without the intelligence, without the will that commands them.

Science remains uncertain and changeable, it is constantly renewed. Its methods, theories, and calculations, built with great difficulty, will crumble before a more attentive observation or a deeper induction, to give way to new theories, which will not be more definitive either.[7] The theory of the indivisible atom, for example, which

---

[7] Prof. C. RICHET admits that, "Science has never been more than a series of errors and approximations, constantly evolving, constantly

for two thousand years was the basis of physics and chemistry, is now considered a debunked hypothesis and pure fantasy by our most eminent chemists. How many similar discoveries have shown in the past the weakness of the scientific thinking! The latter will reach actual reality only by rising above the mirage of material facts, while heading toward the realm of causes and laws.

This is how science has been able to determine the immutable principles of logic and mathematics. This is not the case in other research fields. Scientists too often bring their prejudices, their tendencies, their routines, all the elements of a narrow personality, as we can see in the field of psychical studies, especially in France, where so far we can hardly find brave and truly enlightened scholars to follow a trail already amply blazed by the most beautiful intelligences of other nations.

Nevertheless, the human spirit continues to advance step by step in the knowledge of life and the universe. Our data on force and matter are changing every day; the human personality reveals itself in unexpected aspects. In the presence of so many phenomena experimentally observed, in view of testimonies coming from all sides,[8] no enlightened individual can deny the reality of the soul's survival; and no one can avoid the moral consequences and the responsibilities that it entails.

What was said about science, could also be said of philosophies and religions that have succeeded one another over the centuries. They constitute as many stages or steps traversed by humanity in its infancy, rising towards spiritual planes which are increasingly vast and which connect with each other. In their concatenation,

---

overturned, and all the more quickly as it becomes more advanced." (*Annales des Sciences Psychiques*, January 1905, p. 15).

[8] See Léon DENIS, *Into the Unseen* (Trans. H. M. Monteiro, New York: USSF, 2017), *passim*.

these diverse beliefs appear to us as a gradual development of the divine ideal, reflected in thought with all the more brilliance and purity, as it refines and purifies itself.

That is why the beliefs and knowledge of a time or environment seem to be, for the time or the environment in which they rule, the representation of the truth such as the people of that time could grasp and understand it, until the development of their faculties and their consciences makes them apt to perceive a higher form, a more intense radiation of this truth.

From this point of view, fetishist religion itself is explained, despite its bloody rites. It is the first stammering of the infantile soul trying to spell out the divine language, and which fixes behind coarse features, in forms appropriate to its mental state, a vague, confused, rudimentary conception of a higher world.

Paganism is a higher concept, albeit a very anthropomorphic one. The gods are like humans; they have all our passions, all our weaknesses. But already, the notion of the ideal is purified with that of the good. A ray of eternal beauty comes to fertilize nascent civilizations.

Above all these is the Christian idea, all made of sacrifice, of renunciation in its essence. Greek paganism was the religion of radiant nature; Christianity is that of the suffering humanity, a religion of catacombs, crypts and tombs, which originated in persecution and pain, and still keeps the imprint of its origin. A necessary reaction against pagan sensuality, it will become, by its very exaggeration, powerless to overcome it, because, with skepticism, sensuality is reborn.

Christianity, at its origin, must be considered as the greatest effort attempted by the invisible world to communicate overtly with humanity. It is, according to an expression of F. W. H. Myers, "The first authentic message from a world beyond our own." Already, pagan religions were rich in occult phenomena of all sorts and divination. But the resurrection, that is, the apparitions of Christ materialized after his death, constitute the most powerful manifestation of which humans have been witnesses. It was the sign for an entry into the world of spirits, which occurred in a thousand ways during early Christianity times. Elsewhere[9] I mentioned how and why, little by little, silence fell about the Hereafter which was once again veiled, except for a few privileged ones, such as seers, ecstatic mystics, and prophets.

Today we are witnessing a new thrust of the invisible world in history. The manifestations of the Hereafter, isolated and transient, now tend to become more permanent and universal. A pathway has been established between the two worlds, at first a single track, a narrow path, but then it widened, improving little by little, and turning into a wide and safe road. Christianity began with phenomena of a nature similar to those found today in the field of psychical sciences. It is through these facts that the influence and action of the spiritual world, true abode and eternal homeland of all souls, are revealed. Through them, a blue expanse opens on the infinite life; hope will be revived in anguished hearts, and humanity will be reconciled to death.

---

[9] See Léon DENIS, *Christianisme et Spiritisme* (New ed., Paris: Librairie de Sciences Psychiques, 1910), ch. V.

Religions have powerfully contributed to human education; they put a brake on violent passions and the barbarism of the iron ages, and also strongly engraved the moral notion in the depths of conscience. Religious esthetics has given birth to masterpieces in all fields; it has participated to a large extent in the revelation of art and beauty which has continued through the centuries. Greek art had created wonders. Christian art has attained the sublime in Europe's Gothic cathedrals that stand, like stone bibles, under the sky, with their proudly sculpted towers, their imposing naves, filled by the vibrations of pipe organs and sacred songs, under high ogives, from which light descends and bathes the frescoes and statues; but their role has ended, for it is diluted by copies, or stagnates, as if exhausted.

The error committed by religions, and especially the Catholic error, is not of esthetic nature, which does not disappoint: it is of logical nature. It consists in enclosing religion in narrow dogmas, in rigid formulas. While movement is the very law of life, Catholicism has immobilized thought instead of encouraging its growth.

It is in the nature of humans to exhaust all forms of an idea, to go to extremes, before resuming the normal course of their evolution. Every religious truth, affirmed by an innovator, weakens and deteriorates thereafter, the disciples being almost always unable to maintain the heights to where the master drew them. The religious doctrine then becomes a source of abuse and causes, little by little, an opposing current, in the sense of skepticism and negation. Blind faith is replaced by unbelief; materialism does its work; and it is only when it has shown all its helplessness in the social order that an idealistic renewal becomes possible.

From the earliest times of Christianity, various currents, namely, Judaic, Hellenic, Gnostic, would mingle and collide in the cradle of the nascent religion. Schisms broke out; tears, conflicts succeeded one another, in the midst of which the thought of Christ gradually became obscured and darkened. I pointed out elsewhere[10] the modifications, the successive reworkings of Christian teachings perpetrated by the ages that followed. True Christianity was a law of love and freedom; the churches have made it a law of fear and enslavement. Hence the gradual estrangement of thinkers from the Church; hence the weakening of the religious spirit, for example, in France.

In the wake of the turbulence that has been invading minds and consciences, materialism has gained ground. Its so-called scientific morality, which proclaims the necessity of the struggle for life, the disappearance of the weak, and the selection of the strong, rules today almost as sovereign in public as in private life. All activities are geared toward the attainment of well-being and physical enjoyment. In the absence of moral training and discipline, the springs of the French soul lose tension; discomfort and discord are everywhere, in the family, throughout the nation. This is, like I said, a time of crisis. Nothing dies, in spite of appearances; everything is transformed and renewed. The doubt which besieges souls in our time is paving the way for the convictions of tomorrow, for the intelligent and enlightened faith which will reign over the future and extend to all peoples, to all nations.

---

[10] See Léon DENIS, *Christianisme et Spiritisme* (New ed., Paris: Librairie de Sciences Psychiques, 1910), *passim* (Reprint, Quebec: Librairie Spirite Francophone, 2012).

Although still young and divided by the necessities of territory, distance and climate, humanity has begun to become aware of itself. Above and beyond political and religious antagonisms, groups of intelligences are formed. Humans haunted by the same problems, spurred on by the same worries, inspired by the Unseen, are working on a common ground and pursuing the same solutions. Little by little, the elements of a psychological science and a universal belief emerge, become stronger, and are expanded. Many impartial witnesses see it as the prelude to a movement of thought that tends to embrace all societies on Earth.[11]

The religious idea has completed its lower cycle, and the plans for a higher spirituality are outlined. It can be said that religion is the effort of humanity to commune with the eternal and divine essence. That is why there will always be religions and sects, growing bigger and bigger and conforming to the higher laws of esthetics, which are the expression of universal harmony. Beauty, in its highest rules, is a divine law, and its manifestations, in attaching themselves to the idea of God, will necessarily assume a religious character.

As thought gets more mature, missionaries of all kinds come to trigger religious renewal in different civilizations of humanity. We are witnessing the prelude to one of these renovations, bigger and deeper than the previous ones. It no longer has humans as agents and interpreters, which would make this new dispensation as precarious as the

---

[11] Sir O. LODGE, Rector of the University of Birmingham, member of the Royal Academy of England, saw in psychical studies the coming of a new freer religion (*cf. Annales des Sciences Psychiques*, December 1905, p. 765). See also MAXWELL, Attorney General at the Court of Appeal of Bordeaux, *Metapsychical Phenomena* (Trans. L. I. Finch. London: Duckworth, 1905), "Preliminary Remarks."

others. It is the Inspiring Spirits, the inhabitants of the spirit world, that exert their action both on the whole surface of the globe and in all fields of thought. In all aspects, a new spiritualism emerges. And immediately, a question arises: What is it? Science or religion? Narrow minds, do you believe that thought must eternally follow the ruts that the past has dug!

So far, all the intellectual domains have been isolated from one another, enclosed by barriers and walls: science on one side, religion on the other; whereas philosophy and metaphysics are bristling with impenetrable brushwood. While everything is simple, vast and deep in the domain of the soul as well as in the universe, the mania of system-framing has complicated, narrowed, and divided everything. Religion has been walled up in the dark dungeon of dogmas and mysteries; science, imprisoned in the lowest floors of matter. There is not true religion, nor true science. It suffices to rise above these arbitrary classifications to understand that everything is reconciled and harmonized in a higher vision.

Does not science, although still elementary, as soon as it devotes itself to the study of space and worlds, immediately provoke in us a feeling of enthusiasm, of almost religious admiration? Read the books of great astronomers, or mathematicians of genius. They will tell you that the universe is a prodigy of wisdom, harmony, beauty, and that already, as we penetrate higher laws, the union of science, art, and religion by the reflection of God in Its works, is being accomplished. Having reached such heights, study becomes a contemplation, and thought turns into prayer!

Modern Spiritualism[12] will accentuate, develop this tendency, give it a clearer and more precise meaning. By its

---

[12] [Trans. note] L. DENIS often referred interchangeably to *Spiritism* as *New Spiritualism*, *Modern Spiritualism*, or even as

experimental side, it is still only a science; by the purpose of its research, it plunges through invisible regions and rises to the eternal springs from which all strength and life flow. By this it unites humans to the divine Power and becomes a philosophical doctrine, a religious philosophy. It is, moreover, the link that brings together two forms of humanity. Through it, the spirits imprisoned in flesh and those that are freed from it call each other, answer each other; between them, a true communion is established.

So we must not regard religion in the narrow sense, in the current sense of this word. The religions of our time want dogmas and priests, whereas the new philosophical doctrine does not include them. It is open to all researchers; a sense of free criticism, scrutiny and control governs its investigations.

Dogmas and priests are necessary, and will be so for a long time, to young and timid souls who enter daily into the circle of earthly life, unable go alone in the path of knowledge, nor analyze their needs and sensations.

Modern Spiritualism is directed above all toward evolved souls, to major and free spirits, who wish to find by themselves the solution of the great problems and the formula of their Creed. It offers them a conception, an interpretation of truths and universal laws, based on experimentation, reason, and the teaching of spirits. Add to this the revelation of duties and responsibilities, which alone should give a solid foundation to our instinct for justice. Then, with the moral force, the satisfactions of the heart, the joy of rediscovering, at least by thought,

---

neo-*Spiritualism*. In his books all these expressions mean *Spiritism*. Cf. Allan KARDEC, *The Spirits' Book* (2nd ed., New York: USSC/USSF, 2016), "Introduction to the Study of Spiritism," section I.

sometimes even by form,[13] the beloved departed relatives and friends that one might thought to have lost. To the proof of their survival, one gains the certainty to join them again and to live with them lifetimes without number, lives of ascension, happiness or progress.

Thus, gradually, the darkest problems become clearer; the Hereafter opens up; the divine side of beings and things is revealed. By the force of these teachings, sooner or later, the human soul will rise, and, from the heights it reaches, it will see that everything is connected, that the various theories, contradictory and hostile in appearance, are only different parts of one same whole. The laws of the majestic universe will be summarized in a single law, at once an intelligent and conscious force, a mode of thought and action. And through that, all the worlds, all the beings will be connected in the same powerful unit, associated in the same harmony, driven towards the same goal.

A day will come when all the small, narrow and old systems will merge into a vast synthesis embracing all the realms of the idea. Sciences, philosophies, religions, which are today divided, will join in the light, and will become life, the splendor of the spirit, the reign of Knowledge.

In this magnificent agreement, the sciences will provide precision and method in the order of facts; the philosophies, rigor in their logical deductions; poetry, the irradiation of its lights and the magic of its colors. Religion will add the qualities of feeling and the notion of high esthetics. Thus beauty will be realized in the strength and unity of thought. The soul will move towards the

---

[13] See Léon DENIS, *Into the Unseen* (New York: USSF, 2018), ch. XX, "Spirit Apparitions and Materializations."

highest peaks, while maintaining the balance of necessary relationship that must regulate the parallel and rhythmic march of intelligence and consciousness, in their ascension to conquer Good and Truth.

II

THE CRITERION OF SPIRITISM

MODERN SPIRITUALISM[14] RESTS on a whole series of phenomena: some, simply physical, have revealed to us the existence and mode of action of long unknown forces; the others have an intelligent nature, namely: direct (or automatic) writing; typology;[15] the speeches pronounced in trance or "incorporation" (psychophony). All these manifestations have been reviewed and analyzed elsewhere.[16] As noted, they are frequently accompanied by signs, some evidence establishing the identity and intervention of human souls which have lived on Earth and were released by bodily death.

It is through these phenomena that the Spirits[17] have spread their teachings in the world; and these teachings have been, as we shall see, confirmed in many ways through experience.

New Spiritualism thus addresses both the senses and the intelligence. It is experimental, when it studies the phenomena that serve as its basis; rational, when it controls the ensuing teachings. It constitutes a powerful tool for searching the truth, since it can serve simultaneously all fields of knowledge.

---

[14] [Trans. note] See footnote 12 above.

[15] [Trans. note] *Typtology* or *rappings*, early method of spirit communication in which spirits used raps to convey messages.

[16] See Léon DENIS, *Into the Unseen* (New York: USSF, 2017), Part Two. Here I am referring only to spiritistic facts and not animistic ones, or manifestations of the living from a distance.

[17] We call *spirit* the soul surrounded by its subtle envelope (the *perispirit*).

The revelations of spirits, as I said, are confirmed through experience. Under the name of fluids, the spirits taught us theoretically and demonstrated in practice, as early as 1850,[18] the existence of imponderable forces that science rejected *a priori*. Sir W. Crookes, first among highly influential scientists, has since observed the reality of these forces, and the science of the day recognizes their importance and variety, thanks to the famous discoveries of Roentgen, Hertz, Becquerel, Curie, Gustave Le Bon, and others.

The spirits affirmed and demonstrated the possibility of action of soul upon soul, from all distances, without the aid of physical organs, and this order of phenomena raised no less opposition and incredulity.

Now, the phenomena of telepathy, of mental suggestion, of thought transmission, observed and induced today

---

[18] See Allan KARDEC, *The Spirits' Book* (2nd ed., New York: USSC/USSF, 2016), and *The Mediums' Book* (2nd ed., Brasília: ISC/Edicei, 2010). Also, in *The Spiritist Review* – Year 1860 (New York: USSC, 2016), "Studies about the Spirits of Living Persons: Dr. Vignal," p. 129, a message of the spirit of Dr. Vignal states that the body of living persons emanate a dark light. Perhaps this the radioactivity discovered by current science, but which was ignored by the science of that time?

Note that the following was written by Allan KARDEC, as early as 1867, in his book *Genesis* (Brasília: ISC/Edicei, 2011), ch. XIV, "I. Nature and Properties of the Fluids," item 6:

"Who knows the innermost composition of tangible matter? Perhaps it is compact only in relation to our senses. This may be demonstrated by the ease with which spiritual fluids and spirits pass right through it. It offers no more of an obstacle to them than what transparent objects offer to light. Having as its primitive element the ethereal cosmic fluid, tangible matter should be able to return to the state of etherization upon disaggregation, just as the diamond, the hardest substance known, can be volatilized into intangible gas. *The solidification of matter is in reality only a transitory state of the universal fluid, which can return to its primitive state when the conditions needed for cohesion cease.*"

in all circles, have confirmed, by the thousands, these revelations.

The Spirits teach the preexistence, the survival, the successive lives of the soul.

And now, the experiences of F. Colavida, E. Marata, those of Colonel Rochas d'Aiglun, mine, etc., have established that not only the memories of the tiniest details of current life, even from the earliest childhood, but also those of previous lives, are engraved in the hidden folds of consciousness. A whole past, veiled in the waking state, reappears, lives again during trance. Indeed, these memories have been reconstructed by a number of asleep subjects, as it will be established later on in these pages, where this issue is specifically addressed.[19]

As can be seen, Modern Spiritualism, like the ancient spiritualistic doctrines, cannot be considered a pure metaphysical concept. It presents itself with a very different nature and meets the requirements of a generation raised in the school of criticism and rationalism, made defiant by the excesses of a sickly and dying mysticism.

To believe is not enough today; we want to know. No philosophical or moral conception has any chance of success unless it is based on a demonstration at once logical, mathematical, and positive; and , moreover, if it is not culminated in a sanction which satisfies all our instincts of justice.

It should be pointed out that these conditions were perfectly fulfilled by Allan Kardec in the masterly exposition contained in his *The Spirits' Book*.

This book is the result of an immense work of classification, coordination, and selection concerning innumerable

---

[19] See *Compte rendu du Congrès Spirite et Spiritualiste International*, 1900 (Paris: Librairie de Sciences Psychiques, 1902), pp. 319, 350. See also ROCHAS D'AIGLUN, *Les Vies Successives* (Paris: Charconac Frères, 1911).

messages, coming from various sources unknown to each another. Messages obtained from all corners of the world that this eminent compiler brought together, having made sure of their authenticity. He was careful to dismiss isolated opinions and doubtful testimonies, so as to retain only the items on which the affirmations were concordant.

This work is far from over. It continues every day since the death of the great initiator. Already we possess a powerful synthesis, of which Kardec traced the broad outlines and which the heirs of his thought endeavor to develop with the help of the invisible world. Each of them brings his or her grain of sand to the common building, to this building whose foundations are fortified every day by scientific experimentation, but whose culmination will always rise higher.

I myself can avow to be one of those favored by the teachings of spirit guides, whose assistance and guidance have never failed me for forty years. Their revelations took on a particularly didactic character during a series of seances lasting eight years, of which I have often spoken in a previous book.[20]

In the work of Allan Kardec, the teaching of the Spirits is accompanied, at each question, by considerations, comments, and clarifications which bring out more clearly the beauty of the principles and the harmony of the whole. It is in this that the qualities of the author are shown. He has endeavored, above all, to give a clear and precise meaning to the expressions which usually recur in his philosophical reasoning; then also to define terms that could be interpreted in different ways. He knew that the confusion that prevails in most systems stems

---

[20] See Léon DENIS, *Into the Unseen* (New York: USSF, 2017), *passim*.

from the lack of clarity of expressions only familiar to their authors.

Another rule which Allan Kardec has scrupulously observed, no less essential in any methodical exposition, was that of circumscribing ideas and presenting them in conditions which make them readily comprehensible to every reader. Finally, after having developed these ideas in an order and a sequence that linked them together, he was able to draw conclusions, which already constitute, in their rational order and in their measure of human concepts, a reality, a certainty.

That is why I proposed to adopt herein the terms, the views, the methods used by Allan Kardec, as being the safest, while reserving the right to add to my work all his developments resulting from fifty years of research and experimentation that have passed since the appearance of his books.

Thus we see that, because of all this, the doctrine of the spirits, of which Kardec was the judicious interpreter and compiler, combines, similarly to the most appreciated philosophical systems, the essential qualities of clarity, logic, and rigor.

But, what no other system could offer, is this imposing set of manifestations with which Spiritism was first affirmed in the world, and which after could be checked over, every day, in all circles. It is addressed to people of all ranks and degrees, from all walks of life; and not only to their senses, to their intellects, but also to what is best in them, to their reason and conscience. Do these inner powers not constitute in their union a criterion of good and evil, of truth and falsehood? No doubt, more or less clear or veiled, according to the advancement of souls, but found in each of them as a reflection of the eternal reason from which they emanate.

There are two components in Spiritism: A revelation of the spirit world and a human discovery. In other words, there is, on the one hand, a universal education not of this world, identical only to itself in its essential parts and general meaning; and, on the other hand, a personal and human confirmation, which is achieved following the rules of logic, experience and reason. The conviction which emerges from it is strengthened and becomes increasingly accurate as the spirit communications become more numerous and, for this very reason, the means of verification are multiplied and expanded.

Until now, we had only known personal systems, private revelations. Today, thousands of voices, the voices of the dead, are being heard. The unseen world has entered into action, and among its agents, eminent Spirits have allowed themselves to be recognized through the strength and beauty of their teachings. The great geniuses of the spiritual plane, driven by a divine impulse, are guiding thought toward radiant summits.[21]

Is not there a dispensation otherwise as vast and magnificent as all those from the distant past? The difference of means can only be compared with that of results. Let us compare:

---

[21] See the spirit communications published by Allan KARDEC in *The Spirits' Book* (2nd ed., New York: USSC/USSF, 2016) and *Heaven and Hell* (Trans. A. Blackwell and J. Korngold. New York: SAB, 2003). See also the Spiritualist teachings obtained by M. A. OXON (i.e., W. Stainton MOSES), *Psychography* (2nd ed., London: Psychological Press Association, 1882). Also recommended are General AMADE, *Le Problème de l'Au-delà* (Paris, Leymarie, 1902); Albert PAUCHARD, *Sur le Chemin ...* (Paris : J. Meyer, 1951); and the very interesting messages reproduced in A. NASCHITZ-ROUSSEAU, *La Vie Continue de l'Âme* (Paris: J. Meyer, 1922).

Personal revelations are fallible. All human philosophical systems, all individual theories, as well those of Aristotle, Thomas Aquinas, Kant, Descartes, and Spinoza – and those of our contemporaries – are necessarily influenced by the opinions, tendencies, prejudices, and feelings of those who revealed them. The same is true for the conditions of time and place in which they occur. Or when referring to religious doctrines.

The revelation of spirits, being impersonal and universal, escapes most of these influences, at the same time as it brings together the greatest sum of probabilities, if not certainties. It cannot be stifled or distorted. No individual, no nation, no church has this privilege. It defies all inquisitions and occurs where it is least expected to be found. We have seen people who were most hostile to it at first, changing their views by the power of the demonstrations, moved to the depths of their souls by the appeals and exhortations of their deceased relatives, and turning themselves into vehicles of active dissemination.

Adversaries like St. Paul before his conversion are not lacking in Spiritism, and it is phenomena of an order similar to that "on the road to Damascus" which have caused their change of opinion.

Spirits have awaken many mediums from all walks of life, within the most diverse classes and groups, and even deep into the religious sanctuaries. Priests and preachers have received their instructions and have spread them openly or under the veil of anonymity.[22] Their deceased friends and relatives, all filled the office of masters and

---

[22] See RAPHAEL (pseud.), *Le Doute* (Paris: Librairie Spirite, 1877); P. MARCHAL, *l'Esprit consolateur* (Paris: Didier, 1878); W. Stainton MOSES, *Spirit Teachings* (London: Spiritualist Alliance, 1898).

The priest DIDON wrote (August 4, 1876), in his *Lettres à Mlle. Th. V.* (Paris: Plon-Nourrit, 1902), p. 34:

revelators next to them, adding to their spirit teachings formal and irrefutable proofs of their identity.

It is by such means that Spiritism has been able to take over the world and cover it with enlightening focal points. There is a majestic accord in all these voices that have risen simultaneously to make our skeptical societies hear the good news of the survival of the soul, and to explain the problems of death and pain. The revelation has penetrated mediumistically in the heart of families, down to the bottom of shanties and the underworld. Have we not seen the convicts of the Tarragona galleys address the International Spiritist Congress of Barcelona in 1888? A touching adhesion to a philosophy which, they said, had brought them back to the good path and make them reconcile to their duties![23]

In Spiritism, the multiplicity of sources of teaching and dissemination becomes a source of permanent control (verification), which foils and frustrates all opposition, all intrigues. By its very nature, the revelation made by Spirits escapes the attempts of monopolization or

---

"I believe in the influence that the dead and the saints exert mysteriously upon us. I live in deep communion with these unseen entities and experience with delight the benefits of their secret neighborhood."

Alfred BENÉZECH, eminent preacher of the Reformed Church of France, wrote to me about phenomena observed by himself:

"I feel that Spiritism may well become positively a religion, not in the manner of revealed religions, but as a religion established on facts of experience and fully in accord with rationalism and science. Strange thing! In this era of materialism, where the churches seem to be about to disorganize and dissolve, religious thought returns to us by means of scholars, accompanied by supernatural beings of ancient times. But this preternatural, which I distinguish from miracles since it is only a superior and rare natural, will no longer be at the exclusive service of a Church particularly honored by the favors of divinity; it will be the property of all humanity, without distinction of sects. How greater and more moral it is!"

[23] See *Compte rendu du Congrès Spirite de Barcelone*, 1888 (Paris: Librairie des Sciences Psychiques).

falsification. When facing it, all inclinations toward dissent or domination are frustrated, because if one could extinguish it or distort it at one point, it would be rekindled immediately on a hundred others, thus playing with unhealthy ambitions and deceitfulness.

In this immense, revealing movement, the spirits are obeying orders from above – they say it themselves. Their action is regulated according to a plan drawn in advance, and which proceeds in a majestic scale. An invisible council presides over its execution, from within the spiritual plane. It is composed of great Spirits from all nations, all religions; highly evolved souls which have lived in this world according to the law of love and self-sacrifice. These beneficent powers hover between Heaven and Earth, uniting them with a stroke of light, through which prayers are constantly rising and inspirations descending.

With regard to the concordance of the Spiritist teachings, however, there is a single fact, an exception, which has struck certain observers, and which has been used as a capital argument against Spiritism. Why, they object, do spirits which, in all Latin countries,[24] affirm the law of successive lives and reincarnations of the soul on Earth, deny it, or remain silent about it in Anglo-Saxon countries? How to explain such a flagrant contradiction? Is that not enough to destroy the unity of the philosophical doctrine which characterizes the new revelation?

It should be noted that there is no actual contradiction, just a gradation necessary because of prejudices of class, race, and religion, which are deeply ingrained in certain countries. The teaching of the Spirits, more complete, more extended since the start in Latin circles, was originally restricted and graded for other regions, for practical convenience. Today, it can be seen that

---

[24] [Trans. note] *Latin countries* here refer to Italy, France, Spain, etc., Western European countries whose language derived from Latin.

the number of Spiritist communications affirming the principle of successive reincarnations is growing every day both in England and North America. Many of them even provide valuable arguments in the open discussion among Spiritualists of different schools. The idea of reincarnation has gained enough ground on the other side of the Atlantic, to the point of winning over one of the most important American spiritualistic periodicals. The British journal *Light*, after long disputing reincarnation, discusses it today with impartiality.

Therefore, it seems that, if initially there were some shadows and contradictions, they were only apparent and could barely resist some serious scrutiny.

Like all new philosophical doctrines, the Spiritist revelation has raised many objections and criticisms. Let's take a look at some of them. First, we are accused of being too eager to philosophize; we are blamed for having built, on the basis of phenomena, a hasty system, a premature doctrine, and thus to have compromised the positive character of Modern Spiritualism.

A reputable writer,[25] interpreting a number of psychists, summed up their criticisms in these terms: "Another serious objection to the spiritualist hypothesis is the philosophy with which certain too eager persons have connected it. Spiritualism, which should at present be but the mere beginning of a science, is, according to them, already a philosophy for which the universe holds no secrets."

---

[25] [Trans. note] The unnamed writer was Michel SAGE, *Mrs. Piper* (Trans. N. Robertson, New York: Scott-Thaw, 1904), p. 173.

We might remind this author that the people of whom he speaks have played only the role of intermediaries in all this, limiting themselves to coordinating and publishing the teachings which reached them mediumistically.

On the other hand, it should be noted that there will always be indifferent people, skeptics, and laggards that will think that we are in too much of a hurry. No progress would be possible if we waited for the latecomers. It is really nice to see people who were interested in these issues in the past, led by men like Allan Kardec, for example. He ventured to publish his work only after years of painstaking research and careful considerations, while obeying formal orders and drawing on sources of information that our excellent critics do not even seem to have a idea.

Anyone who closely follows the development of psychical studies, may find that the results obtained have not only confirmed all points but also strengthen even more the work left by Kardec.

F. W. H. Myers, the eminent professor at Cambridge, who was for twenty years, as pointed out by C. Richet, the soul of the Society for Psychical Research, of London; and whom the International Congress of Psychology of Paris, held in 1900, elevated to the dignity of honorary president; in the last pages of his masterful book, *Human Personality*[26] (whose publication in 1903 caused a deep sensation in the world of knowledge) stated that, for any enlightened and conscientious researcher, this research logically and necessarily leads to a vast philosophical and religious synthesis. Starting from these data, he devoted his tenth chapter to a generalization or conclusion "which may place these new discoveries in clearer relation to the existing schemes of civilized thought and belief."

---

[26] F. W. H. MYERS, *Human Personality* (London: Longmans, 1903), vol. II, ch. X, items 1000–1001, p. 278–279.

He concludes thus his lengthy dissertation:

"Bacon foresaw the gradual victory of observation and experiment – the triumph of actual analyzed fact – in every department of human study ; – in every department save one. The realm of "Divine things" he left to Authority and Faith. *I here urge that that great exemption need be no longer made. I claim that there now exists an incipient method of getting at this Divine knowledge also, with the same certainty, the same calm assurance, with which we make our steady progress in the knowledge of terrene things. The authority of creeds and Churches will thus be replaced by the authority of observation and experiment. The impulse of faith will resolve itself into a reasoned and resolute imagination, bent upon raising even higher than now the highest ideals of man.*" (My emphasis.)

Thus, what some shortsighted critics see as a premature attempt, to F. H. W. Myers appears to be "a necessary and inevitable evolution." The philosophical synthesis that crowns his work has received the highest approbation. For Sir Oliver Lodge, the illustrious British academician, it really one of the vastest, most understandable, and best-founded patterns of existence ever seen.[27]

Professor Flournoy, from Geneva (Switzerland), praised Myers's work very highly in the *Archives de Psychologie de la Suisse romande* (June 1903). In France, other scientists, not necessarily Spiritists, stated identical opinions.

J. Maxwell, MD, Attorney General at the Court of Bordeaux, expressed himself thus:[28]

---

[27] The synthesis of F. W. H. MYERS can be summarized as follows: Gradual and infinite evolution, in many stages, of the human soul, both in wisdom and in love. The human soul derives its strength and grace from a spiritual universe. This universe is animated and directed by the Divine Spirit, which is accessible to the soul and in communication with it.

[28] J. MAXWELL, *Metapsychical Phenomena* (Trans. L. I. Finch. London: Duckworth, 1905), pp. 9 and 12.

"This is what makes the success of Spiritism; it comes at its appointed time, and supplies a wide-felt need.... The extent to which this doctrine is spreading is one of the most curious things of the day. I believe we are beholding the dawn of a veritable religion; a religion without a ritual and without an organized clergy, and yet with assemblies and practices which make it a veritable cult. As for me, I take a great interest in these meetings; they give me the impression that I am assisting at the birth of a religious movement called to a great destiny."

Against such testimonies, the recriminations of our opponents fall of themselves. To what should we attribute their aversion to Spiritism? Is it because spiritual teaching, with its law of responsibility, the sequence of causes and effects it shows us in the moral domain, and the examples of sanctions that it provides us, becomes a terrible inconvenience for a lot of people who care little about philosophy?

Speaking of psychical facts, F. W. H. Myers said:[29] "Such a *discovery* opens the door also to revelation." It is evident that the day when relations were established with the world of Spirits, by the very force of things, the problem of life and destiny arose immediately with all its consequences, under new guises.

No matter what one says, it would not be possible to communicate with our deceased relatives and friends by disregarding everything connected with their way of life; by showing no interest in their views, necessarily enlarged

---

[29] F. W. H. MYERS, *Human Personality* (London: Longmans, 1903), vol. II, ch. X, section 1010, p. 287.

and different from what they were on Earth, at least for souls already evolved.

At no time in history have humans been able to escape these great problems of being, of life, death, and pain. In spite of human inability to solve them, they have incessantly haunted us, always coming back with stronger force, each time we tried to dismiss them, slipping into all the events of his life, into all the folds of human understanding; striking, so to speak, at the doors of our conscience. And when a new source of teachings, consolations, moral forces, when vast horizons are open to thought, how could we remain indifferent? Is it not only about us, but our loved ones as well? Is it not our future fate, the fate of our tomorrow that is at stake?

How much might this torment, this anguish at the unknown that besets the soul through time; this confusing intuition of a better, anticipated, desired world; this worry about God and Its justice; be, in a new and greater measure, appeased, enlightened, and quenched – and even so should we despise the means to achieve it? Is it not, in this desire, in this need to think, to probe the great mystery, one of the most beautiful privileges of the human being? Is this not what makes the dignity, the beauty, and the reason of being for one's life?

And every time we have ignored this right, this privilege; every time that, turning our eyes away from the Hereafter, and failing to direct our thoughts toward a higher life, we wished to restrict our horizons to current life. Have we not witnessed at the same time, our moral miseries worsen, the burden of existence weigh more heavily on the shoulders of the unfortunate, despair and suicide multiply their ravages, and whole societies move toward decadence and anarchy?

Another kind of objection is as follows: Spiritist philosophy, we are told, has no consistency. The communications on which it rests come, most often, from the medium itself, from its own subconscious, or from the sitters. The medium in trance "reads in the minds of the consultants the doctrines that are piled up there, eclectic doctrines, borrowed from all the philosophies of the world and especially from Hinduism."

Did the author of these lines[30] really think about the difficulties that such a practice would present? Would he be able to explain to us the processes by which one can read, at first glance, in the brains of others, the doctrines that are "piled up" in them? If he can, let him do it, otherwise we will be justified in seeing in his allegations nothing but empty words, used lightly and for the purposes of a criticism full of bias. Someone who does not want to appear duped by feelings is often fooled by words. Systematic disbelief regarding one point becomes naive credulity regarding another.[31]

Let us first remind that most mediums at the start of spirit manifestations, have opinions which are entirely opposite to those expressed in the communications. Almost all of them had a religious rearing and are imbued with ideas of heaven and hell. Their views of future life, if any, differ appreciably from those of the spirits. This is still frequently observed today; it was so regarding three

---

[30] [Trans. note] Michel SAGE, *Madame Piper* (Paris: Leymarie, 1902), p. 246. The English version, called *Mrs. Piper* (Trans. N. Robertson, New York: Scott-Thaw, 1904), omitted this paragraph.

[31] It is well known that suggestion and the transmission of thoughts can only be exerted upon subjects who have long since been trained, and by persons who have acquired a certain domain over them. So far, these experiments only relate to words, or series of words, and never to a set of "doctrines." A psychic reader of thoughts – allegedly inspired by the opinions of the sitters – if that were at all possible, would not draw from them any precise notions on any principle of philosophy, but the most confused and contradictory data.

mediums in our mediumistic group, all three practicing Catholic ladies who, despite the philosophical teachings they were receiving and transmitting, never completely gave up their old religious habits.

As for the sitters, the listeners, or the people referred to as "consulters," let us not forget that at the dawn of Spiritism in France – that is to say around the time of Allan Kardec – there were very few individuals with notions of philosophy, either Eastern or Druidic, including the theory of transmigrations or successive lives of the soul. They were only found within academies or in some very select scientific clubs.

We ask our adversaries how could an innumerable number of mediums, scattered over all world, unknown to one another, have been able to constitute by themselves the bases of a philosophical doctrine solid enough to withstand all attacks, all assaults; and exact enough so that its principles could be confirmed and corroborated each day through experience, as indicated at the beginning of this chapter.

On the subject of the sincere authenticity of mediumistic communications and their philosophical significance, let us recall the words of an orator whose opinions will not appear suspicious to all those who know the aversion of most churchmen to Spiritism.

In a sermon delivered in New York on April 7, 1899, Rev. Minot J. Savage, a renowned preacher, said:[32]

"There is no end of trash that purports to come as communicated from the other world. At the same time there is a whole library of the noblest morals and spiritual teaching that I am acquainted with. I know one book, for

---

[32] Sermon reproduced in *Light*, vol. XIX, no. 958, p. 231–232, May 20, 1899.

example, the author of which was an Oxford graduate,[33] and who during a large part of his life was connected with the School Board of the city of London, a member of the Church of England when he began, and afterwards a clergyman in that Church, who became a Spiritualist and a medium both. His book was written automatically, as he tells us, through his own hand. Sometimes in order to divert his thoughts from what he was writing, he would sit and read Plato in the original Greek, while his hand was at work on its own account. And this book, contrary to what people ordinarily believe, went squarely against his own religious creeds, and converted him before he got through; and it contains some of the noblest ethical and spiritual teachings to be found in any Bible in all the world...."

"Early Christianity, you will remember, if you will read over the writings of Paul, was made up of the people that the respectable did not have anything to do with. Spiritualism has until modern times been made up of much the same class of people. But now ... others by the score, are associated with it ; and some of the noblest, most intelligent people with whose names you are familiar were open and avowed adherents of Spiritualism. Remember, then, that this is a great and, in the main, genuine, sincere movement ..."

In his speech, Reverend Savage made the difference by calling a spade a spade. It is true that mediumistic communications are not all of equal interest. Many are composed of banalities, repetitions, common places. Not all spirits are able to give us useful and profound

---

[33] The book referred to is W. Stainton MOSES, *Spirit Teachings* (London: Spiritualist Alliance, 1898). It should be pointed out that in the case of Stainton MOSES, as with some others, the messages were not only obtained through automatic writing, but also by direct writing, without the intermediary of any human hand.

teachings. As on Earth and beyond, the scale of beings on the spiritual plane has infinite degrees. One meets there the most noble intelligences as well as the most vulgar souls. Yet sometimes the lower-order spirits themselves, in describing their moral situation, their impressions of death and the Hereafter, by initiating us in the details of their new existence, provide us with precious information for determining the conditions of survival according to the various categories of spirits. So there are elements of instruction to draw from everywhere in our relationship with the Unseen. However, not everything is to be kept in our memory. It is up to the cautious and wise experimenter to know how to separate gold from the baser metal. Truth does not always come to us naked, and action from above gives our faculties and reason the necessary field to be practiced and developed.

In all this, many precautions must be taken, a continual and vigilant control must be exercised. We must beware of frauds, whether conscious or unconscious, and see if there is no case of mere automatism in the writings. For this purpose, one must be ascertained that the communications, both in form and content, are above and beyond the capabilities of the medium. Proof of identity must be required at all times from the communicating spirits, save in cases where the teachings, by their own superiority and majestic magnitude, are self-imposing and evidently surpass the possibilities of the transmitter.

When the authenticity of communications is ensured, one must still compare them, and sift through a severe judgment, all the scientific and philosophical principles they set forth, and accept only those points on which almost unanimous views are established.

Apart from frauds of human origin, there are also mystifications perpetrated by the hidden sources. All serious experimenters know that there are two forms of

Spiritism. One practiced right, the other wrong, without method, without elevation of thought, the latter drawing to us the onlookers of the spiritual world, irresponsible and mocking Spirits, which are numerous in earthly atmosphere. Spiritism practiced right is a serious matter, perfected with restraint and a respectful feeling, it puts us in touch with advanced Spirits, eager to help and enlighten those who call them with a fervent heart. This is what religions have known and referred to as the "communion of saints."

Also, it is often asked how, in this vast set of communications whose authors are invisible, can one distinguish what comes from higher entities and should be preserved? There is only one answer to this question: How can we distinguish the good from the bad books of long-deceased authors? How to distinguish noble and elevated language from banal and vulgar language? Do we not have judgment, a rule to measure the quality of thoughts, whether they come from our world or another? We can judge the mediumistic messages mainly by their moralizing effects; they are great sometimes and have improved many characters, purified many consciences. This is the most certain criterion of all philosophical teaching.

In our relationship with the Unseen, there are also signs of recognition to distinguish good spirits from backward ones. Sensitives can easily recognize the nature of the fluids: soft and agreeable in the good spirits; violent, icy, and painful to endure in evil ones. One of our mediums always announced in advance the arrival of the so-called "Blue Spirit," which was revealed by harmonious vibrations and brilliant radiations. There are some who are distinguished by the smell, perceptible by some mediums. Delicate, soft in some,[34] these smells are repulsive in others. The elevation of a Spirit is measured

---

[34] See J. MAXWELL, *Metapsychical Phenomena* (Trans. L. I. Finch. London: Duckworth, 1905), p. 181.

by the purity of its fluids, and the beauty of its form and language.

In this type of research, what strikes, persuades and convinces the most, are the interviews with those of our relatives and friends who have preceded us in returning to the spiritual plane. If indisputable proof of identity has assured us of their presence, then that intimacy of former days, that trust and abandon, will reign again between them and us, and the revelations thus obtained take on a most suggestive nature. When faced by these facts, the last hesitations of skepticism inevitably vanish to make room for the impulses of the heart.

Can we indeed resist the familiar strains, the appeals of those who have shared our lives, surrounding our first steps of their tender solicitude, of those childhood companions, of our youth, of our virility, which one by one have vanished into death, leaving, at each departure, our road even more solitary, more desolate? They return in the mediumistic trance, with attitudes, voice inflections, reminders of memories, with numerous proofs of identity, banal in their details for those alien to them, but so moving for their nearest and dearest! They teach us about the problems of the Hereafter, while exhorting and comforting us. The coldest individuals, the most learned experimentalists, like Professor Hyslop, could not resist these influences from beyond the grave.[35] This demonstrates that there is not only frivolous and abusive practices in Spiritism, as some claim, but rather a noble and generous motive, that is, our attachment bonds with our dead, the interest we have in their memory. Would this not be one of the most respectable sides of human nature, one of the feelings, one of the forces that elevates

---

[35] See Léon DENIS, *Into the Unseen* (New York: USSF, 2017), ch. XIX, containing the interviews of Professor Hyslop, of Columbia University, with his deceased father, brother, and uncles.

humans above matter and differentiates them from the brute?

Next, above the exhortations of our loved ones, let us point out the powerful surges by Spirits of genius, whose pages were feverishly written in the semi-darkness by mediums of our knowledge, unable of understanding their value and beauty, but where the splendor of style matches the depth of ideas. Or these impressive speeches, often heard in our mediumistic group, delivered by the mouth of a very modest medium both in terms of knowledge and character, and through which a Spirit would tell us of the eternal enigma of the world and the laws that govern spiritual life. Those who had the privilege of attending such meetings know what pervasive influence they can exert on us all. In spite of the skeptical tendencies and the jesting spirit of people of our generation, there are strains, forms of language, impulses of eloquence which they could not resist. The most prejudiced would be obliged to recognize the characteristic, the indisputable mark of a great moral superiority, the seal of truth. When faced with these spirits descending for a moment into our obscure and backward world to let us glimpse a shining flash of their genius, the most demanding criticism is troubled, hesitates, and is silenced.

For twenty years we received communications of this kind at Tours (France). They touched all the great problems, all the important questions of philosophy and morality, and comprised several manuscript volumes. It is a summary of this work, much too extensive, too thick to be published in full, that I would like to present herein. Jerome of Prague, my friend, my spirit guide now and in the past, the magnanimous Spirit that directed the first impulses of my infantile intelligence, in the distant ages, is its author. I wonder how many other eminent Spirits have thus spread their teachings throughout the world, in the intimacy of a few groups! Almost always anonymous, they are revealed only by the high value of their conceptions. It was given to me to lift some of the veils hiding their true identity. But I must keep their secret, for this trait is precisely one of the characteristics of Highly-evolved Spirits, that they hide themselves under borrowed designations and wish to remain incognito. Incidentally, the famous names, found at the bottom of some flat and empty communications, are all too often just a mystifying lure.

By means of all these details, I only wish to demonstrate one thing: this book is not exclusively mine, but rather the reflection of a higher thought that I seek to interpret. It agrees, in all essentials, with the views expressed by the spirit instructors of Allan Kardec; however, any points left obscure by them are herein discussed. I also had to take into account the movement of human thought and science since, new discoveries, and highlight them in this book. In some cases, I added to them my own personal impressions and comments; for in Spiritism, one cannot stress enough, there is no dogma, and each of its principles can and must be discussed, judged, and submitted to the control of reason.

I considered it a duty to make my earthly brothers and sisters benefit from these teachings. A work is worth in itself. Whatever one may think and say about the revelation of the Spirits, I cannot conceive that, while teaching immense metaphysical systems built by human thought in all Universities, one would deem negligible or reject the principles disclosed by the lofty Intelligences of the spiritual world.

If we love the masters of reason and human wisdom, this is no excuse to disdain the masters of superhuman reason, the representatives of a higher and more serious wisdom. The human spirit, compressed by the flesh, deprived of the fullness of its resources and perceptions, cannot come by itself to the knowledge of the unseen universe and its laws. The circle in which our life and thought is moving is limited; our point of view, restricted. The insufficiency of the acquired data makes all generalization impossible or improbable. We need Guides to enter the unknown and infinite domain of universal laws. It is through the collaboration of eminent thinkers of the two worlds, of the two types of humanity, that the highest truths will be attained, or at least glimpsed; and the noblest principles will be established. Much better and more surely than our earthly masters, those of the spiritual plane know how to put us in the presence of the problem of life, of the mystery of the soul, and help us become aware of our greatness and our future.

Sometimes a question is put to me, a new objection is made: In view of the infinite variety of communications and the freedom of anyone to evaluate them, even to control them at will, where can one possibly find, in such circumstances, the unity of this philosophical doctrine, a powerful unity such as the one which has given strength and grandeur, and also assured the permanence and continuation of priestly religions?

Spiritism, as I said, does not rely on any dogmas. It is neither a sect nor an orthodoxy. It is a living philosophy, open to all free spirits, and progressing while evolving. It imposes nothing; it proposes, and what it proposes is based on facts of experience and moral proofs. It excludes none of the other beliefs, but rises above them and embraces them in a larger formula, in a higher and more expansive expression of the truth.

Superior intelligences are opening the way for us. They reveal the eternal principles that each of us should adopt and assimilate in order to extend our understanding, according to the degree of development attained by our faculties in the succession of our lives.

In general, the unity of philosophical or religious doctrine is obtained only at the price of blind and passive submission to a set of principles, fixed formulas in a rigid mold. It is the petrification of thought, the divorce between religion and science – the latter not being able to exist without freedom and movement.

Such an immobility, such a rigid fixation of dogmas, prevents religion from imposing on itself all the benefits inherent social movement and the evolution of thought. In considering itself the only good and true belief, it succeeds in proscribing all that is without, and thus sinks into a tomb, wishing to drag with itself all the intellectual life and genius of the human race.

The greatest concern of Spiritism is to avoid these fatal consequences of orthodoxy. Its revelation is a free and sincere exposition of doctrines that have nothing immutable but constitute a new stage towards the eternal and infinite truth. Everyone has the right to analyze its principles, and they have no other sanction than conscience and reason. But in adopting them, one must conform one's life to it and fulfill the duties that follow from it. Those who do not do so cannot be considered serious adherents.

Allan Kardec has always warned against dogmatism and sectarianism. He constantly recommends in his books not to let Spiritism be crystallized and to avoid the harmful methods that have ruined religious temperament in France.

In these times of discord and political and religious struggles, where science and orthodoxy are at stake, we would like to demonstrate to humans of good will of all opinions, of all beliefs, as well as to all truly free thinkers endowed with a broad understanding, that this is a neutral ground, set by experimental Spiritualism, where we can meet and give one another a hand. Enough of dogmas! No more mysteries! Let us open our minds to all the breaths of the spirit; let us draw from all the sources of the past and the present. Let us say that in every philosophical or religious doctrine there are portions of truth; but none contains it entirely, the truth in its fullness being far larger than the human spirit.

It is only in the agreement of good wills, sincere hearts and disinterested spirits that harmony of thought will be achieved as well as the mastery of the great sum of truth attainable by humans on Earth at this stage in History.

A day will come when everyone will understand that there is no antithesis between science and true religion. There are only misunderstandings. Antithesis exists between science and orthodoxy: by drawing us closer, in a sensible way, to the sacred doctrines from the East and from Gaul, regarding the unity of the world and the evolution of life, recent scientific discoveries have proved it. That is why we can affirm that, by pursuing their parallel march on the great path of the centuries, science and belief will inevitably meet one day, because their goal is identical; and they will end up interpenetrating each other. Science will be analysis; religion will become synthesis. In them the world of facts and the world of causes will unite; the two definitions of human intelligence will reconnect; the veil of the invisible will be torn; the divine work will appear to all eyes in its majestic splendor!

The allusions we have just made to ancient religions and philosophies might give rise to another objection: Spiritist teachings, it will be said, are therefore not entirely new? Indeed, no doubt. At all ages of humanity, light has sprung up, glimmers have enlightened thinking in humanity's march, and the necessary truths was revealed to sages and seekers. Individuals of genius, as well as sensitives and seers, have always received from the Beyond revelations appropriate to the needs of human evolution.[36] It is unlikely that the first humans could have arrived of themselves and only by their own mental capacities to the notion of laws and even to the first forms of civilization. Conscious or not, the communion between Earth and the spiritual plane has always existed.

Also, we would easily find in the religious and philosophical doctrines of the past most of the principles brought to light by the teaching of the spirits. Moreover, these principles, reserved for the few, had not penetrated to the souls of crowds. Their revelation occurred rather in the form of isolated communications, sporadic manifestations; most often they were considered as miraculous. But after twenty or thirty centuries of slow work and silent gestation, critical thinking has developed and reason has risen to the concept of higher laws. These phenomena, with their associated teaching, reappear, become general, and guide hesitant societies in the arduous path of progress.

It is always in the troubled hours of history that great synthetic conceptions are formed within humanity; when old religions and overly abstract philosophies are no longer enough to soothe distress, to revive depleted courage, to drive souls to the summits. Yet these souls still have many latent forces and energy points that could

---

[36] See Léon DENIS, *Into the Unseen* (New York: USSF, 2017) ch. XXVI, "Mediumship in its glory."

be revived. Therefore we do not share the views of some theoreticians who, in this area, rather think of demolishing than restoring – this would be a mistake. Two parts remain to be reappraised in the legacy of the past, and even in esoteric religions, created for childish minds, and all meeting the needs of a particular category of souls. Wisdom would consist in collecting the part referring to eternal life, the elements of moral direction contained in them, while avoiding the useless, superfluous additions later attached to them by the action of the ages and of human passions.

Who could accomplish this work of discerning, sorting out, renovating it? Humans were poorly prepared for the task. In spite of the imperious warnings of the last years, in spite of the moral decay of our time, no authorized voice has risen, neither in the sanctuaries nor from the holders of high academic chairs, to say the strong and serious words that the world was expecting.

From then on, the impulsion could only come from above – and it has. All those who have studied the past with attention know that there is a plan in the convolution of the centuries. Divine thought manifests itself in different ways, and revelation is graded in a thousand ways, according to the needs of societies. Therefore, once the hour of a new dispensation has arrived, the unseen world comes out of its silence. Throughout the Earth, the communications of the dead have poured in, bringing the elements of a doctrine in which the philosophies and religions of two different humanities are summed up and merged. The goal of Spiritism is not to destroy, but to unify and complement by renovating. It comes to separate, in the realm of beliefs, what is alive from what is dead. It collects and collates, in the many systems where hitherto the consciousness of humanity has been locked up, with the relative truths they contain, in order to unite them with the general truths proclaimed by itself. In short, Spiritism attaches to the human soul, still uncertain and feeble, the powerful wings of ample spaces, by this means elevating it to heights from which it can embrace the vast harmony of laws and worlds, at the same time getting a clearer vision of its own destiny.

And this destiny is incomparably superior to all that was preached by the religious philosophies of the Middle Ages or the theories of other times. It is a future of immense evolution that opens up for it and continues from sphere to sphere, from light to light, toward an ever more beautiful goal, increasingly illuminated by the rays of justice and love.

III

THE NATURE OF BEING

THE FIRST PROBLEM that arises in thought is of thought itself, or rather of the thinking being. This is, for all of us, a capital subject, one that dominates all others, and whose solution brings us back to the very sources of life and the universe.

What is the nature of our personality? Does it contain something that can survive death? To this question are attached all the fears and hopes of humanity.

The problem of being and the problem of the soul are one; it is the soul that provides human beings with their principle of life and movement.[37] The human soul is a free and sovereign will; it is the conscious unity that dominates all attributes, all functions, all the material elements of being, whereas the divine soul dominates, coordinates and connects all parts of the universe to harmonize them.

The soul is immortal because nothingness does not exist and absolutely nothing can be destroyed. No individuality can cease to be. The dissolution of material forms merely proves that the soul is separated from the organism by means of which it communicated with the earthly environment. However, it continues to evolve under new conditions, in more perfect forms and without losing its identity. Each time it leaves its earthly body, the soul finds itself living in the spiritual plane, united to its spiritual body, of which it is inseparable, to this

---

[37] As I will demonstrate later in this book, using a whole set of facts of observation, experiments and objective evidence.

imponderable form which it has prepared through its thoughts and deeds.

This subtle body, this fluidic double, exists in us in a permanent state. Although invisible, it serves as a mold for our material body. The latter does not play the most important role in the destiny of a being. This visible body, the physical body, varies. Formed for the necessities of the earthly stage, it is temporary and perishable; it disintegrates and dissolves to death. The subtle body remains; preexisting at birth, it survives decay in the tomb and accompanies the soul in its transmigrations. It is the model, the original matrix, the true human form, in which the molecules of the flesh are incorporated for a period of time, and which remains in the midst of all variations and all material currents. Even during life, this subtle form can be partially detached from the fleshly body under certain conditions, to act, to appear, to manifest itself from a distance, as we shall see later below, so as to prove, irrefutably, its independent existence.[38]

---

[38] Physiological science, to which most laws of life are still elusive, has, however, glimpsed the existence of the perispirit or fluidic body, which is at once the mold of the material body, the envelope of the soul, and the necessary intermediary between them. Claude BERNARD wrote (in *Recherches sur les Problèmes de la Physiologie* [*Research on the Problems of Physiology*]): "There is like a preestablished blueprint of each being and of each organ, so that if, considered in isolation, each phenomenon of the organism is dependent on the general forces of Nature, they seem to reveal a special bond, they seem directed by some invisible condition on the path they follow, in the order that binds them."

Away from the notion of a fluidic body, the union of the soul to the material body remains incomprehensible. From this came the weakening of certain spiritualistic theories which regarded the soul as "pure spirit." Neither reason nor science can admit a being devoid of form. LEIBNIZ (1646–1716) in the preface to his *New Essays concerning Human Understanding* (Trans. A. G. Langley. New York: Macmillan, 1896) said: "I believe with the majority of the ancients that all genii, all souls, all simple created substances, are always joined to a body, and that there are never souls entirely separated."

The proofs of the existence of the soul are of two kinds: moral and experimental. Let us first consider moral and logical proofs, which, having been often used, still retain all their strength and value.

The materialistic and monistic schools affirm that the soul is only the result of brain functions. "The brain-cells," said Ernst Haeckel, "are the true organs of thought, the only organs of our consciousness." The latter would be linked to their integrity. It grows, regresses, and disappears with them. According to him, the material germ contains the entire being, both physical and mental.

Let me answer in substance: Matter is unable to generate qualities that it does not have. Atoms, whether triangular, circular, or crooked, cannot represent reason, genius, pure love, sublime charity. The brain, it is said, creates the function; but would this mean that a function can know itself, possess consciousness and sensibility? How to explain consciousness other than through the spirit? Does it come from matter? Well, it fights it frequently! Does it come from interest and self-preservation instinct? It rebels against both and commands us to self-sacrifice!

The material organism of itself is not the principle of life and faculties; on the contrary, it is its limit. The brain

---

There is, moreover, a great deal of objective and subjective evidence of the existence of the perispirit. First there is the so-called "integrity" sensations, which always accompany the amputation of any member. Magnetizers claim that they can influence their patients by magnetizing the fluidic prolongation of the amputated limbs (see Carl DU PREL, *Die monistische Seelenlehre* [*The Monistic Doctrine of the Soul*], Leipzig: Günther, 1888, ch. VI). Then come the apparitions of phantasms of the living. In many cases, the fluidic body, concretized, impressed photographic plates, left impressions and moldings in soft substances, traces on dust and soot, caused the displacement of objects, etc. (See Léon Denis *Into the Unseen*, New York: USSF, 2017, ch. XII and XX).

is only an instrument by means of which the mind records sensations; it could be compared to a keyboard where each key represents a special kind of sensation. When the instrument is perfectly attuned, these keys, under the action of the will, make sounds specific to them, and harmony reigns in our ideas and our actions. But if these same keys are disturbed, if several of them are destroyed, the sound rendered will be false, generating an incomplete harmony: this will result in disagreement, despite the efforts of the artist's intelligence, who can no longer obtain from this defective instrument a set of regular manifestations. This explains mental illnesses, neuroses, mental impairment, the temporary loss of speech or memory, madness, etc., without the existence of the soul being altered by it. In all these cases, the spirit remains, but its manifestations are thwarted and sometimes even annihilated as a result of a lack of correlation with its organism.

No doubt, generally speaking, the development of the brain denotes high faculties. A delicate and powerful soul requires a more perfect instrument that will lend itself to all manifestations of a high and fruitful thought. The dimensions and convolutions of the brain are often directly related to the degree of evolution of the spirit.[39] As a consequence, it should not be assumed that memory is merely a game of brain cells. These are constantly changing and renewing themselves, says science, to such

---

[39] This rule is not absolute. Gambetta's brain, for example, weighed only 1,246 grams (2.746 pounds), whereas the human average is 1,500 to 1,800 grams. Moreover, let me add that the theory of cerebral localizations, which used to preponderate in physiology, has received a serious blow in the wake of "Famous and frequent cases of extensive lesions in the so-called essential regions, not accompanied by any serious mental disorder, nor any restrictions in personality." See the famous case published by Dr. GUÉPIN in March 1917, and the numerous war-wound cases specially studied by Dr. TROUDE (*Revue Métapsychique*, issue no. 1, 1921–1922).

THE NATURE OF BEING

an extent that the brain and the whole human body are renewed in a few years.[40] In these conditions, how can we explain that we can remember facts dating back ten, twenty, thirty years? How do old men remember with surprising ease the smallest details of their childhood? How can memory, personality, in a word the self, persist and continue in the midst of continual organic destruction and reconstruction? So many insoluble problems for materialism!

Nothing can reach the soul, proclaim contemporary psychologists, except through the senses, and the suspension of the latter causes the disappearance of the former. Let me remark, however, that the state of anesthesia (i.e., a momentary suppression of sensibility) does not at all suppress the action of intelligence; on the contrary, it is activated, in cases where, according to materialistic doctrines, it should be annihilated.

Dr. Buisson wrote: "If there is anything that can demonstrate the independence of the self, it is certainly the proof provided by patients subjected to the action of ether and in whom the intellectual faculties resist in this state to anesthetic agents."

Dr. Velpeau, dealing with the same subject, said: "What a rich mine for physiology and psychology is found in facts like these, which separate the mind from matter, the intelligence from the body!"

We will also see how, in ordinary or induced sleep, in somnambulism and exteriorization, the soul can live, perceive, and act without the help of the senses.

---

[40] Claude BERNARD, *La Science Expérimentale* (Paris: J. B. Ballière, 1878) and *Phénomènes de la Vie* (Paris: J. B. Ballière, 1885).

If the soul, as Ernst Haeckel says, represented only the sum of corporeal elements, there would always be, in humans, a correlation between the physical and the mental. This relation would be direct and constant, and a perfect balance between the faculties and moral qualities, on the one hand, would match one's material constitution, on the other. The best physically fit individuals would also possess the most intelligent and worthy souls. Yet we know that this is not so, for often highly evolved souls have inhabited feeble bodies. Health and strength do not necessarily entail, in those who possess them, a subtle mind and brilliant faculties.

Indeed, although the saying goes, *Mens sana in corpore sano* (*A healthy mind in a healthy body*), there are so many exceptions to this maxim that it cannot be considered as an absolute rule. The flesh always gives way to pain. It is not the same with the soul, which often resists, exalts itself in suffering, and triumphs over external agents.

The examples left by Antigone, Jesus, Socrates, Joan of Arc, Christian martyrs, Hussites and so many others who adorn history and ennoble the human race, are there to remind us that the voices of self-sacrifice and duty can rise well above material instincts. The will of the heroes knows how to subdue the hindrances of the body at decisive hours.

If humans were entirely contained in a physical source, one would find in them only the qualities and flaws inherited from their progenitors, and to the same degree as in the latter. But, on the contrary, children everywhere are seen to differ from their parents, going beyond them or remaining inferior to them. Siblings and twins, strikingly similar in appearance, present traits, in their minds and morals, that are dissimilar to one another and to their ancestors.

The theories of atavism and heredity are powerless to explain the famous cases of child artists or scholars: musicians like Mozart or Paganini, calculating prodigies like Henri Mondeux and Giacomo Inaudi, ten-year-old painters such as Frédéric Van de Kerckhove and so many other child prodigies whose aptitudes are not found in their parents, or when present in them – such as in Mozart's case – are found only to a much lesser degree.

The material properties transmitted by the parents are manifested in the child's physical resemblance and hereditary constitutional ills. But the resemblance remains only during the first period of life. As soon as the character is defined, as soon as the child becomes an adult, we see the features change little by little; at the same time the hereditary tendencies diminish and give way to other elements constituting a different personality, a self which is sometimes very distinct in its tastes, its qualities, its passions, from those of its progenitors. It is therefore not the material organism that forms the personality, but the inner human, the psychical self. As it develops and asserts itself through its own actions in a lifetime, one sees the parents' physical and mental inheritance gradually weakening, and often vanishing.

The notion of good, engraved in the depths of consciousness, is still an evident proof of our spiritual origin. If humans were born only of dust, or as a result of the mechanical forces of the world, we would not know the good from the bad, feel neither remorse nor moral pain. We are told: These notions come from our ancestors, education, social influences! But if these notions were the exclusive heritage of the past, where did the past get them from? And why would they grow in us, if they did not find a favorable terrain and nurture therein.

If you have suffered at the sight of evil, if you have cried over yourself and others at these moments of sadness, of revelatory pain, you have been able to glimpse the secret depths of the soul, its mysterious ties to the Hereafter, and you have understood the bitter charm and high purpose of one's existence, of all existences. This goal is the education of beings through pain; it is the ascension of finite things toward infinite life.

No, thought and consciousness do not derive from a chemical and mechanical universe. On the contrary, they dominate it from above, directing and subduing it. Indeed, is it not thought that measures the worlds and space, which discerns the harmonies of the Cosmos? We only partly belong to the material world, so we feel its evils so strongly. If we belonged to it entirely, we would find ourselves better suited to it in our element, and so much suffering would be spared us.

The truth about human nature, about life and destiny, good and evil, freedom and responsibility, cannot be discovered in the bottom of test tubes or under the tips of scalpels. Material science cannot judge things of the spirit. The spirit alone can judge and understand the spirit, according to one's evolutionary degree. It is from the consciousness of higher souls, from their thoughts, from their labors, from their examples, from their self-sacrifices, that the greatest light and the most noble ideal spring up which can then guide humanity in its path.

Humans are at once spirit and matter, soul and body. Yet perhaps spirit and matter are but words imperfectly expressing the two forms of eternal life, which slumbers in raw matter, awakens in organic matter, becomes active, flourishes and rises in the spirit.

Is there not, as certain philosophers admit, a single essence of things, at once form and thought, the form being a materialized thought, and thought, the form of the spirit?[41] That is possible. Human knowledge is restricted, and the momentary glance of genius is itself only a quick flash in the infinite domain of ideas and laws.

However, what characterizes the soul and absolutely differentiates it from matter is its conscious unity. Matter disperses and vanishes in analysis. The physical atom is subdivided into sub-atoms, which in turn are fragmented indefinitely. Matter – the recent discoveries of Becquerel, Curie, and Lebon have established it – is entirely devoid of unity. The spirit, alone, in the universe, represents the element of a single entity, simple, indivisible and, consequently, logically indestructible, imperishable, and immortal!

---

[41] The spirit is understood here as the *intelligent principle*.

IV

THE INTEGRAL PERSONALITY

Consciousness, the self, is the center of being, the very foundation of one's personality.

To be a person is to have consciousness and a conscience, a self that reflects, examines, and remembers. But can one know, analyze and describe the self, its mysterious folds, its latent forces, its fruitful sources, its hidden activities? Psychologies, philosophies of the past have tried it in vain. Their work only scratched the surface of the conscious being. Its inner and deep layers remained obscure, inaccessible, until the day when the experiments of hypnotism, Spiritism, and the renovation of memory, finally threw some light on it.

And then, we could see that echoes the whole universe are reflected in us, in its double immensity of space and time. We say space, because the soul, in its free and full manifestations, does not know distances. We say time, because a whole past slumbers in it and the future rests there in latent state.

The old schools of thought admitted the unity and continuity of the self, the permanence, the perfect identity of the human personality and its survival. Their studies were based on the inner sense that is currently called introspection.

The new experimental psychology considers personality to be an aggregate, a compound, a "colony." In its view, the unity of the being is only apparent and can be decomposed. The ego is but a transient coordination, said Prof. Théodule-Armand Ribot.[42] These affirmations are based on facts of experience that should not be neglected, such as unconscious intellectual life, alterations of personality, and so on.

How to approach and reconcile theories as dissimilar and yet both based on the science of observation? In a very simple way. By observation itself, more attentively, more rigorously. F. W. H. Myers put it in these terms:[43]

"Deeper, bolder inquiry along their own line shows that they have erred when they asserted that analysis showed no trace of faculty beyond such as the life of earth – as they conceive it – could foster, or the environment of earth employ. For in reality analysis shows traces of faculty which this material or planetary life could not have called into being, and whose exercise even here and now involves and necessitates the existence of a spiritual world."

"On the other side, and in favor of the partisans of the unity of the Ego, the effect of the new evidence is to raise their claim to a far higher ground, and to substantiate it for the first time with the strongest presumptive proof which can be imagined for it a proof, namely, that the Ego can and does survive – not only the minor disintegrations which affect it during earth-life – but the crowning disintegration of bodily death...."

"The 'conscious Self' of each of us, as we call it, – the empirical, the supraliminal Self, as I should prefer to say, – does not comprise the whole of the consciousness or of

---

[42] T. RIBOT, *Les Maladies de la Personnalité* (Paris: Félix Alcan, 1885), pp. 170-171.

[43] F. W. H. MYERS, *Human Personality* (London: Longmans, 1903), vol. I, ch. I, section 111, pp. 11-12. This book represents the most magnificent effort that has ever been made by human thought to solve the problems of life and being.

the faculty within us. There exists a more comprehensive consciousness, a profounder faculty, which for the most part remains potential only so far as regards the life of earth, but from which the consciousness and the faculty of earth-life are mere selections, and which reasserts itself in its plenitude after the liberating change of death."

"Towards this conclusion, which assumed for me something like its present shape some fourteen years since, a long series of tentative speculations, based on gradually accruing evidence, has slowly conducted me."

In some cases we see a human being quite different from its normal state, possessing not only more extensive knowledge and skills than an ordinary personality, but also more powerful and more varied modes of perception. Sometimes, in the phenomena of "second personality," the character changes and differs so much from the usual, that observers have believed in the presence of another individual.

It is important to distinguish between these cases and the phenomena of "incorporation" (psychophony) of the deceased. The mediums, in a state of somnambulistic release, sometimes lend their organism free for entities of the Hereafter, for disembodied Spirits who use it to communicate with humans. But then, the names, the details, the proofs of identities provided by the communicating spirits do not allow any confusion. The invading individuality differs radically from that of the subject. The cases of G. Pelham,[44] of Robert Hyslop, of Fourcade, and others, demonstrate that substitutions of spirits should not be confused with cases of double personality.

However such an error is possible; indeed, like the "incorporations" of spirits, the intervention of secondary personalities is preceded by a short sleep. These

---

44 See Léon DENIS, *Into the Unseen* (New York: USSF, 2017), *passim*.

arise, most often, in a bout of somnambulism or, even, as a result of an emotion. The period of manifestation, initially of short duration, is prolonged little by little, is repeated and specified until acquiring and constituting a sequence of particular memories which are distinguished from the set of memories recorded in the normal consciousness of the individual. This phenomenon can be facilitated or induced by hypnotic suggestion. It is even probable that in spontaneous cases, where no human will intervenes, this phenomenon is due to the suggestion of invisible agents, guides and protectors of the subject; then they act, as we shall see, with a healing, therapeutic purpose.

In the famous case of Félida, studied by Dr. Azam,[45] the two states of consciousness, or variations of the personality, are sharply defined:

"Almost every day, without any known cause or being influenced by an emotion, she is stricken by what she calls her crisis; in fact, she returns to her second state; she sits, holding a sewing book in her hand; suddenly, without being able to foresee it, and after a pain in her temples more violent than usual, her head falls on her chest, her hands remain inactive and descend inert along her body; she sleeps, or seems to be asleep, but in a special sleep, for no sound, no excitement, not even pinching or stinging can awaken her. Moreover this kind of sleep is absolutely sudden. It lasts two or three minutes; formerly it used to last much longer."

"After this period of time, Félida wakes up; but she is no longer in the intellectual state she was in when she fell asleep. Everything looks different. She raises her head and, opening her eyes, greets the people around her with a smile, as if she had just arrived; the countenance,

---

[45] Dr. Alfred BINET, *Altérations de la Personnalité* (Paris: Félix Alcan, 1892), pp. 6–20.

sad and silent before, lights up and exudes gaiety; her speech is brief, and she continues, humming, the needlework which, in the preceding state, she had begun; she rises, moving nimbly, and she scarcely complains of the thousand pains which, a few moments earlier, made her suffer; she goes about the ordinary care of the household, circulates in the city, etc. Her character is completely changed: from sadness, she is now jolly; her imagination is more exalted; for the slightest reason she is moved into sadness or joy; normally indifferent, now she becomes exceedingly sensitive."

"In this state she remembers perfectly all that has happened in the other similar states that preceded, and also during her normal life. In this life as in the other, her intellectual and moral faculties, although different, are incontestably whole: no delusional idea, no false appreciation, no hallucination. Félida is different, that is all. We may even say that, in this second state, this second condition, as Dr. Azam calls it, all her faculties appear to be more developed and more complete."

"This second life, where the physical pain is not felt, is much greater than the other; it is especially so because of the considerable fact that, during her lifetime, Félida remembers not only what happened during the previous accesses, but also during all her normal life, while during her normal life she does not have any memory of what happened during her accesses."

It can be seen that it is not the case of several personalities, but simply several states of the same consciousness. A relation continues to exist among the various aspects of the psychical being. At least, the second state, the most complete, knows everything of what the former state did; while the latter knows nothing of the other, only by hearsay. No. 2's lifestyle treats No. 1 with a certain disdain. Félida, in the second state, speaks of the 'stupid girl' in the same way that we ourselves would speak about the awkward child, the clumsy baby that we once were.

In the case of Louis Vivé,[46] we find ourselves in the presence of a phenomenon of "regression of memory." The subject, under the influence of hypnotic suggestion, relives all the scenes of his life, or, as said by F. W. H. Myers, "Any given condition can be revived in a moment, and the whole gamut of changes rung on his nervous system as easily as if one were setting back or forward a continuous cinematograph." Not only do the past and forgotten mental states come to memory at the same time as the physical impressions of these variations, but when a mental state passed and forgotten is suggested to the patient as being his current state, he immediately experiences the corresponding physical impressions.

We will see later that, thanks to experiments of the same nature, we have been able to reconstruct the previous existences of certain subjects with the same sharpness, the same power of impressions and sensations. And, in this way, we are led to recognize that the deep science of being has many surprises in store for everyone.

In Mary Reynolds,[47] there is a complete character transformation, which presents three distinct phases: one, marked by carelessness; the other, by a tendency to sadness, with a leaning to merge into a third state, superior to the other two.

We cannot overlook the observations of the same nature made by Dr. Morton Prince on Miss Beauchamp.[48]

---

[46] F. W. H. MYERS, *Human Personality* (London: Longmans, 1903), vol. I, ch. II, section 233, p. 62. See also CAMUSET, *Annales médico-psychologiques*, 1882, p. 15.

[47] W. JAMES, *Principles of Psychology*, 2 vols. (New York: Holt, 1890; reprinted Bristol: Thoemmes Press, 1999).

[48] See Dr. Morton PRINCE, *The Dissociation of a Personality* (London: Longmans, Green & Co., 1906). See also ROCHAS D'AIGLUN, *Les*

This one presents several aspects of the same personality, which have been revealed successively and have been denominated, when they appear, as B1, B2, B4, B5.

B1 is Miss Beauchamp in her normal state, a serious person, reserved, scrupulous to excess. B2 is the same person in a state of hypnosis, with more easygoing, carefree, and possessing a larger memory. B4, which was revealed later, is distinguished from the preceding by a complete state of harmonious unity and normal equilibrium, but which lacks the memory of the last six years, as a result of violent emotion. Finally B5, which combines as in a synthesis, the memory of the states already described.

The originality of this case consists in the intervention, in the midst of these various aspects of Miss Beauchamp's personality, of an individuality which is, it seems to us, completely foreign. This is B3 who says her name is Sally, a mischievous, teasing, even facetious entity, controlling Miss Beauchamp, and whose repeated pranks made life very difficult to the latter. Sally adapts, physiologically, rather badly to the subject's organs; it seems totally foreign to them.

In my opinion, this mysterious Sally would be just a disincarnate spirit succeeding in replacing the normal person while asleep, and disposing, for a period of time, of an organism whose state of equilibrium is momentarily disturbed. This phenomenon belongs to the category of "incorporations" of spirits, which was specially covered in another of my books.[49]

Vies Successives (Paris: Charconac Frères, 1911), pp. 398–402.

[49] See Léon DENIS, *Into the Unseen* (New York: USSF, 2017), ch. XIX, "Trance and Incorporations."

Finally, F. W. H. Myers, in his masterful book,[50] reports a case of "multiple personality" studied by Dr. R. Osgood Mason, that I believe should be reproduced here:

"Alma Z. was an unusually healthy and intellectual girl, a strong and attractive character, a leading spirit in whatever she undertook, whether in study, sport, or society. From overwork in school, and overtaxed strength in a case of sickness at home, her health was completely broken down, and after two years of great suffering suddenly a second personality appeared. In a peculiar child–like and Indian–like dialect she announced herself as 'Twoey,' and that she had come to help 'Number One' in her suffering. The condition of 'Number One' was at this time most deplorable ; there was great pain, extreme debility, frequent attacks of syncope, insomnia, and a mercurial stomatitis which had been kept up for months by way of medical treatment and which rendered it nearly impossible to take nourishment in any form. 'Twoey' was vivacious and cheerful, full of quaint and witty talk, never lost consciousness, and could take abundant nourishment, which she declared she must do for the sake of 'Number One.' Her talk was most quaint and fascinating, but without a trace of the acquired knowledge of the primary personality. She gave frequent evidence of supranormal[51] intelligence regarding events transpiring in the neighborhood. It was at this time that the case came under my observation, and has remained so for the past ten years. Four years later, under depressing circumstances, a third personality made its appearance and announced itself as 'The Boy.' This personality was entirely distinct and different from either of the others. It

---

[50] F. W. H. MYERS, *Human Personality* (London: Longmans, 1903), vol. I, ch. II, section 233, p. 62.

[51] [Trans. note] *Supranormal*, the same as *supernormal*.

remained the chief alternating personality for four years, when 'Twoey' again returned."

"All these personalities, though absolutely different and characteristic, were delightful each in its own way, and 'Twoey' especially was, and still is, the delight of the friends who are permitted to know her, whenever she makes her appearance ; and this is always at times of unusual fatigue, mental excitement, or prostration ; then she comes and remains days at a time. The original self retains her superiority when she is present, and the others are always perfectly devoted to her interest and comfort. 'Number One' has no personal knowledge of either of the other personalities, but she knows them well, and especially 'Twoey,' from the report of others and from characteristic letters which are often received from her; and 'Number One' greatly enjoys the spicy, witty, and often useful messages which come to her through these letters and the report of friends."

I have limited myself to quoting these facts alone, so as to avoid extending too much on the subject. However, there are many other cases of the same kind, which the reader can be find in specialized literature.[52]

As a whole, these phenomena demonstrate one thing, namely: that below the level of normal consciousness, apart from the ordinary personality, there exist in us planes of consciousness, layers or zones arranged in such

---

[52] See among others: Doctors H. BOURRU and P. BUROT, *Variations de la Personnalité* (Paris: J. B. Baillière, 1888). Dr. A. BINET, *Altérations de la Personnalité* (Paris: Félix Alcan, 1892). Dr. A. BERJON, *La Grande Hystérie chez l'Homme* (Paris: J. B. Baillière, 1886). Dr. R. Osgood MASON, "Duplex Personality: its Relation to Hypnotism and to Lucidity," in *Journal of the American Medical Association* (November 30, 1895). See also in the *Proceedings of the S. P. R.*, the case of Miss Beauchamp, studied by MORTON, the case of Annel Bourne, described by Dr. HODGSON, and that of Mollie Faucher, observed by the American judge Cain DAILEY.

a way that under certain conditions alternations can be noticed between these planes. We then see emerging on the surface and manifesting themselves for a given time, attributes and faculties which belong to the deep consciousness; then they soon disappear, to where they belong, and plunge back into the shadows, becoming inactive again.

Our ordinary, superficial self, limited by our organism, seems to be only a fragment of our total self. The latter has recorded a whole world of facts, of knowledge and memories related to the long past of one's soul. During normal life, all these reserves remain hidden, as if buried under our material envelope. They reappear in the somnambulistic state.[53] The call of one's will, a suggestion mobilizes them. They come into action and produce those strange phenomena that official physiology observes without being able to explain them.

All cases of duplication of personality, all the phenomena of clairvoyance, telepathy, and premonition, draw attention to new senses and unknown faculties. All this set of phenomena, the number of which increases and already constitutes a formidable array, must be attributed to the intervention of forces and resources deriving from the hidden personality.

The somnambulistic state, which allows the latter to manifest itself, is not a "regressive" or morbid state, as some observers have believed, but rather a superior state which, according to F. W. H. Myers' expression, is also "An advanced stage of evolutionary progress." It is true that the state of degeneration and organic weakening facilitates in some subjects the emergence of the deep layers of the self. This disorder used to be called hysteria. Generally speaking, it should be noted that, everything

---

[53] [Trans. note] *Somnambulistic state*, a trance-like state with no connection whatsoever with *sleepwalking*.

which depresses the physical energies of the body promotes the release, the exit of the spirit. In the dying, their lucidity should give us many testimonies on this point. But in order to judge these facts, it is proper to consider them especially from a psychological viewpoint; all their importance lies there.

Materialistic science has seen in these phenomena what it calls "disintegrations," that is to say, alterations and dissociations of personality. The severing of consciousness sometimes seems so decided, and the types that arise thereby, so different from the normal type, that any observer may believe to be in the presence of several autonomous consciousnesses, alternating in the same subject. I think, with Myers, that this is not so. There is simply a variety of successive states, all coinciding with the permanence of the self. Consciousness is one, but manifests itself variously: in a restricted way, in normal life, as long as it is limited in the field of the organism; fuller, more extended in the out-of-body states; and finally, in its totality, completed at death, after its definitive separation from the body, as demonstrated by the manifestations and teachings of Spirits. The split is therefore only apparent. The only difference to be made among the various states of consciousness is a difference of degrees. These degrees can be numerous. There seems to be a considerable margin, for example, between the state of spirit incorporation and its complete exteriorization. The personality is nonetheless identical through the chain of phenomena of consciousness, in which a continuous link connects them, from the simplest modifications of the normal state, to the cases involving a transformation of intelligence and character: from a simple fixed idea, dreams and visions, to the projection of the personality into the spiritual world, into that Beyond where the soul recovers the fullness of its perceptions and powers.

Already, in the course of our earthly existence, we see from childhood to old age, our self constantly changing; the soul passes through a succession of states; it is incessantly becoming; yet, in the midst of these various phases, its control over the organism does not vary. Physiology has highlighted this wise and harmonious coordination of all the parts of a being, those laws of organic life and nervous mechanism which cannot be explained without the presence of a central unity. This sovereign unity is the source and the preserver of life; it connects all the elements, all the different aspects.

It is by no means less unfortunate, as a the consequence of materialistic theories, that "psychologists" of the official school have come to regard genius as a neurosis, whereas it may actually be the use, to a greater extent, of psychic powers hidden in the human being.

F. W. H. Myers, speaking of the category of hysterics who lead the world, expresses the opinion that the inspiration of genius would only be the emergence, in the realm of conscious ideas, of other ideas in whose development consciousness did not take part, but which formed themselves, so to speak, independently of the will, in the deep regions of our being.[54]

In general, those who are so lightly called "degenerates" are often "progenerators." And among them – sensitives, hysterics and neurotics – the disturbances of the physical organism, nervous disorders, may well constitute a process of evolution that all humanity will have to undergo in order to reach a more intense degree of planetary life.

---

[54] *Cf.* F. W. H. MYERS, *Human Personality* (London: Longmans, 1903), vol. I, ch. III, "Genius," section 304, pp. 73 *et seq*. (I believe, however, that in examining the problem of genius, MYERS did not hold previous achievements in sufficient account, that is, the fruit of accumulated existences, any more than that of mediumistic inspiration, which is very characteristic of certain geniuses, such as discussed elsewhere. See Léon DENIS, *Into the Unseen*, last chapter).

Disorders always accompany the development of the human organism until it is fully developed, just as they precede the coming into light of every new being on Earth. In our painful efforts toward more life, morbid values are transmuted into moral forces. Our needs are merged instincts, which materialize in new senses to gain more power and knowledge.

Even in the ordinary state – the waking state – impulsions of the deep self can reemerge in outer layers of the personality, bringing intuitions, perceptions, sudden flashes of light upon the past and the future of a human being, which denote very extensive faculties not belonging to the normal self.

Most cases of automatic writing are related to this category of phenomena. I say most, because there are others, whose cause is external, by invisible agents.

In us, it is like a reservoir of underground water, from which springs at certain hours a fast and bubbling current, which rises to the surface. The prophets, the martyrs of all religions, the missionaries, the inspired ones, and the enthusiasts of all kinds and all schools of thought, have known these secret and powerful impulses. They have brought us the greatest works which revealed to humans the existence of a higher world.

THE SOUL AND THE DIFFERENT STATES OF SLEEP

THE STUDY OF SLEEP provides most relevant indications on the nature of personality. In general, the mystery of sleep has not yet been fully explored. A careful examination of this phenomenon, the study of the soul and its fluidic form during the part of our existence devoted to resting, will lead us to a wider understanding of our life conditions in the Hereafter.

Sleep not only has restorative properties that science has not sufficiently emphasized, but also a power for coordinating and centralizing the physical organism. It can also, as we have just seen, induce a considerable expansion of psychical perceptions, a greater intensity of reasoning and memory.

But what is sleep after all? It is simply the exit, the release of the soul from the body. It has been said: Sleep is death's sibling. These words express a deep truth. Sequestered in the flesh during the waking state, the soul temporarily recovers in sleep its relative freedom, as well as the use of its hidden powers. Death will be its complete and definitive release.

Already in visions and dreams, we see the senses of the soul in action, those psychical senses, of which those of the body are merely outward, diminished manifestations. As perceptions of the outside become weaker and veiled, when the eyes are shut and hearing is suspended, other, more powerful senses are awakened in the depths of the self. We see, we hear, with the help of internal senses. Images, forms, distant scenes, succeed and unfold; we engage in conversation with living or deceased characters. These actions, often incoherent and confused in natural sleep, become more precise and increase with the release of the soul during induced sleep, in the somnambulistic trance and ecstasy.

Sometimes, the soul moves away while the body is asleep, and then, it is the impressions of its travels, the results of its researches, of its observations, that are translated into dreams. In this state, a fluidic link still keeps it bonded to the material organism, and, through this subtle link – a kind of conducting thread – the impressions and the will of the soul can be transmitted to the physical brain. It is by the same process that, in the other forms of sleep, the soul controls its earthly envelope, commanding it, directing it. This direction in the waking state, during incorporation, is exerted from without; it will be carried out in the opposite direction in the different stages of out-of-body state. The soul, thus emancipated, will continue to influence the body with the help of this fluidic link which never ceases to connect one to the other. From then on, with its reconstituted psychical power, the soul will exert on its fleshly organism a more efficient and sure control. The completely assured walk exhibited by sleepwalkers at night, in perilous places, is an obvious demonstration of this fact.

It is the same with the therapeutic action induced by suggestion. This is effective especially in that it facilitates the liberation of the soul, and gives it its absolute power of control, the freedom necessary to direct the life force accumulated in the perispirit, thereby repairing the losses suffered by the physical body.⁵⁵ We have seen this phenomenon in cases of dual personality. The second personality, more complete, more whole than the normal personality, substitutes the latter for a curative purpose, by means of an external suggestion, accepted and transformed into self-suggestion by the subject's mind. Indeed, this one never relinquishes its rights and its powers of control. As F. W. H. Myers said, "It is not my command, but his faculty, that is the kernel of the whole matter."⁵⁶ The renowned Cambridge scholar also adds elsewhere:⁵⁷ "For what we have in effect been doing with the aid of these hypnotic artifices is simply to energize Life. What Life does for the organism, in slow imperfect fashion, we here train it to do a little faster, a little more completely."

In other words, hypnotism is the activation, to a more intense degree, of the restorative energies that come into play in natural sleep. Therapeutic suggestion is the art of liberating the spirit from the body, opening it up with sleep, and allowing it to exert in their fullness, its powers over the sick body. Suggestible persons are those whose lazy or little evolved souls are incapable of self-reliance and of acting effectively in ordinary sleep to repair the losses of the body.

Therefore, in principle, suggestion is only a thought, an act of will, differing only from the ordinary will by its concentration and intensity. In general, our thoughts

---

⁵⁵ The exteriorized spirit can draw more vital force from the body than the normal being, the incarnate human being, can obtain. Experiments have shown that a dynamometer can be squeezed more strongly by a spirit through the body than by an embodied spirit.

⁵⁶ F. W. H. MYERS, *Human Personality* (London: Longmans, 1903), vol. I, ch. VI, "Sensory Automatism," section 640, p. 233.

⁵⁷ F. W. H. MYERS, *Human Personality* (London: Longmans, 1903), vol. I, ch. V, "Hypnotism," section 580, p. 216.

are multiple and float freely; they are born and pass, or when they coexist within us, they collide and merge. In suggestion, thought and will are fixed on a single point. They gain in power what they lose in extent. By their action, turned more penetrating, more incisive, they induce in the subject the reawakening of the faculties not used in the normal state. Suggestion then becomes a sort of impulsion, a lever that mobilizes the life force and directs it to the point where it should operate.

Suggestion can be exerted whether on the physical domain, through a direct influence on the nervous system, or in the moral domain, on the central self and consciousness of the subject. When well used, it is a very valuable means of education, destroying bad tendencies and pernicious habits. Its action on the character will then produce the most auspicious results.[58]

Now, let us go back to ordinary sleep and dreams. As long as the release of the soul is incomplete, the sensations, the preoccupations of the previous day, the memories of the past, all mingle with the impressions of the night. The perceptions recorded by the brain proceed automatically, in apparent disorder, when the attention of the soul is distracted from the body and no longer regulates the brain vibrations; hence the incoherence of most dreams. But as the soul emerges and rises, the action of the psychical senses prevails and the dreams acquire a remarkable lucidity and clearness. The views become larger and larger, vast perspectives open on the spiritual

---

[58] In summary, these are the fruits that hypnotic suggestion can and should provide, and for which it must be applied: concentration of thought and will; increased energy and vitality; fixing attention on essentially useful things; widening of the field of memory; manifestation of new meanings through internal or external impulsions.

world, the true realm of the soul and where its destiny truly lies. In this state it can penetrate hidden things and even the thoughts and feelings of other spirits.[59]

There exists a double life in every human being, by which we belong to two worlds at the same time, two planes of existence. One is related to time and space, as we conceive them in our planet's environment, by our bodily senses: it is the material life. The other, through the deep senses and the faculties of the soul, connects us to the spiritual universe and the countless worlds. In the course of our earthly existence, it is especially in the state of sleep that these faculties can be exerted and the powers of the soul come into vibration. Our souls then resume contact with this invisible universe which is our real homeland from which flesh has separated them. They renew themselves in the midst of eternal energies in order to reawaken for their painful and obscure tasks in the flesh.

During sleep, the soul can, according to the needs of the moment, either apply itself in repairing energy losses

---

[59] According to the ancients, there are two classes of dreams: the dream proper, in Greek *onar*, of physical origin; and the dream *hypar*, of psychical origin. This distinction is found in Homer, which represents the popular tradition, as well as in Hippocrates, who is the representative of the scientific tradition. Many modern Occultists have adopted similar definitions. According to them, in general, an ordinary dream is produced mechanically by the organism, whereas a spiritual dream would be the product of divinatory clairvoyance. One, illusory, the other, veridical. However, sometimes it is very difficult to establish a clear and definite difference between these two classes of phenomena.

The ordinary dream seems to be generated by automatic brain vibrations which continue during sleep, when the soul is absent; these dreams are often absurd, but their very absurdity is proof that the soul is now free from the physical body and no longer regulating its functions. It is less easy to remember the spiritual dream, because it does not leave any impression in the physical brain, but in the psychical body instead, which is vehicle of the soul, exteriorized during sleep.

caused by the daily toil, thus regenerating the sleeping organism, by infusing it with forces borrowed from the cosmic world; or, after this restorative action is accomplished, resume the course of its higher life, hovering over Nature, exerting its faculties of remote viewing and penetrating things. In this state of independent activity, it already lives by anticipation the free life of the spirit. For this life, a natural continuation of planetary existence, which awaits it after death, it must prepare itself, not only for its earthly labors, but also for its occupations, out-of-body experiences, during sleep. And it is thanks to the reflections of the light from above, extending over our dreams and illuminating the whole hidden side of destiny, that we can glimpse the conditions of living in the Hereafter.

If it were possible for us to encompass the whole extent of our existence at a glance, we would recognize that the waking state is far from constituting its essential part, its most important element. The souls that watch over us take advantage of our sleep to practice fluidic life and the development of our senses of intuition. It is then that a work of initiation for humans eager to evolve higher is accomplished, a work of which their dreams can keep a residual trace. Thus, when we fly, when we glide quickly over the ground, this is the sensation of our fluidic body rehearsing for the higher life.

To dream that one climbs without fatigue, with surprising ease, through space, without feeling any constraint, no fright; or that one hovers over the waters; to cross walls and other material obstacles without being astonished to perform acts that would be unrealizable during wake – is this not proof that we have become fluidic when our soul is released? Such sensations, such images, involving a complete reversal of the physical laws that govern ordinary life, could not come to our mind if they were not the result of a transformation in our mode of existence.

In reality, it is no longer a question of dreams, but of real actions, accomplished in another domain of sensation and whose memory has crept into our brain memory. These memories and impressions are proof that we possess two bodies, and the soul, which is the seat of the consciousness, remains attached to its subtle envelope, while the material body is lying, immersed in inertia.

A difficulty arises, however: The more the soul moves away from the body and penetrates into the ethereal regions, the weaker is the bond that unites them, and the vaguer the memory on waking. The soul hovers far in the immensity, and the brain can no longer record its feelings. As a result, we cannot analyze our most beautiful dreams. Sometimes, the last impression felt during these nocturnal wanderings remains after we awake. And if, at this moment, one has the precaution of fixing it firmly in one's memory, it can remain engraved there. One night, I had the sensation of vibrations perceived while on the spiritual plane, the last chords of a sweet and penetrating melody, and the memory of the last words of a song that ended like this: "There are countless skies!"

Sometimes, on waking, one feels a vague impression of having glimpsed powerful things, without any precise memory of them. This kind of intuition, resulting from perceptions recorded in the deep consciousness, but not in the brain consciousness, continues in us for a certain time and influences our actions. At other times, these impressions are clearly reflected in a dream. Here is what F. W. H. Myers has to say about it:[60]

"The permanent result of a dream, I say, is sometimes such as to show that the dream has not been a mere

---
[60] F. W. H. MYERS, *Human Personality* (London: Longmans, 1903), vol. I, ch. IV, "Sleep," section 409, pp. 126–127.

superficial confusion of past waking experiences, but has had an unexplained potency of its own, – drawn, like the potency of hypnotic suggestion, from some depth in our being which the waking self cannot reach. Two main classes of this kind are conspicuous enough to be easily recognized – those, namely, where the dream has led to a 'conversion' or marked religious change, and those where it has been the starting-point of an 'insistent idea' or of a fit of actual insanity."

These phenomena could be explained as a communication in the dream of a consciousness superior to normal consciousness, or an intervention of some higher intelligence which judges, disapproves, or condemns the conduct of the dreamer and causes him or her an impression of trouble, of salutary fear. A spirit obsession can also be exerted by means of a dream, to the point of causing mental disturbance at one's awakening. This is caused by evil spirits that were given power of us, due to our previous deeds, or any harm we did to them in the past.

Let me continue highlighting this mysterious property of sleep, which, in certain cases, can put us in possession of more wide-ranging layers of memory.

Normal memory is precarious and restricted; it encompasses only the narrow circle of the present life, the set of facts whose knowledge is indispensable for the role to be fulfilled on Earth, and the goal to be attained. Deep memory encompasses the whole history of a being, since its origin, going through its successive stages and modes of existence, whether planetary or celestial. A whole past, with its memories and sensations forgotten or ignored in the waking state, is engraved in us. This past only awakens by means of exteriorization, during ordinary or induced sleep. It is a rule known to all experimenters: When in the different states of sleep, as one moves away from the waking state and normal memory, the deeper the hypnosis, the bigger the increase of memory, with its expansion thus accentuated. F. W. H. Myers further states the following:[61]

"The degree of intelligence, indeed, which finds its way to expression in that trance or slumber varies greatly in different subjects and at different times. But whensoever there is enough of alertness to admit of our forming a judgment, we find that in the hypnotic state there is a considerable memory – though not necessarily a complete or a reasoned memory of the waking state; whereas with most subjects – in the waking state unless some special command be imposed upon the hypnotic self – there is no memory whatever of the hypnotic state."

"Ordinary sleep is roughly intermediate between waking life and deep hypnotic trance; and it seems a priori probable that its memory will have links of almost equal strength with the memory which belongs to waking life and the memory which belongs to the hypnotic trance. And this is in fact the case; the fragments of dream-memory are interlinked with both these other chains."

F. W. H. Myers, in support of his arguments, quotes[62] several cases in which forgotten retrospective facts and others which the sleeper has never known are revealed in dreams.

We will see it when dealing with the issue of reincarnation: the experiences that Myers speaks of have been pushed much further than he expected, and their consequences are immense. Not only has it been possible, by hypnotic suggestion, to reconstruct the least memories of present life, which have disappeared from the normal

---

[61] *Op. cit.*, vol. I, ch. IV, "Sleep," section 412, p. 129.
[62] *Op. cit.*, vol. I, ch. IV, "Sleep," section 412–413, pp. 129 *et seq*,

memory of subjects, but to get the broken sequence of their past lives together again.

At the same time as a wider and richer memory, in sleep, we can see faculties appear which are much greater than all those we enjoy in the waking state. Problems vainly studied or discarded as insoluble, are solved in dreams or somnambulism. Brilliant works, esthetic operations of the highest order – poems, symphonies, funeral anthems – are thus conceived and performed. Should we see here an exclusive action of the higher self or the collaboration of spiritual entities that come to inspire our work? It is probable that these two factors intervene in phenomena of this nature.

F. W. H. Myers cites the case of Agassiz, who discovered in his sleep the skeletal arrangement of disparate bones he had in vain tried to assemble for several times in the waking state. I myself wrote elsewhere about the cases of Voltaire, La Fontaine, Coleridge, Bach, Tartini, and others, who composed important works under similar conditions.[63]

Finally, a form of dreams whose explanation has so far escaped science should also be mentioned. These are the so-called premonitory dreams, a set of images and visions relating to future events, the accuracy of which is verified later. They seem to indicate that the soul has the power to penetrate the future, or that it is revealed to it by higher Intelligences.

There is the dream of the Duchess of Hamilton, who witnessed, two weeks before the event,[64] the death of the Earl of L., in vivid, intimate details. A similar phenomenon was reported by the *Progressive Thinker* of Chicago, on November 1, 1913. A magistrate from Hauser, Mr. Reed,

---

[63] See Léon DENIS, *Into the Unseen* (New York: USSF, 2017), ch. XII, p. 160.

[64] *Proceedings of the S. P. R.*, vol. XI, pp. 505–506, London, 1895.

was killed in an automobile accident. His 10-year-old son had seen this catastrophe in all its details, twice, in a dream. Despite these warnings and his wife's entreaties, Mr. Reed did not think he should give up a planned outing, where he met death in circumstances identical to those perceived in the child's dream.

Mr. Henri de Parville, in the scientific section of the French newspaper *Journal des Débats* (May 1904), reports a case supported by serious testimony:

"A young woman, whose husband has disappeared without a trace and has not been able to be found despite all searches, had a dream: A little dog who lived a long time near her, but was taken away by her husband, appears to her, barking happily, and covers her with caresses. It settles near her and does not leave her gaze; then, after a moment, it gets up and scratches at the door. It made its visit and now must return. She opens it and, in her dream, follows the dog, which runs away. She runs after it and, after a while, sees it enter a house whose ground floor is occupied by a cafe. The street, the house, the neighborhood are all engraved in the memory of the sleeper, who keeps the memory on waking. Constantly worried about this dream, she talks about it to three people around her who have since testified to the authenticity of the facts. She finally decides to follow the trail of the dog and finds her husband in the street and the house seen in a dream."

And, finally, the *Revue de Psychologie de la Suisse Romande*, year 1905, page 379, brings the case of a young man who often saw himself, in an autoscopic[65] hallucination, precipitated from the top of a rock and lying, bleeding and bruised, at the bottom of a ravine. This premonition was confirmed in every detail, when

---

[65] [Trans. note] *Autocospic* refers to hallucinations of one's own body.

he fell off the mountain of Salève, near Geneva, on July 10, 1904.

As we ascend into the realm of psychic phenomena, they are accentuated, more clearly defined, and bring us more decisive proofs of the independence and survival of the spirit.

The perceptions of the soul during sleep are of two kinds. We first detect remote viewing, clairvoyance, lucidity. Then comes a set of phenomena referred to as *telepathy* and *telesthesia* (distant sensations and perceptions). This includes the reception and transmission of thoughts, sensations, motor impulses. To these facts we may add cases of duplication and apparitions, referred to as the *phantoms of the living*. These cases were observed in large numbers by the official psychology, which proved unable to explain them.[66] All these phenomena are linked to one another, forming a continuous chain. In principle, they are basically only one and the same phenomenon, varying in form and intensity, that is, the gradual disengagement (out-of-body state) of the soul. This release has been witnessed in all its various phases, from the awakening of the psychical senses and their manifestations in all degrees, to the distant projection of the whole spirit, that is, the soul and its fluidic body.

Let us start by looking at cases in which psychical sight is exerted with remarkable clearness. I mentioned some of them in my previous books. Here is a more recent one, published by all the London press:

---

[66] See the *Proceedings of the S. P. R.*, London

The disappearance of Miss Holland, a criminal case that fascinated England, was explained by a dream. The police were searching for the victim to no avail. The accused, Samuel Douglas, claimed that she had left for an unknown destination and was about to be released. The London newspapers having published drawings representing the farmhouse inhabited by Miss Holland and the adjoining garden, a young maid saw the engraving and exclaimed, "This is my dream!" And she pointed to a place at the foot of a tree, saying: "There, the corpse is there!" This statement was repeated to the police and, in front of detectives, the girl confirmed what she said. She explained that she had seen this garden in a dream and, in the ground, in the place indicated, a buried body. The police had the ground dug and indeed discovered Miss Holland's corpse there. It has been established that the young chambermaid had never known this person, nor set foot in that garden before.

Camille Flammarion, in his book *L'Inconnu – The Unknown* (London, 1900) mentions a whole series of direct visions from a distance, obtained during sleep, resulting from a research made in France on phenomena of this nature.

Here is a more complicated case. *The Annals of Psychical Science*, Paris, London, contain the detailed relation attested by the legal authorities of Castel di Sangro (Italy) of a macabre dream, which was collective and veridical:[67]

"M. Pascal Cocozza, an excellent man, gamekeeper to Baron Raphael Corrado, dreamed, on the night of the 3rd of March last, that his father, who had been dead for ten years, appeared and reproached him and his brothers for having forgotten him; and, worse still, for having

---

[67] [Trans. note] Original report published in *The Annals of Psychical Science*, vol. II, p. 201–202, London, Sept. 1905.

allowed his poor bones, which had been disinterred by the gravediggers, to remain behind the tower of the cemetery, on the snow, and exposed to the ravages of wolves! M. Cocozza, deeply impressed by this distressing dream, told it to his sister the next morning. To his great surprise, his sister told him that she had had *exactly the same dream*. Then the worthy keeper, without further ado, and in spite of the snowstorm, took his gun and went to the cemetery, which lies on a rocky hill overlooking the town. There, behind the tower, among the bushes and upon the snow ... he saw human bones!"

The *Annals* then give a detailed account of the investigation and the research made by the justice department: they established that the bones were indeed those of the gamekeeper's father, exhumed by gravediggers at the expiration of the legal period. The latter were going to carry them to the ossuary at nightfall, when the cold and the snow compelled them to postpone their work until the following day. The documents relating to this case, which was the subject of a lawsuit, are countersigned by the notary, the justice of peace and the syndic procurator of that district. They were published by the newspaper *Echo del Sangro*, on March 15, 1905.

Professor W. R. Newbold, of the University of Pennsylvania, reports in the *Proceedings of the S. P. R.*, vol XII, page 11, London, in the year 1896, several examples of dreams indicating a great activity of the soul during sleep, and bringing lessons of the invisible world. Among others, we will mention that of Dr. H. Hilprecht, a professor of Assyrian at the same University, who found in sleep the meaning of an ancient inscription, a meaning that had eluded him until then. In a more complex dream, involving a priest from the ancient temple of Nippur (Babylon), he received from him an explanation of an embarrassing enigma. All the details of this dream were recognized as accurate. The priest's archaeological indications were unknown to anyone living on Earth.

It should be noted that, during all these phenomena, the body of the percipient is at rest, the organism completely asleep; but in him or her, the psychical being continues to watch, to act; to see, hear, and communicate without using verbal language, with other beings like the percipient, that is, with other souls.

This phenomenon has a general character and is found in each one of us. When passing from waking to sleep, just when our ordinary means of communication with the outside world are suspended, new outlets are open for us, and through them, a more intense radiation stems from our vision. Already in this another form of life, a psychical life is revealed, which will be amplified with the other phenomena that will be dealt with in this book, proving that there is a mode of perception and manifestation quite different from that of our material senses.

After citing phenomena of vision in natural sleep, here is a case of clairvoyance in induced sleep.

Dr. Maxwell, already quoted above, plunges Mrs. Agullana, a very gifted sensitive, into magnetic sleep. She disengages from her body, by exteriorizing herself, and moves away in spirit from her home. Dr. Maxwell sends her to observe, from a distance, what one of his friends, Mr. Béchade, is doing. It was 10:20 PM. Let the experimenter himself speak:[68]

"To our great surprise, she told us that she saw 'Monsieur Béchade half-undressed, walking barefooted on stones.' This did not seem to us to have any sense. I saw my friend the next day, and, although he is well acquainted

---

[68] J. MAXWELL, *Metapsychical Phenomena* (Trans. L. I. Finch. London: Duckworth, 1905), p. 213.

with spiritistic phenomena, he seemed to be astonished at my recital, and said to me, word for word: 'I was not feeling very well yesterday evening; one of my friends who lives with me advised me to try Kneipp's method, and urged me so strongly, that, in order to satisfy him, I tried last night for the first time to walk barefooted on cold stone. I was, in reality, half-undressed when I made the first attempt; it was then twenty minutes past ten o'clock; I walked about for some time on the first steps of the staircase, which is built of stone.'"

Cases of clairvoyance in the somnambulistic state are numerous; they are reported in all books and journals dealing especially with these phenomena. *La Médecine Française* of April 16, 1906 reports a case of clairvoyance in connection with the accident in the mine of Courrières (France). Mrs. Berthe, the seer consulted, described exactly the mine, and suffered the pangs of the survivors whose death or release she announced.

To this, we may add two recent examples:

Mr. Louis Cadiou, director of a factory at La Grand-Palud, near Landerneau (France), having disappeared by the end of December 1913, could not, despite some meticulous searches, be found. Surveys carried out in the Élorn River had produced no results. A clairvoyant living in Nancy, Mrs. Camille Hoffmann, having been consulted, declared, in a state of magnetic sleep, that the corpse would be found at the edge of a wood near the factory, hidden under a thin layer of earth. The victim's brother, following these indications, discovered the body in a situation identical to that which the seer had described.

All the newspapers, including *Le Matin* of February 5, 1914, reported the details of the Cadiou case, which all France followed with great interest.

A few days later, a similar phenomenon occurred. A young mailman named Charles Chapeland drowned in the River Saône, near Mâcon (France). His brother had recourse to Mrs. Camille Hoffmann to find his corpse. She assured him that the body would be rejected by the waters sixty days after the accident, near the dam of Cormoranche, a prophecy which was fulfilled in every detail.[69]

---

[69] See the French newspaper *Le Matin* of February 23, 1914.

VI
OUT-OF-BODY EXPERIENCES, EXTERIORIZATIONS,[70] AND TELEPATHIC PROJECTIONS

WE NOW COME to an order of manifestations which occur from a distance, without the help of bodily organs, whether in the waking state or during sleep. These phenomena, described under the general and vague term *telepathy*, are not, as I have said, ill and morbid creations of the personality, as certain observers have believed, but quite the opposite, partial cases, isolated outbreaks of the higher life within humanity. We must see in them the first appearance of the future powers of which the earthly human will be endowed. Examination of these facts will lead us to the proof that the exteriorized self during life and the self which survives after death are identical, representing two successive aspects of existence pertaining to one and the same being.

Telepathy – the remote projection of one's thought and even one's own image – makes us move up one more step on the scale of psychical life. Here we are in presence of a powerful act of will. The soul communicates itself by communicating its vibration: an obvious demonstration of the fact that the soul is not a compound, a resultant, or an aggregate of forces, but, on the contrary, the center of life and will in us, a dynamic center that controls the organism and directs its functions. Telepathic manifestations have no boundaries. The power and independence of the soul

---

[70] [Trans. note] In English, also called *externalizations*.

are revealed in a sovereign way, because here the body takes no part in the phenomenon. It is an obstacle rather than a help. Also, they occur with even greater intensity after death, as we shall see later.

"Self-projection," says F. W. H. Myers,[71] "is the one definite act which it seems as though a man might perform equally well before and after bodily death."

Telepathic communications from a distance have been confirmed by experiences which acquired classical status. Let us recall those of Mr. Pierre Janet, who was a professor at the Sorbonne, and of Dr. Gibert, of Le Havre, with their subject Leonie, whom they made come to them, in the night, a kilometer away, using suggestive calls.[72]

Since then, such experiments have multiplied with constant success. I will mention only a few cases of transmission of thought from great distances.

The *Daily Express* of July 17, 1903, reported remarkable attempts at exchanging thoughts that took place at the offices of the *Review of Reviews*, Norfolk Street, Strand, London. These experiments were controlled by a committee of six members, including Dr. Wallace, of 39 Harley Street, and W. Stead, the prominent publicist. The telepathic messages were sent by Mr. Richardson, of London, and received by Mr. Franck, of Nottingham, distant 110 miles.

Finally, the *Banner of Light*, of Boston, on August 12, 1905 reported that an American, Mrs. Burton Johnson from Des Moines, had been the recipient of this kind of transmission. Sitting in her room at the Victoria Hotel, she received four telepathic messages from Palo

---

[71] F. W. H. MYERS, *Human Personality* (London: Longmans, 1903), vol. I, ch. VI, "Sensory Automatism," section 670, p. 297.

[72] See the *Bulletin de la Société de Psychologie Physiologique*, 1885, vol. I, p. 24. [Trans. note: In English, see *Borderland*, vol. II, no. VIII, pp. 113–114, London, April 1895.]

Alto, California, 3,000 miles away. These facts, said the newspaper, were all duly checked and strictly controlled, leaving no doubt whatsoever.

The transmission of thoughts and images takes place, as said before, indistinctly during sleep or in the waking state. I have already reported several cases; others will be found in large numbers in specialized publications; for example, that of a doctor called telepathically during the night, and that of Agnès Paquet, reported by F. H. W. Myers.[73] To these, one may add the case of Mrs. Elgee: she had, in Cairo (Egypt), the vision of one of her friends who was, at that very moment, in England, thinking intensely of her.[74]

In the last days of her life, my own mother often saw me near her, at Tours (France), although I was very far from there, traveling abroad, in the East.

All these phenomena can be explained by the projection of the will of the individual which evokes in the percipient the very image of the acting person. In the following cases, we will see the psychical personality, the soul, disengage itself entirely from its bodily envelope and appear in its phantom form. Testimonies abound of such phenomena.

I have reported elsewhere[75] the results of inquiries held by the Society for Psychical Research (S. P. R.), of London. They have collected about a thousand cases of remote apparitions of living people, supported by high-value certificates. The testimonies were recorded in

---

[73] F. W. H. MYERS, *Human Personality* (London: Longmans, 1903), vol. I, ch. VI, "Sensory Automatism," section 663, pp. 282–283. Previously published in the *Proceedings of the S. P. R.*, vol. VII, pp. 32–35, London, 1891.

[74] F. W. H. MYERS, GURNEY and PODMORE, *The Phantasms of the Living* (London: Trübner & Co., 1886), vol II, ch. XVIII, p. 239.

[75] See Léon DENIS, *After Death* (New York: USSF, 2017), Third Part; and *Into the Unseen* (New York: USSF, 2017), ch. XI.

several volumes, in the form of minutes. They bear the signatures of scientists belonging to various academies or scientific bodies. Among these names are those of Gladstone, Balfour, and others.

These phenomena are generally ascribed to some subjective character. But this opinion does not stand up to scrutiny. Certain apparitions have been successively seen by several persons on the different floors of a house; others have impressed animals: dogs, horses, etc. In some cases, ghosts act upon the material things, open doors, move objects, leave traces on the dust covering the furniture. Voices are heard that give information about facts that are ignored by everyone, and whose accuracy is attested later.

One may recall, among numerous others, the case of Mrs. Hawkins, whose phantasm was sighted by four people at a time and in an identical way.[76]

In France, a whole series of phenomena of the same nature have been collected and published by the *Annales des Sciences Psychiques*, by Doctors Dariex and Charles Richet, and by Camille Flammarion, in his book *Death and Its Mystery* (3 vol. London & New York, 1922–1923).

A case reported by all major London newspapers, *The Daily Express*, *The Evening News*, and *The Daily News*, of May 17, 1905, and also by *The Umpire*, of May 14, among others, tells of the apparition, in Parliament, at the House of Commons, in an absolutely crowded meeting place, the phantom of a member of parliament, Major Sir Carne Rasch, who at this time was ill in bed, at home, suffering from an indisposition. Three other members of

---

[76] F. W. H. MYERS, GURNEY and PODMORE, *The Phantasms of the Living* (London: Trübner & Co., 1886), vol II, ch. XIV, p. 78 and *passim*.

parliament testified to the reality of this phenomenon. Here is how Sir Gilbert Parker described it:[77]

"I wished to take part in the debate in progress, but missed being called. As I swung round to resume my seat, I was attracted first by seeing Sir Carne Rasch out of his place, and then by the position he occupied, I knew that he had been ill, and in a cheery way nodded to him, and said, 'I hope you are better.' But he made no sign and uttered no reply. This struck me as odd. My friend's position was his, and yet not his. His face was remarkably pallid. He sat hunched up, and his expression was steely. It was altogether a stony presentment – grim, almost resentful. I thought for a moment. Then I turned again towards Sir Carne, and he had vanished. That puzzled me, and I at once went in search of him. I expected, in fact, to overtake him in the Lobby. But Rasch was not there. No one had seen him...."

"There is no doubt whatever in the mind of Sir Carne Rasch himself as to the presence in some strange evanescent form. He has been 'precipitated' in the spirit, as he now believes, to 'help Hood [the Ministerial Whip]' of whom he was constantly thinking."

In *The Daily News* of May 17, 1905, Sir Arthur Hayter added his testimony to that of Sir Gilbert Parker. He says that not only did he see Sir Carne Rasch but also drew the attention of Sir Henry Campbell-Bannerman to his presence in the House.

Exteriorization, or out-of-body experience of a human being, can be induced by magnetic action. Experiments have been made that dissipated any doubts about it. The subject, while asleep, goes out of the body and can perform material actions at a distance.

---

[77] [Trans. note] Sir Gilbert PARKER's testimony is also found in the *Annals of Psychical Science*, vol. I, p. 390, London, Jan–Jun 1905.

I have already cited the case of the magnetizer Lewis.[78] In other similar circumstances, the apparition was photographed. Aksakof cites three of these cases in his book *Animisme et Spiritisme* (Paris, 1895). Other similar facts were observed by W. Stead, then director of the British journal *Borderland*.

Thus the objectivity of the soul in its fluidic form, manifesting itself on distant points from where its physical body rests, is positively demonstrated and cannot be seriously challenged.

Moreover, it is enough to look at History to find that the past is full of facts of this kind. Phenomena of *bilocation (or bicorporeality) of the living* are frequently reported in religious annals. The past is no less rich in stories and testimonies concerning the spirits of the dead, and this abundance of affirmations, this continuance through the centuries, is of a nature to indicate that amidst gross superstitions and errors, there must have been a part that was real and true.

In fact, the manifestation and distant communication between incarnate spirits lead, logically and necessarily, to the possibility of communication between incarnate and discarnate spirits.

The inhabitants of the spiritual plane have provided numerous experimental proofs of this law of universal communion, inasmuch as it can be ascertained rigorously on Earth.

Among other facts, the experience of the Society for Psychical Research, of London, should be highlighted, to which the scholarly world is indebted for so many discoveries in the psychical field. It established a system of exchange of thoughts between the United States and England, with no other means than two mediums in a

---

[78] [Trans. note] See *The Spiritualist*, no. 131 (vol. 6, no. 9), p. 97, London, Feb. 26, 1875.

trance. With the aid of these intermediaries, a message was *transmitted by one Spirit to another Spirit*. This message consisted of four Latin words, a language that neither of these mediums knew.

This experiment was monitored and controlled by Professor Hyslop of Columbia University, New York. All necessary precautions have been taken to prevent fraud.[79]

Experiments of the same kind were held during the year 1913 by Madame de Watteville with the help of two mediums. The spirits "Roudolphe," "Charles" and "Emilie" dictated to those mediums, one Mrs. T., in Paris, and another Miss R., in Vimereux (also in France), several simultaneous and absolutely identical messages, 160 miles away.

"This crossed correspondence," says Dr. Geley,[80] "is of an unexpected character, as far as its spontaneity and variety is concerned, which precludes any idea of fraud prepared in advance. It was neither in the mind of Madame de W., nor in the minds of the mediums, to obtain these phenomena."

When one studies the phenomenon of telepathy in all its facets, the general views which emerge from it gradually grow, and one is led to recognize in it a communication process of incalculable significance. First, one saw in it a simple mechanical transmission of thoughts and images between two brains. But this phenomenon will take on the most varied and impressive forms. After the thoughts, it is the remote projections of the phantoms of the living, those of the dying and, finally, without any solution of continuity interrupting the sequence of events, the apparitions of the dead; whereas a seer has, in the most cases,

---

[79] The precautions taken for this experiment are described in the *Proceedings of the S. P. R.* of London.

[80] Dr. Gustave GELEY, *Contribution à l'Étude des Correspondances Croisées* (Paris: Impr. E. Roussel [1914]; or Paris: Durville, 1920).

no knowledge of the deaths of the appearing individuals. There is a continual series of manifestations which are graded in their effects and concur in demonstrating the indestructibility of the soul.

Telepathic action knows no bounds. It removes all obstacles and connects the living of the Earth to the living of the spiritual plane, the visible world to invisible worlds, humans to God; it unites them in the closest, most intimate way.

The means of transmission which it reveals to us constitute the basis of the social relations among spirits, their usual mode of exchanging ideas and sensations. The phenomenon called telepathy on Earth is nothing but the process of communication among all thinking beings of the higher life; and prayer is one of its most powerful forms, one of its highest and purest applications. Telepathy is the manifestation of a universal and eternal law.

All beings, all bodies exchange vibrations. The stars influence each other through the sidereal immensities. Likewise, souls, which are systems of forces and focuses of thought, impress each other and can be communicated at all distances.[81] The attraction extends to souls as to the stars; it attracts them to a common center, an eternal and divine center. A double relationship is established: their aspirations ascend to it in the form of calls and prayers; relief comes down in the form of graces and inspirations.

Great poets, writers, artists, the wise and the pure, all aware of these impetuses, these sudden inspirations, these

---

[81] Speaking about vibrations to the British Association in 1898, Sir W. CROOKES declared that natural law presided over "all psychic communications." Telepathy seems to extend to animals. There are facts indicating telepathic communication between humans and animals. See in the *Annals of Psychical Science*, vol. II, no. 2, of August 1905, pp. 79 *et seq.*, a well-documented study by Ernest BOZZANO, "Animals and Psychic Perceptions."

gleams of genius that illuminate the brain like lightning and seem to come from a higher world, of which they reflect greatness and an intoxicating beauty. Or they are visions of the soul; in an ecstatic impulsion, it sees this inaccessible world open up, it perceives its radiations, its essences, its lights.

All this shows us that the soul is likely to be impressed by other means than the physical organs, collecting knowledge beyond the reach of earthly things, and from a spiritual cause. It is thanks to these gleams and flashes that it can see in the universal vibration the past and the future; it perceives the genesis of forms, art forms and thought forms, of beauty and holiness, from which new forms forever spring, in an inexhaustible variety like the source from which they emanate.

Let us consider these things from a more immediate viewpoint and see their consequences in the earthly environment. Already, through telepathic facts, human evolution is accentuated. Humans conquer new psychical powers, which will enable them one day to manifest their thought at all distances, without any material intermediary. This progress is one of the most beautiful stages of humanity towards a more intense and free life. It could be the prelude to the greatest moral revolution that has occurred on our globe; hence, indeed, evil would be conquered or considerably attenuated. When humans have no more secrets, and their thoughts can be read in their brains, they will not dare think badly and, consequently, do wrong.

Thus, always, the human soul will rise, climbing the ladder of infinite developments. The times will come when, more and more, intelligence will prevail, disengaging itself from the fleshly chrysalis, expanding, asserting its dominion over matter, creating through its efforts new and more extensive means of perception and manifestation. The senses, in turn, once refined, will see their circle of action widen. The human brain will become like a mysterious temple, with vast and deep naves, filled with harmonies, voices, perfumes; an admirable instrument at the service of the spirit that will then become more subtle and more powerful.

And at the same time as the human personality – soul and organism – our earthly homeland will be transformed. For the environment to evolve, individuals must first evolve themselves. Humanity is made of humans, and humankind, by its constant action, transforms its home. There is an absolute balance and a close relation between morals and the physical realm. Thought and will are the tools par excellence with which we can transform everything in ourselves and around us. Let us only have high and pure thoughts; let us aspire to all that is great, noble and beautiful. Gradually we will feel our being regenerate and, with it, step by step, the whole environment, our globe and humanity!

In our ascension, we will eventually better understand and practice this universal communion that connects all beings. Unconscious in the lower states of existence, this communion becomes more and more conscious as the self rises and traverses the innumerable degrees of evolution, eventually leading to that state of spirituality where each soul, radiant with the brilliance of powers acquired, in the impetus of its love, lives of the life of all and feels united to all in the eternal and infinite work.

VII
MANIFESTATIONS AFTER DEATH

IN THE FOREGOING REVIEW, we have followed the human spirit throughout its various phases of out-of-body states: ordinary sleep, magnetic sleep, somnambulism, thought transmission, and telepathy in all its forms. We have seen its sensitivity and its means of perception increase to the extent that the bonds attaching it to the body were loosened. We are now going to see it in a state of absolute freedom, that is, after death, manifesting itself both physically and intellectually to its friends left on Earth. No gap separates these different psychical states. Whether these phenomena take place during or after material life, they are identical in their causes, in their laws, and in their effects; they occur in constant patterns.

There is absolute continuity and gradation among all these facts; in this way that notion of the supernatural vanishes, which has long made them suspect to science. The old adage: Nature does not move in leaps and bounds, is confirmed once again. Death is not a leap; it is the separation and not the dissolution of the elements that constitute the earthly human being; it is the passage from the visible world to the invisible world, the delimitation of which is purely arbitrary and due simply to the imperfection of our senses. The life of each of us in the Hereafter is a natural and logical extension of our current life, the development of the invisible part of our being. There is a sequence in the psychical domain, just as in the physical domain.

As we have seen, in both orders of apparitions, whether of exteriorized living beings or of the deceased, it is always the fluidic form – this vehicle of the soul, its reproduction or rather the canvas of the physical body – which is concretized and becomes perceptible to sensitives. Science, after the labors of Becquerel, Curie, Lebon, and others, is becoming more and more familiar with these subtle and invisible states of matter, in a word, with these fluids used by the spirits in their manifestations, which are well known to Spiritists. Thanks to recent discoveries, science has come into contact with a world of unsuspected elements, forces, and powers, and with the possibility of long-ignored forms of existence of finally coming to the fore.

Scholars and scientists who have studied the Spiritist phenomenon, such as Sir W. Crookes, R. Wallace, R. Dale Owen, Aksakof, O. Lodge, Paul Gibier, F. W. H. Myers, and others, have noted numerous cases of apparitions of the deceased. The spirit of Katie King, which materialized for three years during sittings held by Sir W. Crookes, a member of the Royal Academy of London, was photographed on March 26, 1874, in presence of a group of experimenters.[82]

The same happened with the spirits of Abdullah and John King, both photographed by Aksakof. The British naturalist Alfred Russel Wallace and Dr. Thompson obtained spirit photographs of their mothers, who had been dead for many years.[83]

F. H. W. Myers talks of two hundred and thirty-one cases of apparitions of deceased persons. He quotes some cases borrowed from his book *The Phantasms of*

---

[82] See W. CROOKES, *Researches in the Phenomena of Spiritualism* (London: J. Burns, 1874).

[83] Aksakof, *Animisme et Spiritisme* (French trans. B. Sandow, Paris: Librairie de Sciences Psychiques, 1895), pp. 620–621.

the Living (London, 1886).[84] Let me mention, in their number, an apparition announcing an impending death (as related by Mr. F. G., of Boston):[85]

"This visitation, or whatever you may call it, so impressed me that I took the next train home, and in the presence of my parents and others I related what had occurred. My father, a man of rare good sense and very practical, was inclined to ridicule me, as he saw how earnestly I believed what I stated; but he, too, was amazed when later on I told them of a bright red line or *scratch*[86] on the right-hand side of my sister's face, which I distinctly had seen. When I mentioned this my mother rose trembling to her feet and nearly fainted away, and as soon as she sufficiently recovered her self-possession, with tears streaming down her face, she exclaimed that I had indeed seen my sister, as no living mortal but herself was aware of that scratch, which she had accidentally made while doing some little act of kindness after my sister's death. She said she well remembered how pained she was to think she should have, unintentionally, marred the features of her dead daughter, and that unknown to all, how she had carefully obliterated all traces of the slight scratch with the aid of powder, etc., and that she had never mentioned it to a human being from that day to this.... So strangely impressed was my mother, that even after she had retired to rest she got up and dressed, came to me and told me *she knew* at least that I had seen my sister. A few weeks later my mother died, happy in

---

[84] F. W. H. MYERS, *Human Personality* (London: Longmans, 1903)., vol. II, ch. VII, section 707, p. 11.

[85] *Ibid.*, section 717, p. 28.

[86] Would it be necessary to point out that the Spirit wanted to appear with this "scratch" only to provide, by this means, proof of its identity? It is the same in many of the following cases, where the spirits showed themselves in certain costumes or attributes, among a number of other elements for convincing the percipients.

her belief she would rejoin her favorite daughter in a better world."

The following cases should also be mentioned: That of a young man who had committed himself – if he died first – to appear to a girl without frightening her unpleasantly; he appeared one year later, to the sister of this person, just as she was going to get into a car.[87] The case of Mrs. de Fréville. She loved, during her lifetime, to go to the cemetery and walk around the grave of her husband. She was noticed seven or eight hours after her death by a gardener who was crossing the place.[88]

Then there is the case of a father who died while traveling, and who appeared to his daughter with unknown clothes which he had been clothed with after his death by strangers. He spoke to her of a sum of money which she did not know to be in her possession: these two facts were later proven to be accurate.[89] Finally, the case of Robert Mackenzie. At a time when his boss was still unaware of his death, he appeared to him to exculpate himself of a charge of suicide that weighed on his memory. That accusation was found to be inaccurate, his death having been accidental.[90]

At the Spiritualist Congress held in Paris in 1900, in the session of September 23, Dr. Bayol, senator of Bouches-du-Rhône, former governor of Dahomey, verbally exposed the phenomena of apparitions which he witnessed in Arles and Eyguières (France). The ghost of Acella, an ancient Roman girl whose grave is in Arles, in the famous cemetery of Aliscamps, materialized to the point of leaving a imprint of her face in boiling paraffin,

---

[87] *Proceedings of the S. P. R.*, vol. X, ch. XIV, p. 284, London, 1894.

[88] F. W. H. MYERS, GURNEY and PODMORE, *The Phantasms of the Living* (London: Trübner & Co., 1886), vol. I, p. 212–213.

[89] *Proceedings of the S. P. R.*, vol. X, ch. XIV, p. 283 (?), London, 1894.

[90] *Proceedings of the S. P. R.*, vol. III, p. 95–96, London, April 24, 1885.

not hollow as it usually occurs with casts but in relief, which would be impossible for any living being to do. These experiments, surrounded by all necessary precautions, took place in presence of personalities such as the mayor of Bouches-du-Rhône, the poet Mistral, a general of division, doctors, lawyers, among others.[91]

In a report dated February 11, 1904, published by the *Revue des Études Psychiques*, of Paris,[92] Professor Milesi, of the University of Rome, "one of the most notable champions of the young Italian psychological school," known in France for his lectures at the Sorbonne on the works of Auguste Comte, gave a public testimony of the reality of spirit materializations, including that of his own sister, who had died in Cremona (Italy) three years before. Here is an excerpt from this report:

"The most wonderful things in this seance were the apparitions, which were luminous in nature, though they occurred in the twilight; they were nine in total; all the participants could see them ... The first three were those reproducing the features of [the sister of Professor Milesi], who passed away aged 32 years in Cremona, at the Convent of the Daughters of the Sacred Heart, three years ago. She appeared smiling her exquisite smile, so typical of her."

In his book *Death and Its Mystery – At the Moment of Death* (Trans. L. Carroll, New York: The Century Co., 1922), page 363, C. Flammarion relates the simultaneous apparition at Toulon of Admiral Peyron to two officers who had known him and were still unaware of his death. One, a Lieutenant Commander, the other a Chief Engineer of the Navy, had been on the staff of the admiral when he commanded the evolution squadron of

---

[91] See *Compte rendu du Congrès Spirite et Spiritualiste International*, 1900 (Paris: Librairie de Sciences Psychiques, 1902), p. 241 *et seq.*

[92] Issue of Mars 1904.

the French Mediterranean Fleet. Both, at distant points, were awakened by the apparition, and the details of their visions were entirely consistent.

In the mediumistic group led by myself for a long time in Tours (France), our mediums described apparitions of the dead, visible to themselves alone, it is true, but whom they had never met, nor seen any picture or heard any description of before. The dead were only recognizable to other members of the group as they heard the descriptions given by the mediums.

Sometimes, the spirits materialized to the point of being able to write, in presence of incarnate persons and before their eyes, many messages, which remain like so many other proofs of their visit. This was the case of the banker Livermore's wife, whose writing was recognized as identical to the one she had during her earthly existence.[93]

More often still, the spirits "incorporate" in the envelope of sleeping mediums, then speak and write, make gestures and talk to the sitters, providing the latter with sure proofs of their identity.

In such phenomena, after the medium has momentarily abandoned his or her body, the substitution of personality is complete. The language, the attitude, the writing, the traits of physiognomy belong to a spirit foreign to the organism which it is using for a few moments.

The incorporation phenomena of Mrs. Piper, meticulously observed and controlled by Dr. Hodgson, Professors Hyslop, W. James, Newbold, O. Lodge, and F. W. H. Myers, constitute the most powerful body of evidence of the survival of the soul.[94] The personality of G. Pelham was revealed after death to his own relatives,

---

[93] See AKSAKOF, *Animisme et Spiritisme*, pp. 620–621.

[94] See Mrs. Piper's case in *Proceedings of the S. P. R.*, vol. XIII, pp. 284–582 ; vol. XIV, pp. 6–49, and summarized in Léon DENIS, *Into the Unseen* (New York: USSF, 2017), ch. XIX.

to his parents, as well as to his childhood friends – about thirty of them – to the point of not leaving any doubt in their minds regarding the author of those manifestations.

The same happened with Professor Hyslop, who had asked his diseased father's spirit 205 questions on topics unknown to himself, obtained 152 absolutely accurate answers, 16 inaccurate, and 37 questionable because they were unable to be controlled (i.e., verified). These verifications were made during many travels throughout the United States, to get to know in detail the history of the Hyslop family before the birth of Professor Hyslop; a history to which those questions were related.

The *Annales des Sciences Psychiques*, of Paris, June 1907, reports the following fact, which also occurred in the U.S., about 1860:[95]

"Judge Edmonds had a daughter in whom mediumistic faculties were revealed by the spontaneous phenomena which occurred in her presence, which soon aroused her curiosity to such an extent that she began to frequent seances. When another personality manifested through her she sometimes spoke different languages of which she was ignorant."

"One evening when a dozen persons were assembled in Mr. Edmonds' house, in New York, a Mr. Green, a New York artist, was present, accompanied by a man whom he introduced under the name of Mr. Evangelides, of Greece. Soon a personality manifested through Miss Laura Edmonds, who spoke to him in English and communicated to him a large number of facts, tending to prove that the personality was that of a friend who had died in his home several years ago, a person of whose existence even no one present could ever have known. From time to time

---

[95] [Transl. note] This entire report was published in English by *The Annals of Psychical Science*, vol. V, no. 31, pp. 509–510, London, 1907.

the young girl uttered words and entire phrases in Greek, which suggested to Mr. Evangelides to ask her if she could speak to him in Greek. He himself, as a matter of fact, spoke English with difficulty. The conversation was carried on in Greek on the part of Evangelides, and alternately in Greek and in English on the part of Miss Laura. Now and then Evangelides seemed to be much affected. The next day he resumed his conversation with Miss Laura ; after which he explained to those present that the invisible personality who seemed to be manifesting through the medium was one of his intimate friends, who had died in Greece, the brother of the Greek patriot, Mark Botzaris ; this friend informed him of the death of one of his own sons, who had remained in Greece and was in excellent health at the time that his father left for America."

"Evangelides returned several times to Mr. Edmonds' house, and, ten days after his first visit, he informed him that he dad just received a letter announcing the death of his son ; this letter must have been already posted when the first interview of Mr. Evangelides with Miss Laura took place."

"'I should like,' writes Judge Edmonds on this subject, 'that someone should tell me how I should regard this fact. It is impossible to deny it, it is too obvious. I might as reasonably deny that the Sun shines on us.... This happened in the presence of eight or ten persons, all educated, intelligent, reasonable, and all as capable as anyone of distinguishing between illusion and real fact.'"[96]

"Mr. Edmonds informs us that his daughter had never heard a word of modern Greek up to that day. He adds that on other occasions she spoke as many as thirteen

---

[96] On this subject, see also a letter of the honorable Judge ED-MONDS to Dr. GULLY, published in London in an issue of the *Spiritual Magazine* of 1871, and reproduced by the *Revue Scientifique et Morale du Spiritisme* in its volume of the year 1920.

different languages, including Polish, Italian, Indian, whilst, in her normal state she only knew English and French – the latter only so far as it can be learned in school. And this Judge J. W. Edmonds was not a nobody, far from it. He was President of the Supreme Court of Justice of New York, and President of the Senate of the United States. No one has ever thrown a doubt on the absolute integrity of his character; his writings prove his brilliant intelligence."

I shall now mention a phenomenon of communication during sleep, obtained by Mr. Chedo Mijatovitch, formerly Envoy Extraordinary and Minister Plenipotentiary of Serbia to the Court of St. James, in London, and reproduced by the *Annales des Sciences Psychiques* of January 1st to 16th, 1910:[97]

"Certain Spiritists in Southern Hungary requested me by letter to do them a service by trying to – so to say – interview the spirit of a great sovereign of the Serbians of the fourteenth century on a certain question.... As just about that time my wife read somewhere about the remarkable powers of a certain Mr. Vango ... I went to Mr. Vango...."

"After Mr. Vango had put himself into the trance, he said: 'Yes, here is the spirit of a young man who is most anxious to tell you something, but he talks in a language of which I do not understand a word.'"

"Then he slowly repeated, to my utter astonishment, these words in the Serbian language : '*Molim vas pishite moyoy materi Nataliyi da ye molim da mi oprosti.*' ('I request you write to my mother, Natalie, that I beg of her to forgive me.') Of course, I immediately recognized that it was the spirit of the murdered King Alexander. I asked Mr. Vango how the young man looked, to which

---

[97] [Transl. note] The original English report above was published by *Light*, vol. XXVIII, no. 1419, p. 136, London, March 21, 1908.

he answered at once: 'Oh, horrible, his body is covered with wounds.' If I needed a further proof that it was the spirit of King Alexander, I got it when Mr. Vango said: 'The spirit wants me to tell you that he now very much regrets that he did not follow your advice concerning a certain monument and the policy connected with it.' This related to some confidential advice I gave King Alexander two years before his assassination, and which he thought he could not entertain at that time ..."

In France, among a number of cases, there is that of Father Grimaud, director of the Institution for the Speech-impaired and Profoundly Deaf of Avignon. By means of Madame Gallas' body, while she was asleep, he received from the spirit of Forcade, deceased eight years before, a message by the silent movement of the lips, according to a special method for deaf-mute individuals, which this spirit had invented in his lifetime on Earth, directed at the venerable Abbé Grimaud, who, alone among the sitters knew and could understand. I published elsewhere the minutes of this remarkable seance, with the signature of twelve witnesses and the reasoned affidavit of Father Grimaud.[98]

J. Maxwell, Attorney General at the Court of Appeal of Bordeaux and Doctor of Medicine, in his book *Metapsychical Phenomena*,[99] while studying the phenomenon of "incorporations" (psychophony), which he observed through Mrs. Agullana, the wife of a cement worker, made the following report:

"This sensitive's most curious personality is that of a doctor, who died about eighty or a hundred years ago ... His medical language is archaic. He calls plants by their

---

[98] See Léon DENIS, *Into the Unseen* (New York: USSF, 2017), ch. XIX.

[99] J. MAXWELL, *Metapsychical Phenomena* (Trans. L. I. Finch. London: Duckworth, 1905), p. 252.

ancient medical names; his diagnosis, accompanied with extraordinary explanations, is generally correct, but the description of the internal symptoms which he perceives is such as would astound a doctor of the twentieth century.... During the ten years I have been observing him, he has not changed, and presents a logical continuity which is most striking."

I myself have frequently observed this phenomenon, and have been able to talk, through various mediums, to many deceased relatives and friends, as stated in other books,[100] obtaining from them indications totally unknown to the aforementioned mediums, and which constituted, for me, further proofs of identity.

If we take into account the difficulties involved in the communication of a Spirit to human listeners, with the help of an organism and especially a brain that it did not fashion itself, made flexible by a long experience; if we consider that, because of the difference between planes of existence, we cannot require from a disincarnate soul all the proofs that would be required of a physical human being, it must be recognized that the phenomenon of "incorporation" is one of those which most contribute to demonstrate the spiritual nature of us beings, and the principle of survival.

These facts do not involve merely some remote influence, they are borne out of an impulsion that the subject cannot resist and which, more often than not, takes possession of the whole organism. This phenomenon is analogous to that which we have observed in cases of second personality. In the latter, the deep self replaces the normal self and takes command of the physical body for the purpose of control and regeneration. But in the facts

---

[100] See Léon DENIS, *Into the Unseen* (New York: USSF, 2017), ch. VIII, p. 101 and *passim*; and *Christianisme et Spiritisme* (New ed., Paris: Librairie de Sciences Psychiques, 1910), *passim*.

described above, it is an extraneous spirit that plays this role and substitutes for the normal personality of the sleeping medium.

The word possession, which I have just used, has often been taken in an unfortunate sense. It has been ascribed to facts designating a devilish and terrifying nature. But, as F. W. H. Myers[101] rightly points out: "A devil is not a creature whose existence is independently known to science ... Assuming then, ... that we have to deal only with spirits who have been men like ourselves, and who are still animated by much the same motives as those which influence us ..."

On this subject, Myers raises a question: Is possession ever absolute? To which he answers in these terms:[102] "It seems probable that the thesis of multiplex personality – namely, that no known current of man's consciousness exhausts his whole consciousness, and no known self-manifestation expresses man's whole potential being – may hold good both for embodied and for unembodied[103] men ..."

Here we touch at the central point of the problem of human life, at its secret spring, the intimate and mysterious action of the spirit on a brain, either on the spirit's own or, in cases that concern us, on an extraneous brain. Considered from this angle, this issue becomes of paramount importance in psychology; F. W. H. Myers adds:[104]

"We may hope, indeed, that as our investigations proceed, and as we on this side of the fateful gulf, and

---

[101] F. W. H. MYERS, *Human Personality* (London: Longmans, 1903), vol. II, ch. IX, sections 912 and 914, pp. 199 and 201.

[102] *Ibid.*, section 971, p. 254.

[103] [Trans. note] *Unembodied*, same as *discarnate*.

[104] F. W. H. MYERS, *Human Personality* (London: Longmans, 1903), vol. II, ch. IX, section 972, p. 255.

the discarnate spirits on the other, learn more of the conditions necessary for perfect control of the brain and nervous system of intermediaries, – the communications will grow fuller and more coherent, and reach a higher level of unitary consciousness. Many the difficulties may be, but is there to be no difficulty in linking flesh with spirit – in opening to man, from his prisoning planet, a first glimpse into cosmic things?"

As we can see, thanks to experiments, observations, and testimonies repeated a thousand times, the existence and the survival of the soul are now emerging from the domain of hypotheses or simple metaphysical concepts, to become a living reality, a fact which has been rigorously established. The supernatural has had its day already, a "miracle" is but a word. All the terrors, all the superstitions suggested to humans by the idea of death have vanished. Our conception of universal life and divine work is expanding; at the same time, our confidence in the future is growing stronger. We see, under the alternating forms of physical and fluidic existence, our progress as beings, the continuing development of personality, and a supreme law presiding over the evolution of souls through time and space.

VIII
VIBRATIONAL STATES OF THE SOUL, ONE'S MEMORY

LIFE IS AN IMMENSE vibration that fills the universe and whose focus is in God. Every soul, a spark detached from the divine hearth, becomes, in its turn, a source of vibrations that will vary and increase in amplitude and intensity according to the degree of elevation of a being. This fact can be verified experimentally.[105]

Therefore every soul has a particular, a different vibration. Its own movement, its rhythm, is the exact representation of its dynamic power, intellectual value, and moral elevation.

All the beauty and all the magnificence of the living universe can be summed up in this law of harmonious vibrations. Souls that vibrate in unison recognize and call each other through the spiritual plane; hence the attractions, the sympathies, the friendship, the love! Artists, sensitives, and delicately harmonized beings know this law and feel its effects. The higher soul is a powerful vibration of all its harmonies.

---

[105] Doctors BARADUC and JOIRE built gages and recording devices to measure the radiant force that escapes from each human being and varies according to the subject's psychical state. I myself have often experimented with photographic plates. These, in the revealing bath, reproduce the radiations which emerge from finger ends in the form of spirals or currents of variable intensity according to one's elevation of thought and the action of one's will.

The psychical entity suffuses with vibrations its entire fluidic organism, that is, the perispirit which is its form and its image, the exact reproduction of its personal harmony and its own light. But when an incarnation comes, these vibrations will be reduced, blunted by the veils of the flesh. The inner self will be able to project outside only a weakened, intermittent radiation. Yet, during sleep, somnambulism and ecstasy, as soon as an exit is opened to the soul out of its material envelope that oppresses and chains it, the vibratory current is recovered, and the focus resumes its activity in full. The spirit finds itself in its previous states of power and freedom. All that was slept in it awakes again; its numerous lives are reconstituted, not only with the treasures of its thought, memories and achievements, but also with all the sensations, joys and pains recorded in its fluidic body. That is why, during trance, the soul, vibrating its memories of the past, affirms its previous existences and renews the mysterious chain of its transmigrations.

The smallest details of our life are registered in us and leave indelible traces. Thoughts, desires, passions, good or bad acts, everything is fixed therein, everything is gravitating. In the normal course of life, these memories accumulate in successive layers and the most recent end up erasing, only in appearance, the oldest. It seems that we have forgotten these thousand details of our vanished existences. However, through hypnotic experiments, it suffices to evoke past times and to replace the subject, using one's will, with an earlier period of his or her life, in youth, or even in childhood, so that these memories resurface in large numbers. The subject relives his or her past, not only with the state of mind and the association of ideas which were peculiar to them at that time – ideas that are sometimes very different from those the subject professes today – with own tastes, habits, and language, but also by automatically reconstituting all the series of contemporary physical phenomena of that time. This leads one to recognize that there is a close correlation between psychical individuality and the organic state.

Each mental state is associated with a physiological state; the evocation of one in a subject's memory, brings at once the reappearance of the other.[106]

Given the constant fluctuations and the complete renewal of the physical body every few years, this phenomenon would be incomprehensible without the role of the perispirit, which preserves in itself, engraved in its substance, all the impressions of the past. It is it that provides the soul with the total sum of its conscious states, even after the destruction of brain memory. The spirits demonstrate it by their communications, because they have preserved in space even the smallest memories of their earthly existence.

This automatic recording in one's memory seems to be in the form of groupings or zones, within us, zones

---

[106] This law is known in psychology as psycho-physical parallelism. Wilhem WUNDT (echoing Ernst MACH) in his *Vorlesungen über die Menschen- und Thierseele* (Leipzig: Voss, 1863–1864; 4th rev. ed., 1906), published in English as *Lectures on Human and Animal Psychology* (Trans. from the 2nd German ed., J. E. Creighton and E. B. Titchener. London: Sonnenschein, 1907), already agreed that "Every psychical event corresponds to a physical event and vice versa."

Experiments conducted by materialists themselves also reveal evidence of this law. Thus, for example, when Pierre JANET, when he puts his subject Rose two years back in the course of her current life, sees all the symptoms of the state of pregnancy which she was experiencing at home at that time. (P. JANET, Professor of Psychology at the Sorbonne, *L'Automatisme Psychologique*, p. 160.)

See also the cases narrated by Doctors H. Bourru and P. Burot, *Variations de la Personnalité* (Paris: J. B. Baillière, 1888), p. 152 ; by Dr. SOLLIER, "Des Hallucinations autoscopiques" (*Bulletin de l'Institut Psychique*, 1902, pp. 39 *et seq.*); and those described by Dr. PITRE, Dean of the Faculty of Medicine of Bordeaux (France), in his book *Le Somnambulisme et l'Hystérie*.

corresponding to as many periods of our life. So that, if one's will, by means of self-suggestion or an extraneous suggestion – which is the same, since, as we have seen, a suggestion, to be effective, must be accepted by the subject, who then transform it into self-suggestion – if the will, I say, brings to life a memory belonging to any period of one's past, all the facts of consciousness connected with that same period are immediately set in a methodical sequence. Gabriel Delanne has compared these vibratory states with the concentric layers found in the cross-section of a tree trunk, which make it possible to calculate the number of years in the age of the tree.

This would make understandable the variations of personality of described above. For superficial observers, these phenomena are explained as a dissociation of consciousness; however, when closely studied and analyzed, they represent, on the contrary, aspects of a single self, corresponding to many different phases of the same existence. These aspects come to light as soon as the sleep is deep enough and the degree of disengagement of one's perispirit is sufficient. If instead, some have been able to believe in changes of personalities, it is because the transitory, intermediate states, are missing or have disappeared.

As said before, the disengagement (or out-of-body state) of the perispirit can be facilitated by magnetic action. Magnetic passes applied on a sensitive gradually relax and untie the bonds that unite the spirit to the body. The soul and its ethereal shape issue from the material envelope, and this release constitutes the phenomenon of sleep. The deeper the hypnosis is, the more detached the soul becomes, moving away and recovering the fullness of its vibrations. Active life focuses in the perispirit, while physical life is suspended.

Suggestion further increases the vibratory rhythm of the soul. Each idea contains what psychologists call a tendency to action, and this tendency is turned into action by suggestion. This is, in fact, only a mode of one's will. Brought to its highest intensity, it becomes a driving force, a lever that raises and sets in motion our dormant vital powers, our psychical senses and transcendent faculties.

Then we see phenomena of clairvoyance, of lucidity, of the awakening of one's memory. For these manifestations to become possible, the perispirit must first be impressed by a vibratory shock determined by suggestion. This shaking, by accelerating its rhythmic movement, has the effect of restoring the relation between brain consciousness and deep consciousness, a relation which is broken in the normal state, during our physical life. Then the images, the memories stored in the perispirit can be revived so that the individual becomes aware of them again. But after this momentary awakening, the relation ceases, the veil falls, the distant memories fade away and return to the shadows.

Suggestion is the method that should be employed in these experiments. To bring the subjects back to a certain period of their past, they are put to sleep by means of longitudinal passes, practiced from top to bottom, and then it is suggested to them that they have such or such age. They are thus made to bring back all periods of their existence; one can obtain, for example, facsimiles of their handwriting which vary according to the times the lived and are always consistent, when they are from the same epochs evoked at different sittings. By means of transverse passes, the subjects are then brought back to the present time, passing through the same phases.

It is still possible – and I have proceeded in this way – to indicate to the subject a precise date of his or her past, even the most distant ones, so as to revive it in the subject. If the subject is very sensitive, then scenes of captivating interest will unfold, with details of the environment and the characters who lived then and there, details that are sometimes verifiable. It has been observed, says Colonel Rochas d'Aiglun, "That the memories thus awakened were exact, and that the subjects successively took the personalities corresponding to their age at the time."[107]

Let us insist on these phenomena, whose analysis sheds a bright light on the mystery of being. All the varied aspects of memory, the extinction of memories in normal life, their awakening in the trance and the exteriorization, all are explained by the difference of vibratory movements which connect the soul and its psychical body to the physical brain. At each change of state, these vibrations vary in intensity, becoming faster as the soul emerges from the body. The sensations felt in the normal state are registered with a minimum of force and duration, whereas the total memory remains in the depths of one's self. As soon as the material bonds are relaxed and the soul is restored to itself, it finds, with its superior vibratory state, the consciousness of all the aspects of its life, of all the physical or psychical forms of its integral existence. This is, as we have seen, what can be observed and artificially reproduced under the hypnotic state. In order for it to be well recognized in the labyrinth of these phenomena, it must not be forgotten that this state has many degrees. To each of these degrees is attached one of the forms of consciousness and personality; each phase of sleep corresponding to a particular state of memory; the deepest sleep brings out the most extensive memory.

---

[107] *Annales des Sciences Psychiques*, July 1905, p. 350. See also ROCHAS D'AIGLUN, *Les Vies Successives* (Paris: Chacornac, 1911), pp. 10, 62, 66–109.

It becomes more and more restricted as the soul re-enters its physical envelope. Our waking state corresponds to the narrowest memory, the poorest of all.

This phenomenon of artificial reconstitution of the past makes us understand what happens after death, when the soul, delivered from its earthly body, finds itself facing its enlarged memory, its memory-conscience, an implacable memory which preserves the imprint of all one's faults and becomes one's judge and sometimes executioner.

Yet, at the same time, the self, fragmented into distinct layers during its life on this world, is reconstituted in its superior synthesis and magnificent unity. All the experience acquired over the centuries, all the spiritual riches, fruits of one's evolution, often hidden or at least lessened, diminished during this lifetime, reappear in their brilliance and freshness, to serve as bases for new achievements. Nothing is lost. If the deep layers of one's being recount one's failures and falls, also proclaim the slow, painful efforts accumulated over the ages to build one's personality, which will always grow, ever richer and more beautiful, in the happy fulfillment of one's acquired faculties, qualities, and virtues.

IX

EVOLUTION AND THE ULTIMATE OBJECTIVE OF THE SOUL

THE SOUL, as said before, comes from God; it is the principle of intelligence and life in us. A mysterious essence, it escapes analysis, like everything emanating from the absolute. Created by love, created to love, so dainty that it can be enclosed in a restricted and fragile form, yet so great that, with a momentum of its own thought, it can embrace the infinite, the soul is a particle of the divine essence projected into the material world.

Since the time of its descent into the matter, what path has it followed to go back to the current point of its course?

It had to go through obscure paths, to take on forms, to animate organisms which it discarded at the end of each lifetime, as one does to a mantle that has become useless. All these bodies of flesh perished; the breath of destiny has scattered the dust; but the soul always persists and retains its perpetuity; it continues its ascending course, traverses the innumerable stations of its journey and proceeds toward a greater and desirable goal, a divine goal, which is perfection.

The soul contains, in virtual state, all the embryos of its future developments. It is destined to know everything, to acquire everything, to possess everything. And how would it succeed in a single lifetime? Life is short and perfection is far away! Could the soul, in a single lifetime, develop its understanding, enlighten its reason, strengthen its consciousness, assimilate all the elements of wisdom, holiness, and genius? Never! To achieve these ends, it needs, in time and space, a field without bounds for it to go through. It is through countless transformations, after thousands of centuries, that the coarse mineral finally changes into a pure diamond, sparkling with a thousand hues. The same happens to the human soul.

The goal of evolution, the raison d'être of life is not earthly happiness – as many mistakenly believe – but rather the perfecting of each of us; and this perfecting must be achieved through work, through effort, through all the alternatives of joy and sorrow, until we are fully developed and raised to a heavenly state. If there is less joy than suffering on Earth, it is because suffering is the instrument par excellence for education and progress, a stimulus for the human individual being, which, without it, would linger too long in the realm of sensuality. Pain, whether physical or moral, forms our experience, its price being wisdom.

Little by little the soul rises; and as it rises, it builds up in itself an ever increasing sum of knowledge and virtue. The soul feels more closely connected to its fellow beings; it communicates more intimately with its social and global environment. Ever rising higher and higher, it is soon linked by powerful bonds to the societies of the spiritual plane, and then to the universal Being.

Thus the life of the conscious being becomes a life of solidarity and freedom. Free within the limit assigned by the eternal laws, the individual becomes the architect of its own destiny. One's progress is one's work. No fatality will oppress you, except that caused by your own actions, whose consequences always fall upon yourself. But you can develop and grow only living in community, with the help of everyone and for the benefit of all. The higher one climbs, the more one feels living and suffering in all and for all. In your need for proper elevation, you draw to yourself all the human beings who populate the worlds where you lived, so as to help them achieve their spiritual state. You want to do for them what your eldest brothers, the great Spirits who have guided you on your path, have done for you.

The law of justice requires that all souls be emancipated in their turn, freed from lower life. Every being who has reached full consciousness must work to prepare for their fellow beings a tolerable life, a social state containing only its share of unavoidable evils. Such evils, necessary to the functioning of the law of general education, will never be completely eliminated from on our world. They represent one of the conditions of earthly life. Matter is a useful obstacle; it induces effort and develops the will; it contributes to the ascension of beings, imposing on them needs that compel them to work. And how would we know joy without pain; how to appreciate light without the shadows; how to taste the acquired good, with the satisfaction thus obtained, without deprivation? This is why difficulties are found in all shapes and forms, within and around us.

It is a great spectacle to see the struggle of the spirit against matter, a struggle for the conquest of the globe, fighting against the elements, the plagues, against misery, pain and death. Everywhere matter is opposed to the manifestation of thought. In the field of art, it is the stone that resists the sculptor's chisel. In science, it is the elusive and the infinitely small that escapes observation. In the private sphere as well as in the social, it is countless obstacles, the needs, the epidemics, the catastrophes!

And yet, in the face of blind powers that press and threaten them from all sides, humans have risen up, even as fragile beings; for any resource they can count only on their own our willpower. And with the help of this unique resource, through the times, the bitter struggle has gone on, without mercy, without respite. Then, one day, by means of the human will, those formidable powers were conquered and enslaved. Humans wanted it and matter surrendered. At our command, growling and protesting, the enemy elements, water and fire, were united and started working for us.

This is the law of effort, the supreme law by which all beings assert themselves, triumph, and grow. This is the magnificent epic history, the external struggle that fills the world. The internal struggle is no less moving. At each of its rebirths, the spirit will have to shape and soften the new material envelope that will serve as its home, turning it into an instrument capable of rendering and expressing the conceptions of the spirit's genius. Too often, the instrument resists and the spirit's thought, thus discouraged, folds back on itself, powerless to refine, to lift the heavy burden that stifles and annihilates its efforts. Yet, by its accumulated efforts, by persistent thought and will – notwithstanding many setbacks and reversals through renewed lifetimes – the soul eventually succeeds in developing its higher faculties.

A secret aspiration within us, an intimate, mysterious energy, impels us toward the lofty regions, making us tend toward ever higher goals, and pushing us toward Beauty and the Good. It is the law of progress, the eternal evolution that guides humanity through the ages, which spurs each and every one of us. For humanity is always the same souls; they return from century to century, to resume, with the help of their new physical bodies, and until they are ripe for better worlds, their work of perfecting themselves. The story of an individual soul does not differ much from that of humanity; the scale alone is different, the scale of proportions.

The spirit molds matter. It imparts life and beauty to it. So evolution is, par excellence, a law of esthetics. The forms acquired are the starting point of more beautiful forms. Everything connects. The day before prepares the next day; the past gives birth to the future. The human work, a reflection of the divine work, flourishes in ever more perfected forms.

The law of progress does not apply only to humans. It is universal. There is in all Nature's kingdoms an evolution which has been acknowledged by thinkers of all times. Since the green cell, since the vague embryo floating on the water, through various series, the chain of species has unfolded up to our own.

On this chain, each link represents a form of existence that leads to a higher form, to a richer organism better adapted to one's needs, to the growing manifestations of life. But on the scale of evolution, thought, consciousness, conscience and liberty appear only after going through many degrees. In the plant, intelligence slumbers; in the animal, it dreams; only in humans it awakens, knows itself, takes hold of itself and becomes conscious. Henceforth, the inevitable progress, so to speak, found in the lower forms of Nature, can no longer be accomplished except through an agreement between human will and the eternal laws.

It is by this agreement, by this union of human reason with divine reason, that the preparatory works for the reign of God, that is to say, the reign of Wisdom, Justice and Goodness, of which every rational and conscious being bears an intuition.

Thus, the study of the law of evolution, far from invalidating the spirituality of humans, has, on the contrary, granted them a new sanction. It teaches us how our body can derive from an inferior form through natural selection, but it also shows us that we possess intellectual and moral faculties of a different origin, and this origin, we find it in the invisible Universe, in the sublime world of the Spirit.

The theory of evolution must be completed by that of percussion, that is to say by the action of the invisible forces, which direct and stimulate the slow and prodigious ascensional march of life on the globe. The hidden world intervenes, at certain times, in the physical development of humanity, as it also intervenes in the intellectual and moral domain, by means of mediumistic revelation. When a people has reached its peak, it is followed by another people or nation, so it is rational to guess that a higher family of souls is incarnated among the representatives of the exhausted one so as to raise the latter by one degree in its renewing and shaping it in their image. It is the eternal hymn of Heaven and Earth, the inmost penetration of matter by the spirit, the growing outpouring of psychical life into the evolving form.

The emergence of humans on the scale of beings can be explained as well. Embryogenesis shows that the human being is the synthesis of all living forms that preceded it, the last link of this long chain of inferior lives that unfolds through the ages. But this is only the external aspect of the problem of origins; the inner aspect is otherwise ample and imposing. Just as every birth is explained by the descent into flesh of a soul from the spiritual world, so the first appearance of human beings on the planet must be attributed to an intervention of the invisible forces that generate life. The psychical essence has imparted the breath of a new life to evolved animal forms. It would create, for the manifestation of intelligence, an organ hitherto unknown: speech. A powerful element of all social life, the word appeared and, at the same time, through their fluidic envelope, the incarnate soul retained the ability of making contact with the plane from which it came from.[108]

The evolution of worlds and souls is regulated by the divine will, which penetrates and directs the whole Nature. But physical evolution is only the preparation for psychical evolution, and the ascension of souls goes far beyond the chain of material worlds.

The dominant factor in the lower regions of life is the fierce struggle, the fighting without truce of all against all, the perpetual war in which each being makes an effort to conquer a place in the sun, almost always to the detriment of others. This furious brawl entails and decimates all lower beings in its whirlwinds. Our globe is like an arena where incessant battles are fought.

---

[108] Whichever theory one favors in these matters, whether one adopts the views of Darwin, Spencer or Ernst Haeckel, one cannot bring oneself to believe that Nature, that God, has only one way to produce and develop life. The human brain is limited, whereas the possibilities of life are endless. The poor theoreticians who want to lock up all biological science within the narrow confines of a system, always remind us of the little child of legend who dug a hole in the sand of a beach and wanted to pour therein all the water from the ocean.

Professor Dr. Charles RICHET himself said in his response to SULLY-PRUDHOMME: "The theories about selection are insufficient." To which I add: "If there is unity in a plan, there must be diversity in the means of its execution. God is the great artist that from contrasts extracts harmony. It seems that there are two immense chains of life in the Universe: one ascends from the abyss through animality; the other descends from the divine heights. Both come together to unite, merge, and trigger each other. Is not that the ladder of Jacob's dream?"

Nature constantly renews these armies of combatants. In its prodigious fecundity, it gives birth to new beings; but immediately, death mows down their hurried ranks. This struggle, frightening at first sight, is necessary for the development of the principle of life. It lasts until the day when a ray of intelligence comes to illuminate sleepy consciousnesses. It is through struggle that the will is tempered and asserted; it is from pain that sensitiveness is born.

Material evolution and the destruction of organisms are only temporary: they represent the primary phase of this epic called life. The imperishable realities remain in the spirit. It alone survives these conflicts. All these ephemeral envelopes are only clothes that adapt to its permanent fluidic form. Like costumes, the spirit dons them to play the many acts of the evolution drama on the great stage of the Universe.

Gradually emerging from the abyss of life to become a spirit, a superior genius, and that by its own merits and efforts; conquering its future hour after hour; increasingly disengaging every day from the maze of passions to free itself from suggestions of selfishness, of laziness, of discouragement. Also to redeem itself little by little of its own weaknesses, of its ignorance, by helping its fellow beings redeem themselves in their turn, by dragging the whole human milieu to a higher degree: this is the role assigned to each soul. And to fill this role, we all have a sequence of innumerable existences which are devolved upon us in the magnificent ladder of the worlds.

All that comes from matter is unstable: everything passes, everything is fleeting. The mountains are gradually falling under the action of the elements; the largest cities are changing into ruins; the stars light up, shine, and then go out and die: only the imperishable soul hovers in eternal duration.

The circle of earthly things encloses us and limits our perceptions; but when thought detaches itself from the changing forms and embraces the expanse of time, it sees past and future come together, vibrate and live in the present. A song of glory, a hymn of infinite life fills the spaces; it climbs from the bosom of ruins and tombs; from the debris of dead civilizations new blooms rush forth. There is a union between the two humanities, the visible and invisible one; between those who populate Earth and those who roam the spiritual plane. Their voices are called and answered, and these noises, these murmurs, still deemed vague and confused by many, for us become the message, the vibrating speech which affirms the communion of universal love.

Such is the complex character of the human being – spirit, force and matter – in which all its constituent elements, all the forces of the Universe are summed up. All that is found in us is in the Universe, and all that is in the Universe is found in us. Through its fluidic body and its physical body, we humans find ourselves bound to the immense network of universal life; through our souls, to all the unseen and divine worlds. We are made of light and shadow. We are the flesh with all its weaknesses and the spirit with its latent riches, its radiant hopes, its magnificent flights. And what is in us is found in all other beings. Every human soul is a projection of the great eternal core. This is what consecrates and ensures the loving fellowship among humans. We have in us the instincts of the beast, more or less repressed by the long work and trials of our past existences. And we also have the chrysalis of an angel, this radiant and pure being that we can become through moral training, the aspirations of our heart and the constant self-sacrifice of self. We touch with our feet the dark depths of the abyss and with our forehead the dazzling altitudes of the heavens, the glorious realm of the spirits.

When we lend an ear to what is happening in the depths of our being, we hear like the rustling of hidden and tumultuous waters, like the ebb and flow of that stormy sea of one's personality that the breath of anger may raise, selfishness and pride. Those are the voices of matter, the calls from the nether regions that draw us and can still influence our actions. But these influences can be dominated by our will, these voices can be silenced. When calm has been restored in us, when the murmur of passions subsides, the mighty voice of the infinite Spirit then raises, singing the song of eternal life whose harmony fills the immensity of space.

And the higher the spirit rises, by purifying itself and becoming more enlightened, the more its fluidic organism becomes accessible to the vibrations, to the voices, to the breath from above. The divine Spirit, which animates the universe, acts upon all souls, seeking to penetrate them, to enlighten them, to fertilize them. However, most souls remain obscure and closed; too coarse, they cannot feel its influence or hear its calls. It often surrounds them, envelopes them, trying to reach the deepest layers of their consciences, to awaken them to the spiritual life. Many resist this action, because the soul is free. Others feel it only at the solemn moments of life, in the great trials, in the desolate hours when they feel the need for help from above and call for it. In order to live from the higher life toward which these influences suit our souls, one must have known suffering, practiced self-denial, renounced material joys, lit and maintained in oneself that flame, that inner illumination which never goes out and whose reflections illuminate, already from this world, the perspectives of the Hereafter. Multiple and painful planetary existences prepare us for the latter.

Thus is the mystery of Psyche[109] revealed, that is, the human soul, daughter of heaven, enclosed for a time in flesh, who goes back to her original homeland through thousands of deaths and rebirths.

The task is rough, the slopes steep, the frightful spiral to be traversed unfolds itself without any apparent term; but our strengths are limitless, for we can renew them unceasingly through our willpower and universal communion.

Besides, we are not alone to make this long journey. Not only do we join, sooner or later, other beloved beings, companions of our past lives, those who shared our joys and sorrows; but other great Beings who were also humans but now are heavenly Spirits stand by our side along difficult routes. Those who have overcome us in the sacred path do not lose interest in our fate, and when torment rages on our path, their supportive hands always help us sustain our march.

Slowly, through much pain, we are maturing for higher and higher tasks; we are participating more fully in the execution of a plan whose majesty fills with admiration and deeply touches those who can see its imposing outlines. As our ascension increases, greater revelations are made to us, new forms of activity, new psychical senses are born within ourselves, and more sublime things become

---

[109] [Trans. note] Léon Denis is poetically referring to the Hellenistic legend of *Psyche*.

perceivable. The fluidic universe opens ever wider to our growth, becoming an inexhaustible source of spiritual joys.

Then comes the hour when, after its peregrinations through the many worlds, the soul, in regions of a higher life, contemplates the whole of its existences, the long procession of sufferings that it has undergone. At last, it can understand it: those sufferings were the price of its happiness, those trials have generated only good to itself. And then, its role changes. From protected, the spirit becomes protective. It envelops those who still struggle on Earth or on the spiritual plane with its beneficent influence; it breathes to them the advice of its own experience; it sustains them in their arduous path, through the rough routes that it itself once had to travel across.

Will the soul ever reach the end of its journey? By moving along the path it has always opened up new fields of study and discovery. Similar to a river's current, waves of the supreme science descend towards it in ever more powerful streams. It manages to penetrate the holy harmony of things, to understand that no discordance, no contradiction actually exists in the universe; that everywhere order, wisdom, and foresight reign supreme. And the soul's confidence, its enthusiasm, will still increase with a greater love of the Supreme Power, with which it can savor in a more intense way the felicities of a blessed life.

From then on, it becomes closely associated with the divine work; it is ripe to fulfill the missions devolved upon higher souls, in this hierarchy of Spirits, which, in various different ways, govern and animate the Cosmos. For these souls are the agents of God in the eternal work of Creation. They are, so to speak, the wondrous books in which God has written Its most beautiful mysteries. They are like currents that carry to the spiritual plane the forces and radiations of the Infinite Soul.

God knows every soul It has formed out of Its thought and love. God knows exactly what It can build on later for the realization of Its views. First, It lets our souls slowly travel the winding path, and climb through the dark march of earthly lives, gradually building up in them such treasures as patience, virtue, and knowledge which one acquires in the school of suffering. Then one day, softened by copious rains and gusts of adversity, ripened by the rays of the divine sun, they come out of the shadows of time, from the darkness of innumerable lives, and now have their psychical faculties flourish in dazzling sheaves. Their intelligence is then revealed in works and deeds that are like a reflection of divine genius.

X

ON DEATH

DEATH IS ONLY a change of state, the destruction of a fragile form that no longer provides life with the conditions necessary for its proper functioning and evolution. Beyond the grave, another phase of existence unfolds. The spirit, in its fluidic form, which is imponderable, prepares itself for new reincarnations; its mental state reflects the fruits of the previous existence which has just ended.

Everywhere there is life. The whole Nature shows us, in its marvelous framework, all things in perpetual renewal. Nowhere is death to be found around us, as we generally consider it; nowhere is annihilation. No being can perish in its principle of life, in its conscious integrity. The universe is brimming with physical and psychical life. Everywhere, there is this immense swarming of beings, the elaboration of souls that escape the slow and obscure preparations of matter only to pursue, in stages of light, their magnificent ascension.

Human life is like the sun of Earth's polar regions during summer. It descends slowly, it falls, it weakens, it seems to disappear for a moment in the horizon. In appearance, this seems to be the end; yet behold! Immediately it rises again, describing its huge orb in the sky.

Therefore, death is only an eclipse lasting a fleeting moment in this great revolution of our lives. But such a moment is enough to reveal the deep and serious meaning of life to each of us. Death, too, can have its nobility, its magnificence. We should not fear it, but rather strive to embellish it, by constantly preparing for it through the search and conquest of moral beauty, the beauty of the spirit which has molded the body, adorning it with its august reflection, at the hour of supreme parting. The way in which we know how to die is itself already an indication of what sort of life awaits for us on the spiritual plane.

There is a cold, pure light around the pillow of some deathbeds. Faces, hitherto insignificant, seem to be dazzled by the brightness of the Hereafter. An imposing silence is made around those who have left the Earth. The living, witnesses of death, feel great and austere thoughts freed from the banal background of their usual impressions, imparting a little beauty to their inner life. Hatred, bad passions cannot resist such a display. Before the body of an enemy, all animosity subsides, all desire for revenge vanishes. Near a coffin, forgiveness seems easier, and duty more imperious.

Every death is a birth, or rather a rebirth. It is the manifestation of a life hitherto hidden in us, the invisible life on Earth that will join the invisible life on the spiritual plane. After a time of trouble, we find ourselves on the other side of the tomb, in the fullness of our faculties and our consciousness, near the beloved beings who shared the sad or happy hours of our earthly existence. The tomb contains only vain dust. Let us raise our thoughts and our memories higher, if we want to find the trace of the souls that were once dear to us.

Do not ask the stones of the sepulcher the secret of life. Know that the bones and ashes that lie there amount to nothing. The souls that once animated them has left these places. They relive in more subtle, more refined forms. From the bosom of the unseen, where your prayers reach and touch them, they follow you with their eyes; they answer you and smile at you. Spiritual revelation will teach you to communicate with them, to unite your feelings in the same love, in ineffable hope.

They are often at your side, those mourned people whose graves you visit in the cemetery. They come back and watch over you, those who were the strength of your youth, who cradled you in their arms, friends, companions of your joys and sorrows; and all the forms, all those sweet ghosts of beings that cross your path, that have been mingled with your existence and carried away with them a little of yourself, of your soul, and of your heart. Around you hovers a crowd of fellow beings who have disappeared into death, a confused crowd that is coming back to life, calling you and showing you which path to take.

O death! O serene majesty! You are a scarecrow, for the thinker you are only a moment of rest, the transition between two stages of destiny, one of which ends as the other is preparing! When my poor soul, wandering for so many centuries through the worlds, after many struggles, vicissitudes and disappointments, after having extinguished many illusions and postponed many hopes, will rest again in your bosom, it is with joy that it will greet the dawn of a fluidic life. It is with rapture that it will rise from the midst of earthly dust, through unfathomable spaces, to those which it has cherished here below and now await for its return to the world beyond.

For most humans, death remains the greatest mystery, the dark problem nobody dares to face. For us, however, it is the blessed hour when the tired body returns to Nature, giving Psyche, its prisoner, a free passage toward the eternal homeland.

This homeland is radiant immensity, dotted with suns and spheres. Near them, how poor our Earth would look! Infinity envelops it on all sides. There is no end to their extension or duration anymore, whether for the soul or the universe.

Just as each of our existences has its end and must vanish to make room for another life, so each of the worlds sown in the universe must die to make room for other, more perfect worlds.

There will come a day when human life will be extinguished on the frozen planet. The Earth, as a vast necropolis, will roll bleak and dreary through silent space. Imposing ruins will arise where there used to be Rome, Paris, Constantinople, now corpses of capital cities, last vestiges of extinct races, gigantic books of stone that no eye of flesh will read any more. But humanity will have disappeared from Earth only in order to pursue, on more gifted orbs, other stages of its ascension. The wave of progress will have pushed all earthly souls to planets better equipped for life. It is probable that prodigious civilizations will then flourish on Saturn and Jupiter; there, Renaissance humanities will flourish in incomparable glory. Those are the future destination for humans, their new field of action, the blessed places where they will be given the opportunity to love again and to work on their self-improvement.

In the midst of their new labors, sad memories of planet Earth may come back to haunt these spirits again; but, from the heights already achieved, the memory of the sufferings experienced, the hardships endured, will only serve as an incentive for them to rise higher.

In vain will the evocation of the past bring back to their eyes the specters of flesh, the sad remains lying in earthly burials, for the voice of wisdom will tell them:

"What do the vanished shadows matter! Nothing perishes. Every being transforms itself, becomes enlightened, ascends the degrees which lead from sphere to sphere, from sun to sun, to God. O imperishable spirit, remember this: *There is no death!*"

The teachings and the ceremonial found in churches contributed not a little, by representing death in lugubrious forms, to the rise of terror feelings in our spirits. Also, for their part, materialistic doctrines did nothing in reaction to this misconception.

At dusk, when night descends on Earth, a sort of sadness takes possession of us. We chase it away easily, by saying, "after darkness, light will return; night is but the eve of dawn!" When summer comes to an end and the blossoming of Nature succeeds the dreary winter, we console ourselves by thinking of future blooms. Then why this fear of death, this poignant anxiety concerning an act which does not mean the end of anything?

This often happens because to us death seems to be the loss and sudden deprivation of everything that made us happy.

Spiritualists know that death is nothing; for them, it is the entrance into a way of life which is richer in impressions and sensations. Not only are we not deprived of the living things of the spirit, but these are augmented by new resources, all the more extensive and varied, which the freed soul will be better prepared to enjoy.

Death does not deprive us of things belonging to this world. We will continue to see those we love and left behind. From within the spiritual plane, we will follow the progress of this planet; we will see the changes taking place on its surface; we will witness new discoveries, the social, political and religious development of nations. And until the time of our return, reincarnated in the flesh, we will participate in our fluidic state, by helping and influencing, to the extent of our power and our advancement, those who work for the benefit of all.

Far from banishing the idea of death, as most people do, let us know how to look at it for what it really is. Let us try to get rid of the shadows and chimeras with which it has been enveloped, and ask ourselves how to prepare for this natural and necessary event in the course of one's life.

Necessary, as I said. Indeed, what would happen if death was suppressed? The globe would become too small to contain the crowd of humans. As age and decrepitude mount, at times life seems to us so unbearable, that we would prefer anything to having our lifetime extended indefinitely. A day would come when, having exhausted all the means of study, work and cooperation useful for joint action, our existence would take on an overwhelmingly monotonous character.

Our progress, our elevation, require it: one day or another, we must be rid of this fleshly envelope, which, having rendered its services as expected, becomes unfit to follow us on the other planes of our destiny. How can those who claim to believe in the existence of a Wise Providence, an Ordering Power – whatever form they give to this Power – how can they regard death as evil? If it plays an important role in the evolution of beings, is it not because it is one of the desired phases of this evolution, a natural counterpart of birth, one of the essential elements of life's scheme?

The Universe cannot fail. Its goal is beauty; its means, justice and love. Let us fortify ourselves in the thought of boundless futures. Confidence in survival will stimulate our efforts, make them more fruitful. No patient and lofty work can be achieved without the certainty of a tomorrow. Whenever it strikes around us, death, in its austere splendor, becomes a lesson, an invitation to do better, to act better, to constantly increase the value of our souls.

The apparatus with which burials are surrounded leaves another no less painful impression in the memory of those who attend them. The thought that our deceased body will also have to be deposited into a whole dug in the earth brings a sensation of anguish and suffocation. However, all the bodies that we animated in the past also lie under the ground or have slowly transformed into flowers and plants. These bodies were only worn clothes; our personality has not been buried with them. It does not matter to us today what they have become. Why would the fate of the last of them worry us more than the others? Socrates, when answering the question of his friends regarding how he wanted to be buried, replied: "Just as you please, if only you can catch me."[110]

Too often, human imagination populates the regions of the Beyond with frightening creations that seem formidable and forbidding. Some churches also teach that the good or bad conditions of one's future life are defined permanently at the moment of death, in a definitive, irrevocable way – and this affirmation disturbs the lives of many believers. Others dread being left abandoned in the world beyond, a supposed isolation.

---

[110] I am often asked if cremation is preferable to burial from the standpoint of releasing the spirit. The Unseen, when consulted, answer that in general cremation provokes a quicker release, yet abrupt and violent, painful even, for the soul is still attached to Earth by its habits, tastes, and passions. It requires a certain psychological training, an anticipated detachment from material bonds, for one to undergo the crematory process without any traumatic consequences. This is the case of most individuals in the Far East, for whom cremation is traditionally practiced. In our Western countries, where people are usually underdeveloped and unprepared for death, burial should be preferred because it provides those still attached to matter with a slow and gradual release of the spirit from the body. It should, however, be safeguarded by the greatest precautions. Burials are far too hasty in our society, sometimes leading to some deplorable errors, such as burying people still alive in a state of lethargy.

The revelation of the spirits came to put an end to all these apprehensions; it gave us definite information about life beyond the grave.[111] It has dispelled this cruel uncertainty, this fear of the unknown that haunts us. Death, it tells us, does not change our spiritual nature, our characters, what constitutes our true selves. It only makes us freer, a freedom whose extent is in proportion to our degree of advancement. On both sides, we have the opportunity to do good or evil, the ability to move forward, to progress, and to reform ourselves. Everywhere the same laws reign, the same harmonies, the same divine forces. Nothing is irrevocable. The love that calls us into this world also draw us later to the next; but in all places, friends, protectors, and supporters await us. While here we mourn the departure of one of our nearest and dearest, as if we were going to lose them to nothingness, above us, ethereal beings glorify this individual's arrival in the light, in the same way that we rejoice at the arrival of a new born, whose soul comes to bloom again in our earthly life. The dead are the living of heaven.

Many people fear death because of the physical suffering that accompanies it. True, one suffers in illness that leads to death, but one also suffers of diseases which are eventually cured throughout one's life. The moment of death, so the spirits tell us, is almost always painless. We die the same way as we fall asleep. This opinion is confirmed by all those whose profession or duty frequently bring them close to the bedside of the dying.

However, when comparing the calm and serenity of certain patients at their ultimate hours with the convulsive

---

[111] See Allan KARDEC, *Heaven and Hell* (Trans. A. Blackwell and J. Korngold. New York,: SAB, 2003).

agitation and agony of others, one must recognize that sensations preceding death are very diverse according to the individuals. Suffering is all the more intense as the bonds linking the soul to the body are more numerous and more powerful. Anything that can soften or weaken them will make the soul's release faster, its transition less painful.

If death is often free from suffering for those whose life was noble and dignified, it is not the same for the sensual, the violent, the guilty, or the suicidal.

As soon as the passage is granted, a sort of disturbance, a numbness invade most souls that did not know how to prepare themselves for their departure. In this state, their faculties are veiled; they can only perceive things through a more or less dense fog. The duration of this disorder varies according to their nature and their moral value. It can be very prolonged for the most backward spirits and even last whole years. Then, little by little, the mist clears up, perception becomes clearer and more distinct. The mind recovers its lucidity, it awakens to its new life, the life on the spiritual plane. It is a solemn moment for the soul, more decisive, more formidable than the hour of death, for, depending on its individual value and degree of purity, this awakening will be calm and delicious, or full of anxiety and suffering

During the state of disturbance, the soul is aware of the thoughts directed towards it. Thoughts of love, of charity, the vibrations of affectionate hearts, all shine for the soul like rays in the fog that envelops her; they help it free itself from the last bonds that bind it to Earth, to come out of the shadow where it plunged. That is why the prayers inspired by one's heart, said with warmth and conviction, especially improvised prayers, are salutary, beneficent for the spirit that has left its bodily life. On the other hand, the vague, childish prayers of the churches often remain ineffective. Pronounced mechanically, they do not acquire this vibrational power which makes thought at once a penetrating force and a light.

The religious ceremonials in use usually bring little help and comfort to the deceased. Ignorance of the conditions of survival makes those who participate in these events indifferent and distracted. The casualness with which we take part, in our time, in a funeral ceremony is almost scandalous. The attitude of those present, the lack of any inner retreat, the banal conversations exchanged while driving into the cemetery, all give a painful impression. Few of those who follow the funeral procession think of the deceased and consider it a duty to project an affectionate thought in their direction.

Fervent prayers of friends and relatives are far more effective for the spirits of the dead than the outward manifestations of the most pompous worship. However, it is not good to indulge in the pain of separation. Certainly, the regrets of the departure are legitimate and sincere tears are sacred; but, when extreme, these regrets sadden and discourage the soul to which they are directed and often bears witness to it. Instead of facilitating the spirit flight onto the other plane, they keep it in the places where it has suffered and where those who are dear to it are still suffering.

People sometimes wonder what to make of early deaths, accidental deaths, and catastrophes in which many human lives are destroyed in one single sweep. How to reconcile these facts with the idea of plan, a foresight, a universal harmony? And if one voluntarily quits life in an act of despair, what happens then? What is the fate of suicides?

Prematurely interrupted existences have come to their predestined end. These are, in general, complements of previous existences that have been truncated as a result of abuse or excess. When, owing to unregulated habits, the vital resources have been exhausted before the time set by Nature, we must return to fulfill, in a shorter existence, the lapse of time which the previous existence ought to have lasted. It just so happens that human beings liable to this reparation are gathered together at some point by the force of destiny, so as to undergo, in a tragic collective death, the consequences of acts related to their previous lives. Hence these collective deaths and catastrophes that should serve as a cautionary warning to the world. Those who deceased thus have actually completed the time they ought to have lived here, and will prepare themselves for new and better lifetimes in the future.

As for suicides, they are plunged into a deeply distressing and painful disorder after dying. Anguish sticks and follows them to their new, later reincarnation. Their criminal gesture has shaken their fluidic body with a violent and long-lasting disturbance, which will be carried over into their new fleshly organism at rebirth. Most will reincarnate infirm on Earth. When life is still in all its strength in the suicide, the brutal act that breaks it will produce prolonged repercussions in their vibrational state and determine neurological diseases in their future earthly lives.

A suicide seeks to fade into nothingness and forgetfulness for ever. Instead, one finds oneself in presence of one's own conscience, in which endless memory remains of the pitiful act of desertion in the struggle of life. There is no hard test or cruel suffering on Earth that may be worse than this perpetual reproach of the soul, to the point of bringing shame and an inability to feel any self-esteem. The violent destruction of physical resources that could still be useful and even fruitful to them does not deliver the suicides from the trials that they wanted to flee, for they will have to renew the broken chain of existences and resume the inevitable series, now aggravated by the actions and consequences engendered by themselves.

The reasons for suicide are of a transient and human nature, whereas the reasons for living are of an eternal and superhuman order. Life, is the result of one's whole past, the instrument of becoming. It is, for each of us, what it must be, in the unfailing balance of destiny. Let us accept with courage our vicissitudes, which act as remedies for our imperfections; and let us patiently wait for the hour fixed by the equitable law as the end of our days on Earth.

The knowledge we have acquired of the conditions of future life has a great influence on our last moments. It gives us more assurance; it speeds up the release of our soul. To prepare effectively for life in the Hereafter, we must not only be convinced of its reality, but also understand the laws, see in thought the benefits and consequences of our efforts toward a moral ideal. Our psychical studies, the relations established during life with the invisible world, our aspirations toward higher modes of existence, will have developed our latent faculties and, when the final hour comes, the bodily detachment being already partially carried out, our disturbance will be of short duration. The spirit recovers awareness almost immediately; everything it sees looks familiar to it; it adapts without effort and without emotion to the conditions of its new environment.

With the approach of the last hour, the dying often come into possession of their psychical senses and perceive the unseen beings and things. The examples are numerous. Here are some of them, borrowed from an investigation made by the Italian Ernesto (or Ernest) Bozzano, whose results were published by the *Annals of Psychical Science*, vol. III, no. 2, London, February 1906:[112]

"CASE I – In the life of the Rev. Dwight L. Moody, the celebrated evangelical preacher of the United States, written by his son, his last moments are described as follows: 'Suddenly he murmured: 'Earth recedes, heaven opens up before me. I have been beyond the gates. God is calling. Don't call me back. It is beautiful. It is like a trance. If this is death it is sweet.' Then his face lit up and he said in a voice of joyful rapture: 'Dwight! Irene! I see the children's faces' (referring to two little grandchildren, gone before). Turning to his wife he said: 'Mamma, you have been a good wife to me,' and with that he became unconscious....'"

"Case IV – Mr. Alfred Smedley, on pp. 50 and 51 of his book, Some Reminiscences, gives the following description of the last moments of his own wife: 'A short time before her decease, her eyes being fixed on something that seemed to fill her with pleasant surprise, she exclaimed: 'Why! there is sister Charlotte here; and mother and father, and brother John, and sister Mary! And now they have brought Bessie Heap! They are all here. Oh! how beautiful! Cannot you see them?' she asked. 'No, my dear; I very much wish I could,' I answered. 'Cannot you see them?' she again asked in surprise: 'Why they are all here, and they are come to bear me away with them. Part of our family have crossed the flood, and soon the other part will be gathered home, and then we shall be a family complete in heaven.' 'I may here explain that Bessy Heap had been the trusted family nurse, and my wife had always been a favorite with her.' After the above ecstatic experience she lingered for some time. Then fixing her gaze steadily upward again, and lifting up her hands,

---

[112] [Trans. note] Cases I, IV and V are quoted by the author, leaving out C. II and III as published by the *Annals of Psychical Science*.

she joined the convoy of angel friends who had come to usher her into that brighter spiritual world of which we had learned so little.'"

"CASE V – Dr. Paul Edwards wrote as follows in April, 1900, to the Editor of *Light*: 'While living in a country town in California (U.S.A.) about the year 1887, I was called to visit a very dear lady friend who was very low and weak from consumption. Everyone knew that this pure and noble wife and mother was doomed to die, and at last she herself became convinced that immediate death was inevitable, and accordingly she prepared for the event. Calling her children to her bedside she kissed each in turn, sending them away as soon as goodbye was said. Then came the husband's turn to step up and bid farewell to a most loving wife, who was perfectly clear in her mind. She began by saying: ' Newton' (for that was his Christian name) ... 'do not weep over me, for I am without pain and am wholly serene. I love you upon earth, and shall love you after I have gone. I am fully resolved to come to you if such a thing is possible, and if it is not possible I will watch you and the children, from Heaven, where I will be waiting when you all come. My first desire now is to go.... I see people moving – all in white. The music is strangely enchanting – Oh! here is Sadie; she is with me *and* she knows who I am.' Sadie was a little girl she had lost about ten years before. 'Sissy !'said the husband, 'you are out of your mind.' 'Oh, dear! why did you call me here again?' said the wife; 'now it will be hard for me to go away again; I was so pleased while there – it was so delightful – so soothing.' In about three minutes the dying woman added: 'I am going away again and will not come back to you even if you call me.' 'This scene lasted for about eight minutes, and it was very plain that the dying wife was in full view of the two worlds at the same time, for she described how the moving figures looked in the world beyond, as she directed her words to mortals in this world.... I think that of all my death scenes this was the most impressive – the most solemn' (*Light*, 1900, p. 167)."

The French *Annales*[113] still narrate a large number of cases where the patient perceives apparitions of deceased persons of whose death the patient was unaware. Five sensational cases asserted by testimonials of high value were borrowed from the *Proceedings of the S. P. R.*, of London.

Mr. E. Bozzano, in concluding his presentation, wondered whether these phenomena could be explained by the subconscious or the thought reading. He concludes in the negative and expresses himself in the following terms:[114]

"As will be seen, this hypothesis certainly does not recommend itself by its simplicity, and is not by any means convincing. Everyone will perceive that such intricate theories, more ingenious than serious, go beyond the bounds of scientific induction and enter full sail into the boundless domain of the fantastic."

Here are two other phenomena published by the French *Annales de Sciences Psychiques* of February 1911. They present certain analogies with the previous ones, but in addition, with richer details teaching us how the separation between the fluidic body and material body occurs at death.

Mrs. Florence Marryat has given the following account in her book *The Spirit World* (New York, C. B. Reed, 1894, pp. 115–117):

---

[113] [Trans. note] Elsewhere Léon DENIS refers to French translations published in the *Annales,* of France. Whenever this is the case, their English originals were duly cited and transcribed instead.

[114] *Annals of Psychical Science*, vol. III, no. 2, p. 91, London, February 1906.

"I have a young lady friend, the daughter of a family moving in the highest society, who is a wonderful medium, though the fact is known to no one but her intimate friends. Her father passed on, many years ago, leaving his widow with a large family of sons and daughters to bring up, as well as a large property to manage, which one may say he has done, entirely, for her since, through their mediumistic child. She became controlled by her father, shortly after his death, since which time he has constantly held communication with her mother, giving her advice about her children, and her land, etc. The mother, in consequence, learned shorthand, in order to take down her husband's words, as he uttered them through her daughter's lips ; also typewriting, that she might transcribe them afterwards. She showed me several large volumes of these typewritten words of counsel, to which she is constantly referring. But the circumstance which I was about to relate, concerning this young lady medium, is as follows : Some few years since, she had the misfortune to lose her elder sister, a most beautiful girl of twenty, who died, after a few days' illness, of pleurisy. Edith (as I will call the young medium) told me that she was with her sister during the course of her illness, and that she witnessed, clairvoyantly, the whole process of the spirit leaving the body. She said that, on the last day of her earth life, her sister was flushed, excited, and slightly delirious, tossing about on her pillows, and talking incoherently. About this time, Edith observed a film, like a cloud of smoke, gathering above her head, where it gradually spread out until it had acquired the shape, lengthwise, of her sister's body– a facsimile, as it were, of the dying girl, only without coloring, and suspended in the air, face downwards, about two or three feet above her. As the day wore on, and the delirious restlessness gave way to the weakness of approaching death, Edith could see her sister's feverish color fade, and her eyes grew dimmer, whilst, simultaneously, the vapory form, suspended in the air above her, began to be tinted ; first, very faintly, then, by degrees, more and more, until it glowed with the life that was rapidly departing from the body. The dying girl grew weaker and weaker, until she lay back on her pillows, speechless and unconscious. As she did so, the spirit above her, which was still bound to her brain, heart and vitals by cords of light, like electricity, became, as it were, a living soul. As her sister breathed her last earthly breath, Edith saw the spirit sway from side to side, until it stood upright by the side of the bed, very weak, apparently, and scarcely able to stand, but still the living presentment of the corpse, which now was stretched in death before her eyes. As Edith was watching this wonderful sight, she saw the spirits of her father and grandmother, who had also died in their house, appear, and support the new-born spirit between them, passing their arms beneath hers, whilst her head rested, like that of a fainting person, on her father's shoulder. After they had held her thus for a short time, she seemed to revive somewhat, at which they ruptured, with their hands, the cords which bound her to her body, and, rising, with her between them, passed through the window, where Edith saw them all three floating up a smooth green hill, until they vanished out of her sight."

William Stainton Moses, a professor at Oxford University and priest of the Anglican Church, wrote in the British journal *Light*:[115]

"I have lately had opportunity – the first that has come to me – of studying the transition of the spirit. I have learned so much that I may perhaps be pardoned if I think that I can usefully place on record what I have

---

[115] [Trans. note] *Light*, vol. XXXI, pp. 381–382, August 12, 1911, London (formerly published in *Light*, July 9, 1887, London).

gathered.... It was the deathbed of one very near to me. The threescore years and ten were passed and another ten had been added to them. No actual disease intervened to complicate the departure of the spirit... I was warned that certain symptoms, insignificant in themselves, preluded the end, and I came to discharge the last sad duty. My spiritual sense could discern around and over him the luminous aura or atmosphere that was gathering for the spirit to mold its body of the future life. By slow degrees this increased, and grew more and more defined, varying from hour to hour as the vitality was more or less strong. One could see how even a little nourishment, or the magnetic support that a near presence gave, would feed the body and draw back the spirit. It seemed to be in a state of constant flux. For twelve days and nights of weary watching this process of elimination was carried on. After the sixth day the body showed plain signs of imminent dissolution. Yet the marvelous ebbing and flowing of spiritual life went on, the aura changing its hue, and growing more and more defined as the spirit prepared for departure. At length, twenty-three hours before death, the last noticeable change occurred. All restlessness of the body ceased, the hands were folded over the chest, and from that moment the work of dissolution progressed without a check. The guardians withdrew the split without any interference. The body was lying peacefully, the eyes were closed, and only long, regular breathing showed that life was still there. With the regularity of some exquisite piece of mechanism the deep inspirations were drawn; but .gradually they became less deep and less frequent, till I could detect them no more. The spirit bad left its shell, and friendly helpers had borne it to its rest, new-born into a new state."

"The body was pronounced to be dead. It may be so. The pulse did not beat, nor the heart, nor could the mirror detect the breathing. But the magnetic cord was yet unbroken, and remained so for yet eight-and-thirty hours. During that time I believe it would have been possible, under favoring conditions, to bring back the spirit had anyone so willed, and had his will been powerful enough. Was it by some such means, in some such conditions, that Lazarus was recalled? ... When the spiritual connection – the cord of life – was severed ... the features, which had shown lingering traces of the prolonged struggle, lost all look of pain, and there stole over them an expression of repose very beautiful and very touching to behold."

Finally, let us quote two French attestations: Dr. Haas, president of the Société des Études Psychiques of Nancy (France) wrote in the *Bulletin* of this society, in 1906, page 56: "A fact to point out, witnessed by me, is that often, a few moments before dying, lunatics regain their complete lucidity." Elsewhere, Dr. Teste, in his *Manuel Pratique du Magnétisme Animal* [*Practical Handbook of Animal Magnetism*], also states that he saw patients suffering from mental impairment, recovering a normal mental state during agony, that is, when their consciousness had passed to their fluidic body.

In short, the best way to ensure a soft and peaceful death is to live with dignity, with simplicity, soberly, a life without flaws and weaknesses; and by detaching ourselves in advance of everything that binds us to matter; by filling our existence with ideals, by populating it with lofty thoughts and noble actions.

The same is true of the good or bad life conditions one finds in the world beyond. They also depend solely on how we develop our tendencies, our appetites, our desires. It is in the present that we all must prepare, act, and reform; and not at the moment when the end of our earthly life approaches. It would be puerile to believe that our future situation depends on certain formalities more or less well performed at the time of one's departure. It is entire lifetime that will be accountable for the life to come. One and the other are closely related; they form a series of causes and effects which death does not interrupt.

It is equally important to dispel the chimeras that seem to haunt some brains, about certain regions reserved for souls after death, and where hideous beings must lead them so as to torment them. The one who took care of our birth, placing us in the world in loving arms, stretched to receive us, also holds tender warmth for us upon our arrival in the Hereafter. Let us chase away any vain terrors, infernal visions, and also deceptive beatitudes. The future as the present is made of work and action; it is the conquest of new degrees. Let us trust in the goodness of God, in Its love for Its creatures, and move forward with a steady heart toward the goal It has set for all living beings.

We have no other judge, no other executioner beyond the grave other than our own conscience. Unobstructed by earthly barriers, it acquires a degree of sharpness that is difficult for us to understand. Too often drowsy during life, it wakes up at death and its voice rises. It evokes memories from the past; stripped of all illusion, these appear to it in their true light, and our slightest faults become a cause of regret.

There is no need for purification by fire; self-knowledge is humans' only punishment and only reward – F. W. H. Myers once said. Harmony is everywhere, in the solemn march of worlds as well as in the march of destinies. Each is ranked according to his or her abilities in the universal order. To highly developed spirits, higher tasks and the creations of genius; to weak souls, mediocre tasks, lesser missions. Throughout the growth of our lives, we are moving toward the role that suits us and is ascribed to us legitimately.

Let us, then, make powerful souls, rich in knowledge and virtue, capable of great works, and they will earn for themselves a noble place in the eternal order. By a high moral culture, by the acquiring energy, dignity, goodness, let us strive to reach the level of the Higher-order Spirits which work for the cause of all humanity, and later we will enjoy with them the joys reserved for true merit. Then death, instead of being a scarecrow, will become in our eyes, a blessing, and we will be able to repeat the famous word of Socrates: "Nay, if this be true, let me die again and again!"

XI

LIFE IN THE HEREAFTER

As said before, the human being, already from this life, belongs to two worlds. By its physical body, it is connected to the visible world; by its fluidic body, to the invisible, unseen world. Sleep is the temporary separation of these two envelopes of the soul; death is its definitive separation. In both cases, the soul is detached from the physical body and, together with the soul, life is concentrated in the fluidic body. Life beyond the grave is therefore only the continuance and liberation of the invisible part of our Self.

Antiquity had known this mystery;[116] but for a long time humans possessed nothing but notions of a vague and hypothetical nature regarding the conditions of future life. Religions and philosophies have conveyed to us very uncertain data about these issues, absolutely devoid of control, of sanction, and, in almost every respect, in total disagreement with modern ideas of continuity and evolution.

Science, for its part, has studied and known until now only the earthly surface of the human being, its physical part. Now, this is to the whole being pretty much what the bark is to a whole tree. As for the fluidic, ethereal being, of which our physical brain cannot be aware, science has up to now completely ignored it. Hence, it remains powerless to solve the problem of survival, since it is our fluidic being alone that survives. Science has not been able to understand anything about the

---

[116] See Léon Denis, *After Death* (Trans. J. Korngold. New York: USSF, 2017), First Part, *passim*.

psychic manifestations that occur during sleep, in out-of-body experiences, exteriorization, ecstasy, that is, in all the escapades of the soul to the higher life. Well, it is only by observing these facts that we will be able to acquire, already from this lifetime, a positive knowledge of the nature of the self and its conditions of life in the Hereafter.

Experimentation alone could solve this question. We have to study in current humans what can enlighten us about the humans of tomorrow. There is no other way out for human thought, which has been driven to materialism due to the insufficiency of religions and philosophies. Social salvation lies in this crux, otherwise materialism would inexorably lead us to anarchy.

Only since the advent of experimental Spiritualism that the problem of survival has entered the domain of rigorous scientific observation. The invisible world has been studied using methods and procedures that conform to those adopted by contemporary science in other research fields. Such methods were described elsewhere.[117] So far, this has already been made clear: Instead of digging a gap when trying to establish a solution of continuity between the two modes of life – earthly and spiritual, visible and invisible – as several religions have done in the past, these studies have showed that life in the Hereafter is a natural extension, a continuity of the earthly life we already observe in ourselves.

The continuance of conscious life, with all its attributes – memory, intelligence, affective faculties – has been attested by many proofs of personal identity collected during experiments and surveys led by societies of psychical studies worldwide. The spirits of the dead have manifested themselves by the thousands, not only with

---

[117] See Léon DENIS, *Into the Unseen* (Trans. H. M. Monteiro, New York: USSF, 2017), Part One.

all the traits and set of memories which constituted their moral personality, but also with the physical features and details of their earthly forms, preserved by their perispirit or ethereal body. This latter is, as we know, the mold of one's material body; this is why human traits and forms reappear in phenomena of materialization.

In addition, knowledge of the varied conditions of the life in the Hereafter has been revealed by the spirits themselves, using the means of communication they have. Their indications, collected and recorded in whole volumes of minutes of mediumistic meetings, serve as accurate references for the conception we can now form of the laws of future life.

However, even in the absence of manifestations of the dead, experiments on out-of-body experiences of the living would already have provided us with valuable information on the mode of living of the soul on the invisible plane.

Colonel Rochas d'Aiglun demonstrated this in his experiments: under anesthesia and somnambulism, one's sensitivity and perceptions are not suppressed, only exteriorized, transferred to the outside.[118] This already lead us to assume logically that death is the state of total exteriorization and liberation of the sensitive and conscious self.

Birth is like a death for the soul. It encloses it along with its ethereal body in the tomb of flesh. What we call death is simply the return of the soul to freedom, enriched by the acquisitions it has made during its earthly life. But we have seen that the different states of sleep represent many momentary returns to life on the spiritual plane. The deeper the hypnosis, the more the soul emancipates

---

[118] See ROCHAS D'AIGLUN, *Les États Profonds de l'Hypnose* (Paris: Chamuel, 1892); *L'Extériorisation de la Sensibilité* (6th ed., Paris: Charconac, 1909); *Les Frontières de la Science* (Paris: Librairie des Sciences Psychologiques, 1902).

itself and moves away. The most intense sleep verges on the first phase of the invisible life.

In reality, the words sleep and death are both inadequate. When we fall asleep as to earthly life, we wake up to the life of the spirit. The same phenomenon occurs at death; their difference lies only in duration.

Carl du Prel cites two relevant examples:[119]

"A somnambulist one day described her condition; she regretted that she could not remember it after her awakening; but, she added, 'I will see all this again after my death.' She therefore considered her somnambulistic state as identical with the state after death. (KERNER, *Magikon*, 41)"

"Two spirits visited the seer of Prevorst one day. She did not like these visitors very much: 'Why have you come to my house,' she asked. To which the Spirits replied very judiciously: 'But it is you who came to us!' (Perty, I, 280)"

These phenomena, to which we could add others of the same nature, have proved it: our world and the Hereafter are not separated from each other. They are one in the other; they become entangled in some way and merge closely. Humans and the Spirits mingle. Invisible witnesses associate themselves with our life, share our joys and our trials.

The situation of the spirit after death is a direct consequence of its inclinations, either to matter or to the assets of intelligence and feeling. If sensual inclinations prevail, the individual's soul necessarily lags on the lower planes,

---

[119] [Trans. note] Léon Denis gives no source for these two short excerpts translated into French. In English *cf.* DU PREL, *The Philosophy of Mysticism* (Trans. C. C. Massey, 2 vols. London: George Redway, 1889), who further points to KERNER and PERTY.

which are the densest and coarsest. If it is nourished with beautiful and pure thoughts, it rises towards spheres related to the very nature of its thoughts.

Swedenborg was right when he said, "Heaven is not outside of a man, but within him."[120]

However, neither the placement is immediate, nor the transition is brusque. If the human eye cannot suddenly pass from darkness to bright light, neither can the soul. Death lead us into a transitional state, a kind of prolongation of physical life and a prelude to spiritual life. It is a state of disturbance, already mentioned above, a state which will be more or less prolonged, according to the dense or ethereal quality of the perispirit of the deceased.

Delivered from the material burden that oppressed it, the soul remains still enveloped by a mesh of thoughts and images: sensations, passions, emotions, generated by the soul during its earthly lives. It will have to become familiar with its new situation and aware of its state, before being brought to the cosmic environment for which it is prepared according to its degree of light and density.

First, in the majority of cases, everything will be a matter of astonishment in the Hereafter, where things differ essentially from the earthly environment. The laws of gravity are less rigid. Walls are no longer obstacles. The spirit can cross them and hover in the air. And yet, certain obstacles, although it cannot define why, can still detain it. All these things fill the spirit with fear and hesitation; but its friends from above look after it and guide its first steps.

Advanced spirits quickly emerge out of all earthly influences and regain self-awareness. The material veil is torn under the impetus of their thoughts; immense

---

[120] [Trans. note] See E. SWEDENBORG, *Heaven and Hell* (Trans. from the Latin by John C. Ager. West Chester, PA: Swedenborg Foundation, 2009).

horizons open up to them. They understand their situation almost immediately and adapt with ease. Their spiritual body, which is a volitional instrument and organism of the soul, from which it never separates itself, and which is the work of all its past – because it has built up and woven itself through its activity – floats for some time in the atmosphere. Then, according to its state of subtlety and power, and reacting to distant attractions, it feels naturally drawn to akin associations, to groups of spirits of its same order, whether luminous or veiled spirits, that surround its arrival with solicitude, to introduce it to the conditions of its new mode of existence.

Lower-order spirits retain for a long time the impressions of material life. They believe they are still living physically and continue, sometimes for years, the pretense of their usual occupations. As for materialists, the phenomenon of death remains incomprehensible. In the absence of prior knowledge, they confuse the fluidic body with the physical body. The illusions of earthly life persist in them. By their tastes and even by their imaginary needs, they are like bolts riveted to Earth. Then, slowly, with the help of beneficent spirits, their consciousness awakens, their intellect opens to the understanding of this new state of life. But as soon as they seek to rise and hover, their density makes them fall back to Earth. Planetary attractions and fluidic currents of the spiritual plane bring them back to our regions, like dead leaves swept by the storm.

Conventional believers wander in uncertainty and seek fulfillment of their priest's promises, the enjoyment of promised beatitudes. Sometimes their surprise is great, a long learning is necessary for them to understand the true laws of the spiritual world. Instead of angels or demons, they meet the spirits of humans who, like them, lived on Earth and preceded them. Their disappointment is acute in seeing their hopes postponed, their convictions overthrown by facts to which nothing, in the education they received, had prepared them. But if their life was honest and dutiful – actions that speak louder in one's destiny than mere beliefs – these souls cannot be unhappy.

Skeptical minds and, with them, all those who refuse to admit the possibility of a life independent of the body, see themselves immersed in a dream, the duration of which will be prolonged as long as their error is not be dispelled.

Human impressions are infinitely varied, like the values held by souls. Those who, during their earthly life, have known and served the truth, will receive, from the moment of death, the benefit of their research and of their labors. The following communication, among many others, is proof of this. It emanates from the spirit of a militant Spiritist, a man of heart and enlightened conviction: Charles Fritz, founder of the newspaper *La Vie d'Outre-tombe*, in Charleroi (Belgium). All who have been in contact with this upright and generous individual will recognize him from his language. He describes the feelings felt immediately after his death and adds:

"I felt the bonds being detached little by little and that my spiritual person, my Self, was itself disengaging. I saw around me good spirits all waiting for me; it was with them, finally, that I rose from Earth's surface."

"I did not suffer with this disincarnation, my first steps were those of a child who begins to walk."

"A spiritual light, full of strength and life, was born in me, because the light does not come from others, but from us, it is a ray that emerges from your fluidic envelope and penetrates you completely."

"The more you have worked in truth, love, and charitable love, the greater this light will be, until it becomes dazzling to those who are in a lower level than you."

"Well, my first steps were staggering, yet little by little I regained strength and I asked God for Its help and mercy. After seeing the complete release of my individuality, I finally considered the work I still have to do, I saw the past of my previous life and I worked so that it came back to my memory."

"The past is recorded in the fluid of every human being and, consequently, of the spirit, its perispirit is like a mirage of all human actions, and the soul. If one has lived badly, contemplates with sadness one's faults, which were all recorded, it seems, within the folds of one's perispiritual body."

"I was by no means prevented from recognizing my life as it had been, and of course I found that I had not been infallible, for who can boast of having been so on Earth? However, after finding out about it, I must say that I felt very satisfied and happy with my earthly deeds."

"I have struggled, worked, and suffered for the light of Spiritism, and I have given it, with hope, to many fellow beings on Earth, through words, through my studies and labors – that same light was present in everything I did."

"I am happy to have worked to raise the faith, the hearts and their courage, so I recommend to you all this unshakable faith, drawn from Spiritism, which I possessed."

"I have to develop myself further in order to review the past of my previous incarnations; it is a study involving a lot of work to do on my part. I can see a section of that past, but I am not able to really define it, even though my awakening is complete. In a short time, I hope, these past lives will become clear to me. I do have enough light to walk firmly ahead, by seeing what is before me, my future; and I have already started assisting unhappy spirits."

The law that determine spirit groupings in the world beyond is that of affinities. All spirits are subject to it. The orientation of their thoughts naturally leads them to their own environment; for thought is the very essence of the spiritual world, the fluidic form being only its garment. Everywhere, those who love and understand each other come together.

British philosopher Herbert Spencer, in a moment of intuition, formulated the following axiom, equally applicable to the visible world and the invisible world: "Life is the continuous adjustment of internal relations to external relations."

If inclined to material things, the spirit remains bound to Earth and mingles with individuals who share its tastes and appetites. Instead, if carrying lofty ideals and superior values, it rises effortlessly toward the object of its desires. It joins spiritual societies in the world beyond, participates in their work, and enjoys the scenes and harmonies of the infinite.

Thinking creates, the will builds up. The source of all joys and sorrows is in our reason and consciousness. That is why we find, sooner or later, in the Hereafter, the creations of our dreams and the realization of our hopes. However the feeling of an unfinished task brings back most spirits to Earth together with their affections and memories. Every eventually soul finds the environment yearned by its desires; it will live in dream worlds, united to beings it loves; it will also find regrets, the moral sufferings that its past has engendered.

Our conceptions and dreams follow us everywhere. In the ardor of their faith, when their thoughts gather momentum, the followers of every religion create images in which they believe to recognize the paradises they see. Then, little by little, they realize that these creations are fake, made of pure fantasy and comparable to vast panoramas painted on a canvas, or on immense frescoes. They learn to detach themselves from it and aspire to higher and more sensitive realities. In our present form and within the narrow confines of our faculties, we cannot understand the joys and delights in store for the higher spirits, any more than the deep anxieties felt by the delicate souls that have reached the limits of perfection. Beauty is everywhere; only its aspects vary infinitely, according to the level of evolution and purification of beings.

The advanced Spirit possesses sources of sensations and perceptions infinitely more extensive and more intense than those of the earthly human being. In it, clairvoyance, clairaudience, action at a distance, knowledge of the past and the future, all coexist in an indefinable synthesis, which constitutes, according to the expression of F. W. H. Myers, "The central mystery of human life."[121]

Speaking about the faculties of the average level Unseen, Myers states that the spirit, without being constrained by space and time, still keeps a partial knowledge of space and time. It can orient itself, find a living person and follow him or her at will. It is able to see in the present things that appear to us as situated in the past, and other facts that are located in the future. The spirit is aware of the thoughts and emotions of friends that relate to it.

As for the difference of acuity in the impressions, we can already make an idea of them by the dreams classed as "emotional." The soul, in the out-of-body state, even when this disengagement is only partial, not only can perceive, but also feel, with a much more intensity than

---

[121] [Trans. note] F. W. H. MYERS, *Human Personality* (London: Longmans, 1903), vol. 2, section 972, p. 254.

in the waking state. Scenes, images, pictures which, on the day before, only affected us weakly, in the dream become cause of high satisfaction or acute pain. Here we have a glimpse of what the life of the spirit and its modes of sensation may be when, detached from the fleshly envelope, its memory and consciousness recover the fullness of their vibrations. This also shows how the reconstitution of memories of the past can become a source of torment. The soul carries within itself its own judge, the infallible ratification or punishment of its own deeds, whether good or bad.

This has been found in accidents that could have led to death. In certain falls, during the trajectory of the human body from an elevated location to the ground, or during submerged asphyxia, the victim's superior consciousness reviews one's whole of life, with frightening speed. One sees it all in a matter of minutes, in every detail.

Carl du Prel[122] gives several examples. Citing Dr. Haddock's studies, he quotes, among other facts, the case of Admiral Beaufort:[123]

"He had fallen into the water, and had lost (normal) consciousness. In this condition 'thought rose after thought, with a rapidity of succession that is not only indescribable, but probably inconceivable by anyone who has not himself been in a similar situation.' At first the immediate consequences of his death for his family were presented to him; then his regards turned to the past; he repeated his last cruise, an earlier one in which he was shipwrecked; his schooldays, the progress he then made, and the time he had wasted, even all his small childish journeys and adventures."

---

[122] C. DU PREL, *The Philosophy of Mysticism* (Trans. C. C. Massey, 2 vol. London: George Redway, 1889).

[123] *Id., ibid.* vol. I, pp. 92–93.

"'Thus traveling backwards, every incident of my past life seemed to me to glance across my recollection in retrograde succession, not however, in mere outline, as here stated, but the picture filled up with every minute and collateral feature; in short, the whole period of my existence seemed to be placed before me in a kind of panoramic review, and every act of it seemed to be accompanied by a consciousness of right and wrong, or by some reflection on its cause or its consequences. Indeed, many trifling events, which had long been forgotten, then crowded into my imagination, and with the character of recent familiarity.' In this case also, but two minutes at the most had passed, before Beaufort was taken out of the water."

We can also quote Prof. Perty's[124] account of Catherine Emmerich, who, when dying, has seen her life replayed for her in the same way. We note that this phenomenon is not limited to accident cases; it seems to accompany the death process regularly.

Everything the spirit has done, wanted, thought, is reflected in it. Like a mirror, the soul reflects all the good, and all the evil, it has done. These images are not always subjective; by the intensity of the will, they can take on a substantial character. They live and manifest themselves, for our happiness or our punishment.

Having become transparent in the Hereafter, the soul judges itself, as it is judged by all that contemplate it. Alone in the presence of its past, its sees all its actions reappear and their consequences; all its faults, even the most hidden. There is no rest, no letting go, no oblivion

---

[124] Maximilian PERTY, *Die Mystischen Erscheinungen* [*Mystical Apparitions*], vol. II, p. 443. These three authors (DU PREL, HADDOCK and PERTY) were cited by Dr. PASCAL in his address to the Congrès de Psychologie de Paris, of 1900.

for the criminal. Its conscience, like a ruthless vigilante, pursues the spirit incessantly. In vain it tries to escape its obsessions; its torment cannot cease unless remorse is changed into repentance, and it accepts new earthly trials – the only means of reparation and recovery.

XII

MISSIONS AND A HIGHER LIFE

ANY SPIRIT WANTING to progress in the development of universal solidarity will receive from Higher Spirits a special mission, appropriate to its abilities and its level of advancement.

Some have the task of welcoming humans upon their return to the spiritual life, of guiding them; of helping them to free themselves from the thick fluids that envelop them. Others are charged with comforting and counseling suffering and backward souls. Chemists, physicists, naturalists, astronomers, pursue their research, studying the worlds, with their surfaces and hidden depths, acting in all places upon subtle matter, to which they apply preparations and modifications for the purpose of works that human imagination could hardly conceive. Others devote themselves to the arts, to the study of beauty in all its forms. Less advanced spirits help the former in their various tasks, serving as assistants.

A great number of spirits devote themselves to the inhabitants of the Earth and other planets, stimulating them in their inquiries, rousing their failing courage, guiding the hesitant onto the path of duty. Those who practiced medicine as incarnates, and still possess the secret of curative and restorative fluids, are especially concerned about the sick.[125]

---

[125] Cases of cures by spirits are quite numerous; they are recounted in all Spiritist literature. (See, for example, the case cited by F. W. H. MYERS, *Human Personality*, vol. II, section 833, pp. 124–126). The

Among the most beautiful missions is the one carried out by the Spirits of Light. They descend from celestial spaces to bring the treasures of their science, wisdom and love to humanity. Their task involves constant self-sacrifice, for the contact with material worlds is painful to them; but they face all this suffering because of their devotion to their proteges, so as to assist them in their trials and to pour into their hearts great and generous intuitions. It is right to attribute to them those flashes of inspiration which illuminate one's thoughts, the blossoming of the soul, this moral force which supports us in the hardships of life. If we knew what constraints these noble spirits must undergo in order to reach us, we would respond better to their pleas, making more energetic efforts to detach ourselves from all that is filthy and unclean, and unite with them in divine communion.

In the tormented hours, it is to these Spirits, my beloved guides, that my thoughts and entreaties are directed. It is from them that moral support and supreme comfort have always come to me.

Only through much labor have I managed to climb the paths of life; my childhood was very hard. Early on, I knew manual labor and had to deal with heavy family expenses. Later, in my career as a disseminator, often bruised by the stones of the way, I was bitten by snakes of hatred and envy. And now that twilight time has come to me, shadows rise and surround me; I feel my strength decline and my organs weaken. But I never missed the help of my invisible friends, never did my voice speak to them

---

wife of a renowned doctor highly reputed in all Europe, suffering from an ailment which her husband had been powerless to relieve, was radically cured by the spirit of another physician. See also the case of Mrs. Claire Galichon, who was cured by magnetizations performed by the spirit of the Curé of Ars (the priest of Ars, France). The fact is recounted by Mrs. GALICHON herself in her *Souvenirs et Problèmes Spirites* (Paris: Chacornac, 1908), pp. 174 *et seq.*

in vain. Since my first steps in this world, their influence has enveloped me. Often, I felt their sweet fragrance pass on my forehead like a fluttering of wings. It is to their inspirations that I owe my best pages and my most vibrant traits. They shared my joys and sorrows, and when the storm rumbled, I knew They were standing near me during the struggle. Without them, without their help, I would have had to interrupt my march and suspend my labor a long time ago. But their outstretched hands sustained me, guiding me through the harsh stretches of the way. Sometimes, during the retreat of the evening or the silence of the night, their voices speak to me, cradle me, comfort me; they resound in my solitude like a vague melody. Or they are breaths that convey, like caresses, wise whispered counsels, precious indications of the imperfections of my character, and the means of remedying them.

So I forget my human miseries so as to delight myself in the hope of one day seeing my invisible friends, to join them in the light if God deems me worthy, together with all those I have loved and who, now in the Hereafter, help me to go through the earthly stage.

To all of you, tutelary spirits, protective entities, may my grateful thought rise, the best of myself, the tribute of my admiration and my love!

The soul comes from God and returns to God by going through the immense cycle of its destinies. So low that it has come down, sooner or later, by the divine attraction, it soars back to infinity. What is it looking for? An ever more perfect knowledge of the Universe, an ever more complete assimilation of its attributes: Beauty, Truth, Love! And at the same time, a gradual release from material servitudes, a growing collaboration with the eternal work.

Every spirit, on the spiritual plane, has its vocation and seeks for it with facilities unfamiliar to those on Earth; each finds its place in this superb field of action, in this vast universal laboratory. Everywhere, in the expanse as well as on the worlds, subjects of study and work, means of elevation, of participation in the divine work, are offered to the industrious soul.

This is no longer the cold, empty sky of materialists, nor even the contemplative and blissful heaven of certain believers. It is a living, animated, luminous universe, filled with intelligent beings constantly evolving.

And the more these spiritual beings rise, the more their tasks are highlighted, the more their missions grow in importance. One day they will rank among the messenger souls which will bring to the shores of time and space the forces and wills of the infinite Spirit.

For the lowest order spirit as well as for the most eminent, the domain of life is without borders. Whatever the height we have reached, there is always a superior plan to reach, a new perfection to achieve.

In every soul, even the lowest, a great future is in preparation. Every generous thought that begins to emerge, every outpouring of love, every effort towards a better life is like the vibration, the intuitive feeling, the call of a higher world that attracts and will receive the soul sooner or later. Every moment of enthusiasm, every word of justice, every act of self-abnegation is reflected in growing progress on the scale of our destinies.

As it detaches itself from the lower spheres, where heavy influences reign, where gross, banal or culpable lives are led in existences of slow and painful education, the soul perceives the higher manifestations of intelligence, justice, kindness, and its life becomes more and more beautiful and divine. The confused murmurs, the discordant noises of human circles, gradually weaken for it, then fall into silence. At the same time the harmonious echoes of celestial societies become perceptible to it; it is the threshold of happy regions, where eternal clarity reigns, where there is an atmosphere of benevolence, serenity and peace, where all things come out fresh and pure from the hands of God.

The profound difference which exists between earthly life and life in the spiritual world resides in the feeling of deliverance, of lightness, in the absolute freedom enjoyed by good and purified spirits.

Once the material bonds are broken, the pure soul takes flight toward the lofty regions; it lives there in a free, peaceful, intense life, near which the earthly past seems but a painful dream. In the outpouring of shared tenderness, in a life free of evils, of physical needs, the soul feels its faculties increasingly blossom; they acquire a profundity and an extension whose veiled splendors can somehow be glimpsed in phenomena of ecstasy detected in our realm.

The language of the spiritual world is the language of images and symbols, as quick as thought. This is why our invisible guides prefer to use symbolic pictures to warn us in a dream of dangers or misfortunes. The ether, a supple and luminous fluid, takes on with extreme ease the forms that our guides imprints on it. The spirits communicate with one another and understand each other by processes next to which the most consummated oratorical art, all the magic of human eloquence, would seem to be only a coarse stammer. High intelligences perceive and realize without effort the most wonderful conceptions of art and genius. But these conceptions cannot be conveyed in their entirety to humans. Even in its most perfect mediumistic manifestations, Higher-order Spirits must undergo the physical laws of our world. So, it is only vague reflections or faint echoes of their celestial spheres, only a few sparse notes of the great eternal symphony, that such spirits are able to convey to us.

Everything is set up by degrees in the spiritual life. At each degree of evolution from the Self toward wisdom, light, and holiness, corresponds a more perfect state of its receptive senses, of its means of perception. The fluidic body become more and more transparent and diaphanous, giving free passage to the radiations of the soul. Hence, a greater aptitude to experience, to understand the infinite splendors. From there, a more extensive memory of the past, a growing familiarization with the beings and things of the higher planes, until the soul, in its progression, reaches the supreme altitudes.

Once having reached these heights, the spirit has conquered all passions, all tendencies to evil; it is forever released from the material yoke and the law of rebirths. This is the definitive entrance into the divine realms, from where the spirit will not descend again into the circle of the generations, unless voluntarily and to fulfill sublime missions as an incarnate.

On these summits, existence is a perpetual celebration of intelligence and heart. It is close communion in love with all those who have been dear to us and have traveled with us the cycle of transmigrations and trials. Add to this the constant vision of eternal Beauty, a deep penetration into the mysteries and laws of the Universe, and you will have a little idea of the joys reserved for all those who, by their merits and their efforts, have reached the higher heavens.

PART TWO

THE PROBLEM OF DESTINY

XIII

SUCCESSIVE LIVES, REINCARNATION LAWS

AFTER A TIME spent on the spiritual plane, the soul is reborn in human condition, bringing with it the heritage, whether good or bad, of its past.[126] It is reborn as a little child, it reappears on the earthly stage to play a new act in the tragedy of its life, to pay off its previous debts, to conquer new powers which will facilitate its ascension, speeding its progress forward.

The law of rebirths explains and completes the principle of immortality. The evolution of all beings indicates a plan and a goal: this goal, which is perfection, cannot be accomplished in a single lifetime, no matter how long or fruitful it may be. We must see in the plurality of lives of the soul the necessary condition for its education and progress. It is through its own efforts, its struggles, and its sufferings that it redeems itself from a state of ignorance and inferiority, and rises, step by step, first on Earth, then through other, innumerable dwellings, in the starry sky.

Reincarnation, affirmed by the voices from Beyond, is the only rational concept through which one can admit of any atonement for faults committed, and a gradual evolution of all beings. Without it, we would hardly be able to find a completely satisfactory moral sanction;

---

[126] Residence time on the spiritual plane varies greatly depending on the spirit's progress level. It can last several years. In general, spirits of the same family agree to reincarnate together and form similar groups on Earth.

it would be impossible to conceive of a Supreme Being governing the universe with justice.

If we accepted that each and every human being is living for the first and last time here below, and that a single earthly existence is the only sharing of each one of us, then we would have to admit that there is total incoherence and partiality in the distribution of both goods and evils, aptitudes and faculties, native qualities and original vices among us.

Why then to ones good fortune and constant happiness, while to others, misery and inescapable misfortune? To some, strength, health and beauty; to others, weakness, sickness and ugliness? Why intelligence and genius here, whereas there, only imbecility? How do so many admirable moral qualities are found side by side with so many vices and defects? Why are people so diverse, some inferior to the point where they seem to confine themselves to animality, while others seem favored by all the gifts that assure their supremacy? And what to say of innate infirmities, such as blindness, mental impairment, deformities, and all the misfortunes that fill the hospitals, the asylums, and the houses of correction? Heredity cannot explain everything. In most cases, these afflictions cannot be considered as the result of any current causes. It is the same with so-called favors of fate. Too often, righteous people seem crushed under stress, while selfish and wicked people thrive.

Why also are there stillborn children and those who are condemned to suffer from the cradle? Some existences end in a few years, in a few days even, while others last nearly a century. Still, where do the young prodigies come from: musicians, painters, poets, all those who, from an early age, show extraordinary talents for the arts or sciences, while so many others remain mediocre all their lives, in spite of hard work? In the same way, the early instincts, innate feelings of whether dignity or baseness, sometimes contrasting so strangely with the environment in which they manifest themselves?

If individual life begins only at one's earthly birth, if nothing existed previously for each one of us, we will seek in vain to explain those poignant diversities and appalling anomalies, let alone to reconcile them with the existence of a wise, all-foreseeing and equitable Power. All religions, all contemporary philosophical systems have come up against this problem. None of them could solve it. Considered from their point of view, which is the uniqueness[127] of existence of every human being, destiny remains incomprehensible, the plan of the universe is obscured, evolution stops, suffering becomes inexplicable. Humans, thus inclined to believe in the action of blind and fatal forces, in the absence of all distributive justice, slip insensibly toward atheism and pessimism.

Conversely, everything is explained, everything is enlightened by the doctrine of successive lives. In it, the law of justice is revealed in the smallest details of one's existence. The inequalities that shock us result from different situations experienced by the souls in their infinitely varied degrees of evolution. The destiny of a being is no more than the development, through the ages, of a long series of causes and effects engendered by one's actions. Nothing is lost; the effects of good and evil build up and germinate in us until conditions are favorable for them to emerge. Sometimes they blossom quickly; other times, only after a long period. They are interrelated, and reverberate from one lifetime to another, according to their maturity state, which can be activated or slowed down by ambient influences. However none

---

[127] [Trans. note] *Uniqueness* in the sense of happening only once, as an *unrepeatable singularity*.

of these effects can disappear by itself. Only through self-atonement can someone remove them.

Each and every one carries beyond the tomb and brings back at birth the seed of the past. This seed, according to its nature causing our happiness or misfortune, will spread its fruits on the new life which begins and even on the following ones, if a single lifetime is not enough to exhaust the bad consequences of our previous lives. At the same time, our everyday actions, which are sources of new effects, are added to the old causes, either attenuating or aggravating them. They form with them a chain of goods and evils which, as a whole, will thread the fabric of our destiny.

Thus the moral sanction, so inadequate, sometimes so null, when studied from the standpoint of a single lifetime, is found to be absolute and perfect when seen from the perspective of a succession of lifetimes. There is a close correlation between our actions and our destiny. We suffer in ourselves, in our inner being and in the events of our life, the backlash of our actions. Our actions, in all their forms, is a generator of good or bad components, of instant or distant consequences, which fall on us like rain, like storms, or joyous rays. Humans build their own future. So far, in our uncertainty, in our ignorance, we have been groping our way and suffering our fate without being able to explain it. Soon, better enlightened and suffused with the majesty of the higher laws, we will understand life's beauty, which lies in courageous effort, and will give our work a more noble and higher impulsion.

As said above, the endless variety of aptitudes, faculties, and personalities, is easily explained. All souls are not of the same spiritual age; all have not climbed their evolutionary stages at the same pace. Some have traversed an immense course and are already approaching the apex of earthly progress; others are just beginning their cycle of evolution within the various stages of humanity. These are young souls, emanated at a less distant time from the eternal core, an inexhaustible core, from which spring out intelligent beings that descend on the worlds of matter to animate rudimentary forms of life. When they reach the human stage, they rank among the savage tribes or barbarous peoples that occupy the backward continents, the deprived regions of the globe. And when they finally enter our civilizations, they are still easily identified by their awkwardness, their clumsiness, their incapacity in all things, and especially their violent passions, their sanguinary tastes, sometimes even by their ferocity. But these undeveloped souls will rise one day, by their turn, on the scale of infinite gradations by means of innumerable reincarnations.

Another component of this problem is the free will of the spirit. To some, it allows them to lag behind on the path of ascension, to lose, without concern for the true purpose of life, so many precious hours in pursuit of wealth and pleasure. To others, it makes it possible to speed their passage through difficult paths, and to quickly reach the summits of thought, if they prefer the possession of the goods of the spirit and the heart instead of material seductions. In this number we may count the savants, the geniuses and the saints of all times and places, the noble martyrs of generous causes, and those who have devoted their entire lives to build up, in the silence of cloisters, libraries, and laboratories, the treasures of science and human wisdom.

All the currents of the past find one another, come together and merge into each lifetime. They contribute to making the soul great or feeble, brilliant or obscure, powerful or miserable. In most of our contemporaries, these currents succeed in making only indifferent souls, ceaselessly tossed between the breaths of good and evil, truth and error, passion and of duty.

Thus, during the sequence of our lifetimes on Earth, the great work of our education, the gradual building of our individuality, of our moral personality, goes on until it is completed. This is why the soul must incarnate successively in the most diverse circles, in all social conditions, undergoing alternately the trials of poverty and wealth, learning to obey, then to command. It needs obscure lives, lives of hard work, of privations, so that it can learn the renunciation of material vanities; the detachment from frivolous things; patience, and discipline of the mind. It requires lifetimes of study, missions of devotion, of charity, by which intelligence is enlightened and the heart is enriched with new qualities. Then come the lives of self-sacrifice, sacrifice to the family, to one's homeland, to humanity. It is also necessary to face cruel ordeals, the furnace where pride and selfishness dissolve, and the painful stages which are the redemption of the past, the reparation of our faults, the form under which the law of justice is accomplished. The spirit is thus tempered, refined, purified through struggle and suffering. It returns to expiate in the very environment where lies its guilt. It sometimes happens that these trials make our existence a nightmare, but such an ordeal is a summit that may bring us closer to joyous worlds.

Therefore, there is no inescapable fate. It is we humans who, by our own will, forge the chains with which we shackle ourselves. From birth to death, it is we who weave, day by day, thread by thread, the fabric of our destinies. The law of justice is basically only a law of harmony. It determines the consequences of the actions that we freely perform. It does not punish or reward, but merely presides over order, the balance of the moral world as well as that of the physical world. Any harm to the universal order will cause suffering and a necessary reparation, until, through the efforts of the culprit, the violated harmony is reestablished.

Destiny has no other rule than that of the good or the evil accomplished. On all things hangs a great and powerful law, by virtue of which every living being in the universe can only enjoy a situation in proportion to its merits. Our happiness, despite often misleading appearances, is always in direct relationship with our capacity for good. And this law finds its complete application in the reincarnations of the soul; it is it that fixes the conditions of each rebirth and traces the outlines of our destinies. This is why wicked people seem happy while righteous people suffer in excess. The hour of atonement has come for some; for others, it is nigh at hand.

To associate our actions with the divine plan, acting in concert with Nature, in the sense of harmony and for the general good, is to prepare our elevation, our happiness. To act in the opposite direction, by fostering discord and indulging in unhealthy appetites; to work for oneself at the expense of others; is to plant the seeds of pain in your own future; it is to place yourself under the spell of influences which will retard your advancement and bind you for a long time to the lower worlds.

This is what must be said, repeated and inculcated until each and every human consciousness has only one goal: to conquer moral forces, without which we will always be powerless to improve our condition and that of humanity! By making known the effects of the law of responsibility, and demonstrating that the consequences of our actions fall back on us over time – as a stone thrown in the air falls back to the ground – we will gradually lead our fellow human beings to conform their actions to this law, to achieve order, justice and solidarity in the social environment.

Some Spiritualist schools fight the principle of successive lives and teach that the evolution of souls after death continues only in the invisible world. Others, while admitting reincarnation, believe that it takes place on higher spheres; there is no need to return to Earth, in their opinion.

To the proponents of these theories, I would like to recall that the incarnation on Earth has a goal, and this goal is the perfecting of the human being. Now, given the infinite variety of the conditions of earthly existence, either in its duration or in its results, it is impossible to admit that all humans can attain the same degree of perfection in a single lifetime. Hence the obligation of successive returns, allowing one to acquire all the qualities required to penetrate onto more advanced worlds.

The present can only be explained by the past. It took a whole series of earthly rebirths to reach the point where humans have now reached, and it is hardly acceptable that this evolution stage would be definitive for our planet. Not all its inhabitants are in condition to transmigrate after death to more perfect societies. On the contrary, every detail indicates imperfections in their nature and the necessity of new works, new tests, to perfect their education and enable them to reach a higher level in the scale of beings.

Everywhere nature acts with wisdom, method, and at an unhurried pace. It took many centuries to shape the human form. Civilization arose only after long periods of barbarism. Physical and mental evolution, moral progress, are all governed by identical laws. We cannot accomplish them in a single existence. And why seek far away, on other worlds, the elements of new progress, if we can find them everywhere around us? From savagery to the most refined civilization, does not our planet offer a vast field for the spirit's development? The contrasts and oppositions that good and evil, knowledge and ignorance, present in all their forms, are examples and lessons, with many causes of emulation.

It is no more extraordinary to be reborn than to be born. The soul returns to flesh to undergo the laws of necessity. The needs, the struggles of material life are all major stimulants that compel it to work, increase its energy, temper its character. Such results cannot be achieved by young spirits, whose will is still faltering, if they lived freely only on the spiritual plane. To advance, they need the whip of necessity and the many incarnations in which their souls will focus, retreating in themselves, to acquire the spring, the impetus necessary to later trace their immense trajectory in the skies.

Therefore the purpose of incarnations is, in a way, the revelation of the soul to itself; or rather its own enhancement by the constant development of its forces, knowledge, consciousness and conscience, and of its will. The lower-order, new soul can become conscious of itself only on condition of being separated from other souls, and enclosed in a material body. It will thus constitute a distinct being whose personality will assert itself, with growing experience and progress reinforced by reason of its efforts to triumph over the difficulties and obstacles that earthly life multiplies under its feet.

Our planetary existences connect us to a whole order of things which constitute the initial plan, the basis of our infinite evolution; they are in perfect harmony with our evolutionary level. But this order of things and the series of lifetimes attached to it, however numerous, represent only a tiny fraction of our sidereal existence, a mere moment in the unlimited duration of our destinies.

The transition of souls from Earth to other worlds is carried out under the influence of certain laws. The orbs populating space differ from one another in nature and density. The fluidic envelopes of the souls can adapt to these new environments only under special conditions of purification. It is impossible for lower spirits, while wandering, in the errant state, to penetrate higher worlds and describe their wonders to our mediums. The same difficulty is found, at an even greater degree, when it comes to reincarnations on these worlds. The societies which inhabit them, due to their superior state, are inaccessible to the immense majority of earthly spirits, that are still too primitive and insufficiently evolved by comparison. The latter's psychical senses, still not very refined, would not allow them to live the subtle life that reigns over these distant spheres. They would be there like the blind in the light or the deaf in a concert. The same attraction that connects their fluidic bodies to this planet is the one that bind their thought and consciousness to the lower realm. Their desires, their appetites, their hatred, even their love, bring them down here and link them to the object of their passions.

We must first learn to unravel the bonds that bolt us to Earth, then start to rise to more advanced worlds. To snatch earthly souls from their environment before the special evolution of this environment is concluded, to send them to higher spheres before all the necessary progress is made, would be wanting in logic and proportion. Nature does not act like that. Its work unfolds, majestic, harmonious in all its phases. The beings directed by its law on their ascension leave their field of action only after having acquired the virtues and powers likely to grant them access to a higher domain of universal life.

What rules govern the return of the soul to the flesh? The rules of attraction and affinity. When a spirit is reincarnated, it is drawn to an environment in keeping with its tendencies, its character, and its evolution level. Souls follow each other and incarnate in groups. They constitute spiritual families, whose members are united by tender and powerful bonds, contracted in the course of lives shared in common. Sometimes these spirits are temporarily distant from one another, and change their surroundings to acquire new abilities. This explains, as the case may be, the analogies or dissimilarities that characterize members of the same family, both siblings and parents. But always, those who love each other eventually find one another on Earth, or in the spiritual world.

The concept of reincarnations is accused of ruining the idea of family, of confusing and interfering in the situations that one occupies vis-à-vis the other, of spirits united by kinship ties, for example the relationship of mother and child, of husband and wife, etc. But the opposite is the truth. If one follows the hypothesis of a single life, spirits would disperse after a short coexistence and often become strangers to each other. According to the Catholicism, souls are fixed after death in different places, according to their merits, and the elect are forever separated from the reprobate. Thus, the bonds of family and friendship formed by a transient life would be relaxed in most cases or even break forever. Whereas through the idea of rebirth, the spirits come together again and pursue their goals in common over their lifetimes in the worlds. Their bonds thus become ever tighter and deeper.

Our spontaneous tenderness and affection toward certain beings here below is easily explained. We have already known them; we met them before. How many husbands, how many lovers are connected by innumerable lives traveled two by two! Their love is indestructible, because love is the force of all forces, the supreme bond that nothing can break.

The conditions of reincarnation are such that our reciprocal situations are rarely reversed. Almost always our respective degrees of kinship are maintained. Sometimes, in the event of an impossibility, a son will be able to become the younger brother of his father of a former life, a mother will be able to be reborn as the older sister of his son. In exceptional cases and only at the request of the interested parties, situations will be reversed. The feelings of delicacy, dignity, and mutual respect that we feel on Earth cannot be ignored in the spiritual world. To assume that something like this might happen, one would have to ignore the nature of the laws that govern the evolution of souls.

Advanced spirits, whose freedom increase in proportion to their elevation, choose the environment where they want to be reborn, while lower-order spirits are compelled by a mysterious force which they instinctively obey. Yet, all are protected, counseled and supported in the transition from the life on the spiritual plane to earthly existence, which is more painful and more formidable than death.

The union of the soul with the body is effected by means of the fluidic envelope, that is, the perispirit of which I have often spoken. By its subtle nature, it will serve as a link between the spirit and matter. The soul is attached to the embryo by means of this "plastic mediator,"[128] which will tighten and increasingly condense through the progressive phases of gestation to form the physical body. From conception to birth, this fusion occurs slowly, fiber by fiber, molecule by molecule. Under the increasing inflow of material elements and the vital force provided by the generators, the vibrational movements of the child's perispirit will diminish and be reduced, at the same time as the faculties of the child's soul, such as memory and consciousness, will fade and be blotted out. It is to this reduction of the perispirit's fluidic vibrations, to its concealment in the flesh, that we must attribute the loss of our memory of past lives. An ever thicker veil envelops the soul and extinguishes its inner radiations. All the impressions of its spiritual life and its long past are plunged into the depths of the unconscious. These will emerge from it only at times of exteriorization or at death, when the spirit, recovering the fullness of its vibrational movements, will evoke the sleeping world of its memories.

The role of our fluidic double is considerable; it explains all the vital phenomena from birth to death. Keeping in it the ineffaceable traces of all the states of one's being since its origin, it communicates the imprint, the essential features to the material embryo. The key to embryogenetic phenomena lies here.

During the gestation period, the perispirit is impregnated with vital fluid and materializes sufficiently to become the regulator of energy and supporter of the elements

---

[128] [Trans. note] *Plastic mediator* is a concept formerly introduced by the British philosopher Ralph CUDWORTH (1617–1688).

provided by the progenitors. It thus constitutes a sort of canvas, a permanent fluidic framework, through which will pass the current of matter that destroys and restores ceaselessly, during life, the terrestrial organism. It will be, so to speak, the invisible frame that supports the human statue internally. Thanks to it, individuality and memory will be preserved and perpetuated on the physical plane, in spite of the vicissitudes of the changing and mobile part of human being. And it will likewise ensure the memory of facts of the current existence, memories whose linking, from cradle to grave, provide us with the inner certainty of our identity.

The incorporation of the soul is therefore not spontaneous as certain religions and philosophies preach. It is gradual and becomes complete and definitive only by the end of uterine life. At that moment, matter completely surrounds the spirit, which must vivify it by the action of its acquired faculties. Long will be the period of development, during which the soul will apply itself to mold its new envelope, bending it to its needs, so as to make it an instrument capable of manifesting its inner powers. But in this work, it will be assisted by a Spirit in charge of its guard, which watches over it, inspires and guides it throughout the duration of its earthly pilgrimage. And every night, during sleep, and often at the daytime, during the childish period, the spirit emerges from its fleshly envelope and returns to the spiritual plane to draw strength and encouragement, and then to go down again to its resting envelope, in order to resume the painful course of existence.

Before resuming contact with matter and beginning a new incarnation, the spirit, as I have said, must choose the environment in which it will be reborn in earthly life. But this choice is limited, circumscribed, determined by multiple causes. The preceding time of one's being, its moral debts, its affections, its merits and demerits, the role it is able to fulfill, all these elements intervene in the orientation of the new lifetime in preparation. Hence the preference for a certain race, a certain nation, a certain family. Loved souls that are incarnated attract us. The bonds of the past are renewed in filiation, alliances, new friendships. The very places exert on us a mysterious attraction, and it is rare that destiny does not lead us several times back to the countries where we have already lived, loved, and suffered. Hatred is also a force that bring us closer to our enemies of the past, in order to erase, through better relations, old enmities. Thus we find on our road most of those who made our joy or our torments.

The same occurs with the choice of a certain social class, the conditions of ambience and education, the privileges of fortune or health, the miseries of poverty. All these varied and complex factors will be combined to assure to the new incarnate the fulfillments, the advantages, or the trials which are involved at the latter's evolution level, with its merits or faults, and the debts it contracted in the past.

From this it will be understood how difficult the choice of one's environment is. Also, most often, that choice is inspired by guidelines given by the Intelligences (the Higher Order Spirits), when they do not do it themselves altogether, for our own benefit, if we still do not have the discernment necessary to make, with all wisdom and foresight, the choices which will be most effective in promoting our evolution and purging us of our past.

However, the spirit concerned remains free to accept or postpone the time of its unavoidable atonements. At the moment of attaching itself to a human embryo, when the soul still possesses all its lucidity, its Spirit Guide unfolds before it the panorama of the existence which awaits it, showing it in advance the obstacles and evils which will plague its existence. The Spirit Guide makes the reincarnate soul understand their utility in developing its virtues or stripping it from its vices. If the trial seems too harsh to the soul, if it does not feel sufficiently prepared to face it, the soul is free to set back the deadline and seek a transitional life that should increase its moral strength and willpower.

At the moment of supreme resolutions, before descending into flesh, the spirit perceives and grasps a general idea of the life that is about to begin. It sees it in its outlines, in its culminating events, nevertheless always modifiable by its personal actions and the use of its free will; for the soul is the sovereign of its actions. But as soon as it has been pronounced, as soon as the bond is formed and the incorporation starts, this memory disappears, everything vanishes. Existence will then unfold with all its foreseen, accepted and chosen consequences, without any intuition of the future subsisting in the normal consciousness of the incarnated being. Oblivion is necessary during material life. The anticipated knowledge of adverse events that will take place, the prediction of evils or catastrophes that await us, would paralyze our efforts, would suspend our progress forward.

As for the choice of gender, it is still the soul that decides in advance. It can even change from one incarnation to another by an act of its creative will modifying the organic conditions of the perispirit. Some thinkers admit that the alternation of the sexes is necessary to acquire more special virtues, they say, in each half of the human race. For example, in men, will, firmness, and courage; in women, tenderness, patience, and purity.

Based on instructions received from Spirit Guides, I see the change of sex, always possible for the spirit, as useless and dangerous in principle. Higher-order Spirits do not recommend it. It is easy to recognize, at first glance, those around us who, in a previous existence, had adopted a different sex; they are always, from whatever point of view, atypical. Certain women, with their masculine personality and tastes, some of whom still bear traces of attributes belonging to the opposite sex, such as a stub on the chin, are obviously men who have reincarnated. They do not seem to have anything esthetic or attractive. The same happens with effeminate men, who have all the characteristics of Eve's daughters and are somehow misplaced in life.[129] When a spirit has become accustomed to a sex, it is bad for it to go out and take on another one different from its usual nature.

Many souls, created in couples, are destined to evolve together, united forever in joy as in pain. They have been called kindred souls (soulmates). Their number is greater than is generally believed. They accomplish the most complete form, the most perfect life and feeling, and give to other souls the example of a faithful, unalterable and profound love. They can be recognized by this trait, which is strongly accentuated. What would become of their attachment, their relationship, their destiny, if the change of sex was mandatory, a law? I rather think that, by the very fact of their general ascent, noble characters and high virtues will multiply simultaneously in both sexes. Finally, no quality will remain the prerogative of an isolated sex, but an attribute of both.

There is a situation, the only one, that could make a sex change an act imposed by the law of justice and reparation: it is when mistreatment or serious damage inflicted on persons of one sex draw into this same

---

[129] [Trans. note] In the beginning of the 20th century, and until much later, such prejudiced views prevailed in the world at large.

sex the culpable spirits, so that they undergo, by their turn, the effects of the evils they engendered. But the punishment of retaliation does not rule absolutely over the spiritual world. As we shall see later, there are a thousand manners under which reparation can be accomplished and the causes of evil erased. The all-powerful chain of causes and effects unfolds itself in a thousand different links.

It may be objected that it would be unjust to compel half of the spirits to evolve into a weaker and too often oppressed and humiliated sex, sacrificed by still barbarous societies. We can answer that this state of things tends to gradually disappear, to make room for greater equity. It is through a moral and social valuing and a strong education of women that humanity will elevate itself. As for the pains of the past, these are not lost. The spirit which has suffered social injustice collects, by the law of balance and compensation, the result of the trials that it has undergone. The feminine spirit – so the Spirit Guides tell us – is rising faster to perfection.

The role of women in the lives of nations is immense. As sisters, wives or mothers, they are the great comforters and the sweet counselors. Through their children, they hold the future within them and prepare the humans of tomorrow. Also, any society that debases them, degrades itself. Only respected, honored and enlightened women can make the family strong, and the society great, principled and united!

Certain attractions are too formidable for certain souls in search for conditions of rebirth; for instance, the families of alcoholics, of debauched and insane people.

How to reconcile the notion of justice with the incarnation of beings in such environments? Are there not at stake deep and hidden psychical reasons, and physical causes which are not merely apparent? As we have seen, the law of affinity brings similar beings closer together. A whole culpable past can bring a backward soul to groups that have analogies to its own fluidic and mental state, a state it has created by its thoughts and actions.

In such cases, there is no place for arbitrariness or chance. It is the prolonged misuse of one's free will, the constant pursuit of selfish or evil deeds that draws a soul to progenitors similar to it. They will supply it with materials compatible with its fluidic organism, impregnated with the same coarse tendencies, suitable for the manifestation of the same appetites, the same desires. A new existence will start as a new level of fall towards vice and crime. It is the descent into the abyss.

As master of its destiny, the soul must undergo the state of things that it has wished and prepared for itself. However, after making its conscience an abode of darkness, and becoming a den of evil, it will have to regenerate it into a temple of light. Accumulated faults will give rise to more intense suffering; reincarnations which will then succeed one another will be harder and more painful. This iron ring will be tightened until the soul, milled by the gears of causes and effects created by itself, will understand the need of reacting against its own tendencies, and of overcoming its bad passions, in order to change the course of its path. Therefore, as long as repentance touches the soul, the latter will gain new strength, new impulsions, which will bring it to purer environments. It will then draw on new forms, with elements better suited to its work of reparation and self-reformation. Step by step, progress will be achieved. In the repentant and tender soul, new rays and emanations will penetrate, unknown aspirations, needs for useful action, and a sense of devotion will awaken. The same law of attraction which once pushed the soul into the dregs of society will now act in its favor and become the instrument of its regeneration.

However, such a regeneration will not happen without pain; the ascension will not be without difficulties. The faults, the errors of yesteryear are reflected in causes of obstruction in our future lives. The effort will have to be all the more vigorous and have staying power as responsibilities become heavier, and require a period of resistance against the obstinacy of more extensive evil. Throughout this rough rise, the past will dominate the present for a long time, and its weight will bend the shoulders of the pilgrim more than once. Yet, from above, helping hands will extend to you and help you cross the steepest passages. "There will be more joy in heaven over one sinner who repents than over ninety-nine righteous persons who need no repentance." (Lk 15:7)

Our future is in our hands and our opportunities for doing good will grow as we increase our efforts to achieve it. Every noble and pure life, every higher mission is the result of an immense past of struggles and failures, of victories won over oneself, the coronation of long and patient work, fruits of science and charitable love harvested one by one and built up over the ages. Every brilliant faculty, every solid virtue has required multiple lives of obscure work, violent struggles between spirit and flesh, passions and duty. To achieve talent, genius, our thought has to mature slowly through the centuries. The field of intelligence, painfully cleared, yields at first only meager harvests; then gradually these become richer and more abundant.

At each return to the spiritual plane, the balance of losses and gains is established, one's progress is measured and consolidated. The soul examines itself and judges itself. It painstakingly scrutinizes its recent history, recorded within itself. It reviews the fruits of experience and wisdom that its last lifetime has provided, so as to assimilate its substance more deeply. Life on the spiritual plane, for the evolved spirit, is a period of examination, of recollections, in which the spirit's faculties, after having been directed outside, make a retreat and apply themselves to an inner study, interrogating one's conscience and thus forming a rigorous inventory of whatever is found of beauty or ugliness in one's soul. Life on the spiritual plane is a necessary counterpart of earthly life: it is a life of balance, where forces are reconstituted and energies are renewed, where enthusiasms are revived and the spirit prepares itself for future tasks. It is the resting pause after the effort, the calm after the storm, one's peaceful and serene concentration after a period of active expansion or ardent conflict.

According to Theosophists, the return of the soul to flesh occurs every fifteen hundred years.[130] This theory has never been confirmed by facts or by the testimonies of spirits. The latter, when questioned in large numbers, in totally diverse mediumistic groups, replied that reincarnations happen much faster. Souls eager for progress stay only a short time on the spiritual plane. They demand to come back to live in this world, in order to acquire new credits, new merits. About former existences of certain persons, there are some indications collected at points very far apart from each other, coming from the mouths of mediums who have never met those persons; indications

---

[130] In Theosophy books, it is generally agreed that "Fifteen centuries is the 'average period between incarnations.'" See A. BESANT, *Reincarnation* (New York: Theosophical Publishing Society, 1898), p. 61.

perfectly concordant among themselves. They show that ten, twenty, thirty years at the most have separated their earthly lives. In all this, there is no fixed rule. Incarnations come often or scarcely according to the state of the souls, their desire for work and advancement, and the favorable opportunities available to them. In cases of early death of young children, for example, they sometimes immediately reincarnate.

We already know that the fluidic body is more materialized or ethereal according to the nature of the thoughts and actions of the spirit. Vicious souls, by their tendencies, attract to themselves impure fluids, which thicken their fluidic envelope and reduce their radiations. At death, they are unable to rise above the earthly regions, and instead remain confined in the atmosphere or mixed with humans. If they persist in evil, the planet's attraction becomes so powerful that it precipitates their reincarnation.

The more materialized and coarse a spirit is, the more the law of gravity has influence over it. The opposite is true in pure spirits, whose radiant perispirit vibrates to all the sensations of the infinite, finding in the ethereal regions environments appropriate to their nature and their progress level. Having reached a higher degree, such spirits prolong their stay on the spiritual plane more and more; planetary incarnations become the exception for them. Free life becomes the rule, until the sum of the perfections achieved will free them forever from the bondage of rebirths.

XIV

SUCCESSIVE LIVES, SCIENTIFIC EXPERIMENTS, REGRESSION OF MEMORY

IN THE PRECEDING pages, I explained the logical reasons that militate in favor of a belief in successive lives. Now, I will devote this chapter and the following ones to refute all the objections posed by its opponents, and tackle the scientific proofs which come each day to corroborate it.

The most common objection is as follows: If a human being has already lived, one asks, why does it not remember its past lives? Well, I have already summarily indicated the physiological cause of this forgetfulness. This cause is rebirth itself, that is to say, the action of putting on a new organism, a material envelope which, by superimposing itself on the fluidic envelope, plays, in regard to it, the same role of a candle snuffer. As a result of the diminution of its vibrational state, the spirit, whenever it takes possession of a new body, of a blank brain devoid of any memory, finds itself unable to express the accumulated memories of its past lives. True, the spirit's background will be revealed again in its aptitudes, in its ease of assimilation, in its qualities and defects. But all the details of the facts and events that constitute its distant past will lie buried in the depths of its consciousness, remaining veiled for the duration of the reincarnate spirit's earthly life. The spirit, in the waking state, can only express in the forms of earthly language the impressions recorded by its material brain.

Memory is the sequencing, the association of ideas, facts, and knowledge. As soon as this association disappears, as soon as the thread of memories is broken, the past seems to fade away for us. But this is only an appearance. In a speech given on February 6, 1905, Professor Charles Richet, member of the French Academy of Medicine, declared that, "Memory is an implacable faculty of our intelligence, because none of our perceptions are ever forgotten. As soon as a fact has struck our senses, then, irreversibly, it is fixed in memory. It does not matter whether we keep conscious of it or not; it exists, and is indelible."

It should be added that humans can be reborn. The awakening of memory is only a vibrational effect produced by the action of one's will upon the cells of the brain. To revive pre-birth recollections, one must reposition oneself in vibrational harmony with the dynamic state in which we were at the time when the perception was established. The physical brains that have recorded these perceptions no longer exist; therefore we must look for these perceptions in our deep consciousness. But it will remain silent as long as the spirit is locked in the flesh. It must come out of it and free itself from the body to recover the fullness of his vibrations and retrieve the fabric of memories hidden in itself. Then it can perceive its past again and reconstitute it in its minimal details. This is exactly what happens in the phenomena of somnambulism and trance.

We know that there are mysterious depths within ourselves, in which the sediments of our lives of struggle, study and work have been slowly deposited over the ages. They are all engraved there: all the incidents, all the vicissitudes of our remote past. It is like an ocean of sleeping things rocked by the waves of destiny. A powerful call of our will can revive them. Toward them the glance of our spirit enters moments of clairvoyance, similar to the radiations of stars which slip, into the glaucous depths, even through the vaults and arches of the dark retreats of the ocean.

Let us recall here the essential points of the theory of the Self, to which are attached all the problems of memory and consciousness.

The identity of the Self, of one's personality, persists and remains only through memory and consciousness. Reminiscences, intuitions, aptitudes determine one's feeling of having lived. There exists in the intellect a continuity, a succession of causes and effects that must be reconstituted as a whole for one to possess an integral knowledge of the Self. This, as we have seen, is impossible in our material life, since the incorporation of the soul brings a temporary erasure of the states of consciousness which form this continuous whole. Just as our physical life is subject to the alternations of night and day, so too does a similar phenomenon occur in the life of the spirit. Our memory, our consciousness alternately undergoes periods of eclipse and radiation, of shadow and light, in the spiritual or earthly life, and even on this latter plane, during the wake or in different phases of sleep. And since there are gradations in the eclipse, there are also degrees in the light.

Many dreams leave no trace after we wake up, the same happening to impressions gathered during somnambulistic sleep. All magnetizers are aware of the fact that forgetfulness upon awakening is a constant phenomenon among somnambulists. But as soon as the spirit of the subject, immersed in a new sleep, is found in the dynamic conditions which allow the retrieval of its memories, they reemerge. The subject recalls what he or she has done, said, seen, and expressed at all times of their existence.

In view of this we can easily understand the momentary forgetfulness of past lives. The vibrational movement of the perispiritual envelope, dampened down by matter in the course of one's current life, is far too feeble to reach the degree of intensity and duration necessary for the retrieval of these memories during one's waking state.

In fact, memory is only a mode of consciousness often in a subconscious state. Already, in the restricted circle of our current life, we do not retain the memory of our first years, which is however engraved in us, like all the states we went through during our personal history. The same happens with a large number of actions and facts belonging to other periods of our life. It is said that French philosopher Pierre Gassendi (1592–1655) could remember his life since the age of eighteen months; but this is an exception. Mental effort is needed to awaken these memories of one's normal life, the one most familiar to us; needed, let me stress it, to seize a thousand things studied, learned, forgotten, because they have descended into the deep layers of our memory. At every moment, our intelligence must seek in the subconsciousness our knowledge, the memories that it wants to revive; it strives to make them pass into the physical consciousness, into the material brain, after providing them with the vital elements offered by neurons or nerve cells. Depending on the richness or poverty of these elements, our memory will emerge either clear or diffuse; sometimes it escapes us; communication cannot be established, or its projection occurs only after the fact itself, when we least expect it.

Therefore, to recall one's memory, the first and foremost condition is to want it. This explains why so many spirits, even in the spiritual world, under the influence of certain dogmatic prejudices, neglect all research and remain ignorant of the past that sleeps in them. In this environment, as among us on Earth, during an experiment, hypnotic suggestion becomes necessary. This law of suggestion is manifest everywhere, under a thousand forms; we ourselves endure it at every moment of the day. For example, near us; when a song is played, a certain word or name is spoken, an image strikes our eyes; suddenly, thanks to the association of ideas, a whole series of confused memories, almost forgotten, hidden in the depths of our consciousness, unfolds in our spirit.

Whole periods of our current life can fade from memory. In his book *Metapsychical Phenomena* (Trans. L. I. Finch, London, Duckworth, 1905), pages 187–188, Dr. J. Maxwell, Attorney General at the Court of Bordeaux, speaks in the following terms about known cases of amnesia:

"Sometimes the notion of personality disappears. There are patients who suddenly forget everything, even to their own name. All their antecedent life is effaced, and they appear to return to the state they were in at birth. They have to learn again how to speak, to eat, and to dress themselves. Sometimes the amnesia is not so complete. I have been able to observe a patient, who had forgotten everything which had any connection whatever with his own personality."

The war multiplied these cases and each one of us could read their narrative in the newspapers.

Dr. Pitre, Dean of the Faculty of Medicine of Bordeaux, in his book *Le Somnambulisme et l'Hystérie*, cites a case where he shows that all the facts and knowledge recorded in us from childhood can be retrieved. He calls this phenomenon *ecmnesia*. His subject, a seventeen-year-old girl, could speak only French and had forgotten the Gascon dialect, the idiom of her youth. Put to sleep and reverted in time to the age of five, through hypnotic suggestion, she could no longer understand French and spoke only patois. She told all the details of her childish life; they stood out for her in perfect clarity; but she remained deaf to the questions asked, no longer understanding the language spoken to her. She had forgotten all the facts of her life that had occurred between the ages of five and seventeen.

Dr. Burot carried identical experiments. His subject Jeanne is reverted by him, mentally, back to different periods of her youth, and, in each period, the incidents of her existence are drawn with precision from her memory, but all subsequent facts fade. The progress of her intelligence could be followed backwards. Back at the age of five, she could barely read; her handwriting at that age was clumsy, with spelling mistakes customary of her age at that time.[131]

All these stories have been checked. The above-mentioned researchers made minute inquiries and were able to ascertain the accuracy of the facts reported by the subjects, facts which were erased from their memory in the normal waking state.

As we will see that by a logical and rigorous sequence, these phenomena lead us to the possibility of experimentally awakening in one's memory, in the permanent part of the self, memories prior to one's birth. This is what we find in experiments conducted by F. Colavida, E. Marata, Colonel Rochas d'Aiglun, and others.

The states of fever, delirium, anesthetic sleep, by causing partial disengagement (out-of-the-body experience), can also shake and expand the deep layers of memory, thus awakening old knowledge and specific memories. The famous case of Ninfa Filiberto, of Palermo, certainly

---

[131] Doctors H. Bourru and P. Burot, *Variations de la Personnalité* (Paris: J. B. Baillière, 1888), p. 152.

comes to mind. She spoke, during fever, several foreign languages that she had long forgotten. Here are some other facts reported by medical practitioners.

Dr. Henry Freeborn reports the case of a 70-year-old woman who, seriously ill from bronchopneumonia, was delirious from March 13 to 16, 1902:[132]

According to his article, on the night of the 13th to the 14th, it was found that she spoke a language unknown to the people around her. She sometimes seemed to be saying verses; other times she seemed to be talking. She repeated several times the same composition in verse. We finally recognize that the language was Hindustani. On the morning of the 14th, her Hindustani began to be mixed with a little English; she was either talking to her parents and childhood friends, or talking about them. On the 15th, the Hindustani had disappeared, and the patient was instead addressing friends she had known later, using English, French, and German. The lady in question was born in India, which she left at the age of three to go to England, after four months of traveling, before she had completed her fourth year. Until the day she landed in England, she had been entrusted to Hindu servants and did not speak English at all. It is curious that after a period of sixty-six years, during which she had never spoken Hindustani, delirium had reminded her of the language of her early childhood. At present the patient speaks French and German fluently as well as English; but, although she still knows a few words of Hindustani, she is absolutely unable to speak that language, let alone compose a single sentence in it.

---

[132] The original is in *The Lancet*, vol. 159, no. 4111, pp. 1685–1686, "Temporary Reminiscence of a Long-forgotten Language during the Delirium of Bronchopneumonia," London, June 14, 1902. [Trans. note: due to copyright reasons, the excerpt above was meticulously translated from the French, as a paraphrase.]

The Annals of Psychical Science, of January–June 1906, recorded an interesting case of amnesia in the evening before, reported by Dr. Gilbert-Ballet, of the Hotel-Dieu of Paris:[133]

"'I have observed, during my practice at hospital, a very interesting case of a patient who, in consequence of a violent shock, had completely forgotten a large slice of his former life. He remembered quite well his childhood, and very distant events, but there was a blank with regard to a portion of his existence nearer to the present time, and he could not recollect what bad occurred during that period of his life. This is what we call *retrograde amnesia*.'"

But at this point, this patient, named Dada, falls into the hypnotic state, and immediately all the incidents of his journey are reconstituted in their smallest details, including the memory of the people he met. Dada is in his fourth bout of nervous amnesia. When asleep, he remembers what he has forgotten in the waking state, simply because he is again in the state of second condition, that is, in the state he was in at the moment of his amnesia attack. This case still refers us to the laws and conditions that govern the phenomena of retrieving the memory of past lives.

In short, the whole study of earthly humans provides us with evidence that there are distinct states of consciousness and personality. We have seen in the first part of this book that the coexistence in us of a mental double, whose two parts meet and merge at death, is attested not only by experimental hypnotism, but also by all psychical evolution.

The fact alone of this intellectual duality, considered in its relation to the problem of reincarnations, explains how a whole part of the self, with its immense procession

---

[133] [Trans. note] *The Annals of Psychical Science*, vol. III, "The Mysteries of Amnesia," pp. 189–190, London, Jan–Jun 1906.

of impressions and old memories, can remain hidden in the shadows during one's current lifetime.

We know that telepathy, clairvoyance, premonition of events, are powers related to our deep hidden self. Hypnotic suggestion facilitates this activity; it is a call of the will, an invitation to souls weak and disempowered to emerge from their prison and return temporarily in possession of the riches, the powers that slumber in them. Magnetic passes untie the bonds that attach the soul to the physical body, causing its release. From then on, suggestion, either personal or extraneous, does its work; it is exerted with greater intensity. This action is not only applicable to the awakening of psychical senses; we have just seen that it can also regress to and retrieve the sequence of memories engraved in the depths of the self.

It seems that, in some exceptional cases, this action can be performed even in the waking state. F. W. H. Myers[134] speaks of the faculty of the "subliminal self" to evoke the emotional states that have disappeared from normal consciousness and to relive them in the past. This fact, he says, is frequently encountered in artists, whose revived emotions can exceed the original emotions in intensity.

The same author expresses the opinion that the most probable theory for explaining genius is that of Plato's reminiscences, on the condition of basing it on the scientific data established today.

These same phenomena reappear in another form in an sequence of facts that has already been highlighted. These are the impressions of people who, following accidents, were able to escape death. For example, drowned individuals rescued before complete asphyxiation and

---

[134] F. W. H. MYERS, *Human Personality* (London: Longmans, 1903), vol. 2, ch. VIII, sections 835, pp. 132 *et seq*, and 838, p. 138.

others who suffered serious falls. Many say that between the moment they fell and the moment they lost consciousness, the entire spectacle of their lives unfolded in their brain automatically, in successive and retrograde pictures, with dizzying speed, accompanied by a moral sense of good and evil as well as the awareness of the responsibilities incurred.

T. Ribot, leader of French positivism, in his book *Les Maladies de la Personnalité* (Paris, F. Alcan, 1899), cited numerous phenomena which established the possibility of an spontaneous, automatic awakening of all the scenes or images that populate one's memory, particularly in case of accident.

We should recall, in this regard, the case of Admiral Beaufort, taken from *The Philosophy of Mysticism*.[135] He had fallen overboard and lost for two minutes the feeling of his physical consciousness. This time was sufficient for his transcendental consciousness to sum up all his earthly life in shortened pictures of prodigious clarity. All his acts, including their causes, their contingent circumstances, and their effects, passed through his thoughts. Here is a similar case reported by Mr. Cottin, aeronaut:[136]

"[In its last ascent, the] balloon Montgolfier took Mr. Perron, president of the Académie d'Aérostation, as captain, and F. Cottin, administrative agent of the French Scientific Association."

"Starting from a leap, the balloon was at 700 meters at 4:24; it was then that it broke down and began to descend more quickly than it had climbed; and it rushed at 4:27 a.m. into house No. 20 of the Chevalier alley at Saint-Ouen. After having thrown away all that could worsen

---

[135] See ch. XI above, Carl DU PREL, footnote 123.

[136] See J. Bouvéry, *Le Spiritisme et l'Anarchie* (Paris: Chamuel, 1807), pp. 405–406.

the accident, Mr. Cottin tells us, 'a kind of quietude, of inertia perhaps, seized me; a thousand distant memories hurried, collided before my imagination; then things were highlighted and the panorama of my life unfolded before my attentive spirit.'"

"'Everything was precise: the castles in Spain, the disappointments, the struggle for existence, and all this in the inexorable framework imposed by destiny ... Who would believe, for example, that I saw myself, at twenty, sergeant of the 22nd line regiment, backpack on my shoulders, singing on the road. In less than three minutes, I saw all my life parading in front of my memory.'"

These phenomena can be explained as a beginning of exteriorization. In this state, as in life on the spiritual plane, the subconscious unites with one's normal consciousness and reconstitutes total consciousness, the fullness of the self. For a moment, the association of ideas and facts is retrieved, the chain of memories is resurrected. The same result can be obtained through experimentation; but then the subject, in his or her search, must be helped by a will superior to their own, which associates with them and stimulates their efforts. In the phenomena of trance, this role is fulfilled either by the subject's Spirit Guide or by a magnetizer, whose thought acts upon the subject like a lever.

Then, the two wills, combined, superimposed, acquire an intensity of vibrations which sets in motion the deepest and most veiled layers of the subject's subconscious.

Another essential point should be borne in mind: it is the fact, established by all physiological science, that there is a close link between the physical and the mental in humans. Each physical action corresponds to a psychical act, and vice versa. Both are registered at the same time in the subconscious memory; so that one cannot be evoked without the other immediately appearing. This concordance applies to the tiniest facts of our integral existence, whether for the present or for episodes of our remote past.

The understanding of this phenomenon, not very intelligible for materialists, is facilitated by the knowledge of the perispirit, the fluidic envelope of the soul. It is in it – and not in our physical organism – composed of fluidic matter, incessantly variable in its constituent cells, that all our impressions are engraved.

The perispirit is the precision instrument which records with absolute fidelity the slightest variations in our personality. All the volitions of thought, all the actions of intelligence reverberate in it. Their movements, their distinct vibrational states leave successive and superimposed traces in it. Some experimenters have compared this mode of recording to a living cinematograph, on which our achievements and our memories are fixed successively. It can be activated by a sort of trigger or jolt, caused either by the action of extraneous suggestion, or by self-suggestion, or by an accident, as we have seen above.

The influence of thought upon the body is already revealed by phenomena observable at every moment inside ourselves and around us. Fear paralyzes our movements; astonishment, shame, fear provoke pallor or redness; anguish constricts our hearts; deep sorrow causes our tears to flow, and can eventually lead to morbid depression. These are all clear proofs of the powerful action exerted by the mind over its material envelope.

Hypnotism, by developing the sensibility of humans, shows us even more clearly this reflex action of thought. As we have seen, the suggestion of a burn can produce as much turmoil in a subject as a burn itself. It provokes at will the appearance of wounds, stigmata, etc.[137]

If thought and will can exert such an action upon physical matter, it is clear why this action increases and produces even more intense effects when it applies to fluidic, imponderable matter, of which the perispirit is formed. Less dense, less compact than physical matter, it will obey with much more flexibility the slightest volition of thought. It is by virtue of this law that spirits may take the appearance of one of the forms they had in the past, with all the attributes of their vanished personality. It is enough for them to focus strongly on any phase of their existence, to show themselves to witnesses exactly as they were at the time mentioned in their memory. And if the necessary psychical force is provided by one or more mediums, materializations become possible.

Colonel Rochas d'Aiglun, in his experiments, while succeeding in isolating the fluidic body, has shown that it was the seat of our sensibility and memories.[138] Hypnotism and physiology have been combined to allow us the study of the action of the soul when released from its coarse envelope and united with its subtle body. Soon, they will provide us with the means to elucidate the most delicate problems of the self. Psychical experimentation contains the key to all the phenomena of life; it is called upon to thoroughly renew modern science, shedding a bright light on a great number of questions which had hitherto remained obscure.

We shall now see, in hypnotic phenomena, and particularly during trance, that impressions, recorded by the fluidic body in an indelible manner, form close

---

[137] See Léon DENIS, *Into the Unseen* (Trans. H. M. Monteiro. New York: USSF, 2017), ch. XX.

[138] See ROCHAS D'AIGLUN, *L'Extériorisation de la Sensibilité* (6th ed., Paris: Charconac, 1909)

associations. Physical impressions are related to moral and intellectual impressions, so that one cannot address one without seeing the others also be retrieved. Their reappearance is always simultaneous.

This close correlation of the physical and the moral side, in their application to the memories engraved in us, has been demonstrated by numerous experiments. Mention should be made first of those positivist scientists who, despite their prejudices against any new theory, confirm it without being aware of it.

Positivist researcher Pierre Janet, professor of physiology at the Sorbonne, explains the following facts, while experimenting on his subject Rose during her sleep:[139]

"I suggest to Rose that we are no longer in 1888, but in 1886, in the month of April, simply to observe changes of sensibility that might occur. But, here a very strange accident took place. She moans, complains of being tired and unable to walk. 'Well, what seems to be the problem?' – 'Oh, nothing! ... in my condition!' 'What condition?' She replies with a gesture; her belly was suddenly swollen and tensed with a sudden attack of hysterical tympanites. I had, unwittingly, brought her back to a period in her life during which she was pregnant. More interesting studies were made through this means on Mary; I have been able, by successively reverting her to different periods of her existence, to record all the different states of sensibility through which she went, and the causes of all modifications. So, she is now completely blind of the left eye and pretends to be so since birth. If she is brought back to the age of seven, it is found that her left eye was still insensitive; but if it is suggested to her that she is only six years old, one realizes that she can see well with both eyes, and one can determine the

---

[139] P. JANET, *L'Automatisme Psychologique* (6th ed., Paris: F. Alcan, 1916), p. 160.

time and the very curious circumstances in which she lost sight of her left eye. The memory automatically regressed to a state of health of which the subject believed to have kept no reminiscence."

The possibility of awakening in the consciousness of a subject in a state of trance the forgotten memories of his or her childhood leads us logically to the retrieval of memories prior to birth. This order of events was reported for the first time at the Paris Spiritual Congress of the year 1900, by Spanish experimenters. Here is an excerpt from that report, read during a seance on September 25:[140]

"The medium being deeply asleep by means of magnetic passes, Fernandez Colavida, president of the Psychical Studies Group of Barcelona (Spain)] ordered him to say what he had done the day before, then the day before that, a week, a month, a year before, and so on, until he made the subject go back to his childhood, which he made him explain in full detail."

"Always driven by the same will, the medium told about his life on the spiritual plane, his death in his last incarnation and, continually stimulated to do so, he went back four incarnations, the oldest of which was a totally wild existence as a savage. At each existence, the facial features of the medium changed altogether."

"To bring him back to his normal, usual state, he was gradually brought back to his present existence, then awakened."

Some time later, quite unexpectedly, and for control (checking) reasons, the experimenter made the same

---

[140] See *Compte rendu du Congrès Spirite et Spiritualiste International*, 1900 (Paris: Librairie de Sciences Psychiques, 1902), pp. 349–350.

subject be magnetized by another person, suggesting that the medium's previous stories were imaginary. Despite this suggestion, the medium reproduced the same series of four existences, as he had done before. The awakening of memories, and their sequence, were identical to the results obtained in the first experiment.

In the same session of this Congress, Jacinto Esteva Marata, president of the Spiritist Union of Catalonia, declared that he had obtained analogous facts, by using the same methods while experimenting on his own wife, in a state of magnetic sleep. Following a message given by a spirit relating to one of the past lives of the subject, he was able to awaken in the obscure consciousness of the subject traces of her previous lives.

Since then, these experiments have been attempted in many research centers. Several indications have been obtained about the successive lives of the soul. These experiments will probably multiply from day to day. Note however that they require great caution. Errors and frauds are easy; and there are dangers to be feared. The experimenter must choose very sensitive and well developed subjects. They must be assisted by a spirit powerful enough to ward off any extraneous influences, all causes of trouble, and preserve the medium from possible accidents, the most serious of which would be a complete, irremediable out-of-body state, the impossibility of compelling the spirit to reintegrate its physical body, which would cause a definitive separation, physical death.

Above all, one must warn against the excesses of self-suggestion and be careful to accept only the stories of the subjects that they can be verified and checked; requesting from them names, dates, landmarks, in a word, a collection of evidence of a truly positive and scientific character. In this respect, it would be good to emulate the example given by the Society for Psychical Research of London, by adopting precise and rigorous methods; for example, those which gave great authority to their works on telepathy.

The lack of precaution, the nonobservance of the most elementary rules of experimentation have made Helene Smith's incorporations an obscure and difficult case. However, in the midst of the confusion of facts reported by T. Flournoy, professor at the University of Geneva, I believe the phenomenon of the Hindu princess Simandini deserves attention.

The medium in trance reproduces the scenes of one of her existences, lived in India, in the 12th century. In this state, she frequently uses Sanskrit words, a language she completely ignores in her normal state. It gives about Hindu historical figures indications that are not found in any of the usual history books, and of which Flournoy, after much research, discovered confirmation in a book by Marlès, a little known historian, quite beyond the scope of the subject. Hélène Smith, in somnambulistic sleep, takes on an impressive attitude. In his book, which had a great impact at the time, this is what Mr. Flournoy wrote:[141]

"The religious and solemn gravity of her prostrations ... ; the melancholy sweetness of her chants in a minor key, wailing and plaintive melodies, which unfold themselves in certain flute-like notes ... ; the agile suppleness of her swaying and serpentine movements, ... – all this so varied mimicry and Oriental speech have such a stamp of originality, of ease, of naturalness, that one asks in amazement whence it comes to this little daughter of Lake Leman, without artistic education or special knowledge of the Orient – a perfection of play to which the best actress, without doubt, could only attain at the price of prolonged studies or a sojourn on the banks of the Ganges."

---

[141] T. FLOURNOY, *From India to the Planet Mars* (London, etc: Harper & Bros., 1900), pp. 294–295.

As for the Hindu language and writing employed by Hélène, Flournoy admitted that, in his researches to explain her knowledge of it, "All the trails which I have thought I have discovered ... have proved false."

I myself have observed for many years cases similar to that of Hélène Smith. One of the mediums of the group directed by me reproduced during trance, under the influence of a Spirit Guide, scenes of her different lives. First, there were those of the current life, during her childhood, with all characteristic expressions and youthful emotions. Then came episodes of remote lives, with changes in physiognomy, attitudes, movements, reminiscent of expressions of the Middle Ages, a whole set of psychological and automatic details quite different from the current habits of said lady, who is very honorable and incapable of any simulation, through whom we obtained those strange phenomena.

A researcher of genius, Colonel Rochas d'Aiglun, former administrator of the French Polytechnic School, devoted a lot of his time to this kind of experiments. In spite of any objections they may raise, I believe some of his experiments should be cited, as shown below.

First, in all phenomena of the same order induced by Rochas d'Aiglun, there is this correlation between the physical and the mental, as mentioned above, which seems to be the expression of a law. Pre-birth reminiscences produce tangible effects on the body of the sleeping subjects, noted by all those present, many of whom were medical doctors. However, while taking into account the role that the subjects' imagination may play in these experiments, and even sharing the arabesques that are embroidered around the main phenomena, it is all the more difficult to attribute such effects to some fancy of the subjects concerned, of whom, according to the colonel's own words, "One is perfectly sure of their good faith and that their revelations are accompanied by somatic traces which seem to prove their reality beyond any reasonable doubt."[142]

At this point, let Rochas d'Aiglun speak for himself:

"It has been known for a long time that, under certain circumstances, especially when one is near death, long-forgotten memories follow one another, with extreme speed, in the spirits of certain people, as if the scenes of one's whole life flashed before their eyes."

"I experimentally determined an analogous phenomenon in magnetized subjects; with the difference that, instead of recalling mere memories, I have these subjects take the states of mind corresponding to the ages to which I bring them back, with forgetfulness of all that came after that age. These transformations are carried out by means of longitudinal passes, which usually have the effect of deepening magnetic sleep. Changes of personality, if we are able to invoke the various stages of the same individual, invariably follow one another in the order of time, going back to the past when using longitudinal passes, to return in the same order to the present when using transverse or awakening passes. As long as the subject has not returned to his or her normal state, they have dermal insensibility. Transformations can be precipitated by means of hypnotic suggestion, but we must always go through the same phases and not proceed too fast, otherwise we may cause complaints from the subject, who says that he or she is being tortured and cannot follow you."

---

[142] See *Revue Spirite*, p. 41, Paris, January 1907. See also ROCHAS D'AIGLUN, *Les Vies Successives* (Paris: Charconac Frères, 1911).

"During my first attempts, I stopped at the moment when the subject, brought back to his or her infancy, could no longer answer me; I thought we could not go beyond that. One day, however, I tried to deepen the sleep by continuing with the passes, and I was astonished when, questioning the sleeper, I found myself in the presence of another personality, claiming to be the soul of a dead person, having borne such and such name, and who had lived in such and such country. From then on, a new way seemed to delineate itself: continuing the passes in the same direction, I could revive the dead and go through this resurrection all through the latter's previous life going down the course of time. Here again it was not mere memories that I woke up, but successive moods that I made reappear."

"As my experiences were repeated, this journey into the past was carried out more and more quickly, while passing exactly through the same phases, so that I could thus go back to several previous existences without too much fatigue for the patient or for myself. All subjects, regardless of their opinions when in the waking state, gave the spectacle of a series of individualities, less and less advanced morally as the course of the ages went back; in each existence, with the faults of the previous existence expiated by a sort of pain of retaliation; and the time which separated two incarnations passed in a more or less luminous environment, according to the state of advancement of each individual."

"Waking passes gradually returned the subject to his or her normal state, going through the same steps in exactly the opposite order. When I found out from myself and other experimenters operating in other cities, with other subjects, that there were no simple dreams that could come from chance causes, but a series of phenomena appearing in a regular way with all the visible characters of a vision in the past or in the future, I focused all my efforts in finding out whether this vision corresponded to reality."

The result of the inquiries pursued by Colonel Rochas led him to conclude in these terms:[143]

"It is certain that by means of magnetic operations, one can gradually bring most of the sensitives back to earlier periods of their current life, with the intellectual and physiological peculiarities characteristic of these epochs, and that until the moment of their birth. These are not memories that are awakened; it is the successive states of personality that are evoked; these evocations always occur in the same order and through a succession of lethargy and somnambulistic states...."

"It is certain that by continuing these magnetic operations beyond reaching birth, and without having to resort to any suggestions, the subject is passed through analogous states corresponding to previous incarnations and the intervals which separate said incarnations. The process is the same through successions of lethargy and somnambulistic states."

Let it be said again, the affinities and concordances between facts established by materialistic scholars, hostile to the principle of successive lives – such as Pierre Janet, Dr. Pitre, Dr. Burot, among others – and those reported by Colonel Rochas d'Aiglun, all demonstrate that there is something else besides dreams or subliminal fantasies in these phenomena, but rather a law of correlation which deserves careful and sustained study. This is why I thought it necessary to highlight these facts.

Firstly, it is worth mentioning a series of experiments carried out in Paris with Laurent V—, a twenty-year-old young man, residing at the French École Polytechnique, where he was preparing to graduate in philosophy. The

---

[143] ROCHAS D'AIGLUN, *op. cit.*, "Conclusions," p. 497.

results were published in 1895 in the *Annales des Sciences Psychiques* (pp. 137 *et seq.*) by Rochas d'Aiglun, who summarized them as follows:[144]

"Having found out that he was a sensitive, he had wanted to realize for himself the physiological and psychological effects that could be obtained by means of magnetism. I discovered by chance that by making him sleep by means of longitudinal passes, I could send him back to states of consciousness and intellectual development corresponding to less and less advanced ages; thus, he became successively a student of rhetoric, of secondary, elementary school, etc., knowing nothing of what was taught in higher school. I ended up bringing him back to when he was still learning to read, and he gave details about his schoolteacher and his little classmates which he had completely forgotten during the waking state, but which his mother confirmed to be accurate. By alternating sleeping passes and awakening passes, I made him come back or go down at will through the duration of his current life."

With the following facts, the circle of phenomena will be widened. Rochas d'Aiglun adds:

"More recently, I found in Grenoble and Voiron (France) three subjects with similar faculties, whose veracity I was also able to verify. Having had the idea of continuing the sleeping passes, after having brought them to their childhood, and the awakening passes after having brought them back to their current age, I was very surprised to hear them describe successively the principal events of their past lives, and their state between two lives. The indications, which never varied, were so specific that I could do some research about them. I was thus able to check that the names of places and the surnames which

---

[144] Excerpted from an address given by ROCHAS D'AIGLUN to the Académie Delphinale of France, on November 19, 1904.

entered into their stories actually existed, although they had no memory of them in the waking state. But I have not been able to locate in the civil registers any trace of the more obscure characters they claimed to have been."

I borrowed other complementary details from a study by Rochas d'Aiglun, which is more extensive than the previous one:[145]

"These subjects did not know each other. One, named Josephine, is 18 and lives in Voiron (France); she is not married. The other, Eugénie, is 35 years old and lives in Grenoble (France); she is a widow, has two children and is of an apathetic nature, quite straightforward and not given to curiosity. Both have good health and normal behavior. Knowing their families, *I was able to verify the accuracy of their retrospective revelations* in a host of details that would be of no interest to the reader. I will mention only a few relating to Eugénie, in order to give an idea of it; they are excerpted from the minutes of our sittings with Dr. Bordier, director of the Grenoble School of Medicine."

"Asleep, I take her a few years back. I see a tear bead in her eyes. She tells me that she is twenty years old and that she has just lost a child.

... "Continuation of passes. Sudden cries of horror burst from her; she saw at her beside the ghosts of her grandmother and one of her aunts, who had recently died. (This apparition, which occurred at the age when I brought her back, made a very deep impression on her.)"

... "Now she is 11 years old. She is about to make her First Communion (Catholic Church); her biggest sins are to have sometimes disobeyed her grandmother and especially to have taken a penny out of the pocket of her dad; she was ashamed and asked for forgiveness."

---

[145] ROCHAS D'AIGLUN, *Les Vies Successives* (Paris: Chacornac Frères, 1911), pp. 68–75.

... "At 9 years old. – Her mother has been dead for eight days; she's experiencing much grief. Her father has just made her leave Vinay, where he is a dyer, to send her to Grenoble, to her grandfather's, in order to learn sewing."

... "At 6 years old. – She is attending school in Vinay, and can already write well."

... "At 4 years old. – She looks after her little sister when she is not at school. She starts tracing lines and writing a few letters.

"Transverse passes for awakening her, make her go through exactly the same phases and the same soul states back to the present."

Rochas d'Aiglun tests what he calls "the instinct of modesty" at different stages of sleep; he slightly raises Eugénie's dress, who smacks him vigorously each time, or gives slaps. "As a child, she no longer reacts against this touch; her sense of modesty has not yet developed."

"Joséphine, in Voiron, presented the same phenomena relative to writing at different ages. [There follow five specimens showing the progress of her education from 4 to 18 years old.]"

"So far I have walked on firm ground; I have observed a physiological phenomenon which is difficult to explain, but which many experiments and verifications make it possible to consider as certain. Now I will explore new horizons."

"We left Eugenie as a small child still suckled by her mother. Deepening the magnetic sleep further, I detected a change in personality. She was no longer alive; she floated in a semi-darkness, having neither thought, nor need, nor communication with anybody. Then came even more distant memories."

"In a previous life, she had been a little girl, dead at a very young age, from a fever caused by the dentition;

she can see her parents in tears around her body, from which she was released very quickly."

"Then I woke her up by means of transverse passes, and as she wakes up, she goes in the opposite direction through all the phases I mentioned earlier, and gives me new details that are prompted by my requests. – Some time before her last incarnation, she *felt* that she was to live again in a certain family, she came closer to the person who was to be her mother and who had just conceived ... She came, little by little, 'puff-by-puff,' into the little body. She lived, in part outside the carnal body she saw, in the first months of her life, as if she were standing outside it, and she did not clearly distinguish the material objects that surrounded her, but, on the other hand, she had the perception of spirits floating around her, some of them very bright, protecting her against others, dark and evil. When these latter came, they sought to influence her physical body and provoked fits of rage that moms usually call *whims*."

There follow long, indeed very interesting, details about other existences of the personality who was ultimately Joséphine; and Rochas d'Aiglun concludes as follows:

"*Moreover, it is very difficult to conceive how mechanical actions, such as those of magnetic passes, can induce the phenomenon of memory regression in such an absolutely certain manner, back to a specific moment in the past; and then, these very same actions, continued exactly in the same way, would supposedly incur a sudden change in their effect, so as to produce only hallucinations.*"

I will refrain from adding anything to his comments, for fear of weakening them. I would rather pass without transition to another series of experiments of Mr. Rochas d'Aiglun, made in Aix-en-Provence (France), which were recounted, seance by seance, in the *Annales des Sciences Psychiques* of July 1905.[146]

The subject is an 18-year-old girl, enjoying perfect health and having never heard of magnetism or Spiritism. Miss Marie Mayo is the daughter of a French engineer, who died in the East. She was raised in Beirut (Lebanon), where she was entrusted to the care of local servants; she was learning to read and write in Arabic. Then she was brought back to France and now lives in Aix with an aunt.

The sittings were witnessed by Dr. Bertrand, former mayor of Aix, a family physician, and Mr. Lacoste, an engineer who was in charge of writing most of the minutes. These sittings were very numerous, the listing of facts fills 50 pages of the *Annales*. The first experiments, undertaken in December 1904, concern the retrieval of memories concerning her current life. The subject, immersed in hypnosis by Rochas d'Aiglun, gradually recedes into the past and relives the scenes of her childhood. She gives, at her different ages, specimens of her writing, which could be verified. At age 8, she writes in Arabic and traces characters that she has since forgotten.

Then a retrieval of past lives was obtained. Alternatively, going down the chain of her existences, or up to return to the current one, under the influence of magnetic processes that have already been described above, the subject goes through and repeats the same steps, in the same order, whether directly or retroactively, with a slowness, said the colonel, "Which makes exploration difficult beyond a certain number of lives and personalities."

There was no possibility of faking or simulating. Miss Mayo goes through different hypnotic states and, at each of them, she manifests the symptoms that characterize

---

[146] See also ROCHAS D'AIGLUN, *Les Vies Successives* (Paris: Chacornac Frères, 1911), pp. 123–162.

her. On several occasions, Dr. Bertrand notes catalepsy, contracture, complete insensibility. Miss Mayo passes her hand over a candle without feeling it. "She absolutely cannot feel the smell of ammonia. Her eyes do not react to bright light; the pupil is not impressed by a lamp or a candle advanced abruptly too close to her eye or removed rapidly."[147] On the other hand, sensibility at a distance is very accentuated, obviously demonstrating the phenomenon of exteriorization. Now, let me quote the minutes:

"I revert Mayo to years gone by; she goes to the time of her birth. Pushing her further, she remembers that she had already lived before; that her name then was Lina;[148] that, as Lina, she was drowned, and that, after that, she had risen in the air; that she saw luminous beings there, but that she had not been allowed to speak to them. Beyond Lina's life, she finds herself again in the erratic state,[149] but in a rather painful condition because, previously, she had not been 'not a good person.'"

"In that incarnation she was [a man] called Charles Mauville. She started in public life as an office worker in Paris. People were constantly fighting in the streets. Charles himself killed other people and took pleasure in it; he was mean. Heads were shopped off at the city squares at the time."

"Quitting the office at the age of 50, he was sick (Mayo coughs), and died soon after. He can follow his own burial and hear people say that he had often "painted the town red." He remained attached to his body for a while. He was suffering and unhappy. Finally, he was reborn as Lina in a new body."

---

[147] *Annales des Sciences Psychiques*, July 1905, p. 391.

[148] [Trans. note] Spelled *Line* in Léon DENIS's original.

[149] [Trans. note] *Erratic state* or *erraticity* is a Spiritist term referring to the period comprised between reincarnations of a spirit.

Other sittings retrieved the existence of Lina, the Breton woman: "I slowed down my passes when I reached the time of his death; her breathing then became intermittent, her body swings as if carried by the waves and the patient suffocates."

Sitting of December 29, 1904 – "Col. Rochas d'Aiglun then commands:"[150]

"'Become Lina once more ... at the moment when she is drowned.'"

"Instantly, M[ayo] makes an abrupt movement in her chair; she turns on her right side, her face in her hands, and remains thus for a few seconds. One would say it was the first phase of the act which is accomplished voluntarily, for Lina dies from drowning; but it is a voluntary drowning, a suicide, a fact which gives quite a particular aspect to the scene. It is quite different from an involuntary drowning."

"Then M. returns abruptly to her left side. The respiratory movements are precipitated and become difficult; the chest rises with effort and irregularly; the face expresses anxiety, anguish; the eyes are scared-looking, she makes veritable movements of deglutition[151] as though she were swallowing water in spite of herself: for we see that she resists. At this moment she utters a few inarticulate cries. She writhes rather than struggles, and her face expresses such real pain that M. de R[ochas] orders her to become a few hours older. Then he asks her:"

"Did you struggle a long time ?
A. Yes.
Q. Is it a bad death ?
A. Yes.
A few more transversal passes.

---

[150] [Trans. note] Extracts taken from the British *Annals of Psychical Science*, vol. II, pp. 24 *et seq.*, London, 1905.

[151] [Trans. note] Technical term for *swallowing*.

Q. Where are you ?
A. In the 'gray.' ..."

"*Twenty-third seance*, 30th December, 1904." – Existence of Charles Mauville.

"M[ayo] retraces for us one of the phases of the illness which carried him off. She seems to feel all the characteristics of chest disease: oppression, painful fits of coughing, etc."

"The Colonel [Rochas] causes her to stop at his interment.

"Q. There were many people following the coffin ?
A. No.
Q. What did they say about you? Nothing good, did they? They remembered that you bad been a bad man ?
A. (After hesitation, and in quite a low tone) – Yes."

"She is next in the 'dark'; the Colonel makes her pass through it rapidly, and she reincarnates in Brittany. She sees herself as a child, then as a young girl ; she is 16 years of age, and does not yet know her future husband. At 18 years of age she meets him ; shortly afterwards she marries him and becomes a mother. Here we witness an accouchement[152] scene of striking reality. The subject turns round upon her chair, her limbs become stiff, her face contracts, and her sufferings appear so intense that the Colonel orders her to pass on rapidly."

"(*Note*: Of course this incident was not revealed to her on waking.)"

"She is 22 years of age; she has lost her husband in a shipwreck, and her little child is dead. In despair she drowns herself. This episode, which she has already reproduced at another seance, is so painful that the Colonel orders her to pass on, which she does, but not without suffering a violent shock. In the 'gray' which she next

---

[152] [Trans. note] *Accouchement*, the process of giving birth to a baby.

sees, she does not suffer, as we have said, whereas she suffered in the 'dark,' after the death of Charles Mauville. She reincarnates in her present family, and is brought back to her present age. She is awakened by means of transversal magnetic passes."

"Twenty-fourth seance, 31st December, 1904."

"In this seance I propose to try to obtain some details as to the personality of Charles Mauville, and to try to push Mayo back to a former life. I consequently deepen the sleep rapidly, by means of longitudinal passes, up to the childhood of Mauville."

"At the moment when I question him, be is 5 years old ; his father is foreman in a manufactory, his mother is clothed in black and wears a bonnet. I continue to deepen the sleep. Before his birth, he is in the 'dark,' and suffers; he is tormented by spirits whom he sees shining."

"Before this, she was a lady whose husband was a gentleman attached to the court; her name was Madeleine de Saint-Marc...."

"When I suppose that she has got back home, I make a little inquiry as to her life."

"She has known Mlle. de Lavallière, who was very much in sympathy with her; she hardly knows Madame de Montespan. Madame de Maintenon displeased her.

Q. It is said that the King has married her secretly?

A. Pooh! she is simply his mistress.

Q. And the King, how do you like him?

A. He is very proud.

Q. Do you know M. Scarron?

A. Lord! How plain he was!

Q. Have you seen M. de Molière act?

A. Yes, but I don't like him much.

Q. Do you know M. Corneille?

A. He is a savage.

Q. And M. Racine?

A. I know most about his works; I like them very much."

"I propose to her to make her grow older in order to see what will happen to her later on. She absolutely refuses. In vain do I command her with authority, and I only succeed in overcoming her resistance by means of energetic transversal passes which she tries to avoid by every possible means."

"When I stop, she is 40 years of age; she has left the court; she coughs, and feels ill in her chest. I make her speak of her character; she confesses that she is egotistical and jealous, especially of pretty women."

"Continuing the transversal passes, I bring her to 45 years; she dies of consumption; I witness a short death scene and she enters into the 'dark.'"

Let us pause for a moment to consider all these facts, to look for the guarantees of authenticity they present, and to draw lessons from them.

First of all, a striking detail comes to fore: at each retrieved lifetime, there is a constant repetition, throughout multiple seances, of the same events in the same order, either ascending or descending, in a spontaneous way, without any hesitation, errors or confusion.[153]

Then there is this unanimous observation of experimenters whether in Spain, Geneva, Grenoble, Aix, etc.; a statement that I myself have been able to make whenever I have observed phenomena of this kind: at each new existence which unfolds, there is a change in behavior, gestures, and language of the subject, whose features completely change expression, becoming harder as one moves backward in the order of time. We all have witnessed

---

[153] Another experimenter, M. A. BOUVIER, declared to the *Paix Universelle* of September 15, 1906, Lyon, France: "Whenever the subject goes back to the same lifetime, regardless of precautions taken to deceive or confuse him or her, they always remain the same individuality, with their personal character, even correcting the errors of those who question them, if necessary."

the exhumation of a set of values, prejudices, and beliefs related to the time and environment in which a certain existence took place. When the subject is a woman and passes through a male incarnation, her physiognomy is quite different; the voice is stronger, the tone is louder, its paces more abrupt. Differences are no less pronounced when one goes through a childhood period.

Physical and mental states are linked together, always closely connected, complementing one another, and remaining inseparable. Each memory evoked, each scene revived, mobilizes a whole procession of sensations and impressions, laughing or painful, comical or poignant, as the case may be, but perfectly adequate to each situation. The law of correlation found by Pierre Janet, T. Ribot, and others, is found and manifests itself here in all its rigor, and with a mechanical precision, with regard to the scenes of the present life as well as for those related to past lives. On its own, this constant correlation would suffice to assure that these two orders of memory have the same degree of probability. The memories of the present existence in its primary phases, erased from the subject's normal memory, once verified as accurate, which is a proof of their authenticity, strongly persuades one of the legitimacy of previous lives' memories.

On the other hand, the subjects have reproduced with absolute fidelity, and a vivacity of impressions and sensations not at all fictitious, scenes as moving as they are complex: asphyxia by immersion; agony caused by phthisis[154] at the highest degree; cases of pregnancy followed by childbirth with all the series of physical phenomena associated with it: suffocation, pain, etc.

However, these subjects, almost all young women aged between 16 to 18, are often very shy by nature and have

---

[154] [Trans. note] *Phthisis*, pulmonary tuberculosis or similar diseases.

little scientific knowledge. By acknowledgment of the experimenters themselves, one of whom was the family doctor of the Mayos, their inability to feign any such scenes is notorious. They possess no knowledge whatsoever of physiology or pathology, and have never witnessed in their current lifetime any incident likely to give them indications or lessons about facts of this nature.[155]

All these considerations lead us to dismiss any suspicions of fraud, deception, or the hypothesis of a mere play of the imagination.

What talent, what skill, what perfection of attitude, gesture and accent would not be required to sustain, during so many seances, the imagination and simulation of such realistic scenes – sometimes very dramatic ones – in presence of experimenters who were thoroughly skilled at unmasking imposture, as practitioners always on guard against error or deceit? Such a role cannot possibly be ascribed to young people who had no experience in life, having received only very limited or even elementary education.

Another thing: in the sequence of these stories, in the destiny of the beings in question, in the vicissitudes of their lives, we invariably find the confirmation of this high law of causality or consequence of one's actions, which governs the moral world. We cannot certainly see here a mere reflection of the subjects' opinions, who have no notion whatsoever of this matter, since, as attested unanimously by all observers, the environment where they lived and the education they received had not prepared them for any knowledge of successive lives.[156]

---

[155] This opinion was expressed in my presence, during my stay in Aix (France), by Mr. Lacoste and Dr. Bertrand.

[156] See on this subject, ROCHAS D'AIGLUN, *Les Vies Successives* (Paris: Charconac Frères, 1911), p. 501.

Obviously, many skeptics will think that these phenomena are still too few for one to be able to come up with a firm theory and definitive conclusions. For this, it may be said that it would be necessary to wait for a greater mass of evidence and testimonies. I myself may object to many suspicious-looking experiments in which anachronisms, contradictions and apocryphal facts abound. From these fanciful stories comes the strong impression that volunteer observers have been played, mystified. But in what way would serious experiments be thus diminished? The abuses, the errors that occur here and there, cannot reach the level of serious studies pursued with a precise method and a rigorous spirit of control, of verification.

All in all, I believe that the above-mentioned facts, together with many others of the same nature (that it would be superfluous to enumerate here), are sufficient to establish the existence at the base of the edifice of the self a sort of crypt where a huge cache of knowledge and memories is stored. Therein the long past of one's being has left indelible traces, which alone can tell us the secret of origins and evolution, the deep mystery of human nature.

Herbert Spencer once stated that there are two processes in the construction of consciousness: assimilation and memory. But it must be admitted, that the normal consciousness to which he refers is only a precarious and restricted consciousness. It wavers on the edges of the abyss of the soul like an intermittent flame, illuminating a hidden world where forces and images accumulate impressions collected from the initial point of the self.

And all this, lying hidden during one's life under the veils of the flesh, reveals itself in the trance, coming out of the shadows with all the more clarity as the soul is freer from matter, and more evolved.

As for the reservations made by Col. Rochas d'Aiglun about certain inaccuracies he noticed in the stories told by the hypnotized in the course of his investigations, I must add one observation: it is not surprising that mistakes could have been made, given the mental state of the subjects and the quantity of known and unknown elements – at present – which come into play in these phenomena, all of them so new to science. These could be attributed to three different causes; either to direct reminiscences of the subjects, or to visions, or even to suggestions of some external origin. In the first case, it should be noted, that, in all the experiments aiming to make animic forces vibrate, the subject's self resembles a focus that lights up and expands, and then, in its activity, projects vapors and fumes that from time to time may cloud the inner flame. Sometimes, in the case of poorly evolved subjects with little practice, normal memories and recent impressions may be mingled with more distant reminiscences. It is up to the experimenters' skill to discard such disturbing elements, dispelling these mists and shadows while restoring to the central phenomenon its importance and brilliance.

One might still see in it the results of suggestions exerted by the magnetizers or by extraneous personalities. This is what Col. Rochas d'Aiglun says about this point:[157]

"We are justified, from what we know, in considering them provisionally as suggestions; but what is the origin of these suggestions? They certainly do not come from me, for I have not only avoided everything that could lead the subject into any determined path, but I have often tried in vain to lead her astray by different suggestions; and the same has been the case with the experimenters who have devoted themselves to this study."

---

[157] *Annals of Psychical Science*, vol. III, pp. 25, London, 1906.

"Are they the effects of ideas which, according to the popular expression, 'are in the air,' and which act more forcibly on the mind of the subject when released from the bonds of the body? This might well be the case in a certain measure, for it has been noticed that all the revelations of persons in ecstasy take on more or less the character of the surroundings in which they have lived."

"Are they due to invisible entities who, wishing to spread among men the belief in successive incarnations, proceed like *La Morale en Actions*[158] by the help of little stories under fictitious names in order to avoid complications between living persons? This appears to me very improbable."

The Unseen (i.e., the spirits), when mediumistically consulted about the same subject, replied as follows:[159]

"When a subject is not sufficiently disengaged and unobstructed to read in himself or herself the history of his or her own past, we proceed by showing them successive scenes reproducing before their eyes their previous lifetimes. In this case, these are visions, and that is why they cannot always be accurate."

"We can introduce you to your past, without specifying the dates and places. Do not forget that, once freed from earthly conventions, there is no more time or space for us. Living outside such limits, we may easily make mistakes regarding everything related to it. We consider all these as very small things and would rather talk about your good or bad actions and their consequences. If some dates or certain names are not found in your records, you conclude that everything is wrong – which is a profound error of judgment, since difficulties are great when trying

---

[158] [Trans. note] Laurent-Pierre BÉRENGER, *La Morale en Actions* [*Moral in Action*] (Lyon and Paris: Leroy and Nyon, 1804).

[159] Message received by a mediumistic group of Le Havre (France) in June 1907.

to give you data as precise as you require. But, believe us, do not tire yourself of researching. This is the noblest study of all. Do you not feel that spreading the light is something beautiful? However, alas, on your planet it will take much more time until the masses understand to which dawn they should go!"

It would be easy to add a large number of facts relating to the same type of research.

Prince Adam Wiszniewski, of 7 Débarcadère street, Paris, communicates the following narrative. He cites the witnesses themselves, some of whom still live and have agreed to be named only by initials:

"Prince Gallitzin, the Marquis de B—, and the Count of R—, were all together at the German spa of Bad Homburg during the summer of 1862."

"One evening, after a very late dinner, they were walking in the park of the Casino, when they noticed a poor woman lying on a bench. Having approached and questioned her, they invited her to come and dine at the hotel. After she had supped with great appetite, prince Gallitzin, who was a magnetizer, had the idea of lulling her to sleep. After performing many passes, he succeeded. To the utter astonishment of the people present, the woman who, in the night before, spoke only a bad German dialect, once asleep began to speak very correctly in French, saying that she had reincarnated in poverty as a punishment for committing a crime in her previous life, in the 18th century. She was then living in a castle by the sea in Brittany. Having taken a lover, she wanted to get rid of her husband and hurled him to the sea from the top of a rock. She described the crime scene with great precision."

"Thanks to her indications, prince Gallitzin and the marquis de B— were able, later on, to go separately to Brittany, in the Côtes-du-Nord, and make two inquiries, the results of which were identical. Having questioned many people, at first they could not gather any information. Finally they found old peasants who remembered hearing their parents tell the story of a young and beautiful chatelaine[160] who had killed her husband by throwing him into the sea. Thus all that the poor woman of Homburg had said in a somnambulistic state proved to be exact."

"On his return from France, prince Gallitzin went back to Homburg, where he asked the chief of police about this woman. This officer told him that she had no education, spoke only a vulgar German dialect, and lived on very meager means as a prostitute."

As we can see, the doctrine of successive lives, taught by the great philosophical schools of the past, and nowadays by Kardecian spiritualism (i.e., Spiritism), has received, sometimes directly, sometimes indirectly, many new contributions through the works of scholars and researchers. Through experimentation, the most hidden depths of the human soul are opening up, and our own history seems to be retrieved and reconstituted in the same fashion that geology has been able to reconstruct the history of the globe, by searching through its mighty foundations.

True, there remains the question as to whether these findings are absolutely reliable. We must proceed with extreme caution in drawing conclusions. However, in spite of some obscurities that may still persist, I have considered it a duty to publish these facts and experiences in order to draw the attention of thinkers, and provoke new investigations. As already shed upon so many other issues, it is at this cost that, gradually, light will be completely thrown on this matter.

---

160 [Trans. note] *Chatelaine*, an aristocratic female castellan.

In principle, as mentioned before, forgetting past existences is one of the consequences of reincarnation. However, this forgetfulness is not absolute. For many people, the past is in form of impressions, if not precise memories. These impressions sometimes influence our actions; they are those which come neither from education, nor from the environment, nor from heredity. Among them, we can include sudden sympathies and antipathies, quick intuitions, innate ideas. It is enough to dive into ourselves, to study with close attention, to find in our tastes, our tendencies, in the features of our character, many vestiges of this past. Unfortunately, very few of us engage in analyzing these in a methodical and careful way.

Furthermore, in all periods of history there are a number of individuals who, thanks to the exceptional patterns of their psychical organism, have preserved memories of their past lives. To them, the plurality of existences is not a theory; it is a fact which can be directly observed.

These individuals' testimony is of considerable importance, in the sense that they occupied a high position in the society of their time; almost all of them possessing superior intellects and exerting great influence over their generation. The very rare faculty which they all enjoyed was, no doubt, the result of an immense evolution. When the value of a testimony is directly related to the intelligence and integrity of the witness, we cannot ignore the affirmations made by these individuals, some of whom bore the crown of genius.

It is a well-known fact that Pythagoras remembered at least three of his previous lives and the names he bore in each of them;[161] he claimed to have been Hermotimus, Euphorbus, and one of the Argonauts. Emperor Julian,

---

[161] HERODOTUS, *History* (New York: D. Appleton & Co., 1859), vol. II, ch. 123, p. 168.[Trans. note: See also K. S. GUTHRIE and D. R.

called the Apostate, so slandered by the Christians, but who was actually one of the great figures of Roman history, remembered having been Alexander of Macedonia. Empedocles claimed himself that "By now I have been born a boy and a girl."[162]

According to Johann Gottfried Herder (in his *On Metempsychosis*, 1782), we should add to these names those of the biblical Yarcha (or Jarha) and Apollonius of Tyana.

In the Middle Ages, we find this faculty in Jerome Cardan (or Girolamo Cardano) of Milan, Italy.

More recently, the French writer Lamartine declares, in volume one of his *Voyage en Orient*, to have had very clear reminiscences of a distant past. Here is his testimony:

"I had neither Bible nor travel guide in Judea to give me the names of the places and the ancient names of valleys and mountains. Yet I recognized at once the valley of Terebinth and the battlefield of Saul. When we were at the convent, the Fathers confirmed the accuracy of my guesses. My companions could not believe it. Likewise, at Zipporah, I had pointed out, and designated by name, a hill surmounted by a ruined castle, as the probable place of the birth of the Virgin. The next day, at the foot of an arid mountain, I recognized the tomb of the Maccabees, and I was right without knowing it. Except for the valleys of Lebanon, I have scarcely ever met in Judea a place or thing which was not like a déjà vu memory to me. Have we lived twice or a thousand times? Is our memory only a tarnished image that God's breath is reviving?"

In Lamartine, the concept of successive lives of one's being was so intense that he proposed to make it the

---

FIDELER, *The Pythagorean Sourcebook and Library* (Grand Rapids, MI: Phanes Press, 1987), p. 142.]

[162] Diogenes LAERTIUS, *Lives of the Eminent Philosophers* (Trans. P. Mensch. New York: Oxford University Press, 2018) section 77, p. 426.

master idea, the inspiration par excellence of his books. *La Chute d'un Ange* [*The Fall of an Angel*] was, in his thought, the first link, and *Jocelyn* the last of a series of works that were related to one another, tracing the story of two souls pursuing through times their painful evolution. The turmoil of Lamartine's political life did not leave him time to connect the scattered links of this chain of masterpieces.[163]

French writer Joseph Méry cultivated the same ideas. *Le Journal Littéraire* of November 25, 1864, published the following about him, while he was still alive:

"He has some singular theories, which for him are convictions. He firmly believes that he has lived many times, and remembers the slightest circumstances of his previous existences, which he details with a verve of certitude which imposes itself as being authoritative. Thus, he was one of the friends of Virgil and Horace; he knew Augustus and Germanicus; he fought in Gaul and Germany. He was a general and he commanded the Roman troops when they crossed the Rhine. He recognizes the mountain sites where he encamped; the valleys and battlefields where he once fought. His name then was Minius. Here is an episode that seems to establish that these memories are not just figments of his imagination."

"One day, in his current life, he was in Rome, visiting the Vatican Library. He was received by young men, novices in long brown robes, who began to speak to him the purest Latin. Méry was a good Latinist in all that was related to theory and written texts, but he had not yet tried to talk colloquially in the language of Juvenal. Hearing these Romans today, admiring this magnificent idiom [Latin], so well harmonized with the customs and monuments of the period in which it was in use, it seemed

---

[163] See Louis Petit de JULLEVILLE, *Histoire de la Littérature Française* (Paris: Masson, 1896), vol. VII.

to him that a veil fell from his eyes, and that he himself had conversed at other times with friends who used this divine language. Complete and irreproachable phrases fell from his lips; he immediately found elegance and correction; finally, he was able to speak Latin as fluently he speaks [his native] French. All this could not possibly be achieved without some previous learning – and had he not been a subject of Emperor Augustus, and not traversed that century with all its splendors, he would not have been able to exhibit a proficiency impossible to be acquired in a mere few hours."

Le *Journal Littéraire* goes on to say about Méry:

"His other passage on Earth had been in India: that is why, when he published *La Guerre du Nizan* [*The Nizan War*], not a single of his readers doubted that he had long lived in Asia. His descriptions are so vivid, his scenes are so original, that he encompasses every detail. It is impossible that he did not see what he was describing; the seal of truth is everywhere."

"He claims to have entered that country with the Muslim expedition in the year 1035. He lived there for fifty years; he spent a good few days there, and permanently settled there. He was still a poet, but less literate than in Rome and Paris. A warrior first, then a dreamer, he kept in his soul the striking images of the banks of the sacred Hindu sites and river. He had several houses in the city and in the country and prayed in the Temple of Elephants. He knew the advanced civilization of Java, he saw its splendid ruins that he described, and about which we still know so little."

"One must hear him read his poems, because these are true poems as legitimate as any Swedenborg's memories. He is, no doubt, very serious about them. This is not a mystification arranged at the expense of his listeners. It is rather a reality of which he can totally convince you."

In his book entitled *Victor Hugo à Guernesey* (Paris, 1905), Paul Stapfer, recounts his talks with the great poet. He told him about his belief in successive lives. He thought Hugo had been Aeschylus, Juvenal, etc., but it must be admitted that such remarks do not show an excess of modesty and actually lack demonstrative proof.

Elsewhere, the subtle and profound Swiss philosopher Henri-Frédéric Amiel wrote: "When I think of the intuitions of all kinds that I have had since my adolescence, it seems to me that I have lived many dozens, almost hundreds of lives. Every individuality characterizes this world ideally in me, or rather momentarily forms myself in its image. That is how I was a mathematician, musician, monk, child, mother, etc. In these states of universal sympathy, I was even animal and plant."[164]

Théophile Gautier, Alexandre Dumas, Ponson du Terrail and many other modern writers shared these convictions. Gustave Flaubert, in his *Correspondance* (vol. II, p. 165), writes: "I am sure that under the Roman Empire I was the director of some troupe of traveling comedians ... and, while re-reading the comedies of Plautus, they come back to me like memories."

To these reminiscences of adult individuals, illustrious for the most part, one can add those of a large number of children.

In this case, these phenomena can be easily explained. From birth, the adaptation of the psychical senses to the physical organism takes place slowly and gradually. It

---

164 [Trans. note] H. F. Amiel and Marianne Maurer, *Henri-Frédéric Amiel: fragments choisis et précédés d'un avant-propos* (Lausanne and Geneva: Payot, n.d.), p. 41, "8 mars, 1868."

is complete only towards the age of seven; later still for some individuals.

During that period, the spirit of a child, floating around its physical envelope, still lives to a certain degree the life of the spirit plane. The child enjoys perceptions and visions that sometimes impress the physical brain with fleeting gleams. Thus we have been able to gather from certain juvenile mouths allusions to past lives, descriptions of scenes and characters that have nothing to do with the current life of these young beings.

These visions, these reminiscences generally vanish towards adulthood, when a child's soul has come into full possession of his or her earthly organism. Then, it is in vain that one questions the individual about these fleeting memories. All transmission of perispiritual vibrations will then be ceased; deep consciousness becomes dumb.

So far these revelations have not been given the attention they deserve. The parents, made uneasy by manifestations considered as strange and abnormal, rather than provoking them, seek on the contrary, to prevent their repetition. Science loses useful indications. If the child, when trying to translate, in his or her painful and confused language, the fugitive vibrations of the psychical brain, was encouraged and questioned, instead of being rejected and ridiculed, we could obtain about the past some clarifications of interest, instead of losing them, as it happens in most cases.

In the East, where the doctrine of successive lives is spread everywhere, more importance is attached to such reminiscences. They are collected and verified to all possible extent and often acknowledged as being accurate. Here is some evidence among a thousand others:

A correspondence from Simla (East Indies) to the London *Daily Mail* reports that a young boy, born in the district, is considered the reincarnation of the late Mr.

Tucker, superintendent of the country, murdered in 1894 by a gang of 'dacoits.' The child remembers the slightest incidents of his previous life. He wanted to be taken to various places familiar to the late Mr. Tucker. At the place of the murder, he began to tremble and showed all signs of terror. The newspaper added that these phenomena are quite common in Burma, where reincarnated people who remember their past are called 'minza.'"[165]

French consul C. de Lagrange wrote from Vera Cruz (Mexico) to the *Revue Spirite*, on July 14, 1880:[166]

"Two years ago, in Vera Cruz, there was a seven-year-old who possessed the faculty of healing mediumship. Several people were healed, either by the apposition of his little hands, or with the aid of vegetable remedies which he prescribed and which he claimed to know. When asked where he had learned these things, he replied that when he was a grown-up he had been a doctor. Thus this child has the memory of an earlier existence."

"He spoke with difficulty. His name was Jules Alphonse, born in Vera Cruz. This surprising faculty developed in him at the age of four. Many people, incredulous at first, have been struck and are now convinced. When he is alone with his parents, he often tells them: 'Dad, you must not expect that I will stay with you for a long time; I am only here for a few years, since I must go back there.' And if one asks him: 'But where do you want to go?' he replies 'Far from here, to a place better than here.'"

"This child is very sober and grand in all his actions, also insightful and very obedient." – Soon after that time the boy passed away.

The *Banner of Light*, of Boston, October 15, 1892, published the following statement by the Honorable Isaac G. Forster, also included by the *Globe Democrat*,

---
[165] *Daily Mail*, Tuesday, July 7, 1903, p. 5.
[166] *Revue Spirite*, year 1880, p. 361.

of St. Louis, in its issue of September 20, 1892, and the *Brooklyn Eagle* and the *Milwaukee Sentinel*, of September 25, 1892:

"Mr. Foster says that he buried a daughter in Effingham County, Ill., twelve years ago. She was 'just budding into womanhood,' and so must have been fourteen or fifteen years old. A year after the girl's death he moved to Dakota, where, two years later, a second daughter was born. She was christened Nellie, but when she was old enough to talk she said that her name was not Nellie, but was Maria, the name of the girl who had died. Not long ago Mr. Foster went to his old home in Illinois and took Nellie with him. She had never been in the place before, but she is said to have recognized the dwelling in which her sister had lived, and to have called by name many of her sister's old acquaintances as soon as she saw them. She asked to go to the schoolhouse which her sister used to attend, and when she entered the school-room she went to the desk which her sister had occupied and said: 'This is mine.'"

The *Journal des Débats* of April 11, 1912, in its scientific supplement signed by Henri de Varigny, cites a similar case borrowed from the work of Mr. Fielding Hall, who had engaged in an extensive research on this subject:

"About half a century ago, two children, a boy and a girl, were born on the same day, in the same village, in Burma. Later, they were married, and after forming a family and leading virtuous lives, they died the same day."

"Then came troubled times, and two youngsters of both sexes had to flee the village where the first episode had taken place. They went on to settle elsewhere, and had two twin children who, instead of calling each other by their proper names, gave each other the names of that virtuous couple that were now deceased."

"The parents were utterly surprised, but soon understood. For them, the virtuous couple had reincarnated in their children. Proof was required. They were taken to the village where they the virtuous couple were born. They recognized everything: roads, houses, people, even the clothes worn by the couple, which had been kept for some unexplained reason. One of the twins remembered borrowing two rupees from a certain person. She was still alive and confirmed the fact."

"Mr. Fielding Hall, who saw the twin children when they were six years old, found one to have a more feminine look; this one would house the soul of the deceased woman. Before reincarnation, they say, they lived some time without a body, in the branches of trees. But these distant memories became less and less clear and faded away little by little."

This perception of past lives is also exceptionally found in some adults.

Dr. Gaston Durville, in the Psychic Magazine of January–April 1914, reports a remarkable case of regression of memory in the waking state. Mrs. Laure Raynaud, known in Paris for her cures by means of magnetism, had for a long time asserted that she remembered another life spent in a place described by her, and that she said she would see again some day. She claimed to have lived in clearly defined conditions (gender, social rank, nationality, etc.) and to have disincarnated a number of years before due to some illness. Precise testimonies were collected on this subject.

Mrs. Raynaud, who had gone to Italy in March 1913, recognized the country where she had lived. She traveled around Genoa and found her home exactly as she had described it. "Thanks to the assistance of Mr. Calaure, a scholarly psychologist from Genoa, we found," says the doctor, "in the registers of the parish of San Francesco d'Albaro, an register of death which was that of Mrs. Raynaud, No. 1. All the statements made by her several years ago, about her gender, social status, nationality, age and cause of death, etc. were thoroughly confirmed."

The testimonies from the invisible world are as abundant as they are varied. Not only many spirits claim in their messages that they have lived many times on Earth, but some of them even announce their reincarnation in advance. They designate their future gender and the time of their birth; they provide clues as to their physical appearance or their moral dispositions, which enable them to be recognized on their return to this world; they predict or state some peculiarities of their future existence, which have been able to be verified.

The periodical *Filosofia della Scienza*, of Palermo (Italy), in its issue of January 1911, published a story of the highest interest regarding a case of reincarnation, which I summarize below. It is the chief of the family to which the events happened, Dr. Carmelo Samona, of Palermo, who speaks:

"On March 15, 1910, we lost a little girl whom my wife and I adored; my companion's despair was so intense that I feared for a moment for her sanity. Three days after Alexandrina's death, my wife had a dream in which she thought she saw the child say to her: 'Mother, do not weep any more, I have not abandoned you; I did not get away from you: on the contrary, I will come back to you as a child.'"

"Three days later, there was a repetition of the same dream. The poor mother, whose pain could not be alleviated at all, and who at that time had no idea of the theories of modern Spiritualism, could only draw from these dreams a new reason for stirring up her grief. One morning, when she was mourning as usual, three peals were heard at the door of the room where we were. Believing that it was the arrival of my sister, my children, who were with us, went to open the door saying, 'Aunt Catherine, come in.' Everyone was greatly surprised when they noticed there was no one behind that door, nor in the room that preceded it. It was then that we resolved to begin typtology seances, in hopes that, by this means, we would perhaps have some clarification about the mysterious dreams and blows at the door that we worrying us so much. Moreover, we persisted with our experiments for three months with great regularity."

"Ever since our first seance, two entities appeared: one said to be my sister, the other, our deceased darling daughter. The latter confirmed, by raps on the table, her appearance in the two dreams that my wife had had and revealed that the knocks at the door were for her mother. Again she repeated to her mother: 'Do not be sorry for me, because I will be born again of you before Christmas.' The prediction was welcomed by us with all the more disbelief because an accident resulting from an operation (November 21, 1909) made it unlikely that my wife would have any new pregnancy. And yet, on April 10, a first suspicion of pregnancy was revealed at home. On May 4, our daughter was still present at the mediumistic table and broke the news to us: 'Mother, there is another being in you.' As we did not understand this sentence, the other entity, which, it seems, always accompanied our daughter, confirmed it by saying: 'The little girl is not mistaken another being is developing in you, my dear Adelia.'"

The subsequent communications ratified all these declarations, and even specified them, announcing that the unborn would be twin girls; that one of them would look like Alexandrina and even be a little prettier than she was before. Despite the persistent disbelief of my wife, things seemed to take the announced form, because in August, Dr. Cordaro, who was a reputed obstetrician, prognosticated a twin pregnancy.

"Then on November 22, 1910, my wife gave birth to two girls, without resemblance to each other, one, however, reproducing in her features the special physical features which characterized the physiognomy of Alexandrina, that is to say a hyperemia of the left eye, a slight seborrhea of the right ear, and finally a slight dissymmetry of the face." And, in support of his statements, Dr. Carmelo Samona brought the testimonials of his sister Samona Gardini, Professor Wigley, Mrs. Mercantini, the marquis Natoli, the princess Niscomi, and the count of Ranchileile, who all had been kept abreast of spirit communications obtained in Dr. Carmelo Samona's family, as they occurred.

Since the birth of this child, two and a half years have passed and Dr. Carmona wrote to *Filosofia della Scienza* that the resemblance of this second Alexandrina with the first Alexandrina has only been confirmed, not only in the physical aspect, but especially in the moral one. Same attitudes and quiet playful games, same forms of caresses to her mother; the same childish terrors expressed in the same terms, the same irresistible tendency to use the left hand, even to scribble the names of those around her. Like the former Alexandrina, she opens the shoe closet whenever she can enter the room where this piece of furniture is, wears a shoe, and walks triumphantly into the room. In a word, she absolutely emulates identical traits of the first Alexandria at the corresponding age.

Nothing of the sort was noticed in Maria Pace, her twin sister.

It goes without saying how valuable is an observation of this kind, when followed up years on end by an investigator of Dr. Carmona's caliber.[167]

Mr. T. Jaffeux, a lawyer at the Court of Appeal of Paris, France, communicated the following fact to me (March 5, 1911):

"Since the beginning of 1908, I had as my guide a woman whom I had known in my childhood, and whose spirit communications all had a character of rare precision: names, addresses, medical care, family predictions, etc. In the month of June, 1909, I transmitted to this Entity, on behalf of Fr. Henry, who was the director of the mediumistic group, the advice not to prolong indefinitely a stationary stay on the spiritual plane. The Entity replied to me at that time: 'I intend to reincarnate; I will successively have three very brief incarnations.' Around October 1909, she told me spontaneously that she was going to reincarnate in my family, and she indicated to me the place of this reincarnation: a village in the department of Eure-et-Loir (France). I had, indeed, a cousin who was pregnant at that time. I asked the spirit the following question: 'By what sign can you be recognized?' Answer: 'I'll have a 2-centimeter scar on the right side of my head.' On November 15, the same Entity told me it would stop coming in the following January, and that she would be replaced by another spirit. I thought from that moment on to give that proof all its significance, and nothing would have seemed easier for me to do, after making the spirit prediction officially known, than to have a medical certificate written at the birth of the child. Unfortunately, I found myself in the presence of a family that displayed a fierce hostility against Spiritism; which left me totally disarmed. In January 1910, the child was born with a

[167] *Annales des Sciences Psychiques,* July 1913, no. 7, pp. 196 *et seq..*

2-centimeter scar on the right side of the head. That happened exactly 14 months ago."

Mr. Warcollier, a chemical engineer of Paris, reports the following fact in the *Revue Scientifique et Morale* of February 1920:

"Madame B—, belonging to an aristocratic family of royalist convictions, was introduced to me by a member of my family, Mrs. Viroux. She had lost a son during the war whom she particularly loved. She still has other children, including a married girl, which will be discussed later. The details of this case are known to all Mrs. B—'s friends who were informed of them during the events. A volunteer at the beginning of the war, his son quickly won the rank of second lieutenant and then was killed during an attack. The mother had a dream in which she saw the exact spot, a railway embankment, where the body of her son was buried. Thanks to this dream, she found the body of her son and had him buried in the cemetery of a nearby village."

"A few months later, she had another dream in which she saw her son saying to her, 'Mom, do not cry, I'm coming back, not to your house, but to my sister's.' She did not understand the meaning of those words, but her daughter had a similar dream, in which she saw her brother, who had become a child, playing in his own room. Neither thought nor believed in reincarnation. Mrs. B—'s daughter, having never had children before, was not at all pleased with the idea. Nevertheless, soon after she became pregnant."

"The night before the birth, Mrs. B— saw her son in a dream again. And again he told her about his return and showed her a newborn baby with black hair that she recognized perfectly when she received him in her hands a few hours later. Mrs. B— is now convinced, by a thousand psychological details and by peculiar traits of character, that this child is indeed her son reincarnated and yet she affirms that previously she had never been a believer in reincarnation. A Catholic by birth and rank, while sympathetic toward the clergy, she confessed that she had been an absolute skeptic so far, perhaps even an atheist, and had never attended either Spiritists or Theosophists."

We have indicated in this chapter the physical causes of forgetfulness of past lives. In concluding it, would it not be appropriate to place ourselves in another point of view, asking ourselves if this forgetfulness is not justified by a necessity of a moral nature? The memory of the past does not seem desirable for the majority of humans, fragile "thinking reeds"[168] stirred by the breath of passions. On the contrary, it seems indispensable to our advancement that our past lifetimes be momentarily erased from our memory.

The persistence of memories would lead to a persistence of erroneous ideas, prejudices of social class and caste, of epoch and environment; in short, a whole appendage of mental heritage, a whole set of views and things that we would have all the more trouble to modify, to transform, the more alive it was in us. There would be many obstacles to our education and our progress; our judgment would often be distorted from birth. Forgetfulness, on the contrary, by allowing us to profit more widely from the different conditions that a new life gives to us, helps us reconstruct our personality on a better plane; our faculties and experiences can thus gain in depth and extension.

---

[168] [Trans. note] *Roseaux pensantes*, in the original French (an allusion to the philosopher Blaise PASCAL, who made the term famous when describing human nature as at once fragile and noble).

Another, even more serious, consideration: the knowledge of a blemished, tarnished past, as it might be the case for many of us, would be a heavy burden to carry. It requires a strong will to see without vertigo a long series of faults, failures, shameful acts, perhaps crimes, unfold; to weigh the consequences and resign oneself to undergo them. Most current human beings are incapable of such an effort. The memory of past lives can only be of benefit to a sufficiently advanced spirit, which have already mastered its own self to bear the weight of the past without waning; detached enough from human affairs to serenely contemplate the spectacle of his or her past history, reviving the pains endured, the injustices suffered, the betrayals of loved ones. It is a painful privilege to get to know our vanished past, lived through blood and tears, and also a cause of moral torment and heartbreak.

The visions attached to it would be, in most cases, a source of cruel concern for the weak soul struggling with its destiny. If our previous lives were happy, the comparison between the joys they gave us and the bitterness of the present would make our current life unbearable. Were they guilty ones? Then the perpetual expectation of the evils they would cause would paralyze our actions and render our existence sterile. The persistence of remorse, the slowness of our evolution, would make us believe that perfection is unattainable!

How many things would we not want to erase from our current life, which pose so many obstacles to our inner peace, so many barriers to our freedom! What would it be if the perspective of the centuries gone by unfolded unceasingly before our eyes, with all its details! What is important for us to bring within are the useful fruits from the past, that is to say, our acquired skills and abilities. These are the working instruments, the means of action of the spirit. They also represent everything that constitutes the character, our set of qualities and defects, our tastes and aspirations, all that is carried out from our deep consciousness into our normal consciousness.

A complete knowledge of past lives would present formidable disadvantages not only for the individual but also for the community. It would introduce into social life elements of strife, ferments of hate, which would aggravate the situation of humanity and hinder all moral progress. All the criminals of history, reincarnated in order to atone for their errors, would be unmasked; the shame, the betrayal, the perfidy, the iniquities of all epochs would be revealed again before our eyes. The accusing past, known to all, would become again a cause of profound division and intense suffering.

We, humans, who have come back here to act, to develop our faculties, to conquer new merits, must look forward not backwards. The future is open before us, full of hope and promise. A great law commands us to advance resolutely, and to make it easier for us to deliver ourselves from all ties and burdens, this same law lays a veil over our past. Let us thank the infinite Power which, by lightening the load of our crushing memories, has made our ascension easier, our atonements less bitter.

Sometimes we are told that it would be unfair to be punished for forgotten faults, as if forgetfulness erased the fault! We are told, for example: "A justice that is woven in secret, and which we cannot judge ourselves, must be considered an iniquity."[169]

But at first, is not everything a secret for us? The blade of grass that grows, the wind that blows, the life that moves, the star that glides into the silent night – everything

---

[169] *Journal de Charleroi*, February 18, 1899. This was already argued in the 4th century AD by the sophist AENEAS OF GAZA in his *Theophrastus*.

is mystery. If we are to believe only in things that are well understood, what will be left for us to believe?

If a criminal, convicted by human laws, falls ill and loses memory of his or her actions – since cases of amnesia are not uncommon – does it follow that his or her responsibility vanishes at the same time as their memory? No power can make the past disappear as it had never happened.

In many cases, it would be more atrocious to know than to ignore the past. When the spirit whose distant lives were guilty leaves the Earth and have bad memories awaken for it; when it sees vengeful shadows arise; does it regret the time of oblivion? Does it accuse God of having deprived it of the memory of its faults and of the prospect of the trials they entail?

Let us be content, then, with knowing the purpose of life, with knowing that divine justice governs the world. Everyone is in the place that he or she has earned, and nothing happens that is not deserved. Do we not have our conscience as our guide, and are the teachings of celestial geniuses not shining brightly into our intellectual night?

But the human spirit floats with all the winds of doubt and contradiction. Sometimes it finds that everything is good and it asks for new powers of life; sometimes it curses existence and claims nothingness. Can eternal justice conform its plans to our mobile and changing views? To ask this question is to solve it. Justice is eternal only because it is immutable. In the case at hand, it is the perfect harmony between the freedom of our actions and the inevitability of their consequences. The temporary forgetfulness of our faults does not cancel out their effect. Ignorance of the past is necessary, so that all human activity is toward the present and the future, and so that we all submit to the law of effort and conform ourselves to the conditions of the environment in which we are reborn.

During sleep, the soul acts, thinks, and wanders. Sometimes it goes back to the world of causes and retrieves the notion of past lives. Just as stars shine only during the night, so must our present be veiled in shadows so that the glimmers of the past may turn on brightly in the horizon of consciousness.

Life in the flesh is like sleep for the soul; it is its "dream," whether sad or happy. While it lasts, we forget the previous "dreams," that is, our past incarnations. However, it is still the same individuality that persists under both forms of existence. In its evolution, it alternately passes through periods of contraction and dilation, shadow and light. Personality restricts itself or flourishes in these two successive states, as it is lost and recovered through alternating sleep and waking, until the soul, after attaining its intellectual and moral apex, permanently finishes this "dreaming."

There is in each of us a mysterious book where everything is written in indelible letters. Shut to our eyes during our earthly life, it reopens on the spiritual plane; an advanced spirit can run through its pages at will. Therein it finds lessons, impressions, and sensations that the physical human being can scarcely understand.

This "book," called the subconscious by psychists, is what we Spiritists call the perispirit. The more the latter is purified, the clearer its memories become. Our lifetimes, one by one, emerge from the shadows and parade before us to accuse or glorify ourselves. The most minute facts, acts, thoughts, all things reappear and impose themselves on our awareness. Then the spirit contemplates the dreadful reality; it measures its degree of elevation; its conscience pronounces itself without recourse. How sweet are they to one's soul, at this hour, when good deeds were accomplished, works of self-sacrifice! But, conversely, our failures, works of selfishness and iniquity will weigh very heavily upon us!

During the incarnation, we must bear in mind that matter covers the perispirit with its thick coat; it compresses and extinguishes its radiations; hence our forgetfulness. Once delivered from this bond, the elevated spirit retrieves the fullness of its memory. A lower spirit remembers only its last existence. This is essential for the spirit, since it is the sum of the progress it has made, the synthesis of all its past; through its memory, a spirit can evaluate its situation. Those whose thoughts, in our world, have not been impregnated with the notion of preexistence, of earlier lifetimes, long ignore their first and most remote lifetimes. Hence the assertion of many spirits, in some countries, that there is no such law of reincarnation. These spirits have not questioned the depths of their own selves; they have not opened the fateful "book" where everything is engraved. They retain the prejudices of the earthly environment in which they lived; and such prejudices rather cause diversion, instead of inciting a sense of inquiry and research in them.

Higher Spirits, because of their charitable love, knowing the weakness of these souls, think that the knowledge of the past is not yet necessary to them, and avoid drawing attention to this subject, in order to spare them the sight of painful scenes. But a day comes when, under suggestions from above, their will awakens and searches these hidden folds of memory. Thus past lives reappear to them like a distant mirage. A time will come when, as the knowledge of these things becomes more widespread, all earthly spirits, initiated through a strong education in the law of rebirth, will see the past unfold before them immediately after death and even, in some cases, during their current life. They will have acquired the moral strength necessary to face this spectacle without faltering.

For purified souls, memory is constant. An elevated spirit has the power to relive at will its past, to see the present with all its consequences, and to penetrate into the mysterious future, whose depths are momentarily illuminated for the spirit, flashing in quick insights before plunging again into the dark unknown.

XV

SUCCESSIVE LIVES, CHILD PRODIGIES AND HEREDITY

SOME EARLY MANIFESTATIONS of genius can be considered as proof of earlier lifetimes, in the sense that they are a revelation of the soul's work in other, earlier cycles.

Phenomena of this kind of which history speaks cannot be disconnected facts, without any attachment to the past, just occurring at random in the void of time and space. On the contrary, they show that the organizing principle of life in us is a being that arrives in this world with a whole past of work and evolution, the result of a plan and a goal pursued during successive existences.

Each incarnation finds in the soul that repeats its life a particular culture, aptitudes, mental acquisitions that explain its ease of work and its power of assimilation. This is why Plato said: "To learn is to remember!"

To a certain extent, the law of heredity often interferes with these manifestations of individuality, for the mind shapes its envelope only by means of the elements placed at its disposal by heredity. However, in spite of these material difficulties, we see in certain beings, from the most tender age, faculties erupt that are so superior and unrelated to those of their ancestors, that we cannot, in spite of all the subtleties of materialistic sophistry, ascribe them to any immediate or known cause.

The case of Mozart has often been cited, playing a sonata on the piano at age of four, and at age of eight, composing an opera. Paganini and Teresa Milanollo, while still children, played the violin marvelously. Beethoven, Liszt and Anton Rubinstein were applauded at the age of ten. Michelangelo and Salvator Rosa had suddenly revealed themselves with improvised talents. Pascal, at the age of twelve, discovered projective geometry; and Rembrandt, before reading, already knew how to draw like a great master.[170]

Napoleon was noted for his premature aptitude for war. From his early youth he did not play the little soldier like the children of his age, but with an extraordinary method which he seemed to derive from himself.

The 16th century left us the memory of a prodigious polymath, James Crichton, whom Scaliger called a "monster genius." He was Scottish and, at age of fifteen, could speak Latin, Greek, Hebrew, and Arabic, about any subject. From the age of fourteen, he had earned the degree of master.

Christian Heinrich Heineken, born in Lübeck (Germany) in 1721, spoke almost from birth. At the age of two, he knew three languages. He learned to write in a few days and soon practiced small speeches. At the age of two and a half years, he was submitted to an exam on geography and history, both ancient and modern. He lived only off the milk of his nurse; people tried to wean him, he withered and died in Lübeck on June 27, 1725, in the course of his fourth year of age, while affirming his hopes in the other life. "He was," say the *Mémoires de Trévoux* (1701–1775), "delicate, infirm, and often sick." This toddler prodigy was fully aware of his approaching end. He spoke of it with a serenity at least as admirable as his premature scientific knowledge, and he wished

---

[170] See C. LOMBROSO, *The Man of Genius* (English trans. London: Walter Scott, 1891).

to comfort his parents by encouraging them with ideas extracted from their common beliefs.

The history of the past centuries has pointed out many of these child prodigies.

The young Frédéric Van de Kerckhove of Bruges died at the age of ten years and eleven months on August 12, 1873, leaving 350 small master paintings, some of them, says Adolphe Siret, a member of the Royal Academy of Sciences, Letters and Fine arts of Belgium, "could have been signed by names such as Diaz, Salvator Rosa, Corot, Van Goyen, and others."

Another child, William Rowan Hamilton, was studying Hebrew at the age of three, and at the age of seven had more extensive knowledge than most of the candidates in a high-level competitive examination for teachers. "I can still see him," said one of his relatives, "answer a difficult mathematical question, then go trotting away, dragging his little cart after him." At thirteen years of age, he knew twelve languages. At eighteen, he surprised everyone around him, to the point of making an Irish astronomer exclaim: "I would not say that he will become, but that he is already the top mathematician of his time."

More recently, Italy was honored to possess a formidable polyglot, Mr. Trombetti, who greatly surpassed his former compatriots, the celebrated Giovanni Pico della Mirandola, and the prodigious Giuseppe Mezzofanti, the cardinal who discoursed in seventy languages.

Trombetti was born to a family of poor and *completely illiterate* Bolognese. He learned French and German at school, and after two months he read Voltaire and Goethe. He learned Arabic just by reading a life of the Emir Abd El-Kader in that language. A Persian, passing through Bologna, taught him his language in a few weeks. At the age of twelve, he learned Latin, Greek and Hebrew simultaneously. Since then he has studied almost all living or dead languages; his friends say that he now knows about three hundred Eastern dialects. The King of Italy appointed him Professor of Philology at the University of Bologna.

At the Paris International Congress of Psychology, in 1900, Charles Richet, of the Academy of Medicine, presented in a general assembly, with all sections gathered, a Spanish child aged three years and half, named Pepito Arriola,[171] who played and improvised on the piano a variety of very rich and sonorous tunes. Next, I reproduce the address made by Dr. Richet to the delegates during the meeting of August 21, 1900, concerning this child, before his musical performance:[172]

"This is what his mother says about how, for the first time, she noticed the extraordinary musical gifts of young Pepito. 'The child was about two and a half years old when, for the first time, I discovered, by chance, his musical abilities. At this time one of my friends, a musician, introduced me to one of his compositions, and I began to play it on the piano quite frequently; it is probable that the child was paying attention; but I did not notice it. Now, one morning, I heard the same tune being played in a neighboring room, but with so much authority and accuracy, that I wanted to know who was allowed to play the piano at my home. I went into the living room, and saw my little boy who was alone playing the piano. He was sitting on a high seat, where he had sat down all by himself, and when he saw me, he laughed and said, '*Darling mommy.*' I thought there was a real miracle happening there.' From that moment little Pepito began to play, without his mother giving him any lessons,

---

[171] [Trans. note] José "Pepito" Rodríguez Carballeira (1896–1954).

[172] See the *Revue Scientifique* of October 6, 1900, p. 432, and *Compte rendu du IV Congrès International de Psychologie*, 1900 (Paris: Alcan, 1901), p. 93.

sometimes the tunes she herself played in front of him at the piano, sometimes the tunes he himself invented."

"Soon he was skilled enough to be able, on December 4, 1899, that is to say, before the age of three, to play in front of a rather large audience of critics and musicians. On December 26, that is, when he was aged three years and twelve days, he played at the Royal Palace in Madrid, before the king and the queen-mother, six musical compositions of his own invention, which were transcribed into musical sheets."

"He does not know how to read, whether music or the alphabet; he has no special talent for drawing; but sometimes he likes to write musical tunes. His writing makes no sense, but it is quite amusing to see him take a little piece of paper, make a scribble (which means, it seems, the nature of the piece, a sonata, habanera, or waltz, etc.). Then, underneath the title, he scribbles black lines which, he assures us, are musical notes. 'He looks at this sheet of paper with satisfaction, puts it on the piano, and says: 'I'm going to play this' and indeed, having this formless sheet in front of his eyes, *he improvises in an amazing way.*"

"To tell the truth, what is most amazing about him is not his fingering, nor harmony, nor agility, but his expression. He has an astonishing richness of expression. whether it is a sad, joyful, martial, or energetic piece, *the expression is striking*, and often even this expression is so strong, so tragic, in certain melancholy or funereal tunes, that one has the sensation that Pepito cannot, with his imperfect fingering, express all the musical ideas that quiver in him: *so that I would almost dare to say that he is a much greater musician than he seems to be* ..."

"Not only can he play songs he has just heard playing on the piano, but he can also play on the piano any sung tunes he happens to hear. *It is wonderful to see him then find, imagine, reconstruct the chords of bass and the harmony, as would a skilled musician."*

Since then, that young artist has continued the course of his growing success. Having become an incomparable violinist, he surprised the musical world with his precocious talent. He has already performed at several major concerts in Leipzig (Germany) and has given musical performances in St. Petersburg (Russia).[173]

We may add to this list the name of Willy Ferrero, an American-born Italian conductor and composer who, at the age of four years and a half, directed with skill the Folies-Bergères Orchestra, of Paris, then that of the Casino in Lyon. In his issue of February 18, 1911, the *Comœdia* magazine states: "He is a very little fellow who is already wearing the black coat, the satin pants, the white waistcoat and the patent leather shoes. The baton in his hand, he directs with a clarity, an assurance, and incomparable precision, an orchestra of eighty musicians, attentive to the smallest detail, conscious of the nuances, a scrupulous observer of rhythm ..."

The *Intransigeant* of June 22, 1911 adds that he excels in directing Haydn's Symphonies, Wagner's "Tannhäuser March," and Grieg's "Anitra Dance."

I could also mention *Le Soir*, of Brussels, Belgium, with its catalog of some remarkable children prodigies from overseas:[174]

"The University of New Orleans (USA) has just issued a medical certificate to a five-year-old student named Willie Gwin. The examiners then declared during an open audience that the young medical doctor was the most learned osteologist to whom they had ever issued a certificate."

---

[173] See C. Richet in *Annales des Sciences Psychiques*, April 1908, p. 98.

[174] Issue of July 25, 1900.

"In this regard, some transatlantic journals published a list of their prodigy children. One of them, barely eleven years old, founded a newspaper called *The Sunny Home*, which, from its third issue, already printed 20,000 copies."

"Among famous American preachers, we cite the young Dennis Mahan, from Montana, who at the age of six astonished the faithful with his deep knowledge of the Scriptures and the eloquence of his word."

"We can add to this list the name of the famous Swedish engineer Ericson who, at the age of twelve, was an inspector in the great Suez canal and had 600 workers under his command."

Let us return to the problem of child prodigies, examining it in its various aspects. First, two hypotheses have been proposed to explain it: heredity and mediumship.

Heredity, as everybody knows, is the transmission of an individual's characteristics to his and her descendants. Hereditary influences are considerable both physically and psychically. The parents' transmission of temperament, traits, character and intelligence to their children is very marked in some people. We find in ourselves, in different ways, not only the organic peculiarities of our direct generators or our ancestors, but also their qualities and their defects. In current life, a human being lives again all the mysterious line of beings of which he or she summarizes the efforts of centuries toward a higher and fuller life.

Yet, side by side with these analogies, there exist still even more divergences. Members of a same family, while having similarities and traits in common, sometimes also exhibit very clear differences. This fact can be found everywhere around us, in every family, among brothers and sisters, and even between twins. Many of them, similar in their physical aspect in their early years, to the point that it is difficult to distinguish one from another, present in the course of their development marked differences in features, character, and intelligence.

To explain such dissimilarities, it is therefore necessary to involve a new factor in the solution of the problem; that is, a preexistence of the self that has enabled the individual to increase his or her faculties, life after life, and which constitute an individuality bearing in itself a stamp of originality and its own aptitudes. The law of rebirth alone can enable us to understand how certain spirit show, through incarnation, since their earliest years of age, that ease of work and assimilation which characterize child prodigies. These are the results of immense labors that have previously familiarized these spirits with the arts or sciences in which they excel. Long researches, studies, and practice lasting centuries have left deep imprints in their perispiritual envelopes, creating some sort of psychological automatism. Among musicians in particular, this faculty is manifested early in the performance process, which astonishes the most jaded people and puzzles scientists such as Dr. Charles Richet.

In these young subjects there is a considerable amount of knowledge stored in their deep consciousness, which, from there, overflows into the physical consciousness so as to produce these early manifestations of talent and genius. While apparently abnormal, they are rather only the consequence of the toil and the efforts pursued through the eras. It is this reserve of this indestructible capital of one's being that F. H. W. Myers calls the *subliminal consciousness*, which is found in each and every one of us. It is revealed not only in the artistic, scientific or literary sense, but also through all the acquisitions of the spirit, both moral and intellectual in nature. The concepts of good and justice, the notion of duty, are much more acute in certain individuals and nationalities than in others. They do not result only from one's current education, as can be verified by a careful observation of the subjects in their spontaneous impulses, but rather from a private background which they bring in them when they are born. Education may develop these native rudiments, allowing them to flourish and produce all their fruits. Yet, alone, it could not inculcate so deeply in the newcomers those higher values which dominate their whole existence. This situation is found daily in certain lower human groups, still refractory to moral ideas, and on whom education has little influence.

Previous lives can also further explain these strange anomalies of wild, undisciplined, malevolent beings appearing suddenly within honest and civilized circles. We have seen children of good family commit robberies, start fires, perform crimes with consummated audacity and skill, suffer convictions and dishonor the name they bear. Other children are cited for acts of savage ferocity, which nothing can explain in their surroundings or ancestry. Some teenagers, for example, kill domestic pets that happen to fall in their hands, after having tortured them with refined cruelty.

Conversely, we can also see cases of commitment, extraordinary for one's childhood: rescues have been made with thought and decision by children aged ten and less. Such children, like the preceding ones, seem to have brought into this world certain dispositions which are not found in their parents. As angels of purity and sweetness are seen to be born and grow up in rude and depraved environments, so too are thieves and murderers in virtuous families; and in both cases these anomalies present themselves in conditions such that no atavistic precedent can seem solve this enigma.

All these phenomena, in their infinite variety, find their explanation in the past of the soul, in the many previous lives it has traversed. Each one brings at birth the fruits of its evolution, the intuition of what it has learned, the aptitudes acquired in the various fields of thought and social work: in the arts, science, commerce, industry, sailing, warfare, etc., skills for one thing rather than another, according to the particular activity it has already practiced in other lifetimes.

The spirit is apt for carrying out the most diverse studies. But in the limited duration of an earthly lifetime, through the effect exerted by environmental conditions, and as a result of material and social requirements, the spirit generally applies itself only to the study of a limited number of fields. And as soon as its will is directed toward one of the domains of the vast general knowledge – owing to a spirit's tendencies and the notions built up in itself – its superiority is drawn in one direction, which is brought increasingly into relief. It reverberates from existence to existence, revealing itself at each return to the earthly field, by ever more precocious and prominent manifestations. Hence, children prodigies and, in a more attenuated manner, one's vocations and innate predispositions. Hence, the talent, the genius, which is the result of persevering and a continuous effort toward a specific goal.

However, since one's soul is called upon to approach all forms of knowledge and not to restrict itself to just a few, the necessity of successive stages is demonstrated by the fact alone of the law of boundless development. Just as the proof of past lives is established by the acquisitions made before birth, the necessity of future lives is necessary as a consequence of our present actions. For this consequence to take place, conditions and environments in harmony with the state of souls are required. We have behind us countless reminiscences and memories; before us another countless promises and hopes. But, of all these life splendors, most humans cannot see or do not want to see but this puny fragment of their current lifetimes, the existence of a day that they believe has no precedent and no tomorrow. Hence the weakness of philosophical thought and moral action in our time.

The previous work done by each spirit can be easily calculated, and measured by the speed with which the latter performs again a similar work on the same subject, or by the promptness that it puts in the assimilation of the elements of any science. From this point of view, the difference among individuals is so large that it would remain incomprehensible without this given of previous existences. Two equally smart persons, studying the same subject, will not assimilate it in the same way: one will seize it at first sight when presented with the least elements, the other will penetrate it only through slow work and sustained application. This happens because one has already known these matters and has only to remember them, while the other is tackling them for the first time ever. The same is true of the ease with which some people accept some truth, principle, or point of a political or religious thought, while others are only convinced in the long run, by dint of arguments. For some, this will be something already familiar to their spirits, while it is totally new to others. The same considerations apply, as we have seen, to so great a variety of characters and moral dispositions. Without the given of a preexistence, the boundless diversity of intelligences and consciences would remain an insoluble problem, and the connection of the different elements of the self into one harmonious whole would become a phenomenon without a cause.

As said before, genius cannot be explained by heredity, let alone by conditions in one's environment. If heredity could produce genius, it would be much more frequent. Most famous individuals had ascendants of mediocre intelligence, and their descendants were notoriously inferior. Christ, Socrates, Joan of Arc were born of obscure families. Illustrious scientists have come out of the most lackluster circles; for instance, Bacon, Copernicus, Galvani, Kepler, Hume, Kant, Locke, Nicolas Malebranche, Reaumur, Spinoza, and Laplace, among others. Jean-Jacques Rousseau, son of a Swiss watchmaker, was passionate about philosophy and letters in his father's shop. The mathematician Jean-Baptiste le Rond d'Alembert, a foundling, was picked up during a winter's night on the threshold of a church, and brought up by the wife of a glazier. Neither ancestry nor cultural milieu can explain the brilliant creations of Shakespeare.

Facts are no less significant when it comes to the descents of individuals of genius. Their intellectual power disappears with the latter; we cannot find it in their children. The known children of such and such great poet or mathematician are incapable of the most elementary works in these two fields of thought. Among illustrious personages, most had stupid or unworthy children. Pericles begot two fools called Xanthippus and Paralus. Accentuated differences of other kinds can also be found in the philosopher Aristippus and his son Lysimachus, in Thucydides and Milesias. Sophocles, Aristarchus, and Themistocles were no better represented in their children. What a contrast between Germanicus and his son Caligula; between Cicero and his son Marcus; Vespasian and Domitian; Marcus Aurelius and Commodus! And of the sons of Charlemagne, Henry IV, Peter the Great, Goethe, Napoleon, what is left to say?

There are cases, however, where talent, memory, imagination, and the highest faculties of the spirit, seem to be hereditary. These mental similarities between parents and children are explained by attraction and sympathy. These are akin spirits, attracted to each other by analogous inclinations, and bonded by ancient relationships. *Generans generat sibi simile* [*A begetter begets a thing like to itself*].[175] As far as musical skills are concerned, this can be seen in the cases of Mozart and the young Pepito. But these two characters go above their ancestors. Mozart enthroned among his people like a sun among obscure planets. The musical abilities of his family are not enough to make us understand that at age four he could reveal a knowledge that no one had yet taught him, and show a deep understanding of the laws of harmony. He alone became famous; all other Mozarts have been ignored. Obviously, when these high intelligences can, they choose, in order to manifest their faculties more freely to reincarnate in a milieu where their tastes are shared, and where the physical organisms have practiced from generation to generation in the sense that they are now continuing. This is especially so among great musicians, for whom special conditions of sensation and perception are indispensable. But in most cases, genius appears in a family, unprecedentedly and without successors in the chain of generations. The great moralizing geniuses, founders of religions, such as Lao-tzu, Buddha, Zarathustra, Christ, and Mohammed, belong to this class of spirits. This is also the case of those powerful intelligences who down here had the immortal names of Plato, Dante, Newton, Giordano Bruno, and others.

If brilliant or fatal exceptions, created in a family by the appearance of an individual of genius or a criminal, were mere cases of atavism, we would find in the family genealogy the ancestor who served as a model, a primitive type of this later manifestation. However, this is almost never the case, neither in one direction nor in the other. We might be asked how we can reconcile these dissimilarities

---

[175] [Trans. note] Latin axiom made famous by St. Thomas Aquinas and others after him.

with the law of attractions and similarities, which seems to preside over the bringing together of souls. The penetration into certain families of beings of superior or inferior rank, who come to give or receive teachings, to exert or to undergo new influences, is easily explicable. It can result from the sequence of common destinies which, at certain points, come together and become entangled as a consequence of affections or hatreds exchanged in the past, which are equally attractive forces bringing together souls on successive planes, in the vast spiral of their evolution.

Could we explain through mediumship the phenomena reported above? Some have tried to do it. I myself, in a previous book,[176] have recognized that genius owes a great deal to inspiration, which is a form of mediumship. But I added that, in cases where this special faculty was clearly detected, the individual of genius could not be considered as a mere instrument – this would be above all a medium, properly speaking. Genius, I said, is above all an achievement of the past, the result of patient studies through centuries, of a slow and painful initiation. These antecedents develop in one's being a deep sensibility which opens itself to higher influences.

There is a marked difference between the intellectual manifestations of child prodigies and mediumship taken in its general sense. The latter has an intermittent, transient, abnormal character. The medium cannot exert his or her faculty all the time. Mediums need special conditions, sometimes difficult to meet, whereas child prodigies can

---

[176] Léon DENIS, *Into the Unseen* (New York: USSF, 2017), ch. XXVI, "Mediumship in its glory."

use their talents at any time, in a permanent way, as we ourselves make with our own mental abilities.

If we carefully analyze all the cases reported above, we will recognize that the genius of young prodigies is very personal to them; its application is regulated by their own will. Their works, original and astonishing as they seem, are always affected by their age and do not have the character they would assume, if they emanated from a high, extraneous intelligence. There is in their way of working and acting research, hesitation, trial and error, which would not occur if they were the passive instruments of a superior and occult will. This is what I see in Pepito's case in particular, which has been covered at length above.

Moreover, it may be admitted that in certain individuals these two causes, personal conquests and external inspirations, combine with and complement one another. The concept of reincarnation would not be weakened by that fact.

It is always to the idea of reincarnation that one must resort when approaching some facet of the problem of inequalities. Human souls are more or less developed according to their age and especially according to the use they made of their previous lives. We were not all launched at the same time in the whirlwind of life. We did not all walk at the same pace, unrolling in the same way the beaded rosaries of our lives. We have traveled an infinite road; hence our respective situations and values seeming to be so different. Yet the goal is the same for everyone. Under the whip of trials, under the sting of pain, we all climb and arise. The soul is not made of all pieces, it makes itself; it builds itself through the times. Its faculties, its qualities, its intellectual and moral possessions, far from being lost, are capitalized, growing from century to century. Through reincarnation, everyone comes back so as to continue to strive for perfection, resuming the task of yesterday interrupted by death. Hence, the dazzling superiority of certain souls that have lived much, and acquired a lot, by working hard. Hence, these extraordinary beings who appear here and there in history, projecting bright lights on the road of humanity. Their superiority is made up only of experience and accumulated labors.

Considered in this light, humanity's march a magnificent character. It slowly emerges from the obscurity of the ages, coming out of the darkness of ignorance and barbarism, and advancing step by step through obstacles and storms. It climbs a harsh road, and at every turn of the way, better glimpses the great peaks, the luminous summits where wisdom, spirituality, and love reign supreme.

And this collective march also includes the individual march of each one of us. For this humanity is made of ourselves; the same beings who, after a time of rest in the spiritual world, return from century to century, until they all become ripe for a better society, for a more beautiful world. We were among past generations and we will still be among generations to come. In reality, we are only one immense human family in the march for accomplishing God's design, which is stored in the plan for magnificent destinies written in it.

For those who want to pay attention, a whole past lives and pulsates within us. If history, if all the things ancient are so attractive to us, if they awaken in our souls so many deep impressions, sometimes painful ones; if we feel to have lived the life of individuals of old, and suffer from their troubles, it is because their story is ours. The eagerness placed by us in studying and collecting the work of the ancestors; the sudden impulses that lead us to such a cause or belief, have no other reason to exist. When we travel through the annals of the centuries, we are fascinated for certain eras, when our whole being is animated and vibrates to the heroic memories of Ancient Greece or Gaul, the Middle Ages, the Crusades, the French Revolution, for example, it is our past that comes out of the shadows, coming alive and living again. Through the thread woven through the centuries, we encounter again our own anxieties, aspirations and strifes. Memory is only momentarily veiled in us; but should we question our subconscious, we would hear voices from our own depths, sometimes vague and confused, sometimes completely striking. These voices tell us about great epics, migrations of human beings, furious rides that pass like hurricanes carrying all and everything into the night and into death. They can also tell us of humble, self-effaced lives, silent tears, forgotten sufferings, heavy and monotonous hours spent meditating, working, and praying in the silence of cloisters, or the vulgarity of poor and desolate lives.

Sometimes, a whole world of dark, confused, and mysterious memories awakes and vibrates in us; a world whose rumbling and rumors can move and intoxicate us. This is the voice of the past speaking in the somnambulistic trance and telling us about the vicissitudes of our poor soul, wandering around the world. It tells us that our present self is made up of many personalities that are found in itself as the tributaries of a river; and that our life principle has previously animated many forms, the dust of which rests there among the debris of empires, under the vestiges of dead civilizations. Within us, all these existences have left deep traces, memories and indelible impressions.

Those who study and observe feel that they have already lived and will live again; they inherit from themselves by harvesting in the present what they have sown before, and by sowing for the future.

Thus we find the confirmation of the beauty and magnificence of this concept of successive lives, which completes the law of evolution, which in turn is the subject of science. By acting upon all fields at once, it distributes to each according to his or her works, and shows us above all the majestic law of progress which governs the universe and brings life to ever more beautiful and always better states.

XVI

SUCCESSIVE LIVES, OBJECTIONS AND CRITICISMS

I HAVE RESPONDED to objections which are raised, in the first place, to one's forgetting his or her past lives. All the same, it still remains for me to refute other ones, whether of a philosophical or religious nature, systematically posed by church representatives against the belief in reincarnations.

In the first place, we are told, this belief is insufficient from a moral point of view. By opening to humans such vast perspectives on the future, by allowing them the possibility of repairing everything in their future existence, it encourages them to fall into vices and indolence; it does not offer a stimulus powerful enough, and urgent enough, for the practice of good; being for all these reasons, less effective than the fear of eternal punishment after death.

As I have discussed elsewhere, the theory of eternal punishment is embedded the very thought of the Church,[177] as mere a scarecrow intended to frighten the wicked. But the threat of hell, the fear of torture, effective in times of blind faith, no longer convinces anyone today. In the end, this is an impiety against God, for turning It into a cruel being that punishes unnecessarily and without a goal of improvement.

---

[177] See Léon DENIS, *Christianisme et Spiritisme* (New ed., Paris: Librairie de Sciences Psychiques, 1910), *passim*.

In its place, the belief in reincarnations shows us the true law of our destinies and, with it, the realization of progress and justice in the Universe. By making known to us the earlier causes of our evils, it puts an end to this unjust conception of original sin, according to which all the descendants of Adam, that is to say the whole of humanity, would bear the penalty of his failures as the first man. That is why the moral influence of a belief in reincarnations will be deeper than that offered by childish fables of hell and paradise. It will put a brake on our passions, by showing us the consequences of our actions, which reflect both on our current life and our future lives, sowing seeds of pain or happiness. By telling us that the soul will be all the more unhappy as it is more imperfect and guilty, it will stimulate our efforts toward good deeds. It is true that this doctrine is inflexible, but at least it knows how to proportion the punishment to the fault, and, after our atonements, it speaks to us of recovery and hope. So while the orthodox believer, imbued with the idea that confession and absolution can erase his or her sins, and cradling a vain hope that actually prepares great disappointments in the Hereafter, every individual enlightened by a new clarity learns to rectify his or her conduct, and to be vigilant, in order to carefully prepare the future.

Another objection is thus stated: If we are convinced that our ills are deserved, that they are but a consequence of the law of justice, such a belief will have the effect of extinguishing in us all pity, all compassion for the sufferings of others; we will feel less inclined to succor, to comfort our fellow human beings; we will give free rein to their trials, since these must be for them a necessary atonement and a means of advancement. This objection is only specious; it derives from a hidden agenda.

Let us first consider the matter at hand from the social point of view, followed by a consideration of it in the individual sense. Modern Spiritualism teaches that we all have a common fate. The social imperfections from which more or less we all suffer are the result of our collective mistakes in the past. Each of us bears his or her share of responsibility and has the duty to work to improve the general fate. The education of human souls obliges them in turn to occupy various positions. All humans must alternately undergo the test of wealth and that of poverty, misery, sickness, pain, etc.

When watching the miseries of this world that do not reach them, selfish people become disinterested and say: "After me the deluge!" They believe they are spared death by the action of earthly laws and the convulsions of societies. With reincarnation, their point of view changes. They will have to come back again and suffer the evils that they bequeathed to others. All the passions and iniquities that we tolerated, encouraged, or maintained, either because of weakness or interest, will rise up against us. This social environment, for the improvement of which we will have done nothing, will capture us with all the strength of its embrace. Whoever crushed and exploited others will be exploited and crushed in turn. Whoever has sown division and hatred will suffer the consequences. The proud will be despised and the spoliator stripped. Those who have made others suffer will suffer themselves. If you want to ensure your own future, work now to improve and make better the environment where you must be reborn; also consider improving yourself. So much for the collective miseries that must be overcome by the effort of all. Whoever, being able to help his fellow humans, neglects to do so, lacks a sense of solidarity.

As for one's individual evils, by placing myself in another point of view, I say: We cannot be judges of the precise moment when an atonement begins or ends. Do we even know in which cases there really is an atonement? Many souls, without being guilty, but eager to advance, request a life of hardship to evolve more quickly. The help we owe to these souls may be one of the conditions of their destiny as it is for ours, and it is possible that we may be placed in their path on purpose, to relieve them, to enlighten them, to comfort them. All good and all mischief return to their source with their outcomes; it is always a miscalculation on our part to neglect any opportunity to make ourselves useful and serviceable.

"Without charity there is no salvation," said Allan Kardec. This is the precept par excellence of Spiritist morals. Wherever suffering awakens, it must find compassionate hearts, ready to help and comfort. Charitable love is the most beautiful of virtues; it alone can give access to happy worlds.

Many people for whom life has been rough and tough are frightened at the prospect of renewing it indefinitely. This long and painful ascension through time and worlds overwhelms those who, tired of their weariness, expect immediate rest and endless happiness. It is certain that one must have the soul toughened in order to contemplate without vertigo these immense perspectives. The Catholic conception was more attractive to timid souls and lazy spirits who, according to it, had little effort to make in order to gain salvation. By contrast, the vision of destiny is formidable. It requires vigorous spirits to consider it without faltering; to find in the notion of destiny the necessary stimulus, calm and serenity of thought, a compensation for small denominational customs.

A happiness that must be conquered at the price of so much effort frightens more than it attracts human souls, for the most part still weak and unaware of their magnificent future. But truth must come first! There can be no question here of personal propriety. The law, whether one likes it or not, is the law! It is up to us to adapt our views and actions to it, and not to bend it to our own individual wishes.

Death cannot turn a lower-order spirit into a higher-order spirit overnight. We are, in the Hereafter as here below, what we have done of ourselves, both intellectually and morally. All the Spiritist manifestations demonstrate it. However, we are told that only the perfect souls will enter the heavenly kingdoms and, in addition, our development are restricted to the circle of an ephemeral life. Can anyone possibly overcome one's passions, straighten one's character in a single life? If some have succeeded, what about the crowd of ignorant and vicious people that populate our planet? Is it conceivable for their evolution to be limited to this short passage on Earth? And those who are guilty of great crimes, where will they find the conditions necessary for reparation? If not for later reincarnations, we would inevitably be stuck into the rut of hell. But eternal hell is as impossible as eternal paradise. For there is no act so commendable, or crime so dreadful, that can entail an eternity of rewards or punishments!

To see this it suffices to consider the work of nature since the beginning of time, to see everywhere this slow and quiet evolution of beings and things, which is so well suited to the eternal Power and proclaimed by all the voices of the Universe. The human soul does not escape this sovereign rule. It is the synthesis, the crowning of this prodigious effort, the last link of the chain that unfolds from the shallows of life and covers the entire globe. Is it not in humans that the whole evolution of the lower kingdoms is summed up, and that the sacred principle of perfectibility emerges with brilliancy? Does this principle not represent its very essence, bearing the divine seal affixed to its nature? And if it is so, how can one conceive of human intelligence being placed outside the imposing laws emanating from the first source of all Intelligences?

Can the flow of life that rolled through the ages until it led to human beings, and that, in its course, has been directed by this magnificent rule of evolution, lead to immobility? The principle of progress is written everywhere: in nature and in history. All the movement that it imparts to forces in action on our world culminates in humans, and would we like their essential part, their self, their consciousness, to escape this law of continuity and progression? Absolutely not! Logic, let alone facts, all show it to us: our existence cannot be isolated. The drama of life cannot be composed of a single act; it needs a continuation, an extension, by which the apparent inconsistencies and obscurities of the present are explained and clarified. It requires a series of existences, mutually consolidated, unveiling the plan, the economy that presides over the destinies of human beings.

Does that mean that we are condemned to laborious and incessant toil? Does the law of ascension delays indefinitely the period of peace and rest? Not at all. At the end of each earthly life, the soul harvest the fruit of acquired experiences; it retreats with its forces and faculties toward the inner and subjective life. It makes an inventory of its earthly work, assimilating the useful parts and rejecting the sterile elements. This is our first occupation in the Hereafter, the ultimate work of recapitulation and analysis. An inner retreat between the periods of earthly activity is necessary, and every being that follows the normal path will in turn be benefited from it.

We called it inner retreat because, in reality, the spirit, when in the free state, hardly knows any rest. Activity is its very nature. But do not we see it in sleep? The physical organs of transmission, alone, feel fatigue and gradually collapse. In the life on the spiritual plane, these obstacles are almost unknown; the spirit can devote itself, without any embarrassment or constraint, to the missions devolved upon it, until the time of its next reincarnation.

Its return to life on Earth is a rejuvenation for the spirit. At each rebirth, the soul reconstitutes a sort of virginity. The forgetting of the past, like beneficent and restorative waters of a river Lethe, makes a new being of the same spirit, which again resumes its vital ascension with even more ardor. Each life makes progress, each progress increases the power of the soul and brings it closer to the state of perfection. This law shows us eternal life in its magnitude. All of us have an ideal to achieve: supreme beauty and supreme happiness. We are moving toward this ideal more or less rapidly, according to our momentum and the intensity of our desires. Our will and our conscience, which are living reflections of the universal norm, are our only arbiters. Every human existence conditions the next one. Together they constitute the fullness of destiny, that is, a communion with the infinite.

This question is often posed to me: how can the atonement, the redemption of past faults, be meritorious and fruitful to the reincarnated spirit, since, forgetful and unconscious of the causes which are oppressing it, it is currently ignorant of the purpose and the reason of such trials?

As we have seen, suffering is not necessarily an atonement. All nature suffers; everything that lives: the plants, the animals, and us, humans, are all subject to pain. Suffering is above all a means of evolution, of education. But in the case at hand, it should be remembered that a distinction must be drawn between current unconsciousness and the virtual consciousness of destiny that is found in any reincarnated spirit.

Once the spirit understands, in the intense light of the Hereafter, that a life of trials was absolutely necessary for it to erase the unpleasant results of its previous lives, this same spirit, in a move of full intelligence and full freedom, spontaneously chooses or accepts its future reincarnation with all the consequences it entails, including forgetting the past, which follows the process of reincarnation. This initial, clear and total view of its destiny, at the precise moment when the spirit accepts rebirth, is ample enough to establish the awareness, responsibility, and merit of this new life. Here the spirit keeps the veiled intuition, the dormant instinct, that the slightest reminiscence, the most fleeting dream, are able to awaken and revive. It is through this invisible but real and powerful bond that the current life is connected with the previous life of the same being, constituting the moral unity and relentless logic of its destiny. As previously seen, if we do not remember the past, that is because, most often, we do not do anything to awaken our sleeping memories. Nonetheless the order of things remains, since no link of the magnetic chain of destiny is ever obliterated, let alone broken.

A middle-aged individual usually cannot remember the details of his or her early youth. Does this prevent him or her from being the child of old and to fulfill the promises?

Does a great artist who, in the evening of a laborious day, gives in to fatigue and falls asleep, not keep, during his sleep, the virtual plan, the intimate vision of the work he will take back and resume when he wakes up? Well, it is so with our destiny, which is also a constant work, interspersed several times in its course by rests which are actually different modes of action, illuminated by dreams of light and beauty!

A human life is a logical and harmonious drama whose scenes and scenery change, varying infinitely, but never deviating for a moment from a unity of purpose or harmony of the whole. It is only on our return to the invisible world that we will understand the value of each scene, the sequence of acts, the incomparable harmony of the whole in its relation with universal life and unity.

Let us follow with faith and confidence the line traced by an infallible finger. Let us head for our destinations, as the rivers go to the sea, fertilizing the earth and reflecting the sky.

Two objections still arise: "If the theory of reincarnation were true," says Jacques Brieu, in his journal *Moniteur des Études Psychiques* (Paris), "moral progress ought to have been noticeable since the beginning of historical times. However, quite the opposite happens. Today's humans are as selfish, violent, cruel and ferocious as they were two thousand years ago."

This appreciation seems extreme. Even if it were accurate, it does not prove anything against reincarnation. The best individuals – those who, after a series of lives, have reached a certain degree of perfection – continue their evolution on more advanced worlds, returning to Earth only exceptionally, on special missions. On the other hand, contingents of spirits, coming from lower planes, are added everyday to the population of the globe. How, under such circumstances, should we be surprised that the moral level seems to rise so little?

Second objection: the concept of successive lives, once spread in humanity, will inevitably bring about abuses. Is it not so with all things brought into a world of little progress such as ours, whose tendency is to corrupt, to distort the most sublime teachings, so as to accommodate them to its tastes, passions, and low interests?

It is certain that human pride can find ample satisfaction in doing it, and, with the aid of mocking spirits or hypnotic suggestion, we sometimes witness the most burlesque revelations. Just as many people claim to be descended from an illustrious lineage, so also among contemporary Theosophists and Spiritualists, many faithful believers think that they had been such and such famous personage in the past.

"But in our days Dr. Anna Kingsford and Mr. Edward Maitland must needs have been the Virgin Mary and St. John the Divine," said F. H. W. Myers.[178]

For my part, I have met a dozen people around the world who claim to have been Joan of Arc. I would not be able to finish, if I were to list all cases of this kind. There is, however, a possible grain of truth in these claims. But how can we distinguish it from delusions? When dealing with such matters we must engage in careful analysis and critically screen these revelations thoroughly; first, to find out whether the individuality has striking resemblances to the designated person; and then request from the revealing spirits any evidence of

---

[178] F. W. H. MYERS, *Human Personality* (London: Longmans, 1903), vol. II, ch. VIII, items 836, p. 135.

identity related to these personalities from the past, and some indication of verifiable details and unknown facts that can be checked later on.

Let me point out that such abuses, like so many others, do not depend on the nature of the cause at hand, but on the inferiority of the environment in which they take place. These abuses, the result of ignorance and false judgment, will diminish and disappear over time, thanks to a stronger and more practical learning orientation.

One last difficulty remains: that which results from an apparent contradiction in the Spiritist teachings on the subject of reincarnation. In Anglo-Saxon countries, that subject has long been kept in silence, not being mentioned by spirits in their mediumistic messages. Many even denied it, and this has become a capital argument for the opponents of Spiritism.

I have already partially answered this objection above, when I stated that this anomaly was explained by the necessity that the spirits had, at first, of coping with very inflexible religious prejudices, which prevailed in certain circles. Several points of Spiritism were deliberately left out in Protestant countries, where people were more hostile to the idea of reincarnation. These were disclosed later, at more opportune occasions. In fact, after this period of silence, we now see Spiritist affirmations defending the concept of successive lives in overseas countries as intensely as in Latin countries.[179] There has been some gradation on teaching points, but no contradiction.

---

[179] [Trans. note] See footnote 24 above.

Such negations almost always emanate from spirits which are still too little advanced to know and be able to read in themselves and discern the future that awaits them. We know that these souls undergo reincarnation without foreseeing it and, when the time comes, are immersed in material life as if in anesthetic sleep.

Prejudices of race and religion, which have exerted considerable influence upon these spirits on Earth, still persist in them in the other life. While an elevated entity can easily be freed from it at death, the least advanced ones are long submissive to it.

In the new continent (America), prejudices of color have made the law of rebirth appear in a different light than in the old world (Europe and Asia), where ancient Eastern and Celtic traditions had deposited their seed in many souls. At first it appeared so shocking, it aroused so much revulsion, that the spirits that took part in the Spiritist movement thought it wiser to procrastinate. They first allowed the idea to spread in better prepared environments, and from there, to gain more resistant centers by different means, both visible and hidden, by penetrating them slowly, as it is taking place right now.

Protestant education leaves their orthodox believers no room for the notion of successive lives. According to it, at death, the soul is definitively judged and fixed, either in heaven or in hell. For Catholics, there is an average term, called the purgatory, an imprecise environment, not circumscribed, where the soul must atone for its faults and purify itself by ill-defined means. This concept may be conducive to the idea of earthly rebirths. The Catholic can thus connect their old beliefs to the new ones, while the orthodox Protestant needs to make a clean sweep, and to build upon his or her understanding philosophical ideas absolutely different from those suggested to them by their religion. Hence the hostility that the principle of multiple lives first encountered in the Anglo-Saxon countries, rallied to rooted Protestantism. Hence the prejudices that persist, even after death, among a certain category of spirits.

As we have seen, a reaction is gradually occurring now. Belief in successive lives is gaining more and more ground in Protestant countries every day as the idea of completely hell loses influence. It already has many supporters in England and America. The main Spiritist centers of these countries have adopted it, or are at least discussing it with good impartiality. The testimonies of spirits in its favor, so rare in the beginning, are multiplying today. Here are some examples:

An important work was published in 1904 in New York under the title *The Widow's Mite*,[180] in which the principle of reincarnation is accepted. The author, Isaac K. Funk, says W. J. Colville in the journal *Light*, was a very well known and highly respected individual in American literary circles, as the oldest associate of the publishing house Funk & Wagnalls, who published the famous Standard Dictionary whose authority is recognized wherever English is spoken.

In this book, the author first exposes the conditions of experimentation, which were rigorous. Then, it reviews the communications of the spirit guide Amos, which said one day (*op. cit.*, pp. 203–204):

"A bright spirit is here whom I wish to introduce to you this evening. He will take a little time in teaching you about reincarnation, a subject concerning which you have made inquiry. He is a highly developed spirit, and is a teacher with us. He comes in answer to the invitation of the band [the spirits controlling the circles]. You remember you have asked questions on several evenings

---

[180] [Trans. note] I. K. FUNK, *The Widow's Mite and Other Psychic Phenomena* (1st ed., New York and London: Funk & Wagnalls, 1904).

on this subject which we could not satisfactorily answer, and for this reason we thought it well to request this advanced spirit to come and address you, and he has kindly consented to do so — I am sorry Professor Hyslop is not here, as he asked several questions on this subject the other evening."

"A voice much stronger and seemingly very different spoke as follows: 'Good-evening, friends. Reincarnation is the law of development of the soul or spirit. In the growth of the soul—and we all must grow, slowly it may be and with long cessations and sometimes less, but in the long ages it is growth—the time comes when it is born again and it enters into a higher sphere of existence. I am not talking about reincarnation on earth. A birth does not often take place from the spirit life back to earth life. Sometimes spirits are so much attached to the earth and its enjoyments, the gratification of animal passions and appetites and those pleasures that come through the other senses, that they reenter bodies and live again earth lives; but this is not necessary. In the spirit body and under the conditions here, far greater progress can be made than in the earth life, and this is true in every succeeding sphere.'"

William Stainton Moses (under the pseudonym Oxon), a professor at Oxford University who was an ideal medium because of his high culture and exemplary morality, and the initiator of the Spiritualist movement in England, received and reproduced the affirmation of successive lives in his book *Spirit Teachings* (London, Spiritualist Alliance, 1898, p. 25):

"Love and knowledge help on the soul. The child may have the one qualification; it cannot have the other save by education, which is frequently gained by its being attached to a medium, and living over the earth-life again.... Such an experience is essential; and for the purpose of gaining it many spirits elect to return to earth."

F. W. H. Myers, in his masterly book, *Human Personality* (vol. II, "Syllabuses," "Chapter X," page xx, paragraph 1011) expresses a similar opinion:

"Our new knowledge, confirming ancient streams of thought, corroborates analogically for Christianity the record of Christ's appearances after death, and hints at the possibility of the beneficent incarnation of souls previously on a level higher than man's."

Elsewhere in the same book (vol. II, ch. VIII, section 836, p. 134), he adds:

"Namely, the doctrine of *reincarnation*, or of successive lives spent by each soul upon this planet. The simple fact that such was probably the opinion both of Plato and of Virgil shows that there is nothing here which is alien to the best reason or to the highest instincts of men. Nor, indeed, is it easy to realize any theory of the *direct creation* of spirits at such different stages of advancement as those which enter upon the earth in the guise of mortal man. There *must*, one feels, be some kind of continuity – some form of spiritual Past. Yet for reincarnation there is at present no valid evidence ..."

At the time, Myers did not know the recent experiments discussed herein in Chapter XIV above; even so, he still asserts (*ibid.*, section 1004, p. 281) that there is "An evolution [of souls] gradual with many gradations, and rising to no assignable close."

More recently, Lord Carlingford's *Letters from the Spirit World* (N. P., private print, 1904),[181] published in England, admits reincarnations as a necessary consequence of the law of evolution.

---

[181] [Trans. note] A book whose writer purports to be the late Lord Carlingford.

The doctrine of successive lives, I say, can be found all over the place right now, on the other side of the Channel (the UK). We see a philosopher, such as Professor John M. E. McTaggart, adopt it in preference to other spiritualistic doctrines, when referring immortality, and declare, as Hume had done before him, "absent any better hypothesis, it is the one that is reasonable to accept."

Finally, in his opening address as President of the Society for Psychical Research, the Right Revd. Bishop William Boyd-Carpenter, of Ripon, North Yorkshire, England, in front of a large and distinguished audience, emphasized on May 23, 1912 the usefulness of psychical research in obtaining a more complete knowledge of the human self and in specifying the conditions of its evolution. "The interest of this speech," say the *Annales de Sciences Psychiques* of May, 1912 (pp. 157–158), "lies especially in this: that we see a high dignitary of the Anglican Church assert, like certain Fathers of the Church, the preexistence of the soul, and adhere to the theory of evolution and multiple existences."

XVII
SUCCESSIVE LIVES, HISTORICAL EVIDENCE

THIS STUDY WOULD be incomplete if we did not take a quick look at the role played in history by the belief in successive lives.

This belief dominates all antiquity. It is found in the heart of the great religions of the East, and in the purest and highest philosophical books. It guided in their march the civilizations of the past and has continued from age to age. Despite persecutions and temporary eclipses, it reappeared and persisted throughout the centuries in all countries.

From India, it has spread throughout the world. Long before the appearance of the great revealers of historical times, it was formulated in the *Vedas* and especially in the *Bhagavadgita*. Brahmanism and Buddhism were inspired by it, and even today, six hundred million Asians[182] – the double of all Christian confessions combined – believe in the plurality of existences.

Japan has recently shown what a nation can expect from such beliefs. The magnificent courage, the spirit of sacrifice shown by the Japanese in face of death, their impassibility in face of pain, all these master qualities which astonished the world in memorable circumstances, have no other sources.

After the battle of Tsushima, *Le Journal* tells us, in a scene of grandiose melancholy, before the assembled

---
[182] [Trans. note] 4.54 billion inhabitants, or 60% of the world population, according to current figures.

army at the Aoyama cemetery in Tokyo, Admiral Togo spoke in the name of the nation and addressed the dead in pathetic terms. He asked the souls of these heroes to "protect the Japanese navy, haunt ships and reincarnate in new crews."[183]

If, with Professor Izoulet, commenting at the Collège de France on the work of American historian Alfred Thayer Mahan about the Far East, we admit that true civilization is in the spiritual ideal; and that, without it, people fall into corruption and decadence; it should be necessary for us to recognize that Japan is destined to a great future.

Let us go back to the ancient past. Egypt and Greece adopted this same doctrine. Under a more or less obscure symbolism, universal *palingenesia* (rebirth or reincarnation) is hidden everywhere in their cultures.

The ancient belief of the Egyptians is revealed nowadays by the inscriptions on their monuments and by the books of Hermes: "Taken at the origin ...," says Eugène-Melchior de Vogüé in *Histoires Orientales* (Paris, C. Lévy, 1880), "the [Egyptian] doctrine presents the 'Voyage to the Divine Lands' as a series of trials, at the end of which an ascension into the light takes place." But the knowledge of the deep laws of destiny was reserved only for the initiated.[184] In his recent book, *Life and Death* (Trans. W. J. Greenstreet. London and New York,

---

[183] See in the Parisian newspaper *Le Journal* of December 12, 1907, an article signed by Ludovic NAUDEAU, who witnessed the ceremony. See also about *Yamato-damashii* (*Japanese soul* or *spirit*), and the book *Kokoro: Hints and Echoes of Japanese Inner Life* (New York: Cosimo Classics, 2005. Reprint) by the American professor Lafcadio HEARN, who taught at a Japanese University.

[184] See Léon DENIS, *After Death* (Trans. G. G. Fleurot, J. Korngold. New York: USSF, 2017), ch. 3, "Egypt," p. 26.

Walter Scott, 1911), French physiologist Albert Dastre puts it this way:[185]

"But it was in Egypt that the doctrine of metempsychosis was represented by the most striking images: each being had its *double*. At birth, the Egyptian was represented in duplicate. During the waking state, the two characters are united, but in sleep, while one is resting and repairing its organs, the other rushes into the land of dreams – yet this separation is not complete; only at death, or rather, a complete separation is death itself; and later this active double may return to vivify another body, thus fulfilling a new earthly existence."

In Greece, we find the doctrine of successive lives in Orphic poems. It was the belief of Pythagoras, Socrates, Plato, Apollonius, and Empedocles. Under the name of metempsychosis,[186] they often mention it in their books, in veiled terms, because the majority of them were bound by an initiatory oath. However, rebirth is clearly and undoubtedly affirmed in the last book of Plato's *Republic*, in *Phaedrus*, in *Timaeus*, and in *Phaedo*:

"That souls departing hence exist in Hades, and are produced again from the dead."

---

[185] Actually, this excerpt is a paraphrase authored by Pierre Camille REVEL, in his book *Le Hasard, sa Loi et ses Conséquences dans les Sciences* (Paris: Bibliothèque Chacornac, 1909), "Essai sur la Métempsycose," ch. I, pp. 257–258.

[186] Today, ordinary people can only see in metempsychosis a passage of the human soul into the body of inferior beings. In India, Egypt, and Greece, it was considered more generally as the transmigration of souls to other human bodies. We are led to believe that the descent of the soul into a body inferior to humanity was, like the idea of hell in Catholicism, only a scarecrow intended, in the thought of the ancients, to frighten the wicked. Any retrogression of this kind would be contrary to justice, logic and truth. Moreover, it is rendered impossible by the fact that the development of the fluidic organism (or perispirit) would no longer allow a human being to adapt itself to the conditions of animal life.

"It seems to me to be a sufficient proof that the souls of the dead exist somewhere, whence they come back to life." (*Phaedo*)

Reincarnation was celebrated in Egypt in the mysteries of Isis, and in Greece, in those of Eleusis, under the name of mystery of Persephone. The initiates alone were allowed to participate in the ceremonies.

The myth of Persephone was a dramatic representation of rebirths, the history of the human soul, past, present and future, its descent into matter, its captivity into borrowed bodies, its reascension in successive stages. The Eleusinian feasts lasted three days and translated, in a moving trilogy, the alternations of the double life, earthly and celestial. At the end of these solemn initiations, the initiated were consecrated.[187]

Almost all the great personages of Greece were initiates, devotees of the great goddess. It was in these secret teachings that they drew the inspiration of genius, the sublime forms of art, and the precepts of divine wisdom. As for ordinary people, only symbols were presented. But, under the transparency of myths, the initiatory truth appeared, as through the bark of trees transudes the sap of life.

The great doctrine was also known to the Roman world. Ovid, Virgil, and Cicero, in their imperishable works, make frequent allusions to it. Virgil, in the epic poem *Aeneid*,[188] assures us that the soul, by plunging into the river Lethe, loses the memory of its past lives.

The school of Alexandria gave it a shining brilliance, through the books of Philo, Plotinus, Ammonius Sacchas,

---

[187] See Édouard SCHURÉ, *Sanctuaires d'Orient* (3rd ed., Paris: Perrin et Cie., 1907), pp. 254 *et seq*.

[188] VIRGIL, H. S. FRIEZE, *Virgil's Aeneid* (2nd ed., New York: D. Appleton, 1877), "Notes on the Aeneid," no. 715, "*Securos latices*," p. 528.

Porphyry, Jamblicus, and others. Plotinus says, speaking of the gods: "They assure to each one the human body that suits it best and that is in harmony with one's antecedents, according to one's successive lives."

The sacred books of the Hebrews: the *Zohar*, the *Kabbalah*, the Talmud, also affirm the preexistence of the souls and, under the name of *resurrection*, the reincarnation. It was the belief of both Pharisees and Essenes.[189] The Old and New Testaments, in the midst of obscure or altered texts, still carry many traces of it; for example, in certain passages of Jeremiah and Job, and then in the case of John the Baptist, who once was Elijah; in that of the blind-born; and in the private conversation between Jesus and Nicodemus.

In Matthews, we read:[190] "Truly, I say to you, among those born of women there has arisen no one greater than John the Baptist.... and if you are willing to accept it, he is Elijah who is to come. He who has ears to hear, let him hear."

Another day the disciples of Christ questioned him, saying:[191] "'Then why do the scribes say that first Elijah must come?' He answered, 'Elijah does come, and he will restore all things. But I tell you that Elijah has already come, and they did not recognize him, but did to him whatever they pleased.' ... Then the disciples understood that he was speaking to them of John the Baptist."

---

[189] We read in a French translation of the *Zohar*, II, fol. 99: "All souls are subject to revolution [metempsychosis, the *Aleen t'Gilgulah* of the Hebrews], but humans do not know the ways of God, which is fortunate." Titus Flavius JOSEPHUS, in his *Jewish Antiquities*, XVIII, I, paragraph 3, says that the virtuous will have the power to resurrect and live again.

[190] Mt 11:11,14–15 *ESV*.

[191] Mt 17:10–13.

One day, Jesus asks his disciples what is said of him among the people. They reply:[192] "'Some say John the Baptist, others say Elijah, and others Jeremiah or one of the prophets.'" Jesus, far from dissuading them as if they were dealing in imaginary things, is content to add: "'But who do you say that I am?'"

When Jesus meets the blind-born, his disciples ask him if this man was born blind because of the sins of his parents or the sins he committed before he was born. They therefore believed in the possibility of reincarnation and the possibility of preexistence of the soul. Their language would even lead one to believe that such an idea was widespread among the people, and Jesus seems to allow it instead of fighting it. He speaks of the many dwellings of the Father's house; and Origen, commenting on these words, adds: "The Lord is referring to the different stations which souls must occupy after they have been stripped of their current bodies, and that they occupy new ones."

Therefore, primitive Christianity possessed the true meaning of destiny. But, later, with the subtleties of Byzantine theology, the hidden meaning gradually disappeared; the secret virtue of initiatory rites vanishes like a tenuous perfume. Scholasticism stifled the first revelation under the weight of syllogisms, or altogether ruined it with specious argumentation.

However, the first Fathers of the Church and, above all, Origen and St. Clement of Alexandria, pronounced themselves in favor of the transmigration of souls. St. Jerome and Rufinus (*The Letter of Anastasius*) claim that it was taught as a traditional truth to a certain number of initiates.

---

[192] Mt 16:13–15. Mk 8:27–29.

In one of his major works, *On First Principles*, Book I, Origen (185–254 AD) reviews the numerous arguments which show, in the preexistence and survival of souls in other bodies, the necessary corrective to the inequality of human conditions. He wonders what is the total number of stages that his soul has to travel in its peregrinations through the infinite, what progress is made at each of its stages, the circumstances of this immense journey, and the particular nature of its dwellings.

St. Gregory of Nyssa (335–395 AD) says that "There is a natural necessity why the immortal soul should be healed and purified, and that if it has not been so healed and purified during its life on earth, it must be so in the life to come."

However, this high doctrine could not be reconciled with certain dogmas and articles of faith, which were powerful weapons for the Church, such as predestination, eternal punishment and last judgment. With it, Catholicism should have given more room to the freedom of the human spirit, called in its successive lives to rise through its own efforts and not only by grace from above.

Also, it was an act fraught with fatal consequences the condemnation of Origen's teachings and the Gnostic theories by the Second Council of Constantinople in 553. The principle of reincarnations was thus thoroughly discredited and rejected. Then, in place of a clear and simple conception of destiny, within the reach of the humblest intelligences, by reconciling divine justice with the suffering and the inequality of human conditions, a whole series of dogmas was created. Complete obscurity over the problem of life has revolted reason and, finally, alienated humans from God.

The doctrine of successive lives reappears again at different times in the Christian world, in the form of great heresies and secret schools, but it was often drowned in blood or smothered under the ashes of blazing pyres.

In the Middle Ages, it almost completely disappears and ceases to influence the development of Western thought, to the detriment of the latter. Hence the errors and confusion of that dark age, its narrow fanaticism, cruel persecutions, the jail of the human spirit. A sort of intellectual night was made over Europe.

Yet, from time to time, like a flash of light, the great thought still illuminated by inspirations from above some beautiful intuitive souls. It remained, for choice thinkers, the only possible explanation of what had become, for the masses, the profound mystery of life.

Not only did the finders, in their poems and songs, make discreet allusions to it, but powerful spirits like Bonaventura and Dante Alighieri mention it in a formal manner. Frédéric Ozanam (1813–1853), the Catholic writer, recognized that the plot of Dante's Divine Comedy follows very closely the broad lines of the ancient initiation, based, as we have seen, on the plurality of existences. Cardinal Nicholas of Cusa (1401–1464) supported in the Vatican the theory of the plurality of lives and inhabited worlds, with the assent of Pope Eugene IV.

Thomas Moore, Paracelsus, Jacob Boehme, Giordano Bruno, Campanella either affirmed or taught the great synthesis, often to their own demise. Flemish alchemist and writer Franciscus Mercurius Van Helmont (1614–1698), in *De revolutione animarum humanarum* (London, 1684), expounds in two hundred problems all the arguments in favor of the reincarnation of souls.

Are these high intelligences not comparable to mountains peaks, to the icy summits of the Alps, which are the first to receive the heat of the dawn, and to reflect the rays of the sun, also still preserving them when the rest of the Earth is already immersed in the dark?

Islam itself, especially in the new *Koran*, gives pride of place to ideas of *palingenesia*.[193]

Western philosophy has finally enriched it in these last centuries. Ralph Cudworth and David Hume regard it as the most rational theory on immortality. In Lessing, Herder, Hegel, Schelling, Fichte the younger, we find lofty discussion on the subject.

Giuseppe Mazzini said, while responding to Catholic bishops in his work *The Duties of Man and Other Essays* (New York, Cosimo Classics, 2005, reprint, p. 306):

"We believe in an indefinite series of reincarnations of the soul, from life to life, from world to world; each of which represents an advance from the anterior; and we reject the possibility of irrevocable perdition as a blasphemy against God ..."

Let us now go back to the origins of the French people, where we find the idea of successive lives hovering over the land of Gaul. It vibrates in the accents of the bards, sounding in the great voice of the forests: "I wandered in one hundred worlds, lived in one hundred circles." (Bardic chant: *Barddas, Cad Goddeu*)

It is the French national tradition par excellence; it inspired our ancestors with a contempt for death, with heroism in combat. It must be dear to all those who feel attached by heart or blood to this Celtic race, mobile, enthusiastic, generous, passionate for justice, always ready to fight for great causes.

"During the battles against the Romans," said Mr. d'Arbois de Jubainville, professor at the Collège de France,

---

[193] See *Koran*, sura 2, verse 26; sura 7, verse 55; sura 17, verse 52; sura 14, verse 25.

"the Druids remained motionless as statues, receiving wounds without running away or defending themselves. They knew they were immortal and always expected to find, in another part of the world, a new and freshly young body."[194]

Druids were not only brave, they were also profound scholars.[195] Their worship was that of Nature, celebrated under the dark vault of oaks or on the cliffs beaten by storms. The *Barddas' Triads* proclaim the evolution of souls from "circles of being" – from Annwn (lowest state), slowly rising the long spiral of existences in Abred (probation state), to finally reach, after many deaths and rebirths, Gwynvyd (perfect liberty), the circle of bliss.

The *Triads* are the most wonderful monument left of the ancient wisdom of bards and Druids. They open unlimited perspectives to the astonished eyes of researchers. I will mention only three, those that more directly related to the subject at hand, Triads 19, 21 and 36:[196]

"**19.** The three principal necessities before fullness of knowledge [science and virtue] can be obtained: to traverse Abred; to traverse Gwynvyd; and the remembrance of all as far as Annwn."

"**21.** The three instrumentalities of God in Abred [circle of planetary worlds] for the subduing of evil and Cythraul [the devil], and escaping from them towards Gwynvyd [circle of joyous worlds]: necessity; forgetfulness; and death."

---

[194] Cf. TACITUS, *Libri ab excessu divi Augusti*, book XVI, ch. 30.

[195] This is what Julius CAESAR asserted in *The Commentaries of the Gallic War* (Cincinnati and New York: Van Antwerp, Bragg & Co., 1877), "Commentarius Sextus," 14, p. 136.

[196] *Welsh Triads*, published by Edward WILLIAMS (Swansea: Cyhoeddwyd Gan J. Williams, 1829), after the Welsh original and the translation of Edward DAFYDD. [Trans. note: Triads 19, 21 and 36 above transcribed from *Barddas* (Trans. from the Welsh by J. Williams Ab Ithel, London: Longman, 1862), pp. 173, 175 and 177.]

"36. The three stabilities [foundations] of knowledge: to have traversed every state of life; to remember every state and its incidents; and to be able to traverse every state, as one would wish, for the sake of experience and judgment; and this will be obtained in the circle of Gwynvyd."

Some writers have understood from those bardic texts that the later lives of the soul are pursued exclusively on other worlds. Here are two cases demonstrating that the Gauls also admitted reincarnation on Earth. I drew them from the *Cours de Littérature Celtique* [*Course of Celtic Literature*] of Mr. d'Arbois de Jubainville:[197]

The famous Irish hero Finn Mac Cumail is reborn as Mongan Mac Fiachna, son of Fiachna, King of Ulster (Northern Ireland), around the year 603 AD, and later succeeded him to the throne. The *Annals of Tigernach* fixes Finn's death in the year 273 AD, at Ath Brea on the Boyne. "A second birth," says Arbois of Jubainville, gives him a new life and a throne in Ireland [centuries later]."

The Celts also practiced the evocation of the dead. A dispute had arisen between Mongan and Forgoll about the death of King Fothad, of which he had been an eyewitness, and of the place where the king had lost his life: "He evoked," says the same author, "from the kingdom of dead, Cailte, a companion of his combats. By the time the third day was about to expire, Cailte's testimony provided proof that Mongan had said it right."

The other reincarnation goes back to a much older period. Some time before our era, Eochaid Airem, supreme King of Ireland, had married Etain, daughter of a man

---

[197] Vol. I, pages 266–267. See also Arbois de JUBAINVILLE, Les Druides et les Dieux Celtiques, pp. 137–140. See also the ancient *Book of Leinster*, p. 41; *The Annals of Tigernach*, published by Whitley STOKES; *Revue Celtique*, vol. XVII, page 21; J. O'Donovan, *Annals of the Kingdom of Ireland by the Four Masters* (Dublin: Hodges & Smith, 1848), vol. I, note 1, "Fintain's Grave," p. 4.

called Etar. Etain had previously been born in the Celtic country, several centuries before. In that previous life, she was the daughter of Aillil and wife of Midir, deified after death for her exploits.

It is probable that in the history of Celtic times there were many cases of reincarnation; but we know that Druids did not confide in writing and were content with oral teaching. The documents relating to their science and philosophy are rare and relatively recent.

After centuries of oblivion, Celtic philosophy has reemerged in modern France. It has been reconstituted or supported by a whole host of brilliant writers: Charles Bonnet, Dupont de Nemours, Pierre-Simon Ballanche, Jean Reynaud, Henri Martin, Pierre Leroux, Charles Fourier, Alphonse Esquiros, Michelet, Victor Hugo, Flammarion, Pezzani, Fauvety, and Strada, among others.

"To be born, to die, be reborn again and incessantly progress, that is the law," said Allan Kardec. Thanks to him, thanks to the Spiritist school of thought of which he is the founder, the belief in the successive lives of the soul has become widespread, going throughout the Western world, where it has millions of followers today. Testimonies of the spirits came to give it a definitive sanction. With the exception of a few little evolved souls for whom the past is still shrouded in darkness, all these spirits, in messages collected in France, affirm the plurality of existences and the indefinite progress of beings.

They say in essence that earthly life is only a training, a preparation for eternal life. Limited to a single existence, in its ephemeral duration, it cannot answer to such a vast objective. Reincarnations are the stages of the path that all souls must travel in their ascension; it is the mysterious ladder which, from obscure regions through all the worlds of forms, leads us to the realm of light. Our existences unfold through the centuries; they go by successively and renew themselves. At each of them, we shed a little of the evil that is in us. Slowly, we move forward, penetrating further into the sacred path, until we have acquired the merits that will grant us access to higher circles, from which radiate eternal Beauty, Wisdom, Truth, and Love.

A careful study of the history of peoples shows us not only the universal character of the belief in reincarnations. It also allows us to follow the magnificent sequence of causes and effects that reverberate through time in our social order. Above all we see that these effects are reborn of themselves (palingenesia), and return to their own principle; they enclose individuals and nations in the network of an inescapable law.

From this point of view, the lessons from the past are striking. The testimony of the centuries is imbued with a character of majesty which hits the most jaded individuals, showing the irresistible force of the law. All the evil done, all the blood shed, all the tears shed, fall sooner or later, inevitably, onto their authors, whether individuals or whole communities. The same guilty facts, the same errors will entail similarly harmful consequences. As long as humans continue to live in hostility to one another, by opposing and tearing themselves apart, the works of blood and mourning will continue, and humanity will suffer to the very depths of its bowels. There will be collective expiations, as well as individual atonements. Through time, an immanent justice is brought to bear upon humankind, bringing to life all the elements of decadence and destruction, all the seeds of death, which nations sow in their own bosom each time they violate the higher laws.

If we look at the history of the world, we will see that the youth of humanity, like that of the individual, had its periods of troubles, distractions, and painful experiences. A procession of human misery unfolds through its pages. Deep falls alternate with upward climbs, triumphs with setbacks.

Precarious civilizations signal the first ages. The biggest empires crumble one after the other in the fray of passions. Egypt, Nineveh, Babylon, the empire of the Persians fell. Rome and Byzantium, gnawed by corruption, collapse under the pressure of barbarian invasions.

In Europe, after the Hundred Years' War and the torment of Joan of Arc, England was struck by a terrible civil war, The War of Roses between the houses of York and Lancaster, which brought their nation to the brink of ruin.

What has become of Spain, responsible for so many tortures and slaughtering, proud Spain with its *conquistadores* and its Holy Office? Where now is this once vast empire on which, it used to be said, the sun never set?

See the imperial house of the Habsburgs, heirs of the Holy Roman Empire, and perhaps reincarnations of the executioners of the Hussites! The house of Austria was struck in all its members: Maximilian was shot, Rudolf died during a drunken orgy; the Empress Elizabeth was murdered; then came Franz Ferdinand's turn. The emperor with graying head remained alone in the midst of the ruins of his family, and, finally, with the war, there came defeat, ruin, and the total dislocation of his states.

Where are all these empires now, founded as they were on iron and blood. That of the Caliphs, that of the Mongols, that of the Carolingians, that of Charles V? Napoleon used to say: "Everything has to be paid for." And he himself had to pay. France paid with him: Napoleon's empire passed like a meteor!

Let us stop for a moment on this man's prodigious destiny, which, after having thrown a dazzling brilliance in his trajectory throughout the world, died miserably on a rock in the Atlantic. His life is well known to all, and therefore, better than any other, should serve as an example. As Maurice Maeterlinck puts it, one thing is clearly visible: The three greatest iniquities committed by Napoleon turned into the three main causes of his fall:

"The first was the murder of the Duc d'Enghien, condemned by order, without trial or proof, and executed in the trenches of Vincennes; an assassination that sowed insatiable hatred and vengeance in the path of the guilty dictator. Then the detestable intrigues whereby he lured the too trustful, easy-going Bourbons to Bayonne, that he might rob them of their hereditary crown; and the horrible war that ensued, a war that cost the lives of three hundred thousand men, swallowed up all the morality and energy of the empire, most of its prestige, almost all its convictions, almost all the devotion it inspired, and engulfed its prosperous destiny. And finally the frightful, unpardonable Russian campaign, wherein his fortune came at last to utter shipwreck amid the ice of the Berezina and the snow-bound Polish steppes."[198]

For fifty years the diplomatic history of Europe has not escaped these rules. The faults against fairness and impartiality were struck by its writers, as if touched by an invisible hand.

Russia, after the disintegration of Poland, lent its moral support to Prussia for the invasion of the Danish duchies; "one of the greatest crimes of piracy committed in modern times," said a historian. It was punished, first

---

198 M. MAETERLINCK, *The Buried Temple* (Trans. A. Sutro. London: G. Allen & Unwin Ltd., 1902), pp. 32–33.

by Prussia itself, which, in 1877, at the Congress of Berlin, was deprived of all the advantages gained over Turkey; and then, still more cruelly, by the setbacks of the Manchurian war and their prolonged impact throughout the empire of the Czars, which ultimately culminated in a bloody revolution and the Bolshevik chaos.

In the last centuries, England has often pursued a cold and selfish policy. After the Transvaal War (1880–1881), it has been weakened. Perhaps touching those prophetic times in striking terms, Sir Robert Talbot wrote: "The address of our statesmen will immortalize them by contriving for us a descent which shall not be a fall, by making us rather resemble Holland than Carthage and Venice."[199]

The detachment of Ireland, of Egypt, and the revolt of India have since come to confirm these forecasts regarding the British Empire.

Such will be the fate of all the nations that were great because of their philosophers and thinkers, but had the weakness of putting their destiny back in the hands of too greedy politicians.

Napoleon III in exile, Bismarck in disgrace and painful retreat, thus began to expiate their lack of respect for the moral laws.

There is no need to linger longer over these facts. Did we not see unfold before our very eyes, from 1914 to 1918, the immense tragedy World War I, that vengeful tragedy which left Germany defeated, and punished for its pride and crimes?

At the same time, it must be admitted that France received a terrible lesson, perhaps due to the levity, the improvidence, and the sensualism of a large number of our compatriots. Yet, with the victory in WWI, it regained its prestige before the world. Thus once again its high

---

[199] [Trans. note] in R. TALBOT, *Letters from the French Nation* (London: B. White, 1771), vol. II, p. 204.

mission was confirmed, a providential role which seems to be devolved into it, and which consists in proclaiming and defending, by all forms of the word and by the sword, the right to truth and justice!

Germany and Austria, riveted in a fierce pact of complicity, had dreamed of hegemony over Europe and the domination of the world: one over the East, the other over the West. In the pursuit of their goal, they have trampled on the most solemn commitments, for example to Belgium; they did not shrink from the most heinous deals. What was the result? After four years of fierce struggle, the central empires rolled into the abyss. Austria is no more than a shadow, a phantom of a nation; Germany, weakened and ruined, is beset by all sorts of internal struggles and economic difficulties.

Were they not repercussions of events of the war between France and Germany in 1870–1871? Even though German won the war, it later knew defeat and anarchy.

Perhaps never in any war has the struggle of two principles been more evident. On one side, brutal force, and on the other, law and freedom. What proves that God does not lose interest in the fate of our little globe is that the law and freedom prevailed! It can be said that, like the Greeks at Marathon and Salamis, the soldiers of the Marne and the Verdun, supported by the invisible powers, preserved humanity from the yoke of the sword and saved civilization.[200] Such will be the impartial judgment of history!

Indeed, history contains a great lesson. We can read in its depths the action of a powerful law. Through the succession of events, sometimes we feel as if a superhuman breath is passing; in the middle of the night of the ages,

---

[200] See Léon Denis, *Le Monde Invisible et la Guerre* [*Wars and the Unseen World*] (Paris: Librairie de Sciences Psychiques, 1919), *passim*.

at times we see, in shining flashes, the radiations of an eternal thought.

For the nations as well for the individuals, it is a matter of justice being served. As far as the nations are concerned, we have just seen it manifest itself in the chain of events. For the individual, it is not the same. It cannot be followed, especially when its action, instead of being immediate, takes place only in the long run. The reincarnation, the descent into the flesh, the dark cap of matter that falls on the soul making us forget the past, while hiding the succession of causes and effects. But we have seen them, especially in the phenomena of trance, provided we can lift the veil from the past and read what is engraved in the depths of the human being, the adversities that strike the latter. In great pains, setbacks, and poignant afflictions, we are compelled to recognize the action of an earlier cause of a moral nature, and to bow to the majesty of the laws which preside over the destinies of all souls, societies and worlds!

The great plan unfolds in formidable lines: God sends to humanity Its messiahs, Its revealers, both visible and invisible; Its guides, Its educators of all kinds. Yet humans, free in their thought, in their conscience, either listen to them or deny them. Human beings are free; social inconsistencies are of their own doing. They throw this muddled note into the universal concert; however this discordant note does not always succeed in dominating the harmony of the centuries.

Geniuses, sent from above, shine like torches in the dark night. Without going back to the highest antiquity, without mentioning the likes of Hermes, Zoroaster (or

Zarathustra), and Krishna, since the dawning of Christian times, we saw the prophets rise to enormous stature, giants who still dominate History today. It was they, in fact, who prepared the way for Christianity, the master religion, which came later with the evolution of times, advocating universal fraternity. Then we see Christ, the man of sorrow, the man of love whose thought shines with imperishable beauty, and the drama of Golgotha, the ruin of Jerusalem, the dispersion of the Jews.

On this side of the blue sea, the Mediterranean, there was the flowering of the Greek genius, prime focus of education, splendor of art and science, where humanity came to light. Finally, the Roman power, which taught the world law, discipline, and social life.

Then come the ages of dark ignorance, a thousand years of barbarism, the swirl of invasions, the emergence of savage elements in civilization, the lowering of the intellectual level, the night of thought. But Gutenberg, Christopher Columbus, and Luther appear. Gothic cathedrals are built, unknown continents are revealed, religion is disciplined. Thanks to printing, the new idea spread to all parts of the world. After the Reformation came the Renaissance, then the Revolutions!

And today, after many vicissitudes and struggles, in spite of religious persecutions, civil tyrannies and inquisitions, thought has been emancipated. The problem of life which, with the conceptions of a fanatical and blind Church, remained impenetrable, will have its solution enlightened again. Like a star on the foggy sea, the great law reappears. The world will be reborn to the life of the spirit. Human existence will no longer be an obscure impasse, but a road largely open to the future.

The laws of nature and history complement each other and assert themselves in their imposing unity. A circular law presides over the evolution of both beings and things; it governs the march of the centuries and that of humanity. Each destiny gravitates in an immense circle, each life describes an orbit. The whole human ascension is divided into cycles, spirals, which are enlarged so as to take on an increasingly universal meaning.

Just as nature is constantly renewed in its resurrections, from the metamorphoses of insects to the birth and death of worlds, so human communities are born, develop and die in successive forms. But they die only to be reborn and grow in perfections, institutions, arts and sciences, religions and philosophies.

At times of crisis and misguidance, special envoys come to restore obscured truths and put humanity back on track. And despite the flight of the best human souls to higher spheres, earthly civilizations are changing and societies have been evolving. In spite of the evils inherent to our planet, in spite of the multiple needs which oppress us, the testimony of the ages tells us that, in their centuries-long ascension, personal intelligences are refined, hearts become more sensitive; humanity as a whole has slowly been rising. From today, it aspires to achieve peace in solidarity.

At each rebirth, the individual being plunges back into the mass. The soul, by reincarnating, takes a new mask. Its previous personalities fade for a whole. However, through the centuries, we recognize some great personages from the past. We find Krishna in Christ and, in a lesser order, Virgil in Lamartine, Vercingetorix in Desaix, Caesar in Napoleon.

In a certain beggar with haughty features and imperious eyes, squatting on manure at the gates of Rome, covered in ulcers and reaching out to passers-by, it would have been possible to recognize in the 19th century, a reincarnation of the notorious Roman empress Messalina, according to indications given by some spirits.

How many other guilty souls live among us, hidden in deformed bodies, prey to ills, to infirmities that they themselves have prepared, molded so to speak by their thoughts, by their actions of former times. Dr. Pascal tells us:

"The study of the past lives of some particularly struck individuals revealed some strange secrets: here, a betrayal causing a massacre is punished centuries later by a painful life from childhood, and by an infirmity carrying in it the seal of its origin – the muteness: the lips that betrayed can no longer speak; there, an inquisitor is reincarnated in a sick body from an early age, in a family environment eminently hostile, and with clear intuitions of past cruelty: the most acute physical and moral sufferings pursued him without respite."[201]

Cases like these are more numerous than we think. In them we must see the application of an inflexible rule. All our actions, according to their nature, result in an increase or diminution of liberty. Hence, for the guilty, the rebirth into miserable envelopes, prisons of the soul, images and reflections of their past.

Neither the problems of individual life nor those of social life can be explained without the law of rebirth. All the mystery of being lies there. Through it, our past is lighted up and the future grows. Our personality is unexpectedly vast. We understand that we did not appear just yesterday in the universe, as many still believe; on the contrary, our point of origin, our first birth, recedes into the depths of time. We feel connected to this humanity by a thousand links, woven slowly through the centuries;

---

[201] See T. PASCAL, *Les Lois de la Destinée* (Paris: Publications Théosophiques, 1904), p. 208.

its story is ours; we have traveled with it in the ocean of ages, faced the same perils, suffered the same setbacks. Only temporarily we forget about these things. One day, a whole world of memories will wake up in us. The past, the future, the whole of history will take on a new character, a deep interest. Our admiration will increase for such vast destinies. The divine laws will appear to us greater, even more sublime. And life itself will become beautiful and desirable, despite its trials, despite its many ills!

XVIII

JUSTICE AND ACCOUNTABILITY, THE PROBLEM OF EVIL

THE LAW OF REBIRTH, as said before, governs universal life. With a little attention, we could read in all nature, as in a book, the mystery of death and resurrection.

The seasons follow one another with imposing rhythm. Winter is the sleep of things; spring, their awakening. The day alternates with the night; rest follows the day before; the spirit goes back to higher regions, and then, thus fortified, comes down again and resumes its interrupted tasks.

The transformations of plants and animals are no less significant. The plant dies to be reborn with each return of the sap; everything fades to bloom again. The larva, the chrysalis, the butterfly, are all examples that reproduce, with more or less fidelity, the alternating phases of immortal life.

How could humans alone be placed outside this law? While everything is connected by powerful and numerous bonds, how to admit that our life is like a point thrown, without any ties, in the whirlwinds of time and space? Nothing before, nothing after! No, we humans, like all things, are subject to the same eternal law. All that has lived will revive in other forms, to evolve and to perfect themselves. Nature only makes us die in order to revive us. Already, because of the periodic renewal of the molecules of our body, dispersed and brought back by the vital currents, by daily nutrition and loss, we live in many different envelopes in a single life. So, is it not logical to admit that we will inhabit other envelopes in the future?

The succession of existences is therefore offered to us as a work of improvement and making the most of our opportunities. After each earthly life, the soul reaps and collects in its fluidic body the experiences and the fruits of the past existence. All its progress is reflected in that subtle form of which it is inseparable, that is, in that ethereal body, lucid, transparent, which, being purified together with it, becomes this marvelous instrument, the harp that vibrates to all the breaths of the infinite.

Thus the psychical being is found in all phases of its ascension, as achieved by itself. No noble aspiration is sterile; no sacrifice is in vain. And in this immense work, all are associated, from the most obscure soul to the most radiant genius. An endless chain connects all beings in the majestic unity of the Cosmos. It is an effusion of light and love which, from divine heights, flows and spreads over all, to regenerate and fertilize them. It unites all souls in universal and eternal communion, by virtue of a principle which is the most magnificent revelation of modern times.

The soul must conquer, one by one, all the elements, all the attributes of its greatness, of its power, of its happiness. And for that it needs the obstacle, the resistant nature – hostile even – the adversarial matter, whose demands and rough lessons provoke the soul's efforts and form its experience. From here too, in the lower stages of life, the need of trials and suffering, so that one soul's sensitivity awakens and that at the same time it exercises its free will and develops its choices and its conscience. We must fight to make triumph possible and to bring up the hero in us. Without any iniquity, arbitrariness, or treason, could anyone suffer and die for justice?

Physical suffering and moral anguish are necessary for the spirit to become etherealized, to rid itself of its coarse particles, so that the faint spark that broods in the depths of unconsciousness grows into a pure and ardent flame, a radiant consciousness, the central focus of will, energy and virtue.

We only know, taste and really appreciate the goods slowly and painfully acquired through own efforts. The soul, if created perfect as some thinkers would wish, would be incapable of appreciating and even comprehending its perfection, its happiness. Without terms of comparison, without any possible exchanges with its fellow beings, perfect in itself, without purpose to its activity, the soul would be condemned to inaction, to inertia, which would be the worst of states. Because for the spirit to live is to act, to grow, to always conquer new titles, new merits, a place always higher in the luminous and infinite hierarchy. And to deserve them, one must have suffered, struggled, and suffered. To taste abundance one must have experienced privation. To appreciate the clarity of the day, one must have crossed the shadows of the night. Pain is a condition for finding joy and the price of virtue. And virtue is the most precious good there is in the universe.

To build one's own self, one's individuality, through thousands and thousands of lives, accomplished on hundreds of different worlds; and, under the direction of our elder fellow beings, our friends of the spiritual world, to climb the paths of heaven, climbing higher and higher to make our field of action ever larger, always proportionate to the work accomplished or dreamed, is to ultimately become one of the actors of the divine drama, one of the agents of God in the eternal Work. To work for the universe, as the universe has worked for us, that is the secret of our destiny!

Thus the soul ascends from sphere to sphere, from circle to circle, united to fellow beings that it has loved. It moves on, pursuing its peregrinations, in search of divine perfections. Once arriving at higher regions, it is freed from the law of rebirths. Then reincarnation is no longer an obligation for it, but occurs only as an act of free will, such as the fulfillment of a mission or a work involving self-sacrifice.

When he reaches the highest summits, the spirit sometimes says, "I am free; I forever broke the irons that chained me to material worlds. I acquired science, energy, love. But what I have acquired, I want to share with my fellow human beings, and for that I will return to live among them again; I will go and offer them what is best in me; I will take again a body of flesh. I will come down again to those who toil, to those who suffer, to those who are ignorant, to help them, to console them, to enlighten them!" And then, we have Lao-tzu; we have the Buddha; we have Socrates; we have Christ; in a word, all the great souls which gave their lives to humanity!

Summing up: in this study, the importance of the reincarnation tenet has been demonstrated. Here we have seen one of the essential bases on which New Spiritualism rests. Its reach is immense. It explains the inequality of human conditions, the infinite variety of aptitudes, faculties, characters. It dispels the troubling mysteries and contradictions of life; it solves the problem of evil. Through it, order succeeds disorder; the light is in the midst of chaos; injustices disappear, the apparent iniquities of fate vanish, to give way to the strong and majestic law of repercussions of our actions and their consequences. And this law of immanent righteousness which governs the worlds, God has inscribed it in the depths of all things and in the human conscience.

The tenet of reincarnation gets closer to humans like no other belief, by teaching them their common origins and purposes, showing them the solidarity that binds them all together in the past, in the present, and in the future. It tells them that there is no one among them who is disinherited or favored; each one is the result of one's deeds, master of one's destiny. Our sufferings are the consequences of the past, or the austere school where high virtues and great duties are learned.

We must go through all the stages of this huge road. We will undergo all social conditions, so as to acquire the qualities inherent to different environments. Thus, this solidarity which binds us in a final harmony compensates for the infinite variety of beings, resulting from the inequality of their efforts and also from the necessities of their evolution. With it, no more envy, no more contempt, no more hatred! The smallest among us may have been the greatest, and the greatest will grow small if they abuse their superiority. Each in their turn, to joy as to sorrow! From there, a true communion of souls. We all feel forever united on the degrees of our collective ascension; we learn to help, to support one another, to reach out!

Through the cycles of time, everyone is perfecting and rising. The criminals of the past will become wise men in the future. An hour will come when our defects will be erased, where our vices, our moral wounds will be healed. Frivolous souls will become serious; obscure intelligences will illuminate. All the forces of evil that vibrate in us will be transformed into forces of good. From being weak, indifferent, and closed to all great thoughts, a powerful spirit will emerge one day, which will gather all knowledge, all qualities, and become able to accomplish the most sublime things.

This will be the work built up from successive existences. It will require a great many reincarnations, no doubt, to make such a change, to strip the bark of our imperfections, to remove the asperities of our characters, transforming souls of darkness into souls of light! But nothing is powerful and durable that has not taken the necessary time to germinate, emerge from the shadows, and rise to the sky. This is what the tree, the forest, the layers of the ground, the stars and the worlds tell us in their deep language. No seed is lost; no effort is useless. The stem gives its leaf and its fruit only at the appointed time. Life begins on the orbs of space only after immense geological periods.

See these beautiful diamonds that adorn the beauty of women and sparkle with a thousand lights. How many metamorphoses did they have to undergo to acquire this incomparable purity, this dazzling brilliance? What a slow incubation for them to develop within the dense obscurity of matter!

It is the same when it comes to the human entity. In order to get rid of its coarse elements and acquire all its brilliance, it needs even longer periods of evolution and slow incubation in the flesh.

It is here, in this work of perfecting ourselves, that the utility, the importance of the lives of trials, those modest and effaced lives, fully appear, our lives of toil and duty to overcome savage passions, pride and selfishness, to heal our moral wounds. From this point of view, the role of the humble, the little ones in this world, and their scorned tasks, are revealed in all their greatness: we can now better understand the need to return to the flesh to redeem and purify ourselves.

In solving the problem of evil, New Spiritualism[202] shows once more its superiority over other philosophical doctrines.

For evolutionist materialists, evil and pain are constant and universal. Everywhere, say Taine, Soury, Nietzsche, Haeckel, we see evil flourish and evil will always prevail in humanity. However, they add, with progress, evil will become less frequent, albeit more painful, because our physical and moral sensibility will increase. And it will always be necessary to suffer and cry, without hope, without consolation, for example during catastrophes, irreparable in those philosophers' eyes, such as the death of a loved one. Therefore, evil will always prevail over good.

Some religious philosophies are not much more comforting. According to Catholicism, evil also seems to predominate in the universe and Satan seems much more powerful than God. Hell, according to their fateful word, is constantly peopled with innumerable crowds, while paradise is the sharing of the rare elect. The orthodox believer sees the loss, the separation from beings that were dear to them, as almost as final an event as for the materialist. There is never complete certainty for anyone to find them again, to rejoin them one day.

---

[202] [Trans. note] See footnote 12 above.

With New Spiritualism, this question takes on an entirely different aspect. Evil is no more than a transitory state of being in the process of evolution toward good. Evil is the measure of the inferiority of worlds and individuals; it is also, as we have seen, the sanction of the past. Every scale has degrees. Our earthly lives represent the lower degrees of our eternal ascension.

Everything around us demonstrates the inferiority of the planet we inhabit. Very inclined on its axis, its astronomical situation is in its weather: storms, tidal waves, seismic convulsions, hot heat, rigorous cold. Earthly humanity, to subsist, is condemned to a painful labor. Millions of humans, bent under their excessive burdens, know neither rest nor well-being. Now, there is a close relationship between the physical order of the worlds and the moral state of the societies that inhabit them. Imperfect worlds such as the Earth are reserved, in general, for souls that are still little evolved.

However, our stay in this environment is only temporary and subordinated to the requirements of our psychic education. Other worlds, better shared in all respects, await us. Evil, pain, suffering, all attributes of earthly life, have their obligatory role. They are the whip, the spur that instigates us and carry us forward.

Evil, from this point of view, has only a relative and temporary character; it is a condition of the still infant soul directing its first attempts at life. By the very fact of the progress accomplished, evil diminishes little by little, disappears, and vanishes as the soul ascends the ladder leading to power, virtue, wisdom!

Then justice in the universe is revealed. There are no more the idea of elect or reprobate individuals. Each and every one suffers the consequences of their actions, but all of them repair, redeem themselves and rise up sooner or later, to evolve from the dark and material worlds to the divine light. All loving souls come together, join in their ascension, to cooperate together in the great work and participate in universal communion.

Therefore there is no real evil, no absolute evil in the universe, but everywhere the slow and progressive realization of a higher ideal; everywhere the action of a force, of a power, of a cause which, while leaving us free, draws us and leads us to a better state. Everywhere the great toil of all beings working to develop in them, at the cost of immense efforts, their sensibility, their feeling, their will, and their love!

Let me insist on the notion of justice, which is truly paramount: paramount, because it is a need, an imperative necessity for all to know that justice is not an empty word, that there is actually a sanction for every duty and a compensation for every pain. No system can satisfy our reason, our conscience, unless it realizes the notion of justice in all its magnitude. This notion is engraved in us; it is the law of the soul and also of the entire universe, and it is for having misunderstood it that so many philosophical doctrines have been weakened and extinguished nowadays around us.

Indeed the philosophical doctrine of successive lives is resplendent with the idea of justice. It highlights it, and gives it an incomparable brilliance. All our lives are in solidarity with one another and are linked together rigorously. Our actions and their consequences constitute a succession of elements which are connected to each other by a close relation of cause and effect. We constantly suffer inevitable results in ourselves, in our inner being, as well as in the external conditions of our life. Our active will is a cause generating more or less distant effects, whether good or bad, that fall back upon us and form the fabric of our destinies.

Christianity, by renouncing this world, relegated happiness and justice to the realm of the Hereafter. And if its teachings were sufficient for the simple minds and the believers, it made easy for the skilled skeptics to do without justice, on the pretext that its reign was not of this world. But with the proof of successive lives, the story is quite different. Justice is no longer relegated to a chimeric and unknown domain. It is right here; it is in us and around us that it exercises its empire. Human beings must repair on the physical plane the harm they may have done on the same plane. Humans descend again into the crucible of life, into the very environment where they have been guilty, to those whom they have deceived, defrauded, and robbed, in order to suffer the consequences of their previous actions.

With the principle of rebirth, the idea of justice is clarified and can be verified. The moral law, the law of Good is revealed in all its harmony. Humans can finally understand it: this life is only a link in the great chain of one's existences; whatever one sows, he or she will reap it sooner or later. Therefore, it is no longer possible to ignore our duties or to evade our responsibilities. In this, as in everything else, the next day becomes the product of the day before. Under the apparent confusion of facts, we discover the relations that bind them. Instead of being enslaved to an inflexible destiny whose cause would be external to us, we become its masters and authors. Far from being dominated by fate, we dominate it and create it by our own will and actions. The ideal of justice is no longer relegated to a transcendental world; we can define its terms in every renewed human life, in its relation to the universal laws, in real and tangible things.

This great light is shed precisely at a moment when old beliefs are sinking under the weight of time, where all idle systems are cracking, where the gods of the past are being veiled and removed. For a long time, human thought has been anxious, groping in the night in search of a new moral edifice that would shelter it. And now the tenet of rebirth has come to offer humans the ideal necessary to any actively evolving society, while, at the same time, providing the corrective indispensable to curb violent appetites and excessive ambitions; greed of riches, positions, honors; a rampart raised against the overflow of sensualism that threatens to engulf society.

With this tenet, humans learn to endure, without bitterness or rebellion, the painful existences indispensable to their purification. They learn to submit themselves to natural and transitory inequalities that are the result of the law of evolution; to disdain the artificial and unhealthy divisions stemming from prejudices of castes, religions or races. Such prejudices will vanish entirely on the day when we learn that all spirits, in their ascending lives, must pass through the most diverse environments.

Thanks to the notion of successive lives, together with our individual accountabilities, those shared by whole communities become crystal clear to us. There is a tendency among our contemporaries to relegate the burden of present difficulties to future generations. Convinced that they will never return to Earth, they leave to our successors the task of solving the thorny problems of political and social life.

With the law of destinies, this matter changes completely. Not only will the evil that we have done fall back upon on us, making us pay our debts to the last penny, but the social milieu where we perpetrated our vices and iniquities, will take us back in its heavy gear on our return to Earth; and we will have to suffer all its imperfections.

This society, to which we will have asked a great deal and given back little, will once again become *our* society, a stepmother for its selfish and ungrateful children.

During our earthly stages, whether powerful or weak, leading or led, we will often feel the weight of the injustices we have practiced. And let us not forget one thing: Obscure lives, humble and subdued lives, will be the most numerous for each of us, as long as individuals with facility, education and learning represent only a minority of all the population of the world.

But when the great tenet becomes the basis of human education and is shared by all, when the proof of successive lives appear before everybody's eyes, then, the most educated, the most thoughtful among us, developing in them the intuitions of the past, will understand that they have already lived in all social environments, and they will show more tolerance and kindness towards the lesser ones. They will feel that there is less wickedness and bitterness than actually rebellion and suffering in the souls of the disinherited. And what an admirable advantage it would be for them to draw on their own experience in order to spread enlightenment, hope, and consolation around them.

Then personal interest and individual good will become the good of all. Everyone will feel inclined to cooperate more actively in the improvement of society, within which it will be necessary to be reborn in order to evolve with it and move toward the future.

The current hour is yet another hour of struggle: the nations' struggle for the conquest of the globe, the classes' struggle for the conquest of welfare and power.

All around us blind and deep forces agitate themselves, forces that ignored one another yesterday and today are organizing themselves and coming into action. A society dies, another is born. The ideal of the past collapses. What will tomorrow's society be like?

A transition period has started; a different phase of human evolution has just begun, an obscure phase full of both promises and threats. In the soul of the rising generations, rest the closed buds of new blossoms: will they be flowers of evil or flowers of good?

Many are alarmed; others feel terrified. Let us not doubt the future of humanity, its ascension to the light, and instead spread around us, with indefatigable courage and perseverance, the truths that assure the future and make societies strong and happy.

The defects of our social organization come mainly from this: our legislators, with their narrow conceptions, include only the horizon of material life. Not understanding the evolutionary purpose of existence and the sequence of our earthly lives, they have established a state of things incompatible with the real goals of humans and society.

The conquest of power by the larger number of people is not made to enlarge this point of view. People usually follow the dull instinct that drives them. Unable to measure the merit and worth of their representatives, they too often bring to power those who espouse their passions and share their blindness. Popular education is to be redone entirely; for only enlightened individuals can collaborate intelligently, courageously and conscientiously in social renovation.

Among current claims, one speculates excessively on the notion of right; we thus excite the appetites and whip up moods. We forget that rights are inseparable from duties, and even that is only a resultant effect. Hence, a break in balance, a reversal of relations of cause and effect, that is to say, of the duty to the right in the distribution of social benefits, which constitutes a permanent cause of division and hatred among human beings. The individual who only considers his or her own interest and personal rights is still placed very low on the scale of evolution.

As Jean-Baptiste André Godin,[203] founder of the cooperative Familistère de Guise in France, used to say: "The right is achieved through an accomplished duty." The services rendered to humanity being the cause, the law becomes the effect. In a well-organized society, each citizen will rank according to his or her personal worth, their degree of evolution, and to the extent of their social contribution.

Individuals should occupy only a deserved position. An individual's right is in equal proportion to their capacity for the good. That is the rule, that is the basis of universal order, and as long as social order does not fully reflect it as its faithful image, it will be precarious and unstable.

Under this rule, each member of a community, instead of claiming fictitious rights, must strive to become worthy of it by increasing their own value and participation in the common work. Thus the social ideal is transformed, a sense of harmony develops, the field of altruism widens

Yet in the current state of things, in a society where so many passions still fester, where so many brutal forces agitate themselves; and in the midst of a civilization made of selfishness and greed, incoherence and ill will, sensuality and suffering; many convulsions are to be expected and feared.

---

[203] [Trans. note] The French industrialist, writer, political theorist, and social innovator GODIN (1817–1888) is described by some as "one of the originators of social entrepreneurship" (Boutillier, 2009), and by others as the "inventor of the social economy" (Draperi, 2008).

Sometimes we hear a rumbling stream rise. The complaint of those who suffer is changed into cries of anger. The crowds come gathering. Centuries-long interests are threatened. However a new faith arises, illuminated by a ray from above and supported by facts, on sensible proofs. It says to all, "Remain united, for you are brothers and sister, both here below and in immortality. Work together to soften the conditions of social life, and make your tasks easier tomorrow. Work to increase the treasures of knowledge, wisdom, and power, which are the heritage of humanity. Happiness is not in struggle, in revenge; it is in the union of hearts and wills!"

XIX

THE LAW OF DESTINY

ONCE EVIDENCE OF SUCCESSIVE LIVES is established, the path of our existences is cleared out; the road becomes safe and firmly traced. Now the soul can see its destiny clearly, which is its ascension to the highest wisdom, to the brightest light. Equity governs the world; happiness is in our hands. The Universe can no longer fail, its goal being beauty, its means, justice and love. From then on, all imaginary fears, all terror of the Hereafter vanish. Instead of fearing the future, we taste the joy of eternal certainty. With confidence in the morrow, our strengths redouble; our effort toward good will thus be increased a hundredfold.

Yet one question still remains: by what secret resources does the action of justice exert itself upon the sequence of our lives?

Let me point out, first of all, that the functioning of human justice offers us nothing comparable to the divine law of destinies. The latter is self-fulfilling, without any external intervention, for both individuals and communities. What we call evil, offense, betrayal, murder, determines in those who are guilty a state of mind that delivers them to the blows of fate, to a degree proportional to the gravity of their actions.

This immutable law is, first and foremost, a law of equilibrium. It establishes order in the moral world in the same way that the laws of gravitation and gravity ensure order and balance in the physical world. Its mechanism is both simple and magnificent. All evil is redeemed through pain. What humans accomplish in accordance with the law of good brings them tranquility and contributes to their elevation – any violation of it causes suffering. This law pursues our inner work; it searches the depths of the self; it brings to light the treasures of wisdom and beauty that it contains and, at the same time, eliminates unhealthy tendencies. It will prolong its action and return to the charge as long as it is necessary, until it blossoms in good deeds and vibrates in unison with the divine forces. But in the pursuit of this great work, compensations will be reserved for the soul. Joys, affections, periods of rest and happiness will alternate in the beaded rosary of one's lives with existences of struggle, redemption and reparation. Thus everything is arranged with art, science, and infinite goodness by Providence.

At the start of their race, in their ignorance and weakness, humans often ignore and transgress the law. Hence, the trials, infirmities, and material servitudes. But as soon as the individual becomes enlightened, as soon as he or she learns how to bring the actions of their life into harmony with the universal rule – and for that very reason – they attract less and less misfortunes onto themselves.

Our thoughts and actions are translated into vibrational movements; and their emission focus, by the frequent repetition of these same actions and thoughts, is gradually transformed into a powerful generator for good or for evil. One's self is thus ranked according to the nature of the energies of which it becomes a radiant center. But while the forces of good multiply on their own and grow ever greater, the forces of evil manage only to destroy themselves by their own effects, for these effects invariably come back to their cause, to their emission center, always resulting in painful consequences. Subject like all other beings to an evolutionary impulsion, the wicked see their sensitivity inescapably increase. The vibrations of their actions, of their evil thoughts, after having gone through their trajectory, sooner or later return to them, and oppress them, making them face the necessity of reforming themselves.

This phenomenon could be scientifically explained through the correlation of forces, by this kind of vibrational synchronism which always refers the effect to its cause. There is a demonstration of this well-known fact: in times of epidemics and contagion, it is above all the persons whose vital forces harmonize with the active morbid causes that are struck, while individuals endowed with firm will and free from fear generally remain unscathed.

It is the same when it comes to the moral order. Thoughts of hatred and vengeance, desires to harm others, come from without, cannot act upon us or influence us, unless they find elements that vibrate in unison with them. If there is nothing in us that corresponds to them, these evil forces slip without penetrating us; they return to the one who projected them, to strike the culprits in their turn, either in the present or in the future, when specific circumstances bring them back within the flow of their destinies.

Therefore the law of repercussions for actions taken has something mechanical in it, which is automatic in appearance. However, when it involves hard expiations and painful reparations, higher-order spirits intervene to regulate the trials and accelerate the progress of souls in the process of evolution. Their influence is especially felt at the time of reincarnation, in order to guide these souls in their choice, by determining the conditions and environments favorable to the cure of their moral diseases and the redemption of past faults.

We know that this education is not completely without pain. In this aspect, we must be careful not to see in the trials and ills of humanity the exclusive consequence of past mistakes. All those who suffer are not necessarily guilty in the process of atonement. Many are simply spirits eager for progress, who have chosen painful and laborious lives to draw the moral benefit of any pain they may endure.

However, in general, it is the shock, the conflict between the lower-order being, which is still unaware of itself, and the law of harmony, that generates evil and suffering. It is through the gradual and voluntary return to harmony of this same being that good is restored, that is to say, moral equilibrium. In every thought, in every work, there is action and reaction, and the latter is always proportional in intensity to the action performed. So we can say that the being is reaping exactly what he or she sowed.

It indeed harvests it, since, by its continuous action, it modifies its own nature. It whether etherealizes or materializes its fluidic envelope, which is the vehicle of the soul, the instrument which operates in all its manifestations, and on which the body is modeled physically at each rebirth.

As seen above, our situation in the Hereafter is the result of repeated actions that our will and thoughts constantly exert over the perispirit. Depending on their nature and purpose, they gradually transform it into a subtle and radiant organism, open to the highest perceptions, to the most delicate sensations of spiritual life, able to vibrate harmoniously with the higher-order spirits and to participate in the joys and impressions of the infinite. Conversely, they may turn it into an opaque, coarse form, chained to Earth by its very materiality, and condemned to remain confined to the lower regions.

This continuous action of thought and will, exerted over the perispirit during centuries and through many existences, enables us to understand how our physical aptitudes, as well as our intellectual faculties and our moral qualities, are created and developed.

Our aptitudes for certain types of work, our skills, our dexterity in all things are the result of innumerable mechanical actions accumulated and recorded by our subtle body (the perispirit), just as all the memories and the mental acquisitions are engraved in our deep consciousness. At the time of rebirth, these abilities are transmitted, through a new education, from the external consciousness to the material organs. There lies the explanation for the consummate and almost native skill of certain musicians and, in general, of all those who show a superior performance or execution in some field, which causes surprise at first glance.

The same happens with faculties and virtues, with all the riches of the soul acquired in the course of time. Genius is a long and immense effort of intellectual order, and holiness has been conquered by a centuries-long struggle against passions and inferior attractions.

With a little attention we could study and follow in ourselves the process of our moral evolution. Whenever we perform a good deed, a generous act, a work of charitable love, of commitment; at every sacrifice of one's self; do we not feel a sort of inner elation? Something seems to bloom in us. A flame is ignited or lightens up the depths of one's being.

This sensation is not illusory. The spirit is lighted up by every altruistic thought, every moment of solidarity and pure love. If these thoughts and actions are repeated, multiplied, accumulated, humans find themselves transformed at the end of their earthly existences. The soul and its fluidic envelope will then have acquired a more intense radiation power.

Conversely, every evil thought, every culpable action, every unfortunate habit provokes a constraint, a constriction of the psychical being, whose elements thus become more dense, darken, and charge themselves with coarse fluids.

Violent acts, cruelty, murder, suicide, produce a disturbance in the culprit's organism, a prolonged disruption, which reverberates from rebirth to rebirth on the material body, and is translated into nervous diseases, in tics, convulsions, and even in deformities, infirmities, and in cases of madness, according to the gravity of the causes and the power of the forces in action. Any breach of the law leads to a lessening, a discomfort, a deprivation of liberty.

Impure lives, full of lust, drunkenness and debauchery, bring us back to feeble bodies, devoid of vigor, health and beauty. The human being who abuses his or her vital forces condemns themselves to a miserable future, and to more or less cruel infirmities.

Sometimes the reparation takes place through a long life of suffering, necessary to destroy in us the causes of the evil, or in a short and difficult existence, interrupted by a tragic death. A mysterious attraction sometimes gathers culprits from far away on a given point, to hit them all at once at one place. Examples include famous disasters, major catastrophes, collective deaths, such as the burning of the Charity Bazaar in France in May 1897, the tragic explosion of the Courrières coal mine in the same country, in March 1906, or the great explosion in Jena, Germany; also the sinking of the Titanic among so many other shipwrecks.

This explains such brief existences. They are the complement of previous lives, ended too soon, abridged prematurely, whether by excesses, abuses or by any other moral cause, and which, normally, should have been prolonged.

One must be careful not to equate the deaths of young children with these cases. The short life of a child can be a challenge both for the parents and the spirit who wants to incarnate. In general, it is simply a missed entry into the theater of life, either for physical reason or a lack of adaptation of fluids. In this case, the attempt to incarnate will be renewed a little later in the same family. It reproduces itself until complete success, or, should those difficulties prove insurmountable, it will take place in a more favorable environment.

All these considerations prove it: to ensure the fluidic purification and the good moral state of one's being, one must establish a discipline of thought, and follow a hygiene of cleanliness in one's soul, the same as there is a physical hygiene to observe in order to keep a healthy body.

According to this constant action of thought and will upon the perispirit, we see that reciprocation is absolutely perfect. Each one collects the undying fruit of his or her past and current deeds. They gather it, not by the effect of some external cause, but by a sequence which connects within ourselves pain to joy, effort to success, fault to punishment. Therefore, it is in the secrecy of our most intimate thoughts and in the open visibility of our actions that we must seek the effective cause of our current and future situations.

We are placed according to our merits in the environment where our antecedents call us. If we find ourselves unhappy, it is because we are not perfect enough to enjoy a better fate. But our destiny will improve as soon as we are able to give birth to more selflessness, justice and love. One's being must perfect itself, forever improving its inner nature, increasing its own value, and building up the edifice of its consciousness: this is the purpose of its evolution.

Each of us possesses a particular genius that the Druids used to call *Awen*, that is, the primordial ability of every being to realize one of the special forms of divine thought. God has laid down in the depths of the soul the rudiments of powerful and varied faculties; however, it is one of the forms of its genius that it is called to develop above all others, through constant work, until it has been brought to its point of excellence. These forms are innumerable. These are the multiple aspects of eternal intelligence, wisdom and beauty: music, poetry, eloquence, the gift of invention, the premonition of the future and of hidden things, science or strength, kindness, the gift of teaching, the power to heal, etc.

By projecting the human entity, God's thought impregnates it more particularly with one or another of these forces, for that reason assigning to it a special role in the vast concert of the universe.

The missions of our self, its destiny, its action in the general evolution, will be more and more defined in the sense of its own aptitudes and abilities, which are initially latent and confused in the beginning of its pursuit, but which will awaken and grow, and become prominent as it goes through the immense spiral of its lives. The intuitions and inspirations it receives from above will respond to this special aspect of its character. Depending on its needs and its calls, it is in this form that a spirit will perceive, deep within itself, the divine melody.

Thus God, out of an infinite variety of contrasts, knows how to bring about harmony, both in Nature and in humanity.

And if a soul abuses these gifts, if it applies them to the evil deeds, if it conceives of vanity and pride, it will be necessary, as an atonement, to be reborn in organisms which are powerless to manifest them. It will live, humiliated with its unknown genius, among other humans, long enough for pain to have triumphed over the excesses of personality, thus allowing the soul to resume its sublime growth, its pursuit, interrupted for a moment, toward the ideal.

You, human souls that are going through these pages, raise your thoughts and resolutions to the level of the tasks that fall to you. The roads to infinity are open before you, covered with endless marvels. At whatever point your growth takes you, everywhere, subjects of study await you with inexhaustible sources of joy, dazzling light and beauty. Everywhere and always, unsuspected new horizons will succeed those you have already traveled.

All is beauty in God's work. In your ascension, you are invited to taste its innumerable aspects, smiling or terrifying, from the delicate flower to the flaming stars, to witness the dawn of new worlds and humanities. At the same time, you will feel your understanding of celestial things grow exponentially, and an ardent desire to penetrate God, to plunge into It, into Its light, into Its love – in God, our source, our essence, our life!

Human intelligence cannot properly describe anticipated futures or glimpsed ascensions. Our spirit, enclosed in a body of clay, held by the bonds of a perishable organism, cannot find the necessary resources to express such splendors; expression will always remain below their realities. Nonetheless, the soul, in its deep intuitions, may have the sensation of the infinite things in which it participates and to which it aspires. Its destiny is to live and enjoy them to an increasing extent. But it would seek in vain to express them with the rudiments of our feeble human language; in vain would it strive to translate eternal things into the poor language of Earth. The word would be impotent, yet our evolved consciousness is capable of perceiving the subtle radiations of higher life.

A day will come when the enlarged soul will dominate both time and space. To it, a century will be but a moment in duration and, in a flash of its thought, it will cross the huge distances of the sky. Its subtle organism, refined by thousands of lifetimes, will then vibrate to all breaths, to all ways, to all the calls of immensity. Its memory will be able to plunge into the vanished ages. It will be able to relive at will all that it has lived, to call to itself or to join the cherished souls that have shared in its joys and pains.

Because all those individuals that were dear to us in the past are met again and connected in life on the spiritual plane; new friendships are formed and, step by step, a more powerful communion brings people together, united in life, feeling and action.

Beliefs, love, hope, fellow humans, brothers and sisters, all should please take action! Apply yourselves to convey through your work the reflections and the hopes of your thoughts, the aspirations of your hearts, the joys and certainties of your immortal souls. Communicate your faith to the other thinking beings that surround you and share in your life, so that they assist you in your tasks and that, throughout the Earth, a powerful effort lightens the burden of material oppression, triumphs over gross passions, opens a wide avenue to the flights of the spirit.

Soon a new and rejuvenated science – no longer the science of prejudices, routines, narrow and old methods, but a science open to all research, all investigations, a science of the invisible and the Hereafter – will come to make teaching fertile, to enlighten destiny, to fortify our conscience. Faith in survival will be built up in more beautiful forms, solidly supported by experience and defying all criticism.

A purer and more idealistic art, illuminated by lights that never go out, as an image of the radiant life, a reflection of the glimpsed heavens, will come to vivify and cause joy to the spirit and the senses.

And the same will happen to religions, beliefs, and systems. In their effort to elevate thought from truths of a relative nature to truths of a higher order, they will be able to eventually approach, to join in, and to blend, in order to transform the multiple beliefs of the past, whether conflicting or dead, into a living faith that will bring all humanity closer in one same impetus of adoration and prayer.

You too should employ all the powers of your being to prepare such an evolution. It is necessary that human activity is geared with more intensity toward the roads of the spirit. After a physical humanity, we must create a moral humanity; after physical bodies, there stand our souls! What has been conquered in material energies, in external forces, has been lost in deep knowledge, in revelations of an inner nature. Humans have triumphed over the visible world; their breakthroughs in the physical universe are truly immense; but it remains for them to conquer the inner world, to discover their own nature and the secret of their splendid future.

Do not argue, act instead. Discussion is futile; criticism, sterile. But action can be great, if it consists in growing yourself spiritually, enlarging others, making your being better and more beautiful. Because, do not forget that you work on your own benefit when you work for all by associating yourself with the common task. The universe, like your soul, is constantly renewed, perpetuated and embellished through work and exchange. And God, by perfecting Its work, enjoys it as you enjoy yours by embellishing it. Your most beautiful work is yourself. By your constant efforts, you can make an admirable job of your intelligence, of your conscience, which you will enjoy indefinitely. Each of your lives is a fertile crucible from which you must come out really ready for tasks, ever higher missions, proportional to your strength; and each of them will become your reward and joy.

In this way, with your hands, day by day, you will shape your own destiny. You will be reborn in the forms that your desires build up, that your works generate, until your desires and your summons prepare you forms and organisms superior to those found on Earth. You will be reborn in the circles you love, near the beloved beings who have already been associated with your works, with your lifetimes; and who will live again with you and for you, as you will live with them and for them.

Then, once your earthly evolution is complete, and you have elevated your faculties and forces to a sufficiently powerful degree; when, so to speak, you have emptied the cup of suffering, bitterness and happiness that this world can provide, and exhausted the knowledge of its sciences and beliefs, while communicating with all aspects of human genius: then and only then you will ascend with your loved ones to other, more beautiful worlds where peace and harmony reign supreme.

And, after your last human envelope goes back to earthly dust, and your purified essence has reached the spiritual regions, your remembrance and deeds will still support fellow humans, your brothers and sisters, in their struggles and their trials. And you will be able to say with the joy of a serene conscience: "My passage on Earth will not have been sterile; my efforts will not have been in vain."

PART THREE

THE POWERS OF THE SOUL

WILLPOWER

THE STUDY OF THE SELF'S LIFE, covered in the first part of this book, provided a glimpse of the powerful network of forces and energies which lie hidden within human beings. It demonstrated that the rudiments of our whole future, with its boundless development, is contained in latent state within us. The causes of happiness are not found in certain regions of the spiritual world; they are in us, in the mysterious depths of the soul.

This is confirmed by all the major religious and philosophical doctrines:

"The kingdom of heaven is within you," said Christ.

The same thought is expressed in another form in the Vedas: "You carry inside of you a sublime friend whom you do not know."

Persian wisdom is no less affirmative: "You live in the middle of stores full of riches and you die of hunger at the door." (by Sufi Master Ferdowsi)

All the great teachings converge on this point: it is in our inner life, in the blossoming of our powers, of our faculties, of our virtues, that lies the source of all future felicities.

Let us look carefully deep inside ourselves, closing our minds to all external things and, after having accustomed our psychical senses to darkness and silence, we may see unexpected lights, hear reassuring and comforting voices. However, few are the individuals who are capable to read in them, to explore these retreats in which priceless treasures lie asleep. We spend our life in banal, idle things; we travel the path of existence without knowing anything about ourselves, these psychical riches whose development would bring us countless joys.

In every human soul there are two centers, or rather two spheres, of action and expression: one is external to the other and manifests our personality, the self, with its passions and weaknesses, its mobility, its insufficiency. As long as it presides over our conduct, it is the inferior life, full of trials and ills.

The other, our inner sphere, deep and immutable, is simultaneously the seat of consciousness, the source of spiritual life, the temple of God in us. It is only when this center of action dominates the other, when its impulsions direct us, that our hidden powers are revealed and the spirit asserts itself in all its brilliance and beauty. It is through it that we stand in communion with "The Father" who "dwells in us," according to the words of Christ, the Creator which is the focal point of all love, the principle of all great actions.

By means of one of these spheres we are perpetuated in material worlds where all is inferiority, uncertainty and pain; through the other, we reach the celestial worlds, where all is peace, serenity and greatness. It is only through the growing manifestation of the divine spirit in us that we succeed in overcoming the egoistic self, and in associating ourselves fully with the universal and eternal work, creating a happy and perfect life for ourselves.

By what means will we set in motion these inner powers and guide them toward a high ideal? By our willpower! The persistent, tenacious use of this master faculty will enable us to modify our nature, overcome all obstacles, and prevail over matter, sickness and death.

It is through our will that we direct our thoughts toward a specific goal. In most humans thoughts float nonstop. Their constant mobility and infinite variety leave little room for superior influences. You have to know how to focus, to put your self in tune with divine thought. Then a spiritual fecundation of the human soul by the divine Spirit which envelops it takes place, penetrating it, making it fit to carry out noble tasks, preparing it for the life on the spiritual plane, of which it has a pale glimpse of its splendors from this world. Higher-order spirits see each other and hear each other think. Their thoughts are like penetrating harmonies, while ours are too often only discordance and confusion. Let us learn, therefore, to use our will and, through it, to unite our thoughts toward all that is great, toward universal harmony, whose vibrations fill space and cradle worlds.

Willpower is the greatest of all powers. It is comparable to a magnet in action. The will to live, to develop life in oneself, draws to us new vital resources. This is the secret of the evolution law. Our will can act with intensity upon the fluidic body, activating its vibrations and thereby adapting it to an ever higher mode of sensations, in order to prepare it for a higher degree of existence.

The principle of evolution is not in matter; it is in our will, whose action extends to the invisible order of things as well as to the visible and material one. The latter is only a consequence of the first one. The higher principle, the propelling engine of our existence, is the will. And God's will is the great engine of universal life.

Above all, it is important to understand that everything can be achieved in the psychical realm. No force remains sterile when it is exerted in a constant manner for any purpose consistent with universal law and justice. The same applies to our will; it can also act in sleep or in the wake state, for the valiant soul that has set itself a goal, seeking it tenaciously in both spheres of its life, thus creating a powerful current that gradually and silently vanquishes all obstacles.

And it is for safeguarding as much as it is for action. Our will, our trust and optimism are all safeguarding forces, acting as ramparts against any cause of trouble or disturbance in us, whether inner or outer. Sometimes they alone are enough to avert evil, whereas discouragement, fear or bad humor can often disarm us, making us defenseless and vulnerable to it. The mere fact of fearlessly facing what we call evil, danger and pain, and our resolution of confronting and overcoming them, will diminish their importance and impact upon us.

The Americans, under the name of mind-cure or Christian Science, have applied this method to therapy, and it cannot be denied that the results they achieved have been considerable. This method can be summed up in the following formula: "Pessimism leads to weakness. Optimism leads to power."[204] It consists in a gradual elimination of selfishness by uniting oneself with the supreme Will, source of infinite forces. Cases of healing are numerous and rely on irrefutable evidence.

Moreover, this has been at all times and in various forms the principle of physical and moral health.

For example, in the physical sphere, we cannot completely destroy infusoria,[205] those infinitely small organisms that live and multiply in us; however, as we strengthen up, we give them less grip over our bodies. Similarly, in the moral sphere, vicissitudes of fate cannot always be removed, but we can make ourselves strong enough to bear them with ease. We rise above them by a mental

---

[204] See Prof. William JAMES of Harvard University, *The Varieties of Religious Experience* (London and Bombay: Longmans, Green & Co., 1902), p. 107.

[205] [Trans. note] *Infusoria* is an old term used to describe tiny organisms such as protozoans found in stagnant infusions of organic matter.

effort; thus they are dominated and subjugated in such a way that they lose all menacing character and turn into advantageous elements aiding our progress and wellbeing.

As demonstrated elsewhere, based on recent facts, the soul can exert power over the physical body by means of hypnotic suggestion and autosuggestion.[206] Now I will recall only a few other examples which are even more conclusive:

Louise Lateau, the stigmatized of Bois-d'Haine (Belgium) – whose case was studied by a commission of the Belgian Academy of Medicine – while meditating on the passion of Christ, was able to bleed at will from her feet, hands and left side. The hemorrhage would last for several hours.[207]

Pierre Janet observed similar cases at the Pitié-Salpêtrière Hospital in Paris (France). An ecstatic woman had stigmata on her feet while locked in an apparatus.[208]

Louis Vivé,[209] a hystero-epileptic, gave himself the order to bleed at fixed hours in one of his crises, and the phenomenon occurred exactly as it had been verbally commanded.

The same order of events can be found in certain dreams, as well as in so-called nevi[210] or birthmarks.[211] In all fields of observation, we encounter proof that the will

---

[206] See Léon DENIS, *After Death* (Trans. G. G. Fleurot, J. Korngold. New York: USSF, 2017), ch. 32, "The Will and the Fluids"; and *Into the Unseen* (Trans. H. M. Monteiro. New York: USSF, 2017), ch. XV.

[207] Dr. E. W. Warlomont, *Louise Lateau: Rapport Médical sur la Stigmatisée de Bois-d'Haine* (Brussels: C. Murquardt, 1875).

[208] Dr. P. JANET, "Une Extatique" in *Bulletin de l'Institut Psychologique*, Paris, July–August–September 1901.

[209] [Trans. note] See F. W. H. MYERS, *Human Personality* (London: Longmans, 1903), vol. I, ch. II, item 233 A, pp. 338 et seq.

[210] [Trans. note] *Nevi* (sing. *nevus*) are often raised, usually congenital reddish or brown marks on the skin.

[211] See among other sources the *Bulletin de la Société Psychique de Marseille*, France, October 1903.

can influence matter and can subject it to its purposes. This law is manifested even more intensely in the field of the invisible life. It is by virtue of the same rules that spirits are able to create the forms and attributes that enable us to recognize them in materialization seances.

By the creative will of the higher-order spirits and, above all, of the divine Spirit, a whole wonderful life gradually develops and rises up to infinity and beyond, in the depths of heaven, as an incomparable life, superior to all the fairy tales of human art, and all the more perfect as it reaches closer to God.

If humans knew the extent of the resources that germinate in them, which might dazzle them. Instead of considering themselves weak and helpless, and fearing the future, they would realize their strength and feel that they can create that future themselves.

Each soul is a focal source of vibrations that the will activates. A society is a grouping of wills which, when united and directed toward the same goal, constitute a center of inexorable forces. Human civilizations are even more powerful focuses that vibrate through immensity.

By means of education (upbringing) and training of the will, certain civilizations arrive at results that seem wholly prodigious.

For instance, the mental energy, the vigor of spirit of the Japanese, their contempt for pain, their impassivity in the face of death, have caused astonishment in Westerners, becoming a sort of revelation for them. The Japanese are accustomed from childhood to dominate their impressions, to not betray their frustrations or disappointments, or any suffering that they may endure; to remain impenetrable, never to complain or get carried away, to always make good of a bad situation.

Such an education tempers courage and ensures success in all things. In the great drama of existence and history, heroism plays a vital role, and it is willpower that makes heroes.

This state of mind is not exclusive to the Japanese. In India, its inhabitants also succeed in suppressing the feeling of physical pain in them, by means of what they call hatha yoga, or the exercise of the will.

One can judge by this how the Asian's mental education and goals are different from ours. Everything, in them, tends to develop the inner self, its will and conscience in view of the vast cycles of evolution which are open to it, whereas the European tend to adopt immediate gratification as their goal, seeking the goods confined to his or her current life circle. The goals to be attained are divergent, resulting in completely different outcome deriving in both case from essentially dissimilar conceptions of the role of living beings in the universe. For a long time the Asians have regarded with a mixture of astonishment and pity our febrile agitation, our craze for contingent and untimely things, our ignorance of the stable, deep, and indestructible things which constitute the true strength of humans. Hence the striking contrast offered between the civilizations of the East and the West. Superiority belongs, of course, to those who embraces the broadest horizon and is inspired by the true laws of the soul and its future. This may have seemed backward to superficial observers, as long as the two types of civilization evolved in parallel without running into too much trouble. But since the necessities of existence and the increasing pressure of the peoples of the West have forced Asians into modern progress – and this is the case for the Japanese – we have seen that the eminent qualities of the Asians, manifesting themselves in the material domain, might also assure them supremacy. If this state of affairs increases, as is to be feared; if Japan succeeds in dragging with it all the Far East; it is possible that the domination of the world changes its axis and passes from one civilization to another, especially if Europe continues to lose interest in what constitutes the highest goal of human life, and to be content with an inferior and almost barbaric ideal.

Even in restricting the field of our observations to the Western populations alone, we must observe that, here too, nations that have a firmer, more tenacious will are gradually taking over others. This is the case of the Anglo-Saxon peoples. We see what England has achieved in the pursuit, through the centuries, of its plan of action. Germany itself, with its methodical spirit, has maintained its cohesion despite its setbacks. North America is also becoming more and more prominent in the concert of peoples.[212]

On the other hand, my country, France, is a nation of changing will, generally speaking. We move from one idea to another, with extreme mobility, and this is not unrelated to the vicissitudes of our history. The first impulsions are admirable in us; our enthusiasm is vibrant. But if we undertake a work easily, we sometimes abandon it too early, no sooner it is built up in our thoughts and the elements of realization are already grouped in silence around them. So the world presents many half-erased traces of our transient actions, of our efforts suspended too soon.

Pessimism and materialism, which are increasingly spreading among us, still tend to diminish the generous qualities of the French that war had awakened. The deep resources of the national spirit have atrophied from lack of a strong education and a high ideal.

---

212 [Trans. note] These personal considerations were made by Léon DENIS in the first quarter of the 20th century, long before Word War II and the polarizing hegemony of the USA and Russia.

We must learn to create a powerful will. Let us fortify our hearts and spirits, if we do not want to see our country doomed to irremediable decadence.

To wish is to accomplish! Willpower is limitless. A being conscious of itself, of its latent resources, feels its strength grows because of its efforts. It knows that all that it wishes for good and righteousness is bound to be accomplished sooner or later, inevitably, either in the current lifetime, or in the course of one's existences, when one's thought is in accordance with the divine law. And in this we have the confirmation of Christ's heavenly words: "Faith can move mountains."

Is it not comforting and beautiful to be able to say to oneself: I am a free thinking self with free will? I have made myself, unconsciously, through the ages; I have slowly built up my individuality and my freedom, and now I know the greatness and strength that lie within myself. I will rely on them; I will not let them be veiled by one single doubt, even for a moment; and through them, with the help of God and my fellow souls on the spiritual plane, I will rise above all difficulties. I will overcome evil in myself; I will detach myself from everything that still binds me to coarse matter, so as to take my flight toward joyous worlds.

I clearly see the road unfolding before me, which I am called to travel. It continues throughout the expanse and has no end. But to lead me on this infinite road, I have a sure guide: it is the understanding of the law of life, progress and love that governs all things. I learned to know myself, to believe in myself and in God. Through this I have the key to all elevation. And in this immense way that opens before my steps, I will stand firm, unshakable, in my desire to grow and rise higher and, with the help of my intelligence, which derives from God, I will draw all moral riches to me and participate in all the wonders of the Cosmos.

My will shouts to me: Forward, always forward; more knowledge, more life, divine life, always! And through willpower, I will conquer this fullness of existence, I will build myself a better personality, more radiant and more loving. I left forever the inferior state of ignorant beings, unconscious of their value and power; I affirm myself in the independence and dignity of my conscience and extend my hand to all my brothers and sisters, saying to them:

Wake up from heavy slumber; tear up the material veil that envelops you. Get to know yourself, to know the powers that are within you and how to use them. All the voices of Nature, all the voices of the spiritual plane exhort you: "Get up and walk! hurry up and conquer your destinies!"

Unto all of you who bend under the weight of life; who, believing that you are alone and weak, let yourselves fall into sadness and despair; or aspire to nothingness; I hereby say: Nothingness does not exist; death is but a new birth, a journey to new tasks, new jobs, new harvests. Life is universal and eternal communion which connects God to all Its children.

Unto all of you who believe you are worn out by suffering and disappointments, poor souls afflicted with hearts seared by the harsh wind of human trials, all of you hurt spirits, torn by the iron wheel of adversity, I hereby say: No soul is incapable of rebirths and new blossomings. You just have to wish and you will feel awakened within you unknown forces. Believe in yourself, rejuvenate yourselves in new lifetimes; believe in your immortal destinies. Believe in God, the sun of all suns, this immense hearth of which a spark shines in you which can light a burning and generous flame!

Know that every individual can be kind and happy; to become one, it is enough that you want it with energy and persistence. This mental conception of one's being, matured in the obscurity of painful existences, prepared by a slow evolution through the ages, will blossom in the light of higher lives, when we all will acquire this magnificent individuality which is reserved to us.

Constantly direct your thought toward this truth, that you can become what you want to be, and learn how to be always bigger and better. This is the notion of eternal progress and the means of achieving it; this is the secret of the mental force from which all the magnetic and psychical forces flow. When you have acquired this mastery over yourself, you will not have to fear any setbacks, falls, diseases, or death; you will have turned your inner and fragile self into a high, stable and powerful individuality!

XXI
CONSCIENCE AND INNER AWARENESS

PREVIOUS STUDIES HAVE SHOWN us that the soul is an emanation, a particle of the Absolute. Its multiple lifetimes are aimed at the growing manifestation of what is divine in it, the increase of the domain it is called to exert inside and outside itself, with the help of its senses and latent energies.

This can be achieved through various methods, by science or meditation, by work or moral training. The best method is to use all these modes of application, to complete them with one another. But the most effective of all is still through inner examination and introspection. Add to this the liberation from material bonds, a firm desire to self-improve, the union with God, both in spirit and in truth, and we will see that every legitimate religion, every deep philosophy, finds its source there and is summed up in these tenets. The rest, the doctrines, the worshiping formulas, rites and practices, is only the outer garment which hides from the eyes of crowds the true essence of religions.

French poet and dramatist Victor Hugo wrote in the postscript of his *Intellectual Autobiography (Postscriptum de Ma Vie)*:[213] "It is within us that we must look for the external ... In leaning over this well, our soul, we perceive at an abysmal distance, in a narrow circle, the immense world."

---

[213] [Trans. note] V. HUGO, *Victor Hugo's Intellectual Autobiography* (Trans. L. O'Rourke. New York: Funk & Wagnalls, 1907), p. 305.

American essayist, philosopher and poet Ralph Waldo Emerson once said: "The soul is superior to its knowledge, wiser than any of its works."

The soul connects, through its depths, to the great universal and eternal Soul, of which it is like a vibrational particle. This origin, this participation in the divine nature, explain the irresistible needs of the evolved spirit: a need for infinity, justice and light; a need to probe all the mysteries, to quench one's thirst with the lively and inexhaustible sources whose existence is sensed by it, but which it fails to find on the plane of its earthly lives.

From thence come our highest aspirations, our never-satisfied desire to know, our sense of beauty and goodness. Hence the sudden glimmers which illuminate from time to time the darkness of existence, and these presentiments forecasts of the future, like fugitive flashes in the abyss of time, which sometimes gleam for certain intelligent beings.

Below the surface of the self, a surface agitated by desires, hopes, and fears, lies the sanctuary where an integral, calm, peaceful, and serene Conscience reigns; the principle of Wisdom and Reason, which most human only know by dull impulsions or by vague reflections they can sometimes glimpse.

The whole secret of happiness, of perfection, is in the identification, in the fusion in us of these two psychical planes or focal sources. The cause of all our evils, of all our moral miseries, derives from a conflict between the latter.

In his *Critique of Pure Reason* (*Kritik der reinen Vernunft*), the great philosopher from Königsberg (Germany),[214] Immanuel Kant (1724–1824), demonstrated that human reason, that is to say, the surface reason of

---

[214] [Trans. note] Now called Kaliningrad, Königsberg has belonged to Russia since 1945.

which we speak, could not, of itself, seize anything, prove anything which touches the realities of the transcendental world, the sources of life, the spirit, the soul, God. This argumentation leads logically and necessarily to one consequence: That there exists in us a principle, a deeper reason which, by means of inner revelation, initiates us into the truths and laws of the spiritual world.

William James recognizes it in these terms:[215] "The fact that the conscious person is continuous with a wider self, through which saving experiences come." Then he adds:

"The further limits of our being plunge, it seems to me, into an altogether other dimension of existence from the sensible and merely 'understandable' world.... So far as our ideal impulses originate in this region ... we belong to it in a more intimate sense than that in which we belong to the visible world ..."

Consciousness is thus, as W. James points out, the center of personality, a permanent, indestructible center, which persists and maintains itself through all the transformations of the individual. Consciousness is not only the faculty of perceiving, but also the feeling we have of living, acting, thinking, wanting. It is one and indivisible. The plurality of its states proves nothing, as we have seen, against this unity. These states are successive, like the perceptions attached to them, and not simultaneous. To demonstrate that there are several autonomous centers of consciousness in us, we should also prove that there are simultaneous and different actions and perceptions; but that is not and cannot be.

However, consciousness, in its unity, presents as we know several layers, several aspects. The physical one is confounded with what science calls the *sensorium*, that is to say, the faculty of concentrating the external sensations,

---

[215] W. JAMES, *The Varieties of Religious Experience* (London and Bombay: Longmans, Green & Co., 1902), pp. 515–516.

of coordinating them, of defining them, of grasping their causes and determining their effects. Little by little, by the very fact of the evolution process, these sensations multiply and become more refined and the intellectual consciousness awakens. Henceforth, its development will have no bounds, since it will be able to embrace all the manifestations of infinite life. Then feeling and judgment will hatch, and the soul will perceive itself. It will become both subject and object. In the multiplicity and variety of its mental operations, it will always be aware of what it thinks and wants.

The conscious self affirms itself and grows, completing the personality by the manifestation of the moral or spiritual conscience. The faculty of perceiving the effects of the sensible world will thus be exercised in higher modes. It will become the possibility of feeling the vibrations of the moral world, of discerning its causes and laws.

It is through their inner senses that the human beings perceive transcendental facts and truths. The physical senses are deceptive; they distinguish only the appearance of things and would be nothing without this *sensorium* which groups, centralizes their perceptions and transmits them to the soul. It records everything and releases the useful effects. But beneath this surface *sensorium* there is another more hidden one, which discerns the rules and the things of the metaphysical world. It is this deep, unknown sense, unused by most humans, that some experimenters have referred to as the *subliminal consciousness*.

Most great discoveries have been nothing but the confirmation, in the physical world, of ideas already perceived through intuition or the inner senses. For example, Newton had long conceived of the idea of universal attraction, when suddenly the fall of an apple from a tree served as an objective proof of gravity for the material senses.

Just as there is in us a physical organism and a sensorium which put us in touch with the beings and things of the material plane, there is a spiritual sense with which some individuals can enter, right now, into the field of invisible life. After death, as soon as the veil of the flesh has fallen, this sense becomes the sole center of our perceptions.

It is in the growing extension and liberation of our spiritual sense that lies the law of our psychical evolution, the renovation of all beings, the secret of our inner and progressive illumination. Through it we detach ourselves from relative and illusory things, from all material contingencies, so as to attach ourselves more and more to all that is immutable and absolute.

Also, hard science will never prove sufficient, despite the advantages it offers and the conquests it has achieved, if it is not completed by intuition, this kind of inner divination which makes us discover essential truths. It is a marvel surpassing all those outside; this marvel is ourselves; it is this mirror hidden in humans that reflects the whole universe.

Those who are absorbed in the exclusive study of phenomena, in the pursuit of changing forms and external facts, often search for this certainty very far, for this criterion which is in them. They neglect to listen to their inner voices, to consult the faculties of understanding which develop and become refined in silent and collected study. This is why the things of the invisible, the impalpable, the divine, imperceptible to so many scholars, are sometimes perceived by the ignorant. The most beautiful book is in ourselves. The infinite is revealed there. Happy are those who can read it!

This entire domain remains shut to positivists, who disdain the only key, the only instrument with which one can penetrate it. They strive to experience, by means of their physical senses and material instruments, that which escapes any objective measurements. Also, any individual relying only on the external senses will reason the world and metaphysical beings out as a deaf person would reason the rules of melody out, or a blind person would the laws of optics. But should the inner sense awaken and light up within positivists; then, compared to that light which now floods them; earthly science which now seems so great in their eyes, would immediately diminish and wane.

Again, the eminent American philosopher and psychologist William James of Harvard University, declared it as follows:[216]

"I *can*, of course, put myself into the sectarian scientist's attitude, and imagine vividly that the world of sensations and of scientific laws and objects may be all. But whenever I do this, I hear that inward monitor of which W. K. Clifford once wrote, whispering the word 'bosh!' Humbug is humbug, even though it bear the scientific name, and the total expression of human experience, as I view it objectively, invincibly urges me beyond the narrow 'scientific' bounds. Assuredly, the real world is of a different temperament – more intricately built than physical science allows."

After F. W. H. Myers and Flournoy, whose opinions I have quoted earlier, W. James in turn established that official psychology could no longer disregard these thresholds of deep consciousness, placed below normal consciousness. He says so formally, as follows:[217]

"It is that our normal waking consciousness, rational consciousness as we call it, is but one special type of consciousness, whilst all about it, parted from it by the

---

[216] W. JAMES, *The Varieties of Religious Experience* (London and Bombay: Longmans, Green & Co., 1902), p. 519.

[217] *Ibid.*, pp. 209 and 388.

filmiest of screens, there lie potential forms of consciousness entirely different. We may go through life without suspecting their existence ; but apply the requisite stimulus, and at a touch they are there in all their completeness ..."

Elsewhere in the same book, he writes:

"A man's conscious wit and will, so far as they strain towards the ideal, are aiming at something only dimly and inaccurately imagined. Yet all the while the forces of mere organic ripening within him are going on towards their own prefigured result, and his conscious strainings are letting loose subconscious allies behind the scenes, which in their way work towards rearrangement; and the rearrangement towards which all these deeper forces tend is pretty surely definite, and definitely different from what he consciously conceives and determines."

All this confirms it: the initial cause, the principle of sensation, is not in the body, but in the soul. The physical senses are only its outward and coarse manifestation, an extension, on the surface of the being, of inner and hidden senses.

An issue of *The Chicago Chronicle*, of December 1905,[218] reports an extraordinary case of manifestation of the sixth sense. A 17-year-old girl, blind and deaf-mute from the age of six, developed since that time a new faculty:

"Ella Hopkins comes from a good family of Utica, NY. Three years ago, she was placed by her parents in a New York institution for the education of deaf-mutes. Like other children in this school, she was taught to read, hear and speak with her fingers. Not only did Ella quickly get used to this language, but she eventually could perceive

---

[218] [Trans. note] The American newspaper *The Chicago Chronicle* went out of circulation in 1908. We could not locate a copy of the original issue quoted above, so we translated it from the French text provided by Léon Denis.

what was going on around her as easily as if she enjoyed her normal senses."

"She knows who goes in and out, whether it is a person she knows or a stranger. She follows and catches conversations held in a low voice in the room where she is, and, at your request, can faithfully retrace it in writing. It is not a question of understanding the thought of those present only when they give it vocal expression. But this faculty is intermittent and sometimes shows itself in other ways."

"Ella's memory is most remarkable. Whatever she learns just once – and she learns quickly – is never forgotten. While sitting in front of her typewriter, her eyes fixed – as if they could see – with an intense interest in the keys of the instrument, which she uses with extreme precision, she has all the appearance of a young intelligent woman in full possession of her normal faculties. Her eyes are clear and expressive, her physiognomy animated and changing. There is no doubt that Ella is blind, deaf and dumb."

"One gets the impression that the director of the institution, Mr. Currier, is accustomed to the emergence of abnormal faculties in these poor afflicted, since he does not seem surprised by this girl's case. 'We are all aware,' he says, 'of certain things happening without any apparent help of the ordinary senses' ... Those who are deprived of two or three of the ordinary senses and forced to rely on the development of other faculties to replace them see they grow and strengthen themselves naturally. 'There are in the same class as Ella two other blind girls, also deaf and dumb, who also possess this *sixth sense*, though to a lesser degree. It is pleasure, it seems, to see them all three swiftly exchange the flight of their thoughts, barely needing the light touch of their sensitive fingers.'"

To the facts just enumerated, I will add a testimony of high value given by criminologist and physician Cesare

Lombroso, of the University of Turin (Italy). He wrote in the Italian magazine *Arena* (June, 1907):

"In 1891 I had to struggle, in my medical practice, against one of the most curious phenomena ever presented to me. I had to look after the daughter of a high official of my native town. In puberty, this person was suddenly attacked by a violent fit of hysteria, accompanied with symptoms which neither pathology nor physiology could explain. At times, her eyes completely lost the faculty of sight, and then the patient could see through her ears. She was able to read, blindfolded, some lines of printing that were presented to her ear. When a magnifying glass was placed between her ear and the sunlight, she felt like her eyes were burning; she exclaimed that I wanted to blind her. Although these facts were not new, they were no less singular. I admit that, at least, they seemed to me inexplicable by any physiological and pathological theories established hitherto. Only one thing seemed very clear to me: when put into action in a person who had been entirely normal before, this state triggers particular forces in relation to 'unknown' senses."[219]

Here is another example of development of psychical senses to which I would like to call the reader's full attention. The person I am going to talk about is considered one of the wonders of our time:[220]

Helen Keller was also a blind, deaf and dumb girl. She therefore only possessed the sense of touch to communicate with the outside world. And yet she could converse in three languages with her visitors; her intellectual baggage was considerable. She had an esthetic discernment

---

[219] [Trans. note] See also C. LOMBROSO, *After Death – What?* (Trans. W. S. Kennedy. Boston: Small Maynard & Co., 1909), ch. I, "Transposition of the Senses," pp. 2–4.

[220] See G. HARRY, *Man's Miracle: The Story of Helen Keller and Her European Sisters* (Trans. not named. New York: Doubleday, 1913).

which allowed her to enjoy works of art and harmonies of Nature. By the mere touch of her hands, she was able to discern the character and disposition of the people she met. With her fingertips she picked the word on the lips and read in the books, feeling the embossed characters specially printed for her. She rose to the conception of the most abstract things, and her consciousness was illuminated by the light she drew from the depths of her soul.

Let us hear what Mrs. Georgette Leblanc-Maeterlinck had to say after her visit to Wrentham (USA):

"Helen's personality is so great, her mind is so well-balanced, so strong and sane, her intelligence so fine, that the problem is reversed. We need desire no longer to be understood, we must try to understand."[221]

Elsewhere in the same book we read:

"[Helen] has gained a thorough knowledge of algebra and mathematics, and an acquaintance with astronomy, Latin and Greek; who is able to read Moliere and Anatole France, and express herself in their language – and has mastered Goethe, Schiller and Heine in German, and Shakespeare, Kipling and Wells in English. She writes on philosophy, psychology and poetry ..."[222]

Her biographer, Gérard Harry, assures that the intensity of her perceptions gave her the skills of a thought reader.

Obviously here we are in presence of a very evolved being, coming back to this world's stage with all her achievements of centuries past.

The case of Helen Keller proves that behind momentarily atrophied organs, there exists a consciousness long acquainted with the notions of the external world. This is at once a demonstration of the soul's past lives and of the existence of its own senses independent of

---

[221] G. Harry, *op. cit.*, "Preface."
[222] G. Harry, *op. cit.*, ch. I, p 2.

matter, dominating the latter and surviving any bodily disintegration.

Generally speaking, to develop and refine perception, we must first awaken our inner sense, the spiritual sense. Mediumship shows us that there are human beings who are far more gifted, in terms of inner vision and hearing, than certain spirits living on the spiritual plane, whose perceptions are extremely limited because of their insufficient evolution.

In short, the more disinterested and pure our thoughts and deeds become, the more intense and predominant spiritual life will be over physical life, and the more our inner senses will grow. The veil that hides the fluidic world thus becomes thinner, more transparent, and behind it the soul perceives a marvelous set of harmonies and beauties. At the same time, it becomes more apt to collect and transmit the revelations, the inspirations brought by the higher ones, since the development of our inner senses generally coincides with an extension of the faculties of the spirit, exerting a more energetic attraction of ethereal radiations.

Each plane of the Universe, each life circle corresponds to a number of vibrations which become more accentuated and fast, and subtler, as they come closer to perfect life. The beings endowed with a weak power of radiation are not able to perceive forms of life which are superior to them. But every spirit is capable of obtaining, by practicing its will and educating its inner senses, a power of vibration which will enable it to act upon very extensive planes. Evidence of the intensity of this mode of mental emission is highlighted the fact that many dying individuals, or people in danger of dying, have been seen to telepathically influence, at great distances, several subjects at once.[223]

---

[223] See *Annales des Sciences Psychiques*, October 1906, pp. 611, 613.

Actually, each of us could, if we wanted to, communicate at any time with the unseen world. We are spirits: through our will, we can command matter and free ourselves from its bonds so as to live in a freer sphere, the sphere of superconscious life. For this, one thing is necessary: to spiritualize oneself, to return to the life of the spirit through a perfect concentration of our inner forces. Then we will find ourselves face to face with an order of things that neither instinct nor experience, nor even reason, can grasp.

The soul, in its expansion, can break the wall of flesh that surrounds it and commune by its own senses with the higher and divine worlds. This is what seers and true saints, the great mystics of all times and all religions, have been able to do.[224]

Mediumship, under its multiple forms, is also the result of psychical training, which allows the senses of the soul to come into action, to substitute, for a moment, for the physical senses, and to perceive what is imperceptible to other human beings. It is characterized and developed according to the ability of one's inner sense to predominate one way or the other, and to manifest itself in one of the usual ways of sensation. The spirit wishing to communicate itself recognizes at first sight the organic sense which, in the medium, will serve it as intermediary, and then it acts on this point. Sometimes it is speech, or writing through the mechanical action of the medium's hand; at times it is the brain, when it comes to intuitive

---

[224] W. JAMES, *The Varieties of Religious Experience* (London and Bombay: Longmans, Green & Co., 1902), "Mysticism," pp. 381, 419, 422.

mediumship. In temporary "incorporations," it is the full possession and adaptation of the spiritual senses of the possessor to the physical senses of the subject.[225]

The most common faculty is clairvoyance, that is to say, the perception, with the eyes closed, of what is happening in the distance, either in time or space, in the past or in the future. It is the penetration of the clairvoyant's spirit into fluidic surroundings, where the facts accomplished are recorded and the plans of future things are elaborated. Most often, clairvoyance is exercised unconsciously without any preparation. In this case, it results from the natural evolution of the percipient; but it can also be induced, as well as spirit sight. On this subject, Colonel Rochas d'Aiglun expresses himself as follows:[226]

"Mireille depicted to me the effects of my magnetizations on her: 'When I am awake, my soul is chained to my body, and I am like a person who, locked up on the ground floor of a tower, sees the outside world only through the five windows of the senses, each with glasses of different colors. When you magnetize me, you set me free little by little from my chains; and my soul, which always aspires to rise, climbs up the staircase of the tower – a windowless staircase – and I cannot see more than you who guide me till the moment I reach the upper floor. There, my view extends in all directions with a very sharp sense that puts me in touch with objects, which I could not perceive through the vitreous windows of the tower.'"

One can also acquire clairaudience, the hearing of inner voices, and possible mode of communication among the

---

[225] [Trans. note] In modern Spiritism the term *incorporation* (and all it implies) has been replaced by *psychophony*, since no actual, physical "possession" of the medium takes place.

[226] ROCHAS D'AIGLUN, *Les Vies Successives* (Paris: Chacornac, 1911), p. 499.

spirits. Another manifestation of the inner senses is the reading of recorded events, somehow photographed in the atmosphere, whether of an ancient or modern object. For example, weapon debris, a medal, a fragment of a sarcophagus, a stone from a ruin, may evoke, in the soul of the seer, a series of images related to the times and places to which these objects once belonged. This is called psychometry.

To that list we should add symbolic dreams, premonitory dreams and even obscure presentiments that warn us of unsuspected dangers.

As said above, many people have, without knowing it, the opportunity to communicate intimately with their friends from the spiritual world. This number includes truly religious souls, that is to say, souls exalted to an ideal, in which trials, sufferings, and long moral training have refined the subtle senses, making them more sensitive to the vibrations of external thoughts. Often human souls in distress came to me to ask advice from the Beyond, advice, such as counseling and indications that I could not possibly obtain to them. I recommended the following procedure, which sometimes succeeded: Retreat into yourself in isolation and silence, I told them. Raise your thoughts to God; call your Protective Spirit, this tutelary guide that Providence has attached to your steps in the journey of life. Ask it about the doubts which worry you, on the condition that they are worthy of your protector, that is, free of all mundane interest. Then, wait! listen attentively within yourselves and, after a moment, from the depths of your consciousness, you will hear like the weakened echo of a distant voice, or rather, you will perceive the vibrations of a mysterious thought, which will drive out your doubts, dissipate your anxieties, and soothe you, comfort you.

This is indeed a form of mediumship, and not one of the least beautiful for that matter. Everyone can obtain it and participate in this communion of the living and the dead, which one day will be extended to the whole humanity.

One can even, through this process, correspond with the divine plane. In difficult circumstances of my life, when I hesitated between contrary resolutions about the task entrusted to me of spreading the comforting truths of New Spiritualism (i.e., Spiritism). Appealing to the Supreme Entity, I always heard inside me a grave and solemn voice that dictated my duty. Still clear and distinct, this voice seemed to come from a very distant place. Its tenderness touched me to tears.

That means, intuition is in most cases only one of the forms used by the inhabitants of the unseen to transmit their warnings and instructions to us. Other times, it will be the revelation of deep consciousness to normal consciousness. In the first case, it can be considered as an inspiration. Through mediumship, the spirit infuses his ideas into the understanding of the medium. This latter provides the expression, the form, the language, and, depending on his or her cerebral development, the communicating spirit will find in the medium more or less assurance and abundance of means of conveying its thought in all its extent and brilliance.

The thought of the communicating spirit is at one with its emission principle, but it will vary in its manifestations, according to the more or less perfect state of the instruments that it has at its disposal. Each medium expresses the imprint of his or her own personality together with the inspiration that comes from above. The more the medium's intellect is cultivated and spiritualized, the more the material instincts are compressed in him or her, and the higher they will be to transmit lofty thoughts with purity and fidelity.

The broad stretch of a river cannot flow through a narrow riverbed. Similarly, an inspiring spirit will succeed in transmitting through the organism of the medium only those of its conceptions which find an adequate mediumistic outlet. Through great mental effort, under the excitation of an external force, the medium may express conceptions above his or her own knowledge. Nevertheless, in the expression of the suggested ideas, one will still find some of the medium's favorite terms and habitual turnings of phrases; although the external stimulus by a communicating spirit will lend, for a moment, more amplitude and elevation to the medium's usual language.

We thus see the extent of difficulties and obstacles posed by the human organism against a faithful and complete transmission of the conceptions of the soul; and how long an extensive training through practice, and a prolonged education, are necessary to soften and adapt them to the needs of communicating spirits that make use of them. And this does not apply only to a disembodied spirit wishing to manifest itself with the aid of a mortal intermediary, but also to incarnate souls themselves, whose profound conceptions never succeed in emerging in total plenitude on the earthly plane, a fact asserted by all individuals of genius, especially composers and poets.

At first, inspiration is conscious; but as soon as the action of the spirit is accentuated, the medium fall under the influence of a force which causes him or her to act independently of their will. Or rather, a kind of gravity invades the medium, whose eyes are thus veiled, and he or she loses consciousness of themselves and fall under an invisible domination. In this case, the medium is no more than an instrument, or a reception and transmission device. As a machine obeys the electric current that drives it, the medium then obeys the current of thoughts that invades him or her.

In the practice of intuitive mediumship in the waking state, many feel discouraged by the impossibility of distinguishing the ideas which are their own from those suggested to them by a spirit. It is, however, easy, we believe, to recognize ideas of extraneous origin. The latter spring spontaneously, unexpectedly, like flashes of light emanating from an unknown source; whereas our personal ideas, those which come from our own self, are always at our disposal and occupy, permanently, our intellect. Not only do so-called inspirational ideas arise as if by magic, but they also follow each other, enchained to one another and expressing themselves quickly, sometimes in feverish succession.

The great majority of authors, writers, orators, and poets are mediums on certain occasions: they have an intuition of a hidden assistance that inspires them and takes part in their work. They admit so themselves in moments of effusion.

British-born American writer and Revolutionary leader Thomas Paine once wrote:

"Any person, who has made observations on the state and progress of the human mind, by observing his own, cannot but have observed, that there are two distinct classes of what we call Thoughts: those that we produce in ourselves by reflection and the act of thinking, and those that bolt into the mind of their own accord. I have always made it a rule to treat those voluntary visitors with civility, taking care to examine, as well as I was able, if they were worth entertaining ..." (*Theological Works*, London, 1824)

According to American philosopher and writer Ralph Waldo Emerson, thoughts did not come to him in succession, as in a mathematical problem, but instead penetrated his intellect of their own volition, like a flash shining in the darkness of the night. Truth came to him, not by reasoning, but by intuition.

The speed with which Walter Scott, the Bard of Avon, wrote his novels caused amazement in his contemporaries. Here is the explanation given by Sir Walter himself:

"I sometimes think my fingers set up for themselves, independent of my head; for twenty times I have begun a thing on a certain plan, and never in my life adhered to it (in a work of imagination, that is) for half an hour together.... Having ended the second volume of *Woodstock* last night, I had to begin the third this morning. Now I have not the slightest idea how the story is to be wound up to a catastrophe." (J. G. Lockhart, *Memoirs*, Edinburgh, 1850)

When talking about his novel *The Antiquary*, he adds:

"I shall then set myself seriously to *The Antiquary*, of which I have only a very general sketch at present; but when once I get my pen to the paper it will walk fast enough. I am sometimes tempted to leave it alone, and try whether it will not write as well without the assistance of my head as with it." (J. G. Lockhart, *Memoirs*, Edinburgh, 1850)

The German mystic and philosopher Novalis (1772–1801), whose *Fragments* and *The Novices of Sais* still remain among the most powerful monuments of the human mind, wrote:

"It appears to man as if he were engaged in a conversation, in which some kind of unknown, spiritual being wondrously incites him to develop the most evident thoughts. This being must be a higher being because it is placed in such a relation with himself that it cannot be a being of the world of appearances." (Trans. D. W. Wood, *Notes for a Romantic Encyclopedia*, New York, 2007)

Let me also recall the famous inspiration of Jean-Jacques Rousseau, as described by himself:

"I went to see Diderot, then prisoner at Vincennes. Along the way I started leafing through a *Mercure de France* I had in my pocket. I stumbled on the question of the Academy of Dijon that gave rise to my first piece of writing. If anything ever resembled a sudden inspiration, it was the movement in me after reading this; suddenly I felt my mind blinded by a thousand lights; a crowd of lively ideas presented themselves to me with a force and confusion that threw me into in an inexpressible state of unrest. I felt my head swooning as in a state of drunkenness. A violent palpitation oppressed me, lifting my chest. Unable to breathe while walking, I threw myself under one of the trees of the avenue, and stayed there for half an hour, so agitated that when I finally rose I realized that all the front of my coat was wet with my tears, not even having felt that I shed them. Oh Sir, if I could have written a quarter of what I saw and felt under that tree, with what clarity would I have shown all the contradictions of the social system, with what force would I have exposed all the abuses of our institutions, with what simplicity would I have proved that man is naturally good ... All I could retain of this multitude of great truths, which in a quarter of an hour enlightened me under that tree, is quite feebly dispersed in my three principal writings." (*in* Eli Friedlander, *J. J. Rousseau: An Afterlife of Words*, Harvard, 2004)

Perhaps the most extraordinary modern-day example of psychical inspiration is that of the American Andrew Jackson Davis, also known as the "Poughkeepsie

Seer." This personage appears at the dawn of American Neo-Spiritualism[227] as a sort of powerful apostle. Thanks to a faculty which remained unrivaled, he was able to exert an irresistible influence upon his time and country.

The following details are borrowed from Mrs. Emma Hardinge's book, *Modern American Spiritualism* (2nd ed., New York, 1870):

"About the age of fourteen he was casually magnetized by a Mr. Livingston, of Poughkeepsie, who, discovering that the shoemaker's boy possessed wonderful clairvoyant powers, and an unusually successful gift of prescribing for the sick, gradually drew him from his trade into association with himself until at length they traveled and practiced together as operator and subject, with unbounded success and benefit to the world...."

"The exceedingly humble rank and limited means of his parents deprived young Davis of all chances of culture, save five months at a rustic school and the association of the rude boors of wild country districts...."

"Mr. Davis was about eighteen years of age when He announced to the circle of admirers who had become interested in his wonderful lucidity as a clairvoyant, that a new and astounding phase of spiritual power was about to be revealed through his instrumentality, commencing with the delivery of a course of lectures which were destined ultimately to revolutionize the scientific world and produce a striking effect upon the religious opinions of mankind."

"In fulfillment of this prophecy Mr. Davis proceeded to give the promised course of lectures, for the production of which he selected Dr. Lyon, of Bridgeport, as his

---

[227] [Trans. note] *Neo-Spiritualism* and *New Spiritualism* are neologisms coined by Léon DENIS for *Spiritism*.

magnetizer, the Rev. William Fishbough as his scribe, the Rev. V. N. Parker, R. Lapham, Esq., and Dr. L. Smith, of New York, as his special witnesses, whilst several other gentlemen, high in place or distinguished for literary and scientific attainments, were from time to time invited in, or permitted to be present at the delivery of the lectures ; and thus was produced the vast compendium of literary, scientific, philosophic, and historic knowledge, entitled *Nature's Divine Revelations*. Of the work itself, ... suffice it to say that the marvelously abnormal character of the book, emanating as it did from a person so utterly incapable of its production under ordinary circumstances, excited the most profound astonishment in all ranks and classes. The *Revelations* were quickly followed by *The Great Harmonia*, *Penetralia*, *Present Age* and *Inner Life*, and other voluminous productions, the sum of which, combined with Mr. Davis's lectures, editorial labors, associative movements, and wide-spread personal influence, have effected a complete revolution in the minds of a large and distinguished class of thinkers in the United States ... a belief which emphatically owes its origin to *the poor shoemaker's boy*."

"'Thousands of persons who have witnessed him in his medical examinations or scientific disclosures, live to testify to the astounding exaltation of mind possessed by Mr. Davis in his abnormal state.'"

"His manuscripts were often submitted to the highest intellects of the country for investigation, and his whole career – especially the impossibility of his having acquired the knowledge he exhibited in his clairvoyant state by any ordinary means – was made the subject of searching and rigid scrutiny. One of the most marked results established by the life of this phenomenal personage was the actuality of clairvoyance and the triumphant revelation that the soul of man could commune spiritually with supra-mundane as well as mundane minds, and aspire far beyond this terrestrial sphere in its acquisition of knowledge."

I have spoken incidentally of the method to follow for obtaining the development of psychical senses. It consists in isolating oneself at certain hours of the day or night, suspending the activity of the external senses, removing from oneself the images and the noises of outside life. This is possible even in the most humble social conditions, in the most common occupations. It is necessary, as it were, to fall back on oneself and, in calm contemplation of thought, to make a mental effort to see and read in the great mysterious book which lies within us. At these times, remove from your mind all that is transient, earthly and variable. Material concerns create flatly horizontal vibrational currents that hinder etheric radiation and constrain our perceptions. On the contrary, meditation, contemplation, the constant effort toward goodness and beauty will form ascensional currents that establish a relation with the higher planes, and facilitate the penetration into us of the divine emanations. By this repeated and prolonged exercise, the inner being is gradually illuminated, fertilized, regenerated. This training work is long and difficult; it sometimes requires more than one lifetime. So it is never too early to undertake it. Its good effects will soon be felt. Whatever you lose in lower-order sensations, you will gain in supermundane perceptions, in mental and moral balance, in the joys of the spirit. Your inner sense will acquire delicacy, an extraordinary acuteness; you will be able to communicate one day with the highest spiritual spheres. These powers, the religions sought to constitute them by means of communion and prayer. But the prayer used in churches, a set of formulas learned and repeated mechanically for hours at a time, is powerless to give the soul the necessary impetus, to establish the fluidic link, the thread through which a rapport is established. It requires a call, a stronger impulse, a concentration, and a deeper inner retreat. That is why I have always advocated improvised prayer, the cry of the soul which, in its faith and love, springs from all the forces accumulated in itself toward the object of its desire.

Instead of inviting, by means of evocation, the heavenly spirits to descend toward us, we will thus learn to disengage ourselves and ascend to them.

However, some precautions should be taken. The unseen world is peopled with entities of all kinds, and anyone who enter it must have already attained sufficient perfection, be inspired by sentiments high enough to protect him or her from all suggestions of evil. At a minimum, you must be guided in your research by a reliable and enlightened spirit guide. It is through moral progress that we obtain the authority and the energy necessary to prevail over spirits full of levity and arrogance that swarm around us. The full possession of oneself, the profound and tranquil knowledge of the eternal laws, will preserve us from the dangers, the traps, and the illusions of the Hereafter; they provide us with the means to control forces in action on the invisible plane.

FREE WILL

FREEDOM OR LIBERTY is a necessary condition of the human soul, which, without it, could not construct its destiny. It is in vain that philosophers and theologians have argued as far as the eye can see about this issue. They have obscured it with their theories, their sophisms, relegating humanity to servitude instead of leading it to the liberating light. The concept is simple and clear. The Druids had formulated it from the earliest days of our history. It is expressed in these terms, in that memorable bardic triad which says, "Three things come into existence at the same time: God, light and freedom."

At first glance, human freedom seems to be above all very restricted in the midst of the circle of fatalities that surrounds us: physical needs, social conditions, interests and instincts. But, looking more closely at this issue, we see that this freedom is always enough to allow the soul to break such a circle and escape oppressive forces.

Freedom and accountability are correlative attributes in human beings, and increase as the latter evolve in elevation. A sense of responsibility is what brings about human dignity and morality. Without it, a human being would only be a blind machine, a plaything of the surrounding forces acting upon it. The notion of morality is inseparable from that of freedom.

Responsibility or rather accountability is established by the testimony of the conscience, which approves or blames according to the nature of our actions. A feeling of remorse is a proof more demonstrative than all philosophical arguments put together. To any slightly evolved spirit, the law of duty will shine like a beacon through the mist of passions and interests. Also, we see every day, individuals in the most humble and difficult situations, accept hard trials rather than lower themselves and commit unworthy actions.

If human freedom is restricted, it is at least in the process of perpetual development, for progress is nothing but the extension of free will in the individual as well as in the community. The struggle between matter and spirit is aimed precisely at increasingly liberating it from the yoke of blind forces. Our intelligence and willpower will succeed in prevailing little by little upon what is perceived by us as fatality. Free will is therefore the development of personality and conscience. To be free, one must want to be so and make an effort to become free, by getting rid of one's servitude to ignorance and low passions, and by substituting the empire of reason for one of sensations and instincts.

This can only be achieved through lengthy education and training of the human faculties: physical liberation by limiting appetites; intellectual liberation by conquering truth; moral liberation by the search for virtue. This work takes centuries. But at all stages of their ascension, in the distribution of the goods and evils of life, beside the chain of causes, and without detriment to what our past may have inflicted upon our destinies, there is always place for free will in all humans.

How to reconcile our free will with divine prescience? Given the anticipated knowledge that God has of all things, can we really affirm human freedom? A complex and arduous issue in appearance, which has caused rivers of ink to flow, but whose solution could not be simpler. However humans do not seem to like simple answers. We tend to prefer the obscure, the complicated, and accept the truth only after exhausting all forms of error.

God, whose infinite knowledge embraces all things, knows the nature of each human and his or her impulses, the tendencies according to which they will be able to determine themselves. We ourselves, once knowing the character of a person, could easily foresee in what sense, in a given circumstance, a person would make a decision either by self interest or by a sense of duty. A resolution cannot come out of nowhere. It is necessarily related to a series of causes and previous effects from which it is derived and which explain it. God, knowing the innermost depths of every soul, can therefore rigorously and with certainty deduce from the knowledge which It has of this soul, and from the conditions in which it is called to act, the decisions which the soul will freely make.

Let me stress that God's prediction of our actions does not make them predetermined. If God could not foresee our resolutions, these would still be freely taken, regardless.

It is thus that human freedom and divine foresight are reconciled and combined, when we consider this problem in the light of reason.

Moreover, the circle within which the human will is exerted is in any case too small for it to hinder God's action, the effects of which continually unfold in the boundless immensity. The feeble insect lost in a corner of the garden cannot, by upsetting a few atoms within its reach, disturb the harmony of the whole or hinder the work of the divine Gardener.

Of paramount importance is the question of free will with its serious consequences for the whole social order, through its action and its repercussion on education, morality, justice, legislation, and so on. It has generated two opposing currents: the deniers of free will and those who admit it with certain restrictions.

The arguments of fatalists and determinists can be summarized as follows: "Human beings are subject to the impulses of their nature, which dominate them and force their will, inciting them to take one direction instead of another. Consequently, humans are not free."

The opposite school of thought, which admits free will in humans, raised the theory of indeterminate causes, in face of that negative system. Its most brilliant representative was Charles B. Renouvier (1815–1903).

The views of this philosopher have been confirmed more recently by the fine works of Wilhem Wundt on *apperception* (i.e., volition in action), Alfred Fouillée on his concept of an *idea-force*, and Emile Boutroux on *the contingency of the laws of nature*.

The elements that the neo-Spiritualist revelation brings to the nature and the future of beings give the theory of free will a definitive sanction. They come to seize modern consciousness from the deleterious influence of materialism and to direct our thoughts toward a conception of destiny, which will have the effect, as Carl du Prel said, of rejuvenating the inner life of civilization.

Up to now, from a theological as well as a deterministic point of view, this question has remained almost insoluble. It could not be otherwise, since each of these systems started from the inaccurate premise that a human being goes through only a single earthly existence. It is quite different if one widens the circle of life and considers this problem in the light shed by the doctrine of rebirths. With it, each being conquers its own freedom during the evolution it has to accomplish in successive lives.

Supplied first of all with instinct, which gradually disappears to make room for reason, our freedom is very limited in our inferior stages and throughout the period of our early education. It is considerably expanded as soon as the spirit has acquired the understanding of the law. And always, at all stages of a spirit's ascension, at the moment of important resolutions, it will be assisted, guided and advised by Higher Intelligences, that is, spirits greater and more enlightened than ourselves.

Free will, the spirit's self-determination, is exercised especially at the time of reincarnation. By choosing such and such family or social milieu, the spirit knows in advance what trials to expect, but it also understands the necessity of these trials for developing its qualities, mitigating its faults, and stripping away its prejudices and vices. Such trials may also be the consequence of a bad past which now must be repaired; and the spirit accepts them with resignation and confidence, because it knows that its greater siblings on the spiritual plane will never abandon it in difficult times.

The future then appears to the spirit, not in its details, but in its most salient features, that is, to the extent that the future is the result of previous actions. These facts represent the part of fate or "predestination" that some individuals are inclined to see in all life. Yet these are simply, as we have seen, the effects or reactions of distant causes. In reality, fate does not exist and, whatever the weight of the responsibilities one has incurred, they can always attenuate or modify one's "fate" with works of devotion, of goodness, of charitable love, and by a long self-sacrifice to duty.

As said before, the problem of free will was of great legal importance. While taking into account the right of repression and social conservation, it is very difficult to specify, in all cases in the jury courts, the extent of individual responsibility. This could only be done by establishing the degree of evolution of the culprits. Neo-Spiritualism would perhaps provide us with the means to do it. But human justice, little versed in these matters, remains blind and imperfect in its decisions and judgments.

Often the wicked, the culprit, is in reality only a young and ignorant spirit, in whom reason has not had time to mature. French author Charles Duclos asserts that crime is merely bad judgment (*Considérations sur les Mœurs de ce Siècle* [... *on the Mores of this Century*], 1751). That is why the penalties imposed should be established in such a way as to compel the convict to return to his or her senses, to learn, to enlighten themselves, and to make amends. Society must correct without passion and without hatred, otherwise it makes itself guilty.

As we have shown, all souls are equal at their point of departure. They become different in their infinite degrees of advancement: some, young, others older, and consequently variously developed in their morality and wisdom, according to their absolute age. It would be unfair to ask a juvenile spirit for merits equal to those which can be expected from a spirit that has seen much and learned a lot. Hence there are very great differences in responsibility.

One's self is only ripe for freedom when the universal laws, external to it, have become internalized and conscious by the very fact of the one's evolution. The day we penetrate the law and make it the rule of our actions, we will have reached the moral point where humans take possession of themselves, dominating and governing their own selves. Henceforth, we will no longer need constraints and the social authority to direct ourselves. It is the same for the collectivity as it is for the individual.

A people is truly free and worthy of liberty only when it has learned to obey this inner law, a moral law, both eternal and universal, which emanates neither from the power of a caste or the will of the crowds, but from a higher Power. Without the moral discipline that everyone must impose, public freedoms are only a deception. We have the appearance but not the mores of a free people. Society remains exposed, by the violence of its passions and the intensity of its appetites, to all sorts of complications and disorders.

All that rises toward the light is rising toward freedom. It flourishes, full and whole, into the higher life. The soul will suffer all the more the weight of material fatalities the more backwards and unconscious it proves to be. Conversely, it will enjoy more and more freedom as it rises and approaches the divine. When still in a state of ignorance, it is contented to subject itself to a direction. But, once it becomes wiser and more perfect, the soul enjoys its freedom in the divine light.

As a general proposition, every individual who has reached the state of reason is free and responsible, to the extent of his or her advancement. I will leave aside cases where, under the influence of some physical or moral cause, disease or obsession, a human being has lost the use of his or her faculties. It cannot be ignored that the physical sometimes has a great influence over the moral side. However, in the struggle between them, strong souls always triumph. Socrates said that he had felt the most perverse instincts sprout in him but had tamed them all. There were two currents of contrary forces in this philosopher: one, oriented toward evil, the other, toward good, and it is the latter that won him over.

There are also secret causes often acting upon us. Sometimes intuition comes to fight reasoning. Deep impulsions, which are part of our consciousness, may lead us in an unexpected direction. This is not a negation of free will; it is the action of the soul in its fullness, intervening in the course of its destiny. Also, this can be due to an influence of our invisible guides in action, or the intervention of an intelligent Entity which, seeing from farther above, seeks to pull us out of our lower contingencies, and to carry us up higher. But, in all these cases, it is our own will that alone rejects or accepts, and ultimately makes up its mind.

In short, instead of denying or asserting free will, according to the philosophical school to which we happen to be attached, it would be more accurate to say: Humans are the architects of their liberation. They attain a state of complete freedom only through inner enlightening and education, and by valuing their hidden powers. The obstacles built up along the way are basically only the means of compelling us to escape from our own indifference and to use our latent forces. All material difficulties can thus be overcome.

We are all in solidarity, and the freedom of each of us is related to the freedom of others. By freeing oneself from passions and ignorance, each individual frees their fellow beings. Anything and everything that helps to dispel the dark mists of ignorance, and to reverse evil, sets humanity freer, more aware of itself, of its duties and powers.

Therefore let us rise to the conscience of our true role and goal, and we will be free. Through our efforts, our teachings and our examples, let us make sure that not only willpower but also goodwill and good itself prevail. Also, instead of forming passive beings bent under the yoke of matter, and prey to uncertainty and inertia, let us fashion truly free souls, freed from the chains of fate and hovering over the world by their superior well-earned qualities.

XXIII

THOUGHT

THOUGHT IS CREATIVE. Just as the eternal thought continually throws the rudiments of beings and worlds into space, so also the writer, the speaker, the poet, and the artist, bring forth an endless flowering of ideas, works and concepts, which in their turn influence and impress – either for good or evil, according to their nature – the immense mass of human beings.

This is why the mission of all workers of thought is at the same time great, formidable, and sacred.

Great and sacred, for thought dispels the shadows on the road, solves the enigmas of life and traces the path for humanity. It is the thought's flame that warms souls and beautifies the deserts of existence. Formidable too, since its effects are as powerful for going downwards as they are for going upwards.

Sooner or later, every product of the spirit returns to its originator with all its consequences, incurring, as the case may be, suffering, reduction or suppression of liberty; or conversely, elation, expansion, and elevation of the originator's soul.

Our current lifetime is, as we know, a single episode in our long history, a fragment of the great chain unfolding for all beings throughout immensity. And constantly, the results of our deeds fall back on us, in mists or rays. The human soul walks its way, surrounded by a radiant or a dark atmosphere, populated with the creations of its thought. And therein lies, in the life on the spiritual plane, its glory or its shame.

For thought to develop all its force and magnitude, nothing is more effective than researching big problems. In order to express well, one must feel powerfully; to taste one's sensations high and deep, we must go back to the source from which all life, all harmony, and all beauty pour out.

All that is noble and high in the domain of intelligence emanates from an eternal, living and thinking cause. The greater the flight of thought toward such a cause, the higher it hovers, the more radiant and clear are its glimpses, the more exhilarating the joys felt, the more powerful the forces acquired, the more sparkling the inspirations! After each expansion, thought descends, enlivened and enlightened, into the earthly field, to resume the task by which it will grow further still, because it is work that makes intelligence, as it is intelligence that makes beauty, that is, the splendor of an accomplished work.

Lift up your eyes, O thinker, O poet! send out your cry of appeal, of aspiration, of prayer! In front of the sea with its changing reflections, and at the sight of remote, far away peaks, or the starry skies of infinity, have you ever experienced those moments of ecstasy and exhilaration where the soul feels immersed in a sort of divine dream; where inspiration arrives powerfully, like a flash, a fast messenger from Heaven to Earth?

Listen up! Have you ever heard in the inner depths of your being the vibration of confused harmonies, rumors of the invisible world, hidden voices that cradle your thought and prepare it for supreme intuitions?

In every poet, artist, writer, there are rudiments of mediumship, unconscious, unsuspected and just waiting to hatch. Through them, the worker of thought comes into contact with their inexhaustible source and receives his or her share of revelation. This revelation of esthetics which will be appropriate to his or her nature and type of talent, it is their mission to express it in works that will instill in the souls of the immense human mass a vibration of divine forces, a radiation from eternal truths.

It is through frequent and conscious communion with the world of the spirits that our future geniuses will draw elements for their many works. Nowadays already, penetration in the secrets of their dual life comes to offer humans relief and enlightenment that failing religions can no longer provide them. In all fields, like a fertilizer, the Spiritist idea will put thought into work.

Science will be required to completely reform its theories and methods in view of this idea. It will lead to the discovery of incalculable forces and the conquest of the hidden universe. Philosophy will thus gain a wider and more precise knowledge of human personality. This latter, during trance and exteriorization, will be like a crypt that opens, filled with strange objects, and where lies hidden the key to the mystery of being.

The religions of the future will find in Spiritism the proofs of survival of the soul and the rules of life in the Hereafter, alongside the principle of a tight union between the two worlds, both the visible and invisible humanities, in their ascension to their common Creator. Art, in all its forms, will thus discover inexhaustible sources of inspiration and emotion.

The common person will draw moral courage from it, at times of weariness. These people will understand that the soul can grow as well whether by humble labor or by haughty work, and that no duty is negligible; and that envy is a sibling of hatred; and that often one is less happy in luxury than in austerity. The powerful will learn goodness from the Spiritist idea, with a feeling of solidarity which connects us all through our lives and can force us to return in a lowly condition in order to acquire the virtues of humbleness.

Even skeptics may find faith in it; and the discouraged may also encounter in it hope and vigorous resolutions for their long wait. All those who suffer, therein will discover this profound idea of a law of justice presiding over all things; that there is no effect in any field without a cause, no birth without pain, no victory without a struggle, no triumph without acerbic efforts. But above everything else, there reigns a perfect and majestic sanction: no one is abandoned by God, as everyone is a particle of It.

Thus, slowly, a renovation of humanity takes place, still so young, so ignorant of itself, but whose desire is gradually moving toward the understanding of its duty and purpose; at the same time as it is expanding its field of exploration and the prospect of an endless future. And soon it will move forward, more aware of itself and its strength, and conscious of its magnificent destiny. At each stage, seeing and wanting more, feeling the focal point which is within it shining and alive, humanity also sees darkness recede, with all dark enigmas of the world melting down and being solved, while the path is lighted up by a powerful ray. With all shadows vanishing, little by little, all prejudices and vain terrors, and the apparent contradictions of the universe, are dissipated; and at last harmony is established among all things. Then trust and joyfulness enter our souls, we feel our thoughts and hearts grow. And we advance again, on the road of ages, toward the end of our task; yet this work has no end. For each time humanity moves toward a new ideal, it believes that it has reached the supreme ideal, whereas in reality, it has only achieved the belief or system corresponding to its degree of evolution. Each time also, from our own impulsions and conquests, there arise new felicities and strengths in us, and humanity finds the reward of its labors and anxieties in its very work and in the joy of living and progressing – which is the law for all beings – in more intimate communion with the Universe, and a somewhat more thorough possession of Good and Beauty.

O writers, artists, poets, all of you whose number is increasing every day, whose productions multiply and emerge like a growing stream, often beautiful in form but weak in substance, superficial and material, do not waste your talent in mediocre causes! How many efforts have been spent or put at the service of unhealthy passions, debasing voluptuousness, and vile interests!

While vast and magnificent horizons continually unfold, and the wonderful book of the universe and the spirit opens in its full grandeur, in front of you; and the Genius of the thought itself invites you to noble deeds, to works full of vigor and energy, fecund for the advancement of humanity; too often you indulge in puerile and sterile endeavors, in works devoid of consciousness, in which intelligence sinks and languishes in an exaggerated worship of the senses and of impure instincts.

Who of you will be willing to sing the epic of the soul fighting for the conquest of its destiny throughout the immense cycle of ages and worlds; with its pains and joys, falls and upheavals; its descent into the abysses of life; its quick flutters of wing into the light; its self-immolations, the "burnt offerings" which are a redemption, redemptive missions; and its growing participation in divine conceptions!

Also, who of you will be willing to sing the powerful harmonies of the universe – this gigantic harp vibrating under the God's thought – the song of the worlds, the eternal rhythm that cradles the genesis of stars and different kinds of humanity!

Or rather sing the slow development, the painful gestation of consciousness through its lower stages, the laborious construction of one's individuality, a moral being! Who will sing the conquest of life, ever fuller, wider, and more serene, more enlightened by the rays from above; walking from summit to summit, in pursuit of happiness, power and pure love? Who will sing the toil of humans, immortal wrestlers who, through their doubts, their sorrows, their anxieties and their tears, raise the harmonious and sublime edifice of their thinking and conscious personality? Moving always ahead, always farther, and higher!

We will answer: We have no idea who. And then wonder: Who will teach us all these things?

Who? The inner voices and the voices of the Hereafter! So learn to open, leaf through, and read the book that is kept hidden inside of you, the book of the metamorphoses of being. It will tell you what you have been and what you will be. It will teach you the greatest of all mysteries, the creation of the self through constant effort, the sovereign action which, in silent thought, makes your work sprout and, according to your abilities and the talent you have, will make you paint the more beautiful canvases, sculpt the most ideal forms, compose the most harmonious symphonies, write the most beautiful pages, and create the most beautiful poems.

Everything is right there, in and around you! Everything speaks and vibrates, whether seen or unseen, everything sings and celebrates the glory of living, the intoxication of thinking, of creating, of associating oneself with the universal work. The splendors of the seas and the starry sky, the majesty of mountain peaks, the fragrances of flowers, the various perfumes and rays, the mysterious sounds of forests, the melodies of planet Earth and space, voices of the invisible that speak in the silence of the night the voice of conscience, echo of the divine voice; everything is teaching a lesson and making a revelation to those who can see, listen, understand, think, and act!

Then, above all, stands the Supreme Vision, the formless vision, the uncreated Thought, as the total truth, the final harmony of the essences and laws which, from the bottom of our souls to the most distant stars, connects each one and everything in a resplendent unity. And the chain of life, which spreads and unfolds itself into the infinite, like a ladder of spiritual powers, through prayer, brings to God the appeals of humans, and to humans the response of God in form of inspirations.

And now, one last question remains. Why, in the midst of the immense labors and abundant intellectual productions that characterize our age, is there a scarcity of strong works and brilliant conceptions? Well, that is because we have stopped seeing the divine things through the eyes of the soul! Because we have ceased to believe and to love!

Let us return then to the celestial, eternal sources: it is the only cure for our moral apathy. Let us turn our thoughts to solemn and profound things. Let science be enlightened and completed by the intuitions of consciousness and the higher faculties of the spirit. Modern Spiritualism will help us.

XXIV
DISCIPLINE OF THOUGHT AND INNER TRANSFORMATION

As stated earlier, thought is creative. It does not act only around us, influencing our fellow beings either in a good or a bad way; it acts especially within ourselves. It generates our words and actions, and through it, we build the grand or miserable edifice of our life everyday, both present and future. We shape our soul and its envelope by our own thoughts. These produce forms and images which are impressed on the subtle matter of that composes our fluidic body. Thus, little by little, our being is populated with either frivolous or austere, graceful or horrible, coarse or sublime forms; and our soul is ennobled and bathed in beauty, or debased in an atmosphere of ugliness.

There is no subject more important than the study of thought, its powers, and its action. Thought is the initial cause of our elevation or our fall; it devises all the discoveries of science, all the wonders of art, but also all the miseries and shames of humanity. According a given impulsion, it founds or destroys empires, characters or consciences. Humans are not great in themselves, they are only worth what their thought is worth. Through it, our works and deeds radiate and continue through the centuries.

Experimental Spiritualism, much better than all previous philosophical doctrines, enables us to grasp and understand the whole projection power of thought. It is the principle of universal communion. We see it acting in Spiritist phenomena, which it will facilitate or hinder. Its role in experimental sittings is also considerable. Telepathy has shown us that souls can impress and influence each other at all distances. Thought is the means used by the populations of the spiritual plane to communicate with one another through the sidereal immensities. Throughout the spectrum of solar activities, in all areas of the visible or invisible world, the action of thought reigns supreme. It is no less so – let me repeat it – within ourselves and onto ourselves, by constantly modifying our inner nature.

The vibrations of our thoughts and words, by renewing themselves in a uniform sense, expel from our envelope the elements which cannot vibrate in harmony with them. They attract similar elements that accentuate the tendencies of self. A work, often unconscious, is thus elaborated; a thousand mysterious "mining laborers" keep working in the shadows. In the depths of one's soul, a whole destiny is sketched; in the resulting gangue, the hidden diamond is thus purified or tarnished.

If we meditate abut lofty subjects, including wisdom, a sense duty, and self-sacrifice, our being will gradually become immersed in the qualities of our thought. This is why every improvised, ardent prayer, reflecting the impulsion of the soul toward the powers of the infinite, carries so much virtue. In this solemn dialogue between one's being and its cause, an impetus from above invades us and new senses are awaken. One's understanding, one's awareness of life increases and we feel, better than we can actually express it, the gravity and magnificence of the most humble of existences. Prayer, communion through thought with the spiritual and divine universe, is the effort of the soul toward eternal beauty and truth;

it is the entrance for a moment into the spheres of real and superior life, the one that has no limit.

But if, on the contrary, our thought is inspired by bad desires, by passions, jealousy, or hatred, the images that it gives out follow one another and build up in our fluidic body, entangling it. Therefore we are able to make, at will, light or shade in ourselves. This is what so many communications from beyond the grave have been claiming.

We are what we think, provided we think forcefully, with willpower and persistence. But almost always our thoughts keep constantly moving from one subject to another. We rarely think for ourselves, we reflect the thousand incoherent thoughts of the environment in which we live. Few individuals know how to live by their own thought, to draw from their deeper sources, from this great reservoir of inspirations that each one carries within themselves, but that most of them are unaware of. So one's fluidic envelope ends up populated by the most disparate forms. Their spirit is like a home open to all passersby. The rays of goodness and the shadows of evil are merged into a perpetual chaos. There is an incessant struggle between passion and duty, in which, almost always, passion prevails. Above all, we must learn to control our thoughts, to discipline them, to give them a precise direction, and a noble and worthy goal.

The control of our thoughts leads to the control of our actions, because if the former are good, the latter will be good as well, and our entire conduct will be regulated by a harmonious sequence. Whereas if our actions are good but our thoughts are bad, there can only be a false appearance of good, and we will continue to harbor evil within ourselves, the influences of which will sooner or later impact on our life.

Sometimes we notice a striking contradiction between certain individual's thoughts and writings versus their actions – and by this very contradiction we are led to doubt their good faith, their sincerity. This is often only a false interpretation on our part. The acts of these men result from the dull impulse of the thoughts and forces they have accumulated in them in the past. Their present, higher aspirations, their more generous thoughts, will be realized in action in the future. Thus everything agrees and is explained when we consider things from the enlarged point of view of evolution; while everything remains obscure, incomprehensible, contradictory, with the theory of a unique life for each of us.

It is good to live in contact with great writers of genius, with the truly great authors of all times and countries, by reading, meditating on their works, impregnating our being with the substance of their souls. The radiations of their thoughts will awaken similar effects in us, and in the long run will bring about changes in our character, an inner transformation by the very nature of the impressions they left.

We must choose our readings with care, then mature and assimilate their quintessence. In general, we read too much, we read hastily, and we hardly meditate. It would be better to read less and think more about what you read. It is a sure way to strengthen your intelligence, to collect the fruits of wisdom and beauty that your reading can contain. In this, as in all things, beauty attracts and generates more beauty, just as kindness attracts happiness, and evil draws suffering.

Studying in silence and retreat is always fruitful for the development of thought. It is in silence that powerful works come to fruition. The word is brilliant, but too often it degenerates in sterile, sometimes harmful, phrasing. In this way, thought is weakened and the soul empties itself, whereas in meditation, the spirit will focus, turning to the grave and solemn side of things. Then the light of the spiritual world will bathe it in its waves. There are great invisible beings around thinkers, all eager to inspire the latter. It is in the twilight of quiet hours, or under the discreet light of a working lamp, that such spirits can best communicate with thinkers. Everywhere and always, a hidden life constantly mixes with ours.

Avoid noisy discussions, empty words, frivolous readings. Let us be parsimonious when reading the press. The intense reading of newspapers, by constantly jumping from one subject to another, makes the spirit even more susceptible. We live in times of intellectual inertia, which is caused by the scarcity of serious analyses, by an abusive search of the word for the word's sake, of embellished empty formulas, and especially by the insufficiency of youth educators. Let us attach ourselves to more substantial works, to everything that can enlighten us about the deep laws of life, and facilitate our evolution. Gradually a stronger intelligence and consciousness will be built up within ourselves, and our fluidic body will thus be illuminated by the reflections of a higher and purer thought.

As said above, the soul conceals depths into which thought rarely descends, because a thousand external objects occupy it incessantly. Its surface, like that of the sea, is often agitated, but underneath lie regions that thunderstorms cannot reach. There sleeps these hidden powers, waiting for our call to emerge and appear. The call is seldom heard, and we humans are agitated in our indigence, ignoring the incalculable treasures that lie within ourselves.

It takes the shock brought by our trials, plus sad and desolate hours, for us to understand the brittleness of external things, and end up searching for ourselves, so as to discover our true spiritual riches.

That is why great souls become all the more noble and beautiful as their pains are more vivid. With each new misfortune that strikes them, they feel that they have come a little closer to truth and perfection, and with this thought they experience a bitter pleasure. A new star has risen in the sky of their destiny, a star whose trembling rays penetrate the sanctuary of their consciousness, and illuminate its hidden recesses. Even in intellects of high culture, misery sows: every pain is a furrow where virtue and beauty crops are harvested.

In certain moments of our life, when we lose a parent, or at the collapse of an ardently cherished hope, or still when we lose a beloved partner or child, in short, every time one of the bonds which link us to this world is struck, a mysterious voice rises from the depths of our soul. This solemn voice which speaks to us of a thousand laws more august, more venerable than those of the Earth, opens up a whole ideal world. Yet the sounds of the outside soon stifle it, and we almost always fall back into our doubts, our hesitations, and the flat banality of our lives.

No progress is possible without a careful observation of oneself. We must monitor all our impulsive acts, in order to come to know in which direction we must strive to improve ourselves. First, we must regulate our physical life, and reduce our material needs to the minimum necessary to ensure a healthy body, the indispensable instrument of our earthly tasks. Then, we should discipline our impressions and emotions, to practice curbing them, to use them as agents of our moral perfectioning. To learn, above all, how to forget oneself, to sacrifice oneself, to free oneself from all feeling of selfishness. We are really happy in this world only to the extent that we know how to forget ourselves.

It is not enough to believe and to know, it is also necessary to live one's belief, that is to say, to make the higher principles that we have embraced penetrate into the daily practice of our lives. We must become accustomed to communion by thought and by heart with the eminent spirits that have been the revealers, the elite souls that have served as guides to humankind, in order to live with them daily, in close relationship, be inspired by their views, and feel their influence through this close inner perception that develops our relationship with the unseen world.

Among these great souls, it is good to choose one as our role model, the most worthy of our admiration, and, in all difficult circumstances, in all cases where our conscience oscillates between two options, to ask ourselves what would our model have chosen if placed in that same situation; and then act accordingly.

Thus, according to this model, we will gradually build ourselves a moral ideal that will be reflected in all our actions. Every individual, in their humble everyday reality, can thus model a sublime conscience for themselves. It is a slow and difficult labor, but centuries stand at our disposal to accomplish it.

So let us focus our thoughts often, in order to bring them back, through our will, to the dreamed ideal. Let us meditate on it every day, at a chosen hour, in the morning preferably, when everything is calm and still rests around us; at those moments that a poet would call "the divine hour," when Nature, fresh and rested, awakens in the light of dawn. In the morning hours, the soul, through prayer and meditation, gathers an easier momentum to rise to these heights from where we can see and understand that everything – life, actions, thoughts – each and every thing is connected to something greater and eternal, and we live in a world where invisible powers live and work together with us. In the simplest life, in the humblest task, in the most effaced existence, there are deep sides, a reserve of ideal, latent sources of beauty. Each soul can produce, by its own thoughts, a spiritual atmosphere as beautiful and resplendent as the most enchanting landscape conceivable; and in the most miserable dwelling, in the poorest home, there are openings toward God and the infinite!

Regardless of our social connections, in our relations with our fellow beings, we must constantly keep this in mind: all humans are ongoing travelers, occupying various different points on the scale of evolution which is climbed by all of us. Therefore, we must not demand anything, or expect anything from them, that does not correspond to their degree of advancement.

We owe tolerance, benevolence and even forgiveness to everyone; for if we are harmed, if we are mocked and offended, it is almost always because of a lack of understanding and knowledge that results from insufficient development. God asks of human beings only what they have been able to acquire through their slow and painful labors. We do not have the right to demand more. Were we not like the most backward of them? If each of us could read in our past what we were, what we did, how much more lenient we would be to the faults of others! Sometimes we need the same indulgence we ourselves owe them. Let us be tough on ourselves and tolerant of others. Let us enlighten and guide them gently: this is what the law of solidarity commands us to do.

Lastly, one must know how to bear all things with patience and serenity. Whatever may be the actions of our fellow beings toward us, we must react with no animosity, no resentment. On the contrary, let us make all causes of frustration or affliction instruments for our moral education. No setback would be able to reach us if, through our previous and guilty lives, we had not let adversity take hold. That is what we often have to remember. We will thus be able to accept all trials without bitterness, and consider them as a remedy for our past, or a means of improvement.

Step by step, we will thus attain this peace of mind, this possession of oneself, this absolute confidence in the future, that will give us strength, tranquility, and inner satisfaction, besides allowing us to remain firm even amidst the harshest vicissitudes.

When old age comes, illusions and vain hopes fall like dead leaves; but the high truths only emerge brighter, like the stars in a winter sky, through the bare branches of our gardens.

Then it will matter not that destiny has offered us no glory, no smile, no ray of joy, when it instead has enriched our soul with an additional virtue: a little of moral beauty. Dark and tormented lives are sometimes the most fruitful, while brilliant ones too often and for a long time throw us into a fearsome chain of responsibilities.

Happiness is not found in external things or chance things happening outside, but only within ourselves, in the inner life when we know how to lead it. What does it matter that the sky is black over our heads and bad individuals are around us, if we have light on our forehead, the joy of good and moral freedom in our heart. Yet, if you feel ashamed of yourself, if evil has invaded your mind, if crime and betrayal inhabit you, then all favors, all felicities of the Earth, will not restore to you the silent peace and joy of conscience. The wise individual, already during his or her life in this world, creates in themselves an assured refuge, a sacred place, a deep retreat, where the conflicts and contradictions of the outside cannot reach. Similarly, in the life on the spiritual plane, both the sanction of duty and the realization of justice are of an inner nature. Each soul carries in itself its own luminosity or shadow, its paradise or its hell. Bear in mind, though, that nothing is irreparable: the current situation of a lower-order spirit is but an almost imperceptible point in the immensity of its destiny.

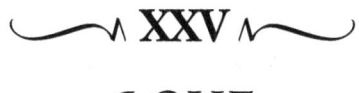

LOVE

LOVE, AS COMMONLY UNDERSTOOD on Earth, is a feeling, an impulse of one being who carries it to another being with a desire to unite with it. But, in reality, love takes on innumerable forms, from the most vulgar to the most sublime. Principle of the universal life, it gives to the soul, in its highest and purest manifestations, an intensity of radiation which warms up and vivifies all that surrounds it; it is through it that the soul feels closely connected to the divine Power, this ardent focus, origin of all life, of all love.

Above all, God is love; it is out of love that It created all beings, to associate them with Its joys, with Its work. Love involves self-sacrifice; God has drawn life from Itself to give it to the souls. At the same time as this vital outpouring, they received the emotional principle destined to sprout and flourish within them, through the trial of centuries, until they learned to give themselves up in their turn – that is, to devote themselves to self-sacrifice for others. Thus, far from being diminished, they grow ever more and become ennobled, while getting closer to the supreme focus.

As a force, love is inexhaustible: it renews itself constantly and enriches both the one who gives and the one who receives it. It is through love, the sun of all souls, that God acts most effectively in our world. In this way It draws to Itself all the poor beings lingering in the depths of passion, spirits captive in matter. It raises them to their feet and leads them into the spiral of infinite ascension toward the splendors of light and freedom.

Conjugal love, parental love, filial or fraternal love, the love of one's country, of one's nationality, of humanity, are mere deflections, broken rays of the divine love, which embraces and penetrates all beings, and by spreading itself in them, hatches and blossoms in a thousand varied forms, a thousand splendid blooms of love.

Down to the depths of the abyss of life, the radiations of divine love slip onto and light up the most rudimentary beings, as reflected by their attachment to their companion and little ones, with the first glimmers which, in an environment of ferocious selfishness, will be like an incipient dawn and the promise of a higher life.

It is the call of one's being to another fellow being, it is love that will cause, in the depths of embryonic souls, the first awakenings of altruism, of pity, of goodness. When we climb higher on the evolutionary ladder, love initiates the human being into its first felicities, the only sensations of perfect happiness that are given to humans to experience on Earth, sensations which are stronger and sweeter than all the physical joys, and granted only to souls that truly learned how to love.

Thus, step by step, under the influence and the radiance of love, ours souls develop, grow, and enlarge the circle of their sensations. Slowly, what was the soul's only passion, carnal desire, will be purified, will turn into a noble and disinterested feeling. The attachment to one fellow being or to only a few becomes an attachment to all, to one's family, to one's homeland, to humanity. And the soul then acquires the fullness of its development when it is able to understand celestial life – which is entirely love – and to participate in it.

Love is stronger than hatred, stronger than death. If Christ was the greatest of all missionaries and prophets, if he exerted so much power over humans, it was because he bore in him a more powerful reflection of divine love. Jesus spent little time on Earth; three years of evangelization that proved enough to seize the attention of whole nations. It was neither through science nor by any oratorical art that he enthralled and captivated the crowds, but rather through love. And since his death, his love has remained in the world as a glowing focus which is always alive, perpetually burning. That is why, in spite of the errors and faults of its representatives, in spite of so much blood shed by them, so many burning flames, and so many veils concealing its teachings, Christianity remained the greatest religion. It disciplined and shaped the human soul, softened the savage mood of barbarians, and wrenched entire nations from sensualism and even bestiality.

Christ is not the only example to draw upon. In general, it is possible in our sphere to observe that all eminent souls emanate from these radiations, these regenerative emanations which form an atmosphere of peace, like a protection, a safeguarding, a particular providence. All who live under this beneficent moral influence feel a calmness, a restfulness of mind, a serenity that gives a foretoken of the elusive celestial tranquility. This feeling is even more pronounced in Spiritist seances directed and inspired by higher souls. I have often experienced it myself, in presence of the spirit entities that presided over the work carried out by our mediumistic group in Tours (France).[228]

These impressions become ever more vividly as one moves away from the lower planes; where selfish and fatal impulses reign; and climbs up the ladder of the glorious spiritual hierarchy to get closer to the divine focus. We can thus see, through an experiment which completes our intuitions, that each soul is a system of

---

[228] See Léon DENIS, *Into the Unseen* (New York: USSF, 2017), ch. XIX, "Trance and Incorporations."

forces and a love generator, whose action power increases as it elevates itself.

In this way, universal solidarity and fraternity are thoroughly explained and affirmed. One day, when the true notion of being emerges from the doubts and uncertainties that still obsess human thought, we will understand this great loving fellowship which connects all souls. We will feel that everyone is enveloped by the divine magnetism, by the great breath of love that fills all planes of space.

Apart from having this powerful bond, souls are also divided in separate groups and families, which have been formed little by little through the centuries, by their common joys and pains. Our real family is that of the spiritual world; whereas the one we have on Earth is only a reflection, a weakened reduction, as are all earthly things as compared to those of heaven. Our true family is composed of spirits that have climbed together the rough paths of destiny, and have come to understand one another and love one another.

Apart from having this powerful bond, souls are also divided in separate groups and families, which have been formed little by little through the centuries, by their common joys and pains. Our real family is that of the spiritual world; whereas the one we have on Earth is only a reflection, a weakened reduction, as are all earthly things as compared to those of heaven. Our true family is composed of spirits that have climbed together the rough paths of destiny, and have come to understand one another and to love one another.

Who could describe the inner tender feelings which unite these beings, the ineffable joys born out of the fusion of their minds and consciences, the fluidic union of souls under the smiling gaze of God?

These spiritual groupings are blessed milieus where all earthly passions subside, where selfishness vanishes, hearts expand, where all those who have suffered, come to reinvigorate themselves and be comforted, when, after being delivered by death, they are reunited with their nearest and dearest, all gathered to celebrate their return.

Who will be able to paint the ecstasies which the purified souls, who have reached the summits of light, experience with the outpouring of divine love? And the celestial betrothal[229] by which two spirits are forever united in the families of the spiritual plane, gathered to consecrate, by a solemn rite, this symbolic and indestructible union? These are the real bonds of marriage, of souls that God brings together by a thread of gold, for all eternity. Through those festivals of love, the spirits that have learned to free themselves, and to use their freedom, merge in one same fluid, under the moved gaze of their fellow spirits. They will follow from then on in their wanderings through the worlds; they will walk hand in hand, smiling at misfortune, and drawing from their mutual tenderness the strength they need in order to bear all the reverses, all the bitterness of fate. Sometimes, separated by rebirths, they will preserve the secret intuition that their isolation is only temporary: after the trials of separation, they foresee the elation caused by their return to the threshold to immensity.

All the power of the soul is summed up in three words: to wish, to know, to love!

---

[229] [Trans. note] *Cf.* A. KARDEC, *The Spirits' Book* (2nd ed., New York: USSC/USSF, 2016), question 202, "Spirits ... have no gender."

To wish, that is to say, to make all your activity, all your energy converge toward a goal you want to achieve; by developing your will and learning how to focus it.

To know, because without thorough study, without the knowledge of things and laws, your thought and the will can go astray amidst the forces they seek to conquer, and the elements they aspire to command.

But, above all, we must love, for without love, our will and science would be incomplete and often sterile. Love enlightens them, fecundates a hundredfold their resources. This is not a question of love contemplating without action, but rather of love working to spread good and truth in the world. Earthly life is a conflict between the forces of evil and those of good. The duty of every courageous soul is to take part in the combat, bringing to it all their vigorous will and their means of action, in order to fight for others, for all those who are still agitating the dark ocean. The most noble use that one can make of his or her faculties is to work in order to expand and develop a sense of good and beauty in our civilization; this human society, which has its wounds and ugliness, no doubt, but that nonetheless is still rich in hopes and wonderful promises. These promises will be transformed into living realities, the day when humanity will have learned to commune, through thought and heart, with the inextinguishable focus of love which is the splendor of God.

Therefore let us love with all the power of our heart and soul; let us love to the point of self-sacrifice, as Joan of Arc loved France, as Christ loved humanity; and all those around us will thus be influenced, feeling born to a new life.

O fellow human beings, search around you for wounds to be dressed, ills to be healed, afflictions to be soothed. Help expand knowledge; bring back lost hearts; bring together forces and souls. Work to construct a higher city of peace and harmony that will be the city of love, the city of God! Enlighten, raise, purify! And what does it matter if others laugh at you? What does it matter if ingratitude and wickedness stand in your way? The one who loves does not back down for so little. Even if he or she only harvests only thorns and brambles, they persevere in their work because therein lies their duty. They know that self-denial can only make us grow.

Besides, self-denial too has its joys; when accomplished with love, it turns tears into smiles, it gives rise in us to joys unknown to the selfish and wicked. For those who know how to love, the most banal things become interesting: everything seems to light up, a thousand new sensations awaken in them.

It takes wisdom and science long-standing efforts and a slow and painful ascension to lead us to the summits of thought. Love and self-sacrifice succeed in a single leap with one stroke of the wing. In their stride, they gain patience, courage, benevolence, and all strong and sweet virtues. Love refines intelligence, expands the heart, and it is in relation to the sum of love built up in ourselves that we can measure the progress we have actually made toward God.

To all the questions posed by human beings – their hesitations, their fears, their blasphemies – a big, powerful and mysterious voice replies: "Learn to love!" Love is the summit of everything, the ultimate goal of everything, the culmination of everything. From this summit the immense network of love, woven of gold and light, continually unfolds and extends in the universe. Loving is the secret of happiness. In a word, love resolves all problems and dispels all obscurities. Love will save the world; its blazing heat will melt the ice of doubt, selfishness and hatred. It will soften even the hardest and most resistant hearts.

Even in its splendid derivatives, love is always an effort toward beauty. Even sexual love, that of a man and a woman, all material as it may seem, can only display an ideal, express poetry and thus lose all vulgarity, if it combines a feeling of esthetics with a lofty thought. And this depends mostly on the woman. She who loves feels and sees things that a man cannot know. She possesses in her heart inexhaustible reserves of love, a kind of intuition that can give an idea of eternal love.

In some ways, women always remain like sisters of mystery, and the part of their being which touches the infinite seems to reach deeper than that of men's. When men respond like women to the calls of the unseen, when their love is free from all brutal desire, if they become one in spirit as in body, then, in the embrace of these two beings, interpenetrating each other, complementing each other in order to transmit life, they will pass like a flash, like a flame, a reflection of the highest felicities they have glimpsed. Yet the joys of earthly love are fugitive and mixed with bitterness. They are not exempt from disappointments, setbacks and falls. God alone is love in all its fullness. God is the ardent fire and, at the same time, the abyss of thought and light, from which emanate and to which return, eternally, the warm emanations of all the stars, the passionate tenderness of all women's, mothers', and wives' hearts, and the virile affections of all men. God generates and calls back love, because It is the infinite, perfect Beauty – and what is proper of beauty is to induce love.

On a summer's day, when the sun is shining while the immense azure dome is unfurled over our heads, and from the meadows and the woods, from the mountains and the sea, rises a worship, a silent prayer of beings and things, who can say that he or she did never feel these radiations of love filling the infinite?

You must never have opened your soul to these subtle influences to be able ignore or deny them. Too many earthly souls, it is true, remain hermetically closed to anything divine. Or, should they feel its harmonies and beauties, they carefully hide the secret in themselves. They seem ashamed to confess what they know from experience to be bigger and better.

But try the experience! Open your inner being, open the windows of the prison of your soul with the emanations of universal life, and suddenly this dungeon will be filled with lights and songs; a whole luminous world will penetrate you. Your delighted soul will experience ecstasies, joys that cannot be described; it will understand that there is an ocean of love, power and divine life surrounding it, in which it is immersed; and that it is enough for it to wish to be bathed in that ocean's regenerative waves. It will feel in the universe a sovereign and marvelous Power that loves us, envelops us, supports us, watches over us like a zealous guardian over a precious jewel; and that by invoking It, by sending It an ardent appeal, the soul will be penetrated immediately by Its presence and love. These things can be felt, but hardly be expressed; only those who have tasted them can really understand them. Yet all of us can come to know them, to possess them, by awakening the divine in ourselves. There is no human being so dark and wicked, that, in an moment of abandonment and suffering, cannot see the way through which a little light of superior things, a little love, filter up toward itself.

It suffices to have once experienced these impressions to keep their memory forever. And when the night of life falls upon us with its disenchantments, when the twilight shadows loom over, these powerful sensations awaken with the memory of all the joys we had felt. And this memory of a time when we truly loved, like a delicious dew, descends upon our souls parched by the harsh winds of trials and sufferings.

XXVI

PAIN

ALL THAT LIVES here below, suffers: Nature, animals and humans. And yet love is the law of the Universe, and it is out of love that God has formed all beings. A formidable contradiction, in appearance, and an agonizing problem, which has troubled so many thinkers, leading them to doubt and pessimism!

Animals are subject to a fierce struggle for life. Among the grasses of the prairie, under the foliage and branches of the woods, in the air, in the water, everywhere, a multitude of dramas take place. In our cities, a hecatomb of innocent, harmless animals, sacrificed to our needs, or delivered to laboratories, to the torments of vivisection, goes on continually.

As for humanity, its history has been nothing but a long martyrology. Through the ages, over the centuries, the sad chant of human suffering unravels; the complaint of the unfortunate rises with a heart-rending intensity with the regularity of sea waves.

Pain follows closely each of our steps; it watches us at every turn of the road. And in front of this sphinx which fixes us with its strange guise, we humans ask ourselves the same eternal question: Why pain?

Is it, as far as it is concerned, a punishment, an atonement, as some say? Is it an atonement for past misdeeds, the redemption from mistakes?

Basically, pain is only a law of balance and education. Doubtless, our faults in the past fall upon us with all their weight and determine the conditions of our destiny. Suffering is often only the counterblow to violations committed against the eternal order; but, being shared of all beings, it must be considered as a necessity of a general nature, as an agent of development, a condition of progress. All beings must undergo it in their turn. Its action is beneficial for those who know how to understand it. Yet only those who have felt its powerful effects can really understand it. It is to them especially that I address these pages, to all those who suffer, and have suffered, or are worthy of suffering!

Pain and pleasure are the two extreme forms of sensation. To abolish one or the other, sensitivity would have to be suppressed. They are, therefore, inseparable in principle, and both are necessary for the education of beings, which, in their evolution, must exhaust all the unlimited forms of pleasure as well as pain.

Physical pain produces sensations; moral suffering produces feelings. But, as we have seen above, in the inner sensorium,[230] sensation and feeling merge with one another and become one.

Therefore pleasure and pain reside much less in external things than within ourselves. And that is why they belong to each one of us, when we regulate our sensations, discipline our feelings, and commanding both by limiting their effects. Greek philosopher Epictetus once said: "Remember that all things are only what we think they are." Thus, through will, we can tame and overcome pain, or at least turn it to our advantage, by transforming it into an instrument of elevation.

---

[230] [Trans. note] (*inner*) *sensorium* is the seat of sensation in humans and animals. Also called *common sensorium* or *sensorium commune*.

The idea we have of happiness and misfortune, of joy and sorrow, varies infinitely according to our individual evolution. The pure soul, which is good and wise, cannot be happy in the same way as an ordinary soul. What may charm one leaves the other indifferent. As one climbs up, the appearance of things changes. As children, while growing up, disdain the games that once captivated them, the rising soul seeks ever more noble, serious and deep satisfactions. The spirits that have a lofty judgment and consider the grand purpose of life will find more happiness and serene peace in a beautiful thought, a good work, an act of virtue, and even in the misfortune that purifies be it in material goods or in the glories of earthly rewards, for these disturb us, corrupt us, and make us drunk with illusory intoxication.

It is quite difficult to make humans understand that suffering is good for them. Everyone would like to reshape and embellish life at will, to adorn it with all amenities, without thinking that there can be no lasting good without pain, no ascent without effort.

The general tendency is to shut oneself up in the narrow circle of individualism, of each one for himself; hence humans are getting smaller, by reducing to narrow limits all that is great in them, everything that is destined to expand, to dilate, to take flight: thought, consciousness, in a word, all their soul. Now, enjoyments, pleasures, sterile idleness, only serve to tighten these limits even more, to make our lives and our hearts to further shrink with narrowness. To break this vicious cycle, so that all hidden virtues are spread out, it takes pain. Unhappiness and trials bring forth in us the sources of an unknown and more beautiful life. Sadness and suffering make us see, hear, and feel a thousand things, both delicate and powerful, that the happy individual or ordinary humans are not able to perceive. The material world is usually darkened; another world is taking shape, vaguely at first, but one that will become more and more distinct as our gaze detaches itself from inferior things and plunges into infinity.

Genius is not only the result of a centuries-old work; it is also the apotheosis, the crowning of suffering. From Homer to Dante, Camoens, Tasso, Milton, and after them, all the great individuals and poets have suffered. Pain made their souls vibrate; it inspired them with that nobility of feeling, that intensity of emotion which they knew how to render with the accents of genius that immortalized them. The soul never sings better than in pain. When it touches the depths of one's being, it brings forth these eloquent cries, these powerful calls that move and drag entire crowds.

It is the same with all heroes, all great personages, all generous hearts, and the most eminent spirits. Their elevation is measured by the sum of the sufferings they endured. In the face of pain and death, the soul of a hero, of a martyr, reveals itself in its touching beauty, in its tragic grandeur which sometimes borders on the sublime, with the halo of an inextinguishable light.

Abolish pain and at the same time you will be suppressing what we have most worthy of admiration in this world, that is, the courage to endure it. The noblest teaching that can be offered to human beings is not the memory of those who have suffered and died for truth and justice? Is there anything more august, more venerable than their graves? Nothing equals the moral power that emerges from it. The souls who gave such examples grow in our eyes as the centuries go by and look even more imposing. They are like so many sources of strength and beauty where generations have come to rediscover themselves. Through time and space, their radiance, like the light of the stars, still extends to Earth.

Their death has given birth to life, and their memory, as a subtle aroma, will everywhere throw the seeds of future enthusiasms.

They have taught us, these souls, that it is by devotion, through sufferings worthily supported that we climb the paths of heaven. And the history of the world is nothing but the crowning of the spirit through pain. Without it, there can be no complete virtue or imperishable glory.

We must suffer in order to achieve and to conquer. Acts of sacrifice increase the psychical radiations. There is like a luminous trail that follows, on the spiritual plane, the spirits of heroes and martyrs.

Those who have not suffered can hardly understand these things, because in them only the surface is cleared and developed. Their feelings are not extensive; they have no effusions of the heart; and their thoughts embrace only narrow horizons. It is necessary that they go through misfortunes and anxieties, to give their souls a velvety moral beauty, awakening their sleeping senses. A painful life is an alembic where beings are distilled for better worlds. Both the form and its core, everything is embellished by having suffered. There is, since this life, something grave and tender in the faces that tears have often soaked. They take on an expression of austere beauty, a kind of majesty that impresses and enchants.

Michelangelo had adopted as a rule of thumb the following precepts: "Retreat into yourself and do as the sculptor does on the work he wants to make beautiful ... Take away all that is superfluous, make clear what is dark, bring light everywhere, and never stop chiseling out your own statue."[231]

A sublime axiom, which contains the principle of all inner perfection. Indeed, our soul is our work, a capital

---

[231] [Trans. note] Quoted from Jules Barthélemy SAINT-HILAIRE, *De l'École d'Alexandrie* ... (Paris: Lib. Phil. de Ladrange, 1845), p. 195.

and fruitful work which exceeds in size all the partial manifestations of art, science and genius.

However, difficulties of the execution are closely related to the splendor of the goal. And in face of this painful task of inner transformation, in this incessant combat against passions, against matter, how often does the craftsperson become discouraged? How many times do we drop the chisel? Well, that is when God sends us help: pain! It carves boldly into those depths of consciousness that the hesitant and clumsy worker could not or would not reach; it digs its folds, shaping its contours; it eliminates or destroys what was useless or bad.

And this cold marble, without form or beauty, from which we had barely sketched an ugly and rough statue with our own hands, will in time yield a living statue: the incomparable masterpiece, the harmonious and sweet contours of our divine Psyche!

Pain does not strike only the guilty ones. In our world, good and honest people suffer as much as the wicked. And this can be explained. Firstly, the virtuous soul being more evolved, is more sensitive. In addition, it often likes and seeks pain, being well aware of its price.

There are still among these souls those that do not come here below for anything else but to give an example of greatness in suffering. These are also missionary souls, and their mission is no less beautiful and touching than that of the great revealers. We meet them in all times, present in all walks of life. They are standing on the resplendent peaks of history and we can also find them, humble and hidden, among the crowds.

We admire Jesus Christ, Socrates, Antigone, Joan of Arc; but how many obscure victims of duty and love perish every day, relegated to silence and oblivion! Their examples, however, are never lost: they illuminate the whole life of the few people who witnessed their efforts.

To be full and fruitful, it is not essential that one's life be sprinkled with these great deeds of self-sacrifice, or crowned by a death that is sacred to everyone. Such a gloomy and sad existence, colorless and effaced in appearance, is deep inside only a continual effort, a constant struggle against misfortune and suffering. We are not judges of all that happens in the inner sanctum of souls; many of these, out of modesty, hide painful wounds, cruel evils, which would make them as worthy of interest in our eyes as the most famous martyrs. By the incessant combat they fight against destiny, these souls are great and heroic too. Their triumphs are ignored, but all the treasures of energy, of generous enthusiasm, of patience, and of love which they have built up in this everyday effort, will revert to them as a wealth of strength and moral beauty, which can render them a place in the Hereafter as high as that occupied by the noblest figures in history.

In the imposing workshop where souls are cast, genius and glory are not enough to make them truly beautiful. To give them the ultimate sublime trait, one needs pain. If certain obscure existences have become as sacred and hallowed as famous revered personages, it is because suffering was continuous in them. In such circumstances, it is not only once, or at the hour of death, that pain has raised them above themselves, and has been offered to the admiration of ages: it is because their whole life was a constant immolation.

And this slow work of purification, this long parade of painful hours, this mysterious refinement of beings who are thus preparing for the ultimate ascensions, cause admiration in the Higher-order Spirits themselves. It is this touching spectacle that inspires them to be reborn among us, to suffer and die again for all that is great, for all that they love; and, by this new sacrifice, to make their own brilliance even brighter.

After these general considerations, let us return to the main question in its primary elements.

Most often, physical pain is a warning from Nature, which seeks to preserve us from excesses. Without it, we would abuse our organs to the point of destroying them prematurely. When a dangerous evil slips into us, what would happen if we did not immediately feel its unpleasant effects? It would gradually creep inside us, invading and drying up the very sources of life.

And even when persisting in ignoring the repeated warnings from Nature, we allow disease to develop in us, this can still be a blessing if, caused by our abuses and vices, it teaches us to hate them, and us to correct them. You have to suffer in order to know yourself and to understand life better.

Again, the ancient Greek philosopher Epictetus, whom I like to quote, says: "Even in regard to what is false, something good arises: ... The same should be true in life also: ... Is health a good and illness an evil? No, ... Health is good when put to right use, and bad when put to bad use.... By God, isn't it possible to draw advantage even from death?"[232]

To weak souls, illness comes to teach them patience, wisdom, and self-control, whereas to strong souls, it may offer compensation in their ideals, by leaving the human

---

[232] [Trans. note] EPICTETUS, *Discourses, Fragments, Handbook* (Trans. Robin Hard. Oxford: OUP, 2014), 3.20, 2–4.

spirit free to develop its own aspirations, to the point of forgetting all about physical sufferings.

The action of pain is no less effective in whole communities than it is for individuals. Is it not thanks to it that the first human groupings were formed? Were it not the threat of wild beasts, of hunger, of plagues which first compelled humans to seek their fellow beings so as to associate with them? And from their common life, from their common sufferings, their intelligence, and their labors, all civilization was born, with its arts, sciences and industry!

One might say that physical pain results from the disproportion between our bodily weakness and all the forces that surround us, these colossal and prolific forces which correspond to as many manifestations of universal life. We can only assimilate a tiny part of the latter, yet, by acting upon us, they work in increasing and continually enlarging the sphere of our activities and the range of our sensations. Their action over our organic body has repercussions on our fluidic one: it helps to enrich the latter, to dilate it, to make it more impressionable, in a word, apter to new improvements.

Any suffering, by its chemical action, always has a useful result, but this result varies infinitely according to the individuals and their progress. By refining our material envelope, it gives more strength to our inner being, which then can more easily detach itself from earthly things. In other, more advanced people, it will act in the moral sense. The pain is like a wing lent to the soul enslaved to the flesh, in order to help it emerge and rise higher.

The first reaction of an unhappy individual is to revolt under the blows of fate. But later on, when the spirit has climbed the slopes, and then contemplates the harsh road traversed – and the moving parade of its lifetimes – it is with joyful tenderness that the spirit will recall the trials and tribulations of the world which ended up helping it reach the summit.

If, during times of trial, we learned how to observe the inner work, the mysterious action of pain in ourselves, in our conscience, we would better understand its sublime work of education and improvement. We would see that it always strikes at sensitive spots. The hand that directs the chisel belongs to an incomparable artist; it never tires of acting until the angles of our character are carved, rounded and polished. To attain that result, it will return to the fray for as long as necessary. And under repeated hammering, first our arrogance and excessive personality will have to subside; then softness, apathy and indifference will also be effaced; and finally hardness, anger and fury will all disappear under a third blow of the chisel. For each and every one, it will use different processes, infinitely varied according to our individuality, but always acting effectively with no exception, so as to give birth or to develop sensitivity, delicacy, goodness, and tenderness; and to bring out of heartaches and tears some unknown quality that was silently asleep in the depths of our being; or even a new nobility, adornment of the soul, thus retrieved to last forever.

And the more it rises, grows, and becomes beautiful, the more pain is spiritualized and becomes subtle. To the wicked it takes many trials, as on a tree it takes a lot of flowers to produce just a few fruits. But the more perfect the human being, the more the fruits of pain become admirable. To rough souls, still badly trimmed, incumbent physical sufferings and violent pains; to the selfish, the mischievous, losses of fortune, dark anxieties, torments of the spirit. As to delicate beings, mothers, lovers, married partners, there will be hidden tortures, wounds of the heart. To noble thinkers, to the inspired, a subtle and profound pain that gives rise to a sublime cry, the gleam of genius!

Yes, behind the pain, there is someone invisible who conducts its action and rule it according to the needs of each one, with art and infinite wisdom, thus working to increase our inner beauty, which is never complete, but always pursued, from light to light, virtue to virtue, until we become celestial spirits.

Surprising as it may seem at first sight, pain is only a means used by the Infinite Power to draw us toward itself and, at the same time, to bring us more quickly to spiritual joy, the only lasting happiness. It is therefore out of love for us that God sends us suffering. It strikes us, it corrects us as a mother corrects her child to straighten us and make us better. It works ceaselessly to soften, to purify, and to beautify our souls, because these can be truly and completely happy only to the extent of their perfection.

And for that, on this planet of learning, God has put, alongside scarce and fleeting joys, frequent and prolonged pains, to make us feel that our world is a place of transition and not an end in itself. Joys and sufferings, pleasures and pains, God has distributed them all in our existences like a great artist who, on his vast canvas, combines shadows and lights to produce a masterpiece.

In animals, suffering already serves as evolutionary work for the principle of life which inhabits each of them. Thereby they acquire the first rudiments of consciousness. Similarly, human beings also evolve in their successive reincarnations. If, from the very first earthly stages, a soul lived without facing any evils, it would remain inert, passive, and oblivious to the profound things and moral forces that lie within it.

Our goal is forward; our destiny is to walk toward this goal, without lingering on the way. Now, the happiness of this world may immobilize us; we linger here; we forget about the goal. But when we linger for too long, pain comes to push us forward.

As soon as a source of pleasure is open to us; for example through youth, love, or marriage; and that we forget ourselves in the enchantment of blissful hours, it is not rare that, shortly after, an unforeseen circumstance happens, and its sting is felt.

As we move forward in life, our joy decreases as pain increases. Our body becomes more unwieldy, the burden of the years, heavier. Almost always, existence starts in happiness and ends in sadness. For most individuals, decline brings the morose period of old age, with its lassitude, its infirmities, its neglects. Lights are extinguished; sympathies and consolations withdraw; dreams and hopes vanish. More and more pits crop up around us. Open long hours of immobility, inaction and suffering. These end up forcing us to retreat into ourselves, to often review the deeds and memories of our lives. This trial is necessary, so that the soul, before leaving its physical envelope, acquires this maturity, this judgment, this clear sight of things which will be the crowning of its earthly career. Thus, when we curse the seemingly barren and desolate hours of our infirm, solitary old age, we disregard one of the greatest blessings nature offers us: We forget that painful old age is the crucible where purifications are completed.

At that moment of our existence, the rays and forces that, during our years of youth and vigor, were dispersed on all sides of our activity and exuberance, concentrate and converge toward the depths of being, rousing our awareness and providing us with more wisdom and maturity. Little by little, harmony is made between our thoughts and external radiations; our inner melody agrees with the divine melody.

Therefore there is in resigned old age more grandeur and serene beauty than in the radiance youth and the strength of mature age. Under the action of time, what is profound and immutable in us tends disengage itself, and the brow of some old individuals is wreathed by halos of light from the Hereafter.

To all those who ask, "Why pain?" I answer: Why polish stone, carve marble, melt stained glass, or hammer iron? It is in order to build and decorate the magnificent temple, full of rays, vibrations, hymns, perfumes, where all the arts combine to express the divine, prepare the apotheosis of conscious thought, celebrate the liberation of the spirit!

And behold the result! From what was just scattered elements and shapeless materials in us; and sometimes, in the vicious and the fallen, even ruins and debris; pain has erected and built in the heart of humans a splendid altar to moral beauty, to eternal Truth.

A statue, in its ideal and perfect shape, lies buried, hidden in the rough block. When an individual does not have the required energy and knowledge, or the necessary will to strike it, then, as I said before, pain emerges. It takes the hammer, the chisel, and little by little, with violent blows, or under the slow and persistent work of the burin, outlines the living statue in its flexible and marvelous contours – under the broken quartz, the emerald sparkles!

Yes, indeed, for the form to emerge in its pure and delicate lines, the spirit to triumph over material substance, one's thought to spring up in sublime impulses, and for the poet to find immortal accents, and the musician sweet harmonies, the sting of destiny must be felt in our hearts, together with mourning and weeping, the ingratitude, the betrayals of friendship and love, anguish and heartache. We need the cherished coffins that descend beneath the earth, the fleeting youth, the icy old age that comes to us, the disappointments, the bitter sorrows that follow one another. Suffering is a necessity for humans, as much as a press is needed to extract the exquisite liquor from grapevine to wine!

Let us consider again the problem of pain from the point of view of penal laws.

Allan Kardec has been criticized for insisting too much in his books on the idea of retribution and atonement. For this he has received many reproofs. It gives, we are told, a false notion of God's action; it entails a plethora of punishments, which is incompatible with the supreme Goodness.

This judgment results from a superficial exam of the books of the great Codifier of Spiritism. The idea, the word punishment, may seem excessive, perhaps if one focuses on certain isolated passages, which in many cases were poorly interpreted. But this impression diminishes and completely disappears when we study his whole work.

As we know, it is above all in one's conscience, that the sanction of good and evil takes action. It painstakingly records all our actions and, sooner or later, becomes a harsh judge for the culprit, who, as a result of his or her evolution, always ends up hearing this voice and suffering its judgments. For the spirit, memories of the past unite with one's present on the spiritual plane, forming an inseparable whole. It lives outside of time, beyond the limits of time, and suffers as much from distant faults as from the most recent ones. So the spirit often asks for a quick and painful reincarnation, which will redeem the past, while at the same time giving some truce to its haunting memories.

With the difference of planes, suffering changes in nature. On Earth, it becomes both physical and moral and will be a way of atonement. It will plunge the culprit into its flame in order to purify him or her; it will recast in the rolling mill of trials the soul twisted by evil. Thus, each one of us has been able or will be able to erase his or her past; the sad pages of the beginning of our personal history, the serious faults committed when we were only an ignorant or impetuous spirit. Through suffering we will learn humility, together with indulgence and compassion for all those who succumb under the impulse of lower instincts, as happened to ourselves so many times in the past.

It is not therefore through vengeance that the law strikes us, but because it is good and profitable to suffer, since suffering frees us by satisfying conscience, whose verdict it executes.

All is redeemed and repaired through pain. As we have seen, there is a profound art in the processes it uses to shape the human soul and, when the latter is astray, bring it back to the sublime order of things.

People have often spoken of a law of talion, a law of retaliation. In reality, the reparation does not always appear in the same form as the fault committed. Social conditions and historical evolution are opposed to it. At the same time as the torments of the Middle Ages, many plagues have disappeared. Nevertheless, the sum of human sufferings, in their varied and innumerable forms, is always proportional to the cause that produces them. In vain progress is achieved, civilization spreads, hygiene and well-being develop. New diseases appear that human beings are powerless to heal. In this we must recognize the manifestation of a superior law of equilibrium of which we have spoken earlier. Pain will be necessary as long as humans do not put their thoughts and actions in harmony with the eternal laws; it will stop being felt as soon as such an agreement is attained. All our ills come from the fact that we act in a direction opposite to the current of divine life. If we return to this current, pain will disappear with the causes that gave birth to it.

For a long time yet, earthly humanity – ignorant of the higher laws, unconscious of the future and of duty – will need pain to stimulate it in its path, to transform what predominates in itself, that is, primitive and gross instincts, into pure and generous sentiments. For a long time we humans will have to go through a bitter initiation in order to get to know ourselves and our true purpose in life. Human beings are currently only thinking of applying their faculties and energies on the combat of suffering on the physical plane, so as to increase well-being and wealth, and make the conditions of material life more pleasing. But this will all be in vain. Sufferings may vary, move, change their appearance, yet pain will persist regardless, as long as selfishness and interest govern earthly societies, as long as thought turns away from deep issues, and as long as the flowers of the soul fail to bloom.

All economic and social theories are powerless to transform the world, to mitigate the evils of humanity, because they are founded on a very narrow basis placed solely in the present time, as the raison d'être of a single lifetime, which then would be the only goal of everyone's life and efforts. Well, to extinguish all social evil, it would be necessary instead to elevate the human soul to the consciousness of its role, making it clear to it that its fate depends on this elevation alone, and that its happiness will always be proportional to the extent of its triumphs over itself, and its dedication to others.

Then the social issue will be solved by replacing exclusive and narrow self-interest with altruism. Humans will feel like brothers and sisters, fellow beings and equals before the divine law which distributes to everyone the goods and ills necessary for their evolution, the means of overcoming the latter and hastening their ascension. Only when this happens, pain will have diminished its domain. Fruit of ignorance and inferiority, fruit of hatred, envy and selfishness, all animal passions are still agitating at the bottom of human beings. These ills will only vanish with the causes that produce them, by means of a higher education, and the realization in us of moral beauty, justice and love.

Moral evil is in the soul alone, in its dissonances with the divine harmony. But as it ascends to a brighter light, to a greater truth, to a more perfect wisdom, the causes of suffering will diminish, at the same time as its vain ambitions and material desires will dissipate. And step by step, from lifetime to lifetime, the soul will enter the great light and complete peace, where evil is unknown and good alone reigns!

Very often, I have heard from some people whose life was painful and fraught with hardship: "I would not want to be reborn in a new life; I do not want to return to Earth." When one has suffered a lot and has been violently shaken by the storms of this world, it is quite legitimate to long for respite. I understand that an overwhelmed soul recoils at the thought of resuming this battle of life, where it gained wounds which are still bleeding. But the law is inexorable. To ascend higher in the hierarchy of worlds, we must have left behind all the cumbersome baggage of inclinations and appetites which binds us to Earth. These binds are too often carried with us into the Hereafter, and it is them that keep us in the lower regions. Sometimes we think that we are capable and worthy of reaching the altitudes while, without our knowledge, a thousand chains still bolt us to this lower planet. We do not understand love in its sublime essence, nor self-sacrifice as it is practiced in these purified human groupings where no one lives for oneself or for a select few, but for all. Only those who are ripe for such a life can enjoy it. To make yourself worthy of it, it will be necessary that you go down again into the crucible, in the furnace where the hardness of our heart will melt like wax. And when our souls are purified from the slag, which is totally eliminated; when our essence becomes unalloyed; then God will call us to a higher life, to a more beautiful task.

Above all, it is necessary to measure with their just value the worries and sorrows of this world. For us, these are very cruel things; but all this becomes smaller and fades in significance if we consider it from a distance, if the spirit, rising above the details of existence, embraces the perspectives of its destiny with a broader view. The spirit alone will know how to weigh and to measure these things. Its thought will probe without difficulty the two oceans of space and time: immensity and eternity!

O you who bitterly complain of disappointments, of petty misery, of tribulations of which each and every existence is sown; and you who feel overcome by lassitude and discouragement: if you want to recover your resolution, your lost courage; if you want to learn how to happily brave bad fortune, or to bear with resignation the fate that befalls you, take a good look around you. Consider the pains that are ignored by the little ones, the disinherited, think about the sufferings of thousands of beings who are humans like you; meditate about these afflictions without number: the blind devoid of sight, of the rays of light which guide and bring joy; the paralytic, impotent in the body that existence has maimed; those who suffer from ankylosis, due to hereditary ills! And those who lack the bare essentials for living, on whom the winter blows with freezing winds! Think of all those sad, obscure, sickly lives and compare your often imaginary evils with the tortures of your brothers and sisters in pain, and you will judge yourself less unhappy. You will regain patience and courage and, with your heart, will descend on the crowd of human beings, on all those pilgrims of life who drag themselves along, overwhelmed on the arid road, with a feeling of boundless pity and immense love!

XXVII

REVELATION THROUGH PAIN

IT IS ESPECIALLY in the presence of suffering that the necessity and the effectiveness are revealed of a robust belief powerfully based simultaneously on reason, feeling and facts; and explaining the enigma of life, the problem of pain.

What comforting can materialism and atheism offer to individuals suffering from an incurable disease? What will they say to soothe despair, to prepare the soul of the person who will die? What language will they use for the parents kneeling in front of the cradle of a dead child? And for all those who see the coffins carrying their beloved ones descend into the grave? In situations like this, all the deficiency, all the insufficiency of such doctrines of nothingness are laid bare.

Pain is not only the criterion of life par excellence, but also the judge of our characters, the conscience and measure of true greatness in humans. It is also an infallible process for recognizing the value of philosophical theories and religious doctrines. The best among these will obviously be the one that comforts us, the one that tells why tears are the lot of humanity, but provides the means to quench them. Through pain, we more surely discover the focus from which emanates the most beautiful, the sweetest ray of truth, the one that never goes out.

If the universe is merely a restricted field open to the whimsical and blind forces of Nature, as an odious fatality that crushes us; if there is no conscience, no justice, no kindness in it, then pain is meaningless, has no utility; and does not involve consolation. There is nothing to do but to silence our broken hearts, for it would be puerile and vain to bother other human beings and the heaven with our complaints!

For all those whose lives are limited by the narrow horizons of materialism, the problem of pain has no solution, and there is no hope for the one who suffers.

Is it not really strange this impotence of so many scientists, philosophers and thinkers, for thousands of years, in explaining and soothing pain, their failure to make us accept it when it is inevitable? Some have even denied it, which is puerile. Others have advised to forget it, to distract from it, which is vain, and which is cowardly when it comes to the loss of our beloved ones. In general, we have been taught to dread, to fear, and to hate pain. Very few people have understood it; fewer still could explain it!

Also, around us, in our everyday relations, how poor, banal and childish have become the words of sympathy and comfort lavished on those whom misfortune has touched. How cold are those words on the lips, what an absence of warmth and light in the thoughts and in hearts! What a weakness, what a void in the processes used to comfort the mourners' hearts, processes which end up aggravating and redoubling their sorrows, their sadness. All this results solely from the obscurity that reigns over the problem of pain, false information spread in people's minds by negative doctrines and certain spiritualistic philosophies. Indeed, it is characteristic of all erroneous theories to discourage, to overwhelm, and to darken the soul at difficult moments, instead of providing it with the means to face destiny with a firm resolution.

And what about religions, could anyone tell me? Indeed, no doubt, religions have brought spiritual help for souls in distress; yet the comfort they offer rest on a too narrow conception of the purpose of life and of the laws of destiny. I have sufficiently demonstrated it above, so there is no need to return to this subject now.

Christian religions in particular have understood the majestic role of suffering, but they have exaggerated and distorted its meaning. Paganism expressed joy; its gods were crowned with flowers, and presided at festivals. Yet the Stoics and with them some secret sects of antiquity already considered pain as an indispensable element of the world order. Christianity glorified and deified it in the person of Jesus. In front of the Cavalry, humanity found his own less heavy to bear. The memory of the great tortured in the cross helped individuals to withstand suffering and to die. However, by pushing things to the extreme, Christianity has given life, death, religion, and God, some gloomy, sometimes terrifying, aspects. It is necessary to react against this and to put things in the right perspective, because thanks to their excesses, religions now see their empire shrink each day. Materialism gradually gains terrain in the field that religions have lost; the conscience of the masses has darkened, the notion of duty collapsed, for want of a body of thought adapted to the necessities of current time and to the needs of human evolution.

That is why I would like to say to priests of all religions: "Expand the frame of your teachings; give human beings a more extended notion of their destinies, a clearer view of the Hereafter, a higher idea of the goal to be attained. Make humans understand that their work consist in building their own selves, with the help of pain, their conscience, and their moral personality, through infinity times and spaces. If, at the present hour, your influence is weakened, if your power is shaken, it is not because of the morality you teach. It is because of the insufficiency of your conception of life, which does not clearly show justice in laws and things and, consequently, does not show God. Your theologies have locked thought into a circle that suffocates it; they have fixed a too limited basis for it, and on this basis the whole building is staggering and threatening to crumble. Stop talking about texts, stop oppressing consciences; get out of the crypts where you shut up the spirit; move on and act!"

A new doctrine rises, grows, expands, which will help thought to accomplish its work of transformation. This New Spiritualism contains all the necessary resources to soothe afflictions, to enrich philosophy, to regenerate religions, to draw the affection of the most humble disciple as well as the respect of the proudest genius.

It can satisfy the noblest impetus of intelligence and all the aspirations of one's heart. And, at the same time, it explains the reason for human weakness; the dark, tormented side of an inferior soul surrendered to passions; and gives us the means to rise to knowledge and fullness.

Last but not least, it is the most powerful moral remedy against pain. In the explanation which it gives of it, in the comfort which it succeeds to offer us regarding misfortunes, Spiritism gives the most evident proof, the most touching aspect of its truthful character and unshakable solidity.

Better than any other philosophical or religious system, it reveals the magnificent role of suffering and teaches us to accept it. By turning it into an educational or restorative process, it shows us divine justice and love intervening even in our trials and ills. Instead of making despairing people of us, like some negative religions and philosophies do; instead of fallen reprobates; or accursed individuals, Spiritism highlights the unfortunate as apprentices and neophytes enlightened by pain, as initiates and candidates to perfection and happiness.

In giving life an infinite end, New Spiritualism (i.e., Spiritism) has just given us a reason to live and suffer that really deserves to be lived and explains why we suffer; in a word, a goal worthy of the soul and worthy of God. In the apparent disorder and confusion of things, it shows us the order that slowly is being sketched out and realized, the future that is being elaborated in the present, and, above all, the unfolding of an immense and divine harmony.

And see the consequences of such teaching. Pain loses its scary character; it is no longer an enemy, a dreaded monster; it is a helper, an auxiliary, and its role is providential. It purifies, making one's being grow, melt again and temper in its flames; it adds to the individual a beauty that was not there before. The human being, at first astonished and anxious at its appearance, learns to understand pain, to appreciate it, to become acquainted with it, and almost ends up loving it. Some heroic souls, instead of fleeing and turning away from it, will go straight to it and voluntarily plunge into it in order to regenerate themselves.

Destiny, being unlimited, provides us with ever new possibilities of improvement. Suffering is only a corrective to our abuses, our mistakes, and a stimulus in our path. Thus the sovereign laws are perfectly just and good. They do not inflict on us any unnecessary or unmerited punishment. The study of the moral universe fills us with admiration for the Power which, by means of pain, gradually transforms the forces of evil into forces of good, extracting virtue out of vice, love out of selfishness!

Once assured of the result of their efforts, humans courageously accept the inevitable trials. Old age can come, life may decay and roll on the fast slope of the years; regardless, our faith will help us go through the rugged patches and sad hours of our existence. As life declines and becomes shrouded in mist, the great light of the Hereafter becomes more vivid, and a feeling of justice, of kindness, of love which presides over the destiny of all beings, becomes a force for the individual in hours of weariness. It makes it easier for us to prepare for our departure.

For materialists and even for many believers, the death of loved ones leave between us and the departed a gap that nothing can fill, an abyss of shadow and night where no ray of light or hope may shine. Protestants, uncertain of their destiny, do not even pray for the dead. Catholics, being no less anxious, fear that their nearest and dearest may undergo judgment which forever separates the elect from the reprobate.

But now, new tenets have been brought by Spiritism with unshakable certainty. For those who adhered to it, death, like pain, will be without fear. Each grave that is hollowed out is a portico of deliverance, an exit open to free spaces. Each friend who disappears will prepare the future home and mark the road to follow on which we all join in. The separation is only apparent. We know that these souls have not left us to never come back again; inner communion can still be established with them. If their manifestation, in the physical plane, meets with obstacles, we can at least correspond with them through thought.

We know the law of telepathy. There is no cry, no tear, no call of love, that goes without repercussion and response. The admirable solidarity of the souls for which we pray and which pray for us, by exchanging vibrational thoughts and regenerating calls that cross the two planes, penetrate our anxious hearts with radiation, strength and hope that never miss their goal!

You thought you were suffering alone, but that is not so: near and around you, and even in the boundless expanse, there are beings who vibrate with your suffering and participate in your pain. Try not make it too lively, so as to spare them themselves.

To sorrow, to human sadness, God has given celestial sympathy as companion. And this sympathy often takes the form of a loved one who, in the days of trial, descends full of solicitude, and collects each of our pains to make us a crown of light on the spiritual plane.

How many spouses, betrothed, and lovers separated by death, live in a new union, even closer and more intimate. At times of affliction, the spirit of a parent, all the friends of heaven, lean towards us and bathe our foreheads with their gentle and affectionate fluids. They envelop our hearts with warm vibrations of love. How to let oneself slip to evil or despair in presence of such witnesses, when we think that they see our concerns, read our thoughts, and that they wait for us and get ready to receive us on the threshold of immensity!

As we leave the Earth, we will meet them all again, and with them a much greater number of friendly spirits than we had forgotten during our last earthly stay; the crowd of those who shared in our past lives and make up our spiritual family.

All our companions in this great eternal journey will come together to welcome us, not as pale shadows, not as vague ghosts animated by a wavering life, but in the fullness of all their increased faculties, as active beings, still interested in the things of the Earth. They participate in the universal work, by cooperating with our efforts, our work, and our projects.

Our bonds from the past will reconnect with renewed force. Love, friendship, parenthood, once sketched in many lives, will be cemented by new commitments made for the future, in order to constantly increase and elevate to their supreme power the sentiments which we unite us all. And the sadness of temporary separations, the apparent distance of souls caused by death, will be melted in effusions of happiness, in the delight of homecomings and ineffable reunions.

Therefore, do not give credit to any dark religions and philosophies that preach iron laws and eternal condemnation, that speak of hell and paradise keeping beings far from one another, and forever keeping apart those who have loved each other.

There is no abyss that cannot be filled with love. God, which is all love, could not condemn to extinction the most beautiful, the most noble feeling of all that vibrates in the human heart. Love is immortal, like the soul itself.

In periods of suffering, of anguish, of despondency, collect yourself and, with ardent appeal, draw to you those beings which once were, like you and I, men and women who are now celestial spirits, and unknown forces will penetrate inside you, helping you bear your miseries and your ills.

Human beings, poor travelers who painfully climb the painful rise of existence, know that everywhere, on our path, invisible beings, both powerful and good, walk by our side. In difficult stretches, their helping fluids support our faltering march. Open your soul to them; put your thoughts in accord with their thoughts, and immediately you will feel the joy of their presence; an atmosphere of peace and blessing will envelop you; a wonderful soothing comfort will descend on you.

In the midst of trials, the truths we have just recalled do not dispense with emotions and tears; that would be against nature. At least, they teach us not to murmur, not to be overwhelmed by the blows of pain. These truths take away from us those fatal thoughts of revolt, despair, or suicide, which often haunt the brain of those who believe in nothing.[233] Should we go on crying, it would be without bitterness and blasphemy.

Even when it comes to the suicide of young individuals carried away by the ardor of their passions, when faced with the immense pain of a parent, Spiritism does not remain without resources. It still pours hope into the hearts of those who are mourning. It gives them, through prayer, through ardent thought, the possibility of relieving those souls that now wander in spiritual darkness between Earth and the spiritual world, or remain captive by their own coarse fluids in the environments in which they have lived. It mitigates their grief by telling them that there is nothing irreparable, nothing definitive about evil; any hindered development resumes when the culprit has paid his or her debt to justice.

In everything and everywhere, Spiritism offers us a foundation, a point of support from which the soul can take flight toward the future and find comfort for current issues through the perspective of things to come. Trust and faith in our destinies throw a light before us that illuminates the meaning of life, establishes a duty, broadens our sphere of action, and teaches us to act for others. We feel that there is incomparable strength, power and wisdom in the universe; but also that we

---

[233] [Trans. note] In the French original, L. DENIS calls them *néantistes*, a philosophical term meaning both atheists and nihilists.

ourselves are part of that strength and power from whence we come.

We understand that God's views regarding our souls, Its plan, Its work and Its purpose, all have their principle and source in Its love. In all things, God wants our good and pursues it by ways which are sometimes clear, sometimes mysterious, but invariably appropriate to our needs. If God separates us from those we love, it is to make us rediscover the joys of reunion. If it allows disappointments, abandonments, diseases, misfortunes, it is in order to force us to detach our eyes from Earth and to raise them toward It, to seek joys superior to anything we can experience in this world.

The universe is justice and love; in the infinite spiral of ascensions, the sum of sufferings, through divine alchemy, is changed up there into streams of light and sheaves of joy.

Have you noticed, in the depths of certain pains, something like a peculiar new flavor, that we cannot help but recognize as a beneficent intervention? Sometimes the struck soul sees an unknown light shine, the more so as the disaster seems greater. Suddenly, pain takes it to such heights that it would take twenty years of study and effort to reach them.

I cannot resist to single out two examples, among many others that are known to me. These concern two men, who have since become my friends, fathers of two charming young girls who were all their joy in this world, but who were abruptly removed from Earth, taken by death in a few days' time. One was a high-ranking officer in the East. His eldest daughter possessed all the gifts of intelligence and beauty. Furthermore, she had a serious character and willingly disdained the pleasures of her age and instead shared in the work of her father, a military writer and a talented publicist. So he had devoted to her an affection that verged on worship. Then, in a short time, a disease without remedy removed the girl from the tender shelter of her family. In her papers, he found a notebook with the title, "To my father when I'm gone!" Although she enjoyed perfect health as she was writing those pages, she had a presentiment of her impending death, and addressed to her father very touching consolations. Thanks to a book he found in his child's office, we got acquainted. Gradually, proceeding methodically and persistently, he revealed himself a medium with the gift of spirit sight, and today not only enjoys the favor of being introduced to the mysteries of survival, but also of often seeing his daughter next to him, giving further testimonies of her love. Yvonne's spirit has also communicated with her fiancé and one of her cousins, a non-commissioned officer in the regiment that was under her father's command at the time. These manifestations were complementary and verified by one another. Moreover, they were perceived by two family pets, as attested by her father, the general, in his letters.[234]

The second case is that of Mr. Debrus, a merchant in Valencia (Spain), whose only child, Rose, born after many years of marriage, was tenderly loved. All the hopes of her parents rested on her darling head. But at the age of twelve, the child was suddenly struck by acute meningitis and perished. The parents' despair was beyond description and the idea of suicide haunted the poor father's mind more than once. However, he recovered, for having some knowledge of Spiritism, and also because of the joy of becoming a medium himself. Today, he communicates freely and surely, without any intermediaries, with his daughter. She frequently intervenes in the private life of

---

[234] See L. DENIS, in his monograph *L'Au-delà et la Survivance de l'Être* [*Beyond the Survival of the Self*], "Le colonel français L. G., aujourd'hui général ..."

her family and sometimes produces around them luminous phenomena of great intensity.

Both knew little of the Hereafter and lived in culpable indifference to the problems of future life and destiny. Now everything has been lighted in their eyes. After having suffered, they have been comforted and now console others in their turn, working to spread the truth around them, impressing all who approach them with the height of their views and the firmness of their convictions. Transfigured and radiant, their children came back to them. And they came to understand why God had separated them and how they are reunited in the light and peace of the two planes. This is the work of pain!

Materialists, as said earlier, can conceive of no explanation for the enigma of the world, nor the problem of pain. In their eyes, all the magnificent evolution of life, of all forms of existence and beauty slowly developed over the centuries, are due to the caprice of blind chance, and that its sole outcome is nothingness. According to this view, at the end of time, it would be as if humanity had never existed. All human efforts to rise to a loftier state, all human complaints and sufferings, and accumulated miseries, absolutely everything will vanish like a shadow, all will have been useless and vain.

But instead of this theory of impotence and despair, we, who are certain of future life and a spiritual plane, see in the universe an immense laboratory where the human soul is refined and purified alternately through celestial and earthly existences. The latter have only one goal: the education of intelligent beings associated with physical bodies. Matter is an instrument of progress. What we call evil or pain is only a means of elevation.

Sometimes we hear that the ego is hateful. However, allow me a confession. Whenever the angel of pain touched me with its wing, I felt unknown forces stir inside me; I heard inner voices sing the eternal song of life and light. And now, after having experienced all the ills of my travel companions, I came to bless suffering. It helped shape my being; it gave me a more secure judgment, a more precise sense of the eternal higher truths. More than once, my life was shaken by misfortune, like an oak by the storm; but no trial has ever failed to teach me more about myself, and how to get hold of myself better.

And there comes old age. The end of my work is approaching. After fifty years of study, work, meditation, and experiments, it is sweet for me to be able to affirm to all those who suffer, to all the afflicted of this world, that there is one infallible justice in the universe. Our troubles are never in vain; there is no pain without compensation, no labor without gain. We all walk through vicissitudes and tears toward a grand goal fixed by God, and we have on our side a sure guide, an invisible counselor to support and comfort us.

My fellow human beings, learn to suffer, for pain is sacred! It is the noblest agent of perfection. It is the noblest instrument for perfection. Penetrating and fecund, it is indispensable to the life of anyone who does not want to remain paralyzed by selfishness and indifference. It is a philosophical truth that God sends suffering to those It loves: "I was a slave and a cripple," wrote the ancient Greek philosopher Epictetus, "poor as the beggar in the proverb, and [yet] the favorite of heaven."[235]

Learn to suffer! I am not telling you to search for pain. But when it stands inevitably on your way, welcome it as a friend; get to know it, to appreciate its austere beauty,

---

[235] [Trans. note] As famously translated by British writer Samuel JOHNSON in *Works* ... (Oxford: Talboys & Wheeler, 1825), p. 266.

to seize its secret teachings. Study its hidden labor, instead of revolting against it, or remaining overwhelmed, inert and cowardly under its action. Associate your will, your thought, with the goal that it has set for itself; seek to remove from its passage in your life all byproducts it can leave behind in your spirit and your heart.

Strive to be an example for others through your attitude toward suffering, your voluntary and courageous acceptance, your confidence in the future; in short, make pain more acceptable to others.

In a word, make pain more beautiful. Harmony and beauty are universal laws and, in this context, pain has its esthetic role. It would be childish to grumble against this element, so necessary to the beauty of the world. Let us rather highlight it by choosing loftier views and hopes! Let us see in it the supreme remedy for all vices, all deceptions, and all downfalls!

All of you who bend under the burden of your trials or who cry in silence; whatever happens, never despair. Remember that nothing happens in vain or without a reason. Nearly all our pains come from ourselves, from our past; and they open a road to heaven. Suffering acts as an initiator. It reveals the serious meaning, the imposing significance of life, which is not a frivolous comedy, but rather a poignant tragedy. It is the struggle for the conquest of spiritual life, and in this struggle, the greatest virtues are resignation, patience, resoluteness, and heroism. Essentially, the allegorical legends of Prometheus, the Argonauts, the Nibelungen, and the sacred mysteries of the East, have no other meaning.

A deeply rooted instinct makes us admire those whose existence was only a perpetual struggle against pain, a constant effort to climb the steep slopes which lead to virgin peaks and inviolate treasures. And we do not only admire heroism in broad daylight, those actions that provoke the enthusiasm of the crowds; we also revere obscure and hidden struggles against deprivation, disease, destitution, in short, everything that can detach material bonds and transitory things.

Temper your willpower; toughen your character for the fight of life. Develop the strength of resistance; remove from the soul of the child all that can soften it; elevate the ideal to a higher level of strength and greatness: this is what modern education should adopt as its essential goal. However, in our time, moral struggles have been discarded in order to seek the pleasures of body and mind. Also sensuality overflows in us, characters collapse, and social decadence is accentuated.

Up with our hearts, thoughts and wills! Let us open our souls to the great breaths of the spiritual plane! Let us lift up our eyes to a future without limits; let us remember that this future belongs to us: our task is to conquer it.

We live in times of crisis. For intelligent beings to open to new truths, for hearts to speak, vivid warnings have become necessary. It takes hard lessons from adversity. We have experienced dark days and difficult times. Misfortune must bring humans together. We only really feel like fellow human beings through pain.

It seems that this nation is following a road lined with precipices. Alcoholism, immorality, suicide, crime, are wreaking havoc. At every moment, scandals burst, awakening unhealthy curiosities, stirring up mud and fermenting corruption. Thought crawls without ever elevating itself. The soul of France, which was often the initiator of other nations, guiding them in the sacred way; the great soul of France suffers from the feeling of having to live in a tainted body.

O living soul of France, extricate yourself from this gangrenous envelope. Evoke the great memories, the high thoughts, the sublime inspirations of your genius!

For your genius is not dead; it is asleep. Tomorrow it will wake up again!

Decay precedes renewal. From social fermentation another life may emerge, purer and more beautiful. Under the influence of the new idea, France will regain belief and confidence. It will rise and grow stronger to accomplish its work in this world!

PROFESSION OF FAITH[236]
OF THE 20ᵀᴴ CENTURY

AT THIS POINT in evolution reached by human thought; and also considering, from the top of all philosophical and religious systems, the formidable problem of being, of the universe, and of destiny; in what terms could we summarize our acquired notions; in a word, what could be the philosophical creed of the twentieth century?

I have already attempted to summarize in my book *After Death*,[237] the essential principles of Modern Spiritualism. If we analyze that book from another angle, adopting as a basis – as Descartes did – the very notion of a thinking being, yet developing and expanding it, we may say:

1. *The first principle of knowledge is the idea of Being (Intelligence and Life). The idea of being imposes itself:* I am! *This statement is indisputable. One cannot doubt oneself. But, alone, this idea cannot suffice; it must be completed by the idea of action and progressive life:* I am and I want to be always more and better!
   The Being, in its conscious self: the soul, is the only living unity, the only indivisible and indestructible monad of simple substance, which is sought in vain in matter, for it exists only in ourselves. The soul remains invariable in its unity, through thousands and thousands of forms, thousands and thousands of bodies of flesh that it constructs and animates, for the needs of its

---
[236] [Trans. note] Nowadays also called a *mission statement*.
[237] Léon DENIS, *After Death* (New York: USSF, 2017).

eternal evolution. The soul is always diverse in acquired qualities and progress, becoming more and more conscious and free in the infinite spiral of its planetary and celestial existences.

2. *However, only half the soul pertains to this order of things. The other half belongs to the universe, of which it is an integral part. That is why a soul can know itself by studying the universe.*

   The pursuit of this double knowledge is the very reason and object of the soul's existence, of all its lives. Death is but the renewal of the vital forces necessary for a new step forward.

3. *The study of the universe shows, first of all, that a superior, intelligent, and sovereign action governs the world.*

   The essential character of this action, by the very fact that it is perpetuated, is duration. Being necessarily absolute, this duration cannot have any limit: hence eternity.

4. *Eternity, being living and active, implies an eternal and infinite being: God, first cause, generating principle, source of all beings. We say eternal and infinite because unlimited duration mathematically leads to unlimited extension.*

5. *Infinite action is linked to the necessities of duration. Now, where there is connection or relation, there is Law.*

   The law of the universe is conservation, which entails order and harmony. From the order flows the good; from harmony flows beauty.

   The highest goal of the universe is Beauty in all its aspects: material, intellectual and moral. Justice and Love are its means. In essence, Beauty is therefore inseparable from Good; and both, by their close union, constitute absolute Truth, supreme Intelligence, and Perfection!

6. *The purpose of the soul in its evolution is to reach and realize in and around it – through the eras and ascending stations of the universe – by the blossoming of powers it already possesses in latent form, this eternal notion of Beauty and Good, as expressed in the idea of God, the very idea of perfection.*

7. *From the law of ascension, when well understood, comes the explanation of all the problems of being: the evolution of the soul, which first receives through atavistic transmission all its ancestral qualities, and then develops them by its own action to add new qualities: The relative freedom of the relative being in the absolute Being; the slow formation of human conscience through the centuries, and its successive growth in the infinities of the future; the unity of essence and the eternal solidarity of souls in their march to conquer the high summits.*

―⁀ THE END ⁀―

TESTIMONIES OF SCIENTISTS AND EXPERTS

WILLIAM CROOKES (United Kingdom)

Opinion on Spiritist phenomena as stated by the famous English physicist who discovered thallium, made known the radiant state, invented the radiometer, experimented with cathodic rays and facilitated the study of the X-rays (the tubes of Crookes):

"Having satisfied myself of their *truth*, it would be moral cowardice to withhold my testimony ..."

After six years of experiments on Spiritualism, in which he devised many devices intended either to allow a scientific control or to record the phenomena, William Crookes wrote about spiritualistic facts:

"I never said it was possible, I only said it was true."

OLIVER LODGE (United Kingdom)

Opinion of another great English physicist whose work in the field of electricity, including the theory of ions, is known all over the world:

"If anyone cares to hear what sort of conviction has been born in upon my own mind, as a scientific man, by some twenty years' familiarity with these questions which concern us (Psychical Research), I am very willing to reply as frankly as I can."

"First, then, I am, for all personal purposes, convinced of the persistence of human existence beyond bodily death; and though I am unable to justify that belief in a full and complete manner, yet it is a belief which has been produced by scientific evidence; that is, it is based upon facts and experience, though I might find it impossible to explain categorically how the facts have produced that conviction. Suffice it to say for the present that it is not in a simple and obvious way, nor one that can be grasped in an hour or two, except by those who have seriously studied the subject, and are consequently equally entitled to an opinion of their own."

Continuing his research, the same scholar, who was both Rector of the University of Birmingham and a member of the Royal Academy, wrote elsewhere that he confessed to being a Spiritist, because he was compelled to accept phenomena as realities.

Cesare Lombroso (Italy)

Opinion of the illustrious Italian criminal lawyer and professor of the University of Turin, who for long fought the Spiritist theories, but agreed to study them:

"I am forced to express my conviction that spiritual phenomena are of enormous importance and that it is science's duty to direct its attention, without delay, to these manifestations."

This scholar again gave the following precise testimony:

"Spiritism is treated as trickery, which dispenses with thinking. I am embarrassed for having fought the possibility of Spiritist phenomena."

A. Russel Wallace (United Kingdom)

Opinion of the eminent naturalist, explorer, anthropologist, and biologist, emulator of Darwin, and president of the anthropology section of the British Association:

"I was so thorough and confirmed a materialist that I could not at that time find a place in my mind for the conception of spiritual existence, or for any other agencies in the universe than matter and force. Facts, however, are stubborn things.... The facts beat me.... *The facts of Spiritualism are ubiquitous in their occurrence and of so indisputable a nature as to compel conviction in every earnest inquirer."*

CAMILLE FLAMMARION (France)

Opinion of the famous French astronomer:

"I do not hesitate to say that anyone who declares that Spiritist phenomena are contrary to science does not know what he or she are talking about. In fact, in nature there is nothing occult or supernatural, only the unknown; but yesterday's unknown becomes tomorrow's truth."

In the third volume (*After Death*) of his book *Death and Its Mystery*,[238] he concludes in the following terms:

"*The soul survives the physical organism and may manifest itself after death."*

---

[238] C. FLAMMARION, *Death and Its Mystery* (Trans. L. Carroll. New York and London: The Century Co., 1923), vol. III, p. 348.

www.ingramcontent.com/pod-product-compliance
Lightning Source LLC
Chambersburg PA
CBHW071618170426